THE ROUTLEDGE COMPANION TO CONSUMER BEHAVIOR

T0330483

The key to marketing is understanding and satisfying consumer needs, thus a knowledge of consumer behavior is essential to any organization dealing with customers, users, or clients. This book promises to be a contemporary classic. It brings together an international set of scholars, many of whom are "household names", to examine the diverse approaches to consumer behavior topics.

The editors employ a micro to macro structure, dividing each topic into three parts: one reflecting foundational work, one focused on emerging trends, and one covering practical applications. Each part examines the relationship between consumer behavior and motivation, including well-being, gender, social class, and more, and concludes with practitioner perspectives on the challenges and opportunities that come with understanding customers. Readers will gain insight into how drives that are constantly in flux relate to other aspects of human cognition and behavior, allowing them to reach customers successfully, and to meet their needs. With contributions from leading scholars, including Sidney Levy and Jagdish Sheth, this volume sets the standard as the most comprehensive, cutting-edge resource on the subject of consumer behavior.

Students of consumer behavior and marketing will find this a useful exploration of a fast-moving field, fundamental to the welfare of companies, government, nonprofits, and consumers. It will also benefit new and established academic researchers as well as practitioners who want to stay on top of current knowledge.

Michael R. Solomon is Professor of Marketing at Saint Joseph's University, USA.

Tina M. Lowrey is Professor of Marketing at HEC Paris, France.

"This volume is an excellent companion to the study of consumer behavior. It covers the basic components such as perception, motivation, attitudes, and learning. More importantly, it provides cutting-edge updates and new topics including effects of climate, the quantified self, retail therapy, and poverty. It clearly deepens and broadens our understanding of consumers."

Russell Belk, *York University, Canada*

"Featuring leading scholars in the field, this book surveys the breadth of consumer behavior research while providing sufficient depth for readers to appreciate both the existing knowledge and knowledge gaps in the domains it covers. It is a must-have reference for anyone wishing to perform research in consumer behavior."

David Gal, *University of Illinois at Chicago, USA*

"In this new edited volume on consumer behavior, Solomon and Lowrey bring together a broad range of contributions that address many relevant topics in contemporary consumer research. The book not only reports on a broad range of topics, but also provides insights from many of the different scientific disciplines involved in consumer studies, making it a showcase of the multidisciplinary nature of the field."

Arnout Fischer, *Wageningen University, the Netherlands*

"Bringing together world-class researchers from diverse fields, this book is a grand tour of the fast-changing area of consumer behavior. It's up-to-date, easy-to-read, and comprehensive. A must-have for all researchers, graduate students, and practitioners who want to keep up with the research developments in this area!"

Yuwei Jiang, *The Hong Kong Polytechnic University, China*

THE ROUTLEDGE COMPANION TO CONSUMER BEHAVIOR

Edited by Michael R. Solomon and Tina M. Lowrey

Routledge
Taylor & Francis Group

LONDON AND NEW YORK

First published 2018
by Routledge

2 Park Square, Milton Park, Abingdon, Oxfordshire OX14 4RN
52 Vanderbilt Avenue, New York, NY 10017

Routledge is an imprint of the Taylor & Francis Group, an informa business

First issued in paperback 2020

Library of Congress Cataloging-in-Publication Data
A catalog record for this book has been requested

ISBN: 978-1-138-69516-0 (hbk)
ISBN: 978-0-367-65617-1 (pbk)

Typeset in Bembo
by Sunrise Setting Ltd, Brixham, UK

PART VIII

Attitudes and Branding

15

HOW CONSUMERS' ATTITUDES TOWARD BRANDS ARE SHAPED

Danielle J. Brick[1] and Susan Fournier[2]

[1]PETER T. PAUL COLLEGE OF BUSINESS AND ECONOMICS,
UNIVERSITY OF NEW HAMPSHIRE, DURHAM, NH, USA
[2]QUESTROM SCHOOL OF BUSINESS, BOSTON UNIVERSITY, BOSTON, MA, USA

Introduction

A central value-creating mechanism in the marketing arsenal is the brand: the entity through and with which close connections with consumers are established. Decades of academic research have sought insight into the nature of consumers' brand connections and the mechanisms that govern them such that brand value can be captured by the firm. Practical theoretical insights have been sought using many disciplinary lenses—psychological, sociological, cultural, and economic—and our knowledge about brands from the psychology perspective is especially deep. In this disciplinary realm, brand connections are conceptualized using the construct of attitude: summary evaluative judgments of a target object that are qualified by properties of valence (positive, negative, neutral) and strength (Fazio, 1986). Attitudes comprise webs of associations that variously include cognitive (beliefs and knowledge), affective (evaluative), and behavioral components (Fazio, 1990). Keller's oft-cited customer-based brand equity paradigm (1993) builds squarely from attitudinal frameworks to offer managers insight into building brands.

Brand research in the psychology tradition focuses largely on understanding the nature and strength of brand attitudes and the mechanisms that govern their (re)formation and use. Research supports that both attitude valence (the positive-negative dimension) and strength matter in driving consumer responses (Park et al., 2010; Thomson, MacInnis & Park 2005). As with attitudes toward people and other focal objects, the nature and strength of a given brand attitude are influenced by many factors, including characteristics of the object and evaluator, the manner in which information is processed, and the way in which the object is presented. Research has repeatedly shown that consumers form attitudes toward brands similarly to the way that they do with other objects, ideas, or people, and that attitudes toward brands (A_B) are influenced by the same factors as attitudes for other objects or people. For example, mere exposure to a brand, like other stimuli, is sufficient to increase brand liking (Rindfleisch & Inman, 1998) and awareness of the exposure need not be conscious (Ferraro, Bettman, & Chartrand, 2009;

Janiszewski, 1993). Marketers capitalize on this knowledge to encourage strong, positive brand associations through product placement (Homer, 2009; Redker, Gibson, & Zimmerman, 2013), celebrity endorsements (Agrawal & Kamakura, 1995), and side-advertising on social media sites (De Vries, Gensler, & Leeflang, 2012).

Through the years, we have learned that consumers' brand attitudes are more complicated than mere liking or disliking, and many constructs have been offered to capture the summary judgments contained in consumers' brand attitudes. Park and colleagues (2010) introduced brand attachment (i.e., the strength of the bond connecting the brand with the self) as a key driver of purchasing behavior; an updated conceptualization considers the salience of brand attitudes and negative brand affect (Park, Eisingerich, & Park, 2013). Fournier's (2009) brand relationship quality (BRQ) construct captures brand attitude as a composite of self-connection, social-connection, behavioral interdependence, love/passion, commitment, intimacy, and brand partner quality. Brand love provides another attitudinal lens that borrows from relational constructs (Batra, Ahuvia, & Bagozzi, 2012). Within the relationship paradigm, various positive and negative relational frames have been identified to qualify consumer-brand attachments including marriages (Fournier, 1998), friendships (Price & Arnould, 1999), flings, one-night stands (Alvarez & Fournier, 2012), master-slaves (Miller, Fournier, & Allen, 2012), adversaries (Paharia, Avery, & Keinan, 2014), and ex-friends (Grégoire, Tripp, & Legoux, 2009). The nature and strength of consumers' brand relationships drive cognition (Aggarwal, 2004; Aggarwal & Law, 2005), brand behaviors (Alvarez & Fournier, 2012; Fournier, 2009), and brand equity overall (Wittenbraker, Zeitoun, & Fournier, 2015).

The goal of this chapter is to review current research on how consumers' attitudes toward brands are shaped in order to gain a more informed understanding of consumer-brand dynamics for marketing practitioners and academics. We explore characteristics of both brands and consumers, cognitive science concerning how consumers process brand information, and the medium of brand information. We attempt contributions not just through review of past research but also by suggesting four high potential areas for future research.

Factors Influencing Consumers' Attitudes Toward Brands

Brand Characteristics

Brand personality affects the brand associations that provide the basis for consumers' attitudes toward brands. The Big Five brand personality traits (i.e., sincere, exciting, sophisticated, competent, or rugged, cf. Aaker, 1997) influence brand attitudes, expectations, and interactions. Consumers' brand attitudes after the event of a brand transgression depend centrally upon the personality of the brand (Aaker, Fournier, & Brasel, 2004). For sincere brands, a transgression weakens the relationship; for exciting brands, the relationship and brand attitude strengthen in response. When a focal brand is seen with a brand that has a dissimilar personality, consumers have more positive reactions than if the focal brand has a similar personality (Yang, Cutright, Chartrand, & Fitzsimons, 2014). Alvarez and Fournier (2016) demonstrated that consumers' unique experiences and connections with a brand, as subsequently represented in the personalized meanings they develop for the brand, may be more predictive of attitudes and behavior than general brand personality traits.

More recently, brand personality research has evolved from the Big Five to focus on the "Big Two," namely warmth and competence. Building on the Stereotype Content Model (Fiske, Cuddy, Glick, & Xu, 2002), this research explores how the social perception of brands influences attitudes and behaviors (Kervyn, Fiske, & Malone, 2012). Within this framework, brands are viewed as possessing intentions (i.e., warmth) and ability (i.e., competence), and how these two brand characteristics interact predicts consumers' attitudes and emotions toward brands. Of the 16 well-known brands that Kervyn and colleagues (2012) tested, popular mass brands (e.g., Campbell's, Coca-Cola) loaded in the high ability and high intentions quadrant. These are generally leading brands with charismatic CEOs or major corporate sponsorships and are viewed with admiration and pride. Brands that were controversial (e.g., BP, Marlboro) loaded in the low ability and low intentions quadrant. These are brands that may be seen as unethical and often elicit feelings of contempt or disgust in consumers. Brands that loaded in the high ability and low intentions quadrant (e.g., Porsche) generally constituted luxury brands and were viewed with envy or jealousy. Finally, brands that loaded in the low ability and high intentions quadrant were generally non-profits and government brands (e.g., USPS) and elicited feelings of sympathy or pity. Further research has found that perceptions of warmth are especially diagnostic. Consumers react more severely to scandals that affect warmth versus competence perceptions (Kervyn et al., 2014), and CSR initiatives that increase warmth also increase consumers' perceptions of product performance (Chernev & Blair, 2015). Further, consumers are less willing to buy products from a non-profit company as consumers view non-profits as warmer but less competent than for-profit companies (Aaker, Vohs, & Mogilner, 2010). The importance of age, education, and income on warmth and competence evaluations has been highlighted (Bennett & Hill, 2012). Fournier and Alvarez (2012) suggest attention to additional social perception dimensions including power and capacity for excitement.

The degree to which consumers view brands as having human-like characteristics and agency also influences their brand attitudes. Anthropomorphization can be facilitated through the use of brand characters and celebrities (Fournier, 1998), product designs evoking the human form (Aggarwal & McGill, 2007), or communication strategies that showcase the management behind the brand. While enlivening brands through human-like interactions can help build brand relationships (Fournier, 1998), anthropomorphized brands are also held to higher moral standards (Kwak, Puzakova, & Rocereto, 2015; Puzakova, Kwak, & Rocereto, 2013), prompting harsh evaluations in the face of wrongdoings. Anthropomorphization can also influence consumers' receptiveness toward brand messages (Touré-Tillery & McGill, 2015). Aggarwal and McGill (2012) found that anthropomorphized brands (i.e., brands that consumers imagined coming to life as a person) primed individuals' goals for a successful social interaction and consequently resulted in assimilative or contrastive behavior depending upon the brand's image. These effects of brand anthropomorphism are shaped by the specific relational or marketplace role that consumers assign to the brand. Brands viewed as liked "partners" or "disliked servants" resulted in assimilative behavior. For example, participants primed with Kellogg's (a liked partner brand associated with healthfulness) were more likely to take the stairs compared with the elevator. On the other hand, disliked partners and liked servants resulted in contrastive behavior (Aggarwal & McGill, 2012). Further research has found that consumers' characteristics can influence attitudes toward anthropomorphized brands with materialistic consumers preferring anthropomorphized servant brands over partner brands (Kim & Kramer, 2015). When a brand is viewed as an underdog, this increases positive brand attitudes, purchase intentions, and loyalty (Kao, 2015; Paharia, Keinan, Avery, & Schor, 2011). Not all brands are anthropomorphized, however, and cross-cultural differences do exist (Ghuman, Huang, Madden, & Roth, 2015).

Brand logos are also important factors as these meaning-laden signals increase brand awareness and serve as an efficient means of conveying brand information. Research has demonstrated that circularity and angularity of a brand logo affect perceptions of product and company attributes (Jiang, Gorn, Galli, & Chattopadhyay, 2016). Whereas circular-logo shapes activate softness associations, angular-logo shapes activate hardness associations. Brand loyal consumers respond more negatively and have a lower brand attitude after a logo redesign, even if the redesign is culturally supported (Walsh, Winterich, & Mittal, 2010).

The linguistic factors of a brand's name also drive memorability, evaluations, and performance expectations (Pavia & Costa, 1993). Yorkston and Menon (2004) found that consumers use information they gather from phonemes (individual sounds) to make inferences about and evaluate brands. Lowrey and Shrum (2007) demonstrated that consumers preferred brand names more when the attributes implied by the vowel sounds were positive for a product category. For example, participants preferred brand names with front vowels more for a hypothetical convertible because front vowels connote smallness and fastness, whereas they preferred back vowels for a hypothetical SUV brand name because back vowels connote largeness. Words with negative vowel sounds (i.e., vowels similar to the word disgust) were least preferred. Alphanumeric brand names also affect consumers' brand attitudes. Comparing identical sets, product options whose brand names have a higher versus lower numeric position (e.g., X-200 vs. X-100) are preferred even when the option is objectively less favorable (Gunasti & Ross, 2009). Not surprisingly, meaningful brand names that convey information about the product are evaluated more favorably on overall liking than non-meaningful brand names (Klink, 2001). Although attitudes stemming from names that lack inherent meaning improve at a greater rate after repeated exposure, consumers evaluate meaningful brand names more favorably overall (Kohli, Harich, & Leuthesser, 2005). Congruence between a brand name and attributes is also an important tactic for enhancing positive brand attitudes, and this factor holds across cultures and languages. For example, Shrum and colleagues (2012) found that French-, Spanish-, and Chinese-speaking participants preferred a match between the phonetic symbolism of the brand name and the product attributes. This effect held regardless of language used and indicates that marketers can embed universal meaning in their brand names. However, marketers must use care when using cultural branding. Researchers have found that incongruence between the actual country of origin of a product and implied country of origin (based upon the brand name) decreases purchase likelihood (Melnyk, Klein, & Völckner, 2012). This effect is prominent for hedonic categories from emerging countries, but does not occur for utilitarian products.

Consumer Characteristics

Aspects of consumers' identities and personalities interact with aspects of brands to influence attitudes and behavior, and the personalized meanings an individual consumer develops in light of his/her brand experiences may promote the strongest and most enduring attitudes (Alvarez & Fournier, 2016). The underdog effect was shown to be driven by consumers who strongly self-identified as underdogs (Paharia, Keinan, Avery, & Schor, 2011). Researchers have found that attachment style and individual personality traits like extraversion, openness, and agreeableness are important predictors and moderators of brand attitudes (Mende, Bolton, & Bitner, 2013; Mulyanegara, Tsarenko, & Anderson, 2009). For example, Swaminathan, Stilley, and Ahluwalia (2009) found that whereas individuals with high relationship avoidance and anxiety preferred exciting brands, individuals with low relationship avoidance and anxiety preferred sincere brands. The preference for sincere (vs. exciting) brands occurred in public (vs. private) settings, and those where relationship expectations are high, highlighting how brand personality can influence brand attitudes. Further research has shown that a match between the brand's personality and the consumer's personality can influence emotional brand attachment, with actual self-congruence, as opposed to ideal self-congruence, having the greatest impact (Malär, Krohmer, Hoyer, & Nyffenegger, 2011). There is also research to suggest that highly attached consumers can be slow to forgive a brand for its transgressions, exhibit increased complaint behavior, and seek payback and revenge (Thomson, Whelan, & Johnson, 2012). The consumer's resource level, which can be defined as a stock or supply of money, materials, or assets that an individual possesses, also influences brand attitudes. Individuals with greater resources rate brands as more important overall and have stronger brand connections than do individuals with fewer resources (Brick, Chartrand, & Fitzsimons, 2016).

Extensive research highlights how consumer beliefs and expectations influence judgments, including attitudes toward brands. Consumers believe lower-priced brands to be of lower quality (Rao & Monroe, 1989); a beer with a brand label tastes better than one that is not labeled, even when this is the same beer (Allison & Uhl, 1964). Research on what is commonly referred to as the "placebo effect" in marketing (Shiv, Carmon, & Ariely, 2005) shows that beliefs and expectations influence behavior for both better and worse. For example, the slogan "Red Bull gives you wings" positively influenced individual performance, but also made consumers behave recklessly (Brasel & Gips, 2011). Along related lines, research has shown that coordinating brands makes consuming multiple products at the same time more enjoyable because consumers believe the products were made to go together (Rahinel & Redden, 2013). Many of these processes are related to consumers' tendency to associate brands with success or failure, and the degree to which consumers are affected by personal beliefs is driven by factors including motivation (Irmak, Block, & Fitzsimons, 2005), self-efficacy (Garvey, Germann, & Bolton, 2016), reward-seeking tendency, need for cognition (Plassmann & Weber, 2015), and the desire for control (Hamerman & Johar, 2013).

Consumers' beliefs about personal control (Chaxel, 2016) are especially powerful drivers of brand attitudes and behaviors. When consumers are feeling low in personal control they increase their preferences for brand logos that have clear boundaries (Cutright, 2012) and reject brand extensions that do not fit well with the parent brand (Cutright, Bettman, & Fitzsimons, 2013). Park and John (2010; 2012) focused on how consumers' implicit self-theories, or beliefs about control over personality, influence brand attitudes, experiences, and advertising effectiveness. They find that entity theorists, or people who believe that personal qualities are fixed, enhance their self-perceptions through brand usage, choosing brands to signal positive qualities in line with the brand's personality. Incremental theorists, or people who believe personal qualities are malleable through effort, are not influenced by brands in the same manner. Park and John (2010) also find that brands using signaling ads are more effective for entity theorists (Park & John, 2012), whereas brands whose ads focus on self-improvement appeals are more effective for incremental theorists. Park and John (2014) add that brand usage can help an individual's performance, but that this depends upon implicit self-theory. While entity theorists demonstrated better task performance and increased self-efficacy, incremental theorists were unaffected by brand use. Implicit self-theories also influence attitudes toward brand extensions. Mathur, Jain, and Maheswaran (2012) demonstrated that extension fit with a parent brand can enhance brand personality when extension fit is poor, but only for incremental theorists.

From research highlighting the power of reference groups (Escalas & Bettman, 2003, 2005) and brand communities (Muniz & O'Guinn, 2001) to the mere presence of other persons (Pozharliev, Verbeke, Van Strien, & Bagozzi, 2015), research consistently shows how other consumers magnify self-brand connections and attitudes. Self-brand connection has been shown to both increase (Choi & Winterich, 2013) and decrease (White & Dahl, 2007) preference for out-group brands, magnify the effects of celebrity endorsement on brand attitudes (Escalas & Bettman, 2009), and help consumers to maintain favorable views in the face of conspicuous or attention-getting brand users (Ferraro, Kirmani, & Matherly, 2013).

Brand Information Processing

Interestingly, the manner in which consumers process information about brands influences their attitudes toward them. Advertising is an important driver of how consumers process brand information. When advertising promotes self-association, consumers have more positive implicit attitudes, self-reported attitudes, and greater purchase intentions (Coulter & Grewal, 2014; Perkins & Forehand, 2012). The tactics advertisers use to encourage self-association are important. For example, saying "we" has more favorable effects on brand evaluations when consumers want a close relationship with the brand, and more negative effects when consumers expect a more distant relationship or less involvement with the brand (Sela, Wheeler, & Sarial-Abi, 2012).

The fluency or ease of processing brand information also informs brand attitudes. Research has shown that when a brand comes to mind more readily, either by conceptual activation or semantic priming, consumers develop more favorable brand attitudes (Labroo, Dhar, & Schwarz, 2008; Lee & Labroo, 2004). Thematic brand extensions (e.g., Budweiser chips) are processed more rapidly and are judged more positively than taxonomic extensions (e.g., Budweiser cola; Estes, Gibbert, Guest, & Mazursky, 2012). Although sub-branding (e.g., Quencher by Tropicana Cola) evokes slower, more thoughtful processing than family branding (e.g., Tropicana Cola), this process can enhance evaluations and protect the parent brand from negative feedback (Sood & Keller, 2012). Empirical studies do not support this, however: using financial models of shareholder value and stock performance data, Hsu, Fournier and Srinivasan (2016) show greater financial risk for brand architectures designed around sub-brands.

Not surprisingly, consumers process and use brand information differently depending upon whether the brand is familiar or unfamiliar (Grewal, Krishnan, Baker, & Borin, 1998). Strong brands, or brands that are familiar, are processed using areas of the brain associated with information retrieval and positive emotions (Esch et al., 2012). Brands that are weak, or unfamiliar, are more likely to be processed in areas of the brain that are associated with negative emotions. Overall, this research highlights that consumers use experienced emotion, as opposed to declarative information, to evaluate and form attitudes toward brands. Because individuals process brand information emotionally, marketers should associate brands with positive affectively-laden stimuli such as celebrity endorsers or pictures, to encourage engagement in evaluative conditioning in order to change brand attitudes (Sweldens, Van Osselaer, & Janiszewski, 2010).

Perceptual information beyond fluency can guide consumers' processing of information about brands. The use of sensory perception to guide cognition, or embodied cognition, has significant effects on consumers' attitudes toward products and brands (Krishna & Schwarz, 2014). Visual aesthetics have long been considered key drivers of ad effectiveness (McQuarrie & Mick, 2003), and research has shown that enhanced mental simulation through visual appeals can increase positive brand attitudes and purchase intentions (Elder & Krishna, 2012). Dynamic imagery and auditory appeals can also lead to more favorable brand attitudes (Cian, Krishna, & Elder, 2014), especially when the brand or product is viewed as hedonic

(Roggeveen, Grewal, Townsend, & Krishnan, 2015). Music in ads also improves message processing and brand attitudes, but only when it is congruent with the features of the ad and brand (Hung, 2000; Strick, de Bruin, de Ruiter, & Jonkers, 2015). Representations of the brand and the brand extension can also influence attitudes with concrete representations resulting in a preference for higher-quality brands as opposed to better-fitting ones (Meyvis, Goldsmith, & Dhar, 2012).

Consumer characteristics also influence information processing and subsequently affect brand attitudes. Consumers inherently organize and utilize brand information differently (Puligadda, Ross, & Grewal, 2012). This concept, known as brand schematicity, affects how consumers pay attention to brand information, store it in memory, and evaluate brand extensions, with brand-schematic consumers using more abstract brand-level information to guide their attitudes. In addition, the degree to which consumers use lay rationalism, that is, decisions made based on reason, to process information affects brand preferences (Hsee, Yang, Zheng, & Wang, 2015). So too does the extent to which consumers engage in analytic (as opposed to holistic) thinking, which has been shown to result in less favorable attitudes toward functional brands that engage in distant extensions (Monga & John, 2010). Recent research has also found that effortful cognitive evaluation—something previously deemed critical for the formation of strong attitudes—is not necessary for consumers to form strong brand attitudes (Kwon & Nayakankuppam, 2015). Entity theorists, consumers who believe personality traits are fixed, form strong attitudes quickly and with less effort than incremental theorists who believe that traits are malleable, but hold these attitudes toward brands more strongly (Kwon & Nayakankuppam, 2015). Entity theorists are also less accepting of brand extensions than are incremental theorists (Yorkston, Nunes, & Matta, 2010). Age is also important. Brand names acquired at a younger age are recognized more quickly and consumers are better able to access semantic knowledge about these brands (Ellis, Holmes, & Wright, 2010). Researchers have also shown that consumers begin to develop stronger self-brand connections as they move through middle childhood and adolescence, highlighting the importance of age of brand exposure and formation of initial brand attitudes (Chaplin & John, 2005).

The Brand Information Medium

With current internet use among American adults at 87%, and closer to 100% for young and higher-income adults (Stephen, 2016), many marketers have shifted toward online advertising as a context for brand building, prompting research that explores the different effects and drivers of on- versus offline behaviors on consumers' attitudes toward brands. Some research suggests that television advertising remains the main vehicle for brand equity development (Srinivasan, Vanhuele, & Pauwels, 2010); other research puts internet ads on par with television ads in terms of recall and attitudinal change (Draganska, Hartmann, & Stanglein, 2014). Other research comparing online versus offline effects on brand attitudes has focused on word of mouth (WOM) effects (Pauwels, Aksehirli, & Lackman, 2016). Individuals transmit information about brands using WOM differently and at different rates depending on the medium. Whereas social and functional drivers are more important for online WOM, emotional drivers are more important for offline WOM (Lovett, Peres, & Shachar, 2013). This finding is in accord with work showing that WOM valence is enhanced when the conversation occurs offline (Baker, Donthu, & Kumar, 2016). Research has also found that the difference in the desire to engage in online versus offline WOM is mediated by consumers' perception of social risk, which can be mitigated by consumers' need to self-enhance (Eisingerich, Chun, Liu, Jia, & Bell, 2015).

Research in the online context has begun to examine effects of the specific location of brand messages on webpages. Brand posts at the top of a page increase brand popularity (a key driver of brand equity, Keller, 1993) and positive comments about the brand (De Vries et al., 2012). Differences in the online interface—for example, desktop computer versus touch-screen laptop—also matter, with touchscreens driving increased psychological ownership and endowment effects (Brasel & Gips, 2014). Although this research did not specifically consider brands, it found that touch-based devices, particularly ones that are owned by the consumer like a mobile phone, lead to higher product valuations than interactions driven through traditional desktop devices. Apropos for the mobile marketing space, researchers have begun to organize a framework and research agenda for understanding the effects of mobile advertising on consumers and brands (Grewal, Bart, Spann, & Zubcsek, 2016).

Recent online advertising research has also delved into more specific processing mechanisms and effects. Of note is research on how to overcome backlash, or psychological reactance, resulting from a barrage of targeted, personalized ads. Schumann and colleagues (2014) find support for normative reciprocity appeals as opposed to utility appeals; Lambrecht and Tucker (2013) offer ad retargeting, a strategy where personalized advertising recommendations are made based on the individual's prior web-browsing history, by refining personalized preferences. Another strategy resulting in more favorable online advertising reception and hence brand attitudes gives customers control over the ads that are shown to them (Tucker, 2014).

Social media is a crucial space attracting research attention as we seek a deeper understanding of how the online environment affects brand attitudes and brand relationships (Labrecque, 2014). Laroche, Habibi, and Richard (2013) found that brand communities housed on social media have positive effects on brand relationships, including brand trust, which positively affects brand attitudes and loyalties. Kim and Ko (2012) demonstrated that social media marketing activity in the form of entertainment, interaction, trendiness, customization, and word of mouth, can positively increase relationship and brand equity for luxury brands. Choudhury and Harrigan (2014) built off a traditional framework of customer relationship management (CRM) to focus on social media technologies and their influence. Their paper on social CRM includes a new construct of customer engagement and contributes to an understanding of the change in communication between marketers and consumers – communication that ultimately shapes brand attitudes and relationships.

Future Research

Negative and "Mixed Valence" Brand Attitudes

Most research on consumers' psychological connections with brands focuses on positive attitudes and drivers of attitude strength. Limited work explores the negative valence dimension, and most of this focuses on mitigating or changing negative attitudes, leaving our understanding of the nature, causes, and outcomes of negative brand attitudes underdeveloped. Filling this hole in our conceptual framework is critical since negative brand relationships are more common than positive ones (Fournier & Alvarez, 2013). Future research on various negative relationship forms including addictions, adversaries, stalkers, compulsions, and other forms of dependency is needed for a more holistic understanding of consumers' psychological responses to brands.

The online space is hyper-critical (Fournier & Avery, 2011), and it is easy for brands to come across as inauthentic or incite consumer backlash (Spiggle, Nguyen, & Caravella, 2012). The potential for the propagation of negative or dysfunctional brand relationships also increases with negative online reviews and technological advances that make advertising, purchasing, and over-indulgence easier than ever. Anti-branding and anti-brand communities proliferate online (Dessart, Morgan-Thomas, & Veloutsou, 2016) and these manifestations of brand attitude deserve closer investigation. Researchers have begun to separate forms of consumer-brand sabotage and hostile aggression from other negative behaviors, such as negative word of mouth, to highlight how different negative attitudes can lead to different behaviors and have different consequences for marketers (Kähr, Nyffenegger, Krohmer, & Hoyer, 2016). Some mechanisms and antecedents of online anti-branding have been investigated, including brand moral violations, inauthentic behavior, and oppositional attitudinal loyalty (Romani, Grappi, Zarantonello, & Bagozzi, 2015). Additional research is needed to fully understand why, when, and how these negative online attitudes arise.

Mixed or ambivalent brand attitudes present a related opportunity. Research on interpersonal relations has illustrated that consumers can hold both positive and negative attitudes toward other people, including loved ones, at the same time (Zayas & Shoda, 2014). Love-hate relationships and secret affairs are evocative bivalent brand relationship examples (Avery, Fournier, & Wittenbraker, 2014). What are some potential causes and outcomes of these mixed relationships and how are they different from univalent ones? Complex approach-avoidance relationships present interesting opportunities for future research.

Temporal Dynamics

Attitude change is fundamental to attitude theory, and though we have learned a great deal about these processes by studying persuasion (Friestad & Wright, 1994), more focused work on brand attitude dynamics over time is needed. There are natural ebbs and flows in consumer-brand interactions and the resultant strength of the relationship, and longitudinal designs can do much to illuminate consumers' attitude changes while contributing to brand relationship theory. An ambitious undertaking would embrace the systematic variation in attitudes across the life span (Erikson, 1968) and explore how consumers' brand attitudes change as a function of stage in life. Previously mentioned research examined how age influences consumers' brand attitudes (Chaplin & John, 2005; Ellis, Holmes, & Wright, 2010), but this research has mostly compared one cohort with another. Future research could investigate the same group of consumers over an extended period of time to estimate the lifetime value of consumers' interactions with a given brand.

Another future research area related to brand attitude dynamics recognizes that not all brands last. What happens when a brand has failed or been discontinued? Who cares about a brand that is no more? For managers and researchers interested in consumers' brand relationships this is an important space. Individuals have relationships with brands as they do with other people (Fournier, 1998; 2009), and research has shown that consumers too can undergo deeply felt emotional losses when their relationships with brands are forced to end (Russell & Schau, 2014). Loss and mourning have been documented with television shows that reach their natural conclusion (Russell & Schau, 2014) and binge watching that leaves consumers in a "showhole" once available content has been used up. More research, particularly experimental and empirical research, is needed to investigate the effects of discontinuation and loss on consumer attitudes. Another direction recognizes that while brands may continue, not all brand *relationships* last. Future research could investigate not only how select brand relationships end but also why and how consumers change from positive to negative brand attitudes, or from various attitudinal frames (e.g., marriage to addiction).

Attending to Content, Context and the Meaning behind Consumers' Connections with Brands

As research on brand attitudes advances, the need for attending not just to their valence and strength, but also to their content and context becomes critical. Multitudinous attitudinal constructs have been offered to capture consumers' psychological connections to a brand: brand attitude, the summation of brand beliefs weighted by their evaluative strength; brand attachment, as per self-concept connection or brand salience plus self-connection; brand love; satisfaction; brand relationship quality; and so on. Little is known about the discriminant and predictive validity of these different constructs, and the research that reveals these as highly correlated gives significant pause. Do our various constructs add meaningful distinction? What is the incremental value and explanatory power of these alternative valenced attitudinal ideas?

The consumer context can also be more expressly built into our investigations of people's attitudes toward brands. Implicit attitude theory (Greenwald & Banaji, 1995) can be tapped to identify and better understand the stereotypes that consumers apply when considering companies and brands. This perspective highlights the importance of unconscious or implicit attitudes that may deviate from consumers' stated attitudes and preferences. How can differences between explicit and implicit attitudes help inform consumer attitudes toward brands, particularly brands that are stigmatized? Building from early work on the "schemer schema" (Wright, 1986), the Persuasion Knowledge Model (Friestad & Wright, 1994), and commercial attachment styles (Gustafsson, Johnson, & Roos, 2005), can we identify attitudinal templates that guide judgments, consumer-brand interactions, and approach-avoidance behaviors in the marketplace?

One cannot opine on context factors without considering further how brand attitudes are influenced by online advertising and social media. Brands claim thousands of Facebook friends, Twitter followers, and YouTube fans, and with the advent of new social media platforms such as Snapchat, brand presence in daily conversation grows. With online engagement available and accessible 24/7 through the ubiquitous cellphones in consumers' hands, marketers can for the first time capture brand attitudes and behaviors in real time—unfiltered and unadulterated through scientific observation. With targeting available through big data analytics, marketers can now engage in tailored conversations to build brand associations and encourage brand engagement. Brands in the online space are also more readily anthropomorphized by their active, reciprocating behaviors. The dynamics behind and long-term effects of building brands through heightened, natural, customized, and anthropomorphized online interactions remain largely unknown. Future research could also further investigate differences in and complementarities between online and offline brand attitudes. Are those most vocal online the biggest brand supporters in daily life? Are vocal online supporters good for building brand awareness, vibrancy, and energy, but problematic for maintaining strong brand relationships? It will be important to distinguish those who support the brand online as a "means" for self-expression from those who support it for the "ends" obtained through authentic engagement with the brand.

Cross-Disciplinary Work

Attitude theory has provided a strong foundation in consumer research for decades, and research exploring the nature of consumers' brand attitudes, the cognitive beliefs and evaluations that comprise them, and the moderators of strength and valence has informed the practice and discipline of marketing. Still, attitude is a psychological construct, and the theoretical contributions made possible through this lens are at once advanced and limited by this individuated perspective. There exists a world of contribution made possible through cultural and sociological theories that at present remain largely untapped. True scientific advances come from cross-disciplinary work that challenges basic assumptions and merges ideas to form new insights. Our exploration of consumers' connections with brands deserves illumination through the cross-fertilization of ideas.

References

Aaker, J., Fournier, S., & Brasel, S. A. (2004). When Good Brands Do Bad. *Journal of Consumer Research*, *31*(1), 1–16.

Aaker, J., Vohs, K. D., & Mogilner, C. (2010). Nonprofits are Seen as Warm and For-Profits as Competent: Firm Stereotypes Matter. *Journal of Consumer Research*, *37*(2), 224–237.

Aaker, J. L. (1997). Dimensions of Brand Personality. *Journal of Marketing Research*, *34*(3), 347–356.

Aggarwal, P. (2004). The Effects of Brand Relationship Norms on Consumer Attitudes and Behavior. *Journal of Consumer Research*, *31*(1), 87–101.

Aggarwal, P., & Law, S. (2005). Role of Relationship Norms in Processing Brand Information. *Journal of Consumer Research*, *32*(3), 453–464.

Aggarwal, P., & McGill, A. L. (2007). Is That Car Smiling at Me? Schema Congruity as a Basis for Evaluating Anthropomorphized Products. *Journal of Consumer Research*, *34*(4), 468–479.

—— (2012). When Brands Seem Human, Do Humans Act Like Brands? Automatic Behavioral Priming Effects of Brand Anthropomorphism. *Journal of Consumer Research*, *39*(2), 307–323.

Agrawal, J., & Kamakura, W. A. (1995). The Economic Worth of Celebrity Endorsers: An Event Study Analysis. *The Journal of Marketing*, *59*(3), 56–62.

Allison, R. I., & Uhl, K. P. (1964). Influence of Beer Brand Identification on Taste Perception. *Journal of Marketing Research*, *1*(3), 36–39.

Alvarez, C., & Fournier, S. (2012). Brand Flings: When Great Brand Relationships are Not Made To Last. *Consumer-Brand Relationships: Theory and Practice*, 74–96.

—— (2016). Consumers' Relationships with Brands. *Current Opinion in Psychology*, *10*, 129–135.

Avery, J., Fournier, S., & Wittenbraker, J. (2014). Unlock the Mysteries of Your Customer Relationships. *Harvard Business Review*, *92*(7), 72–81.

Baker, A. M., Donthu, N., & Kumar, V. (2016). Investigating How Word-of-Mouth Conversations About Brands Influence Purchase and Retransmission Intentions. *Journal of Marketing Research*, *53*(2), 225–239.

Batra, R., Ahuvia, A., & Bagozzi, R. P. (2012). Brand Love. *Journal of Marketing*, *76*(2), 1–16.

Bennett, A. M., & Hill, R. P. (2012). The Universality of Warmth and Competence: A Response to Brands as Intentional Agents. *Journal of Consumer Psychology*, *22*(2), 199–204.

Brasel, S. A., & Gips, J. (2011). Red Bull "Gives You Wings" for Better or Worse: A Double-Edged Impact of Brand Exposure on Consumer Performance. *Journal of Consumer Psychology*, *21*(1), 57–64.

—— (2014). Tablets, Touchscreens, and Touchpads: How Varying Touch Interfaces Trigger Psychological Ownership and Endowment. *Journal of Consumer Psychology*, *24*(2), 226–233.

Brick, D. J., Chartrand, T. L., & Fitzsimons, G. J. (2016). The Effects of Resources on Brand and Interpersonal Connection. *Journal of the Association for Consumer Research*, *2*(1), DOI: 10.1086/688755.

Chaplin, L. N., & John, D. R. (2005). The Development of Self-Brand Connections in Children and Adolescents. *Journal of Consumer Research*, *32*(1), 119–129.

Chaxel, A.-S. (2016). Why, When, and How Personal Control Impacts Information Processing: A Framework. *Journal of Consumer Research*, *43*(1), 179–197.

Chernev, A., & Blair, S. (2015). Doing Well by Doing Good: The Benevolent Halo of Corporate Social Responsibility. *Journal of Consumer Research*, *41*(6), 1412–1425.

Choi, W. J., & Winterich, K. P. (2013). Can Brands Move in from the Outside? How Moral Identity Enhances Out-Group Brand Attitudes. *Journal of Marketing*, *77*(2), 96–111.

Choudhury, M. M., & Harrigan, P. (2014). CRM to Social CRM: The Integration of New Technologies into Customer Relationship Management. *Journal of Strategic Marketing*, *22*(2), 149–176.

Cian, L., Krishna, A., & Elder, R. S. (2014). This Logo Moves Me: Dynamic Imagery from Static Images. *Journal of Marketing Research, 51*(2), 184–197.

Coulter, K. S., & Grewal, D. (2014). Name-Letters and Birthday-Numbers: Implicit Egotism Effects in Pricing. *Journal of Marketing, 78*(3), 102–120.

Cutright, K. M. (2012). The Beauty of Boundaries: When and Why We Seek Structure in Consumption. *Journal of Consumer Research, 38*(5), 775–790.

Cutright, K. M., Bettman, J. R., & Fitzsimons, G. J. (2013). Putting Brands in their Place: How a Lack of Control Keeps Brands Contained. *Journal of Marketing Research, 50*(3), 365–377.

De Vries, L., Gensler, S., & Leeflang, P. S. (2012). Popularity of Brand Posts on Brand Fan Pages: An Investigation of the Effects of Social Media Marketing. *Journal of Interactive Marketing, 26*(2), 83–91.

Dessart, L., Morgan-Thomas, A., & Veloutsou, C. (2016). What Drives Anti-Brand Community Behaviours: An Examination of Online Hate of Technology Brands. In *Let's Get Engaged! Crossing the Threshold of Marketing's Engagement Era* (pp. 473–477). New York: Springer International Publishing.

Draganska, M., Hartmann, W. R., & Stanglein, G. (2014). Internet Versus Television Advertising: A Brand-Building Comparison. *Journal of Marketing Research, 51*(5), 578–590.

Eisingerich, A. B., Chun, H. H., Liu, Y., Jia, H. M., & Bell, S. J. (2015). Why Recommend a Brand Face-to-Face but not on Facebook? How Word-of-Mouth on Online Social Sites Differs from Traditional Word-of-Mouth. *Journal of Consumer Psychology, 25*(1), 120–128.

Elder, R. S., & Krishna, A. (2012). The "Visual Depiction Effect" in Advertising: Facilitating Embodied Mental Simulation through Product Orientation. *Journal of Consumer Research, 38*(6), 988–1003.

Ellis, A. W., Holmes, S. J., & Wright, R. L. (2010). Age of Acquisition and the Recognition of Brand Names: On the Importance of Being Early. *Journal of Consumer Psychology, 20*(1), 43–52.

Erikson, E. H. (1968). *Identity, Youth and Crisis*. New York: W.W. Norton Company.

Escalas, J. E., & Bettman, J. R. (2003). You Are What They Eat: The Influence of Reference Groups on Consumers' Connections to Brands. *Journal of Consumer Psychology, 13*(3), 339–348.

—— (2005). Self-construal, Reference Groups, and Brand Meaning. *Journal of Consumer Research, 32*(3), 378–389.

—— (2009). Self-Brand Connections: The Role of Reference Groups and Celebrity Endorsers in the Creation of Brand Meaning. In D. MacInnis, C. W. Park & J. Priester (Eds.), *Handbook of Brand Relationships* (pp. 107–123). Armonk, NY: M. E. Sharpe.

Esch, F.-R., Möll, T., Schmitt, B., Elger, C. E., Neuhaus, C., & Weber, B. (2012). Brands on the Brain: Do Consumers use Declarative Information or Experienced Emotions to Evaluate Brands? *Journal of Consumer Psychology, 22*(1), 75–85.

Estes, Z., Gibbert, M., Guest, D., & Mazursky, D. (2012). A Dual-Process Model of Brand Extension: Taxonomic Feature-Based and Thematic Relation-Based Similarity Independently Drive Brand Extension Evaluation. *Journal of Consumer Psychology, 22*(1), 86–101.

Fazio, R. H. (1986). How Do Attitudes Guide Behavior?. In R. M. Sorrentino & E. T. Higgins (Eds.), *The Handbook of Motivation and Cognition: Foundations of Social Behavior* (pp. 204–243). New York: Guilford Press.

—— (1990). Multiple Processes by Which Attitudes Guide Behavior: The MODE Model as an Integrative Framework. *Advances in Experimental Social Psychology, 23*, 75–109.

Ferraro, R., Bettman, J. R., & Chartrand, T. L. (2009). The Power of Strangers: The Effect of Incidental Consumer Brand Encounters on Brand Choice. *Journal of Consumer Research, 35*(5), 729–741.

Ferraro, R., Kirmani, A., & Matherly, T. (2013). Look at Me! Look at Me! Conspicuous Brand Usage, Self-Brand Connection, and Dilution. *Journal of Marketing Research, 50*(4), 477–488.

Fiske, S. T., Cuddy, A. J., Glick, P., & Xu, J. (2002). A Model of (Often Mixed) Stereotype Content: Competence and Warmth Respectively Follow from Perceived Status and Competition. *Journal of Personality and Social Psychology, 82*(6), 878–902.

Fournier, S. (1998). Consumers and Their Brands: Developing Relationship Theory in Consumer Research. *Journal of Consumer Research, 24*(4), 343–373.

—— (2009). Lessons Learned about Consumers' Relationships with Their Brands. *Handbook of Brand Relationships, 5*, 23.

Fournier, S., & Alvarez, C. (2012). Brands as Relationship Partners: Warmth, Competence, and In-Between. *Journal of Consumer Psychology, 2*(22), 177–185.

—— (2013). Relating Badly to Brands. *Journal of Consumer Psychology, 23*(2), 253–264.

Fournier, S., & Avery, J. (2011). The Uninvited Brand. *Business Horizons, 54*(3), 193–207.

Friestad, M., & Wright, P. (1994). The Persuasion Knowledge Model: How People Cope with Persuasion Attempts. *Journal of Consumer Research, 21*(1), 1–31.

Garvey, A. M., Germann, F., & Bolton, L. E. (2016). Performance Brand Placebos: How Brands Improve Performance and Consumers Take the Credit. *Journal of Consumer Research, 42*(6), 931–951.

Ghuman, M. K., Huang, L., Madden, T. J., & Roth, M. S. (2015). Anthropomorphism and Consumer-brand Relationships. *Strong Brands, Strong Relationships*, 135–148.

Greenwald, A. G., Banaji, M. R. (1995). *Implicit Social Cognition: Attitudes, Self-Esteem, and Stereotypes. Psychological Review, 102*(1), 4–27.

Grégoire, Y., Tripp, T. M., & Legoux, R. (2009). When Customer Love Turns into Lasting Hate: The Effects of Relationship Strength and Time on Customer Revenge and Avoidance. *Journal of Marketing, 73*(6), 18–32.

Grewal, D., Bart, Y., Spann, M., & Zubcsek, P. P. (2016). Mobile Advertising: A Framework and Research Agenda. *Journal of Interactive Marketing, 34*, 3–14.

Grewal, D., Krishnan, R., Baker, J., & Borin, N. (1998). The Effect of Store Name, Brand Name and Price Discounts on Consumers' Evaluations and Purchase Intentions. *Journal of Retailing, 74*(3), 331–352.

Gunasti, K., & Ross, W. T. (2009). How Inferences About Missing Attributes Decrease the Tendency to Defer Choice and Increase Purchase Probability. *Journal of Consumer Research, 35*(5), 823–837.

Gustafsson, A., Johnson, M. D., & Roos, I. (2005). The Effects of Customer Satisfaction, Relationship Commitment Dimensions, and Triggers on Customer Retention. *Journal of Marketing, 69*(4), 210–218.

Hamerman, E. J., & Johar, G. V. (2013). Conditioned Superstition: Desire for Control and Consumer Brand Preferences. *Journal of Consumer Research, 40*(3), 428–443.

Homer, P. M. (2009). Product Placements. *Journal of Advertising, 38*(3), 21–32.

Hsee, C. K., Yang, Y., Zheng, X., & Wang, H. (2015). Lay Rationalism: Individual Differences in Using Reason Versus Feelings to Guide Decisions. *Journal of Marketing Research, 52*(1), 134–146.

Hsu, L., Fournier, S., & Srinivasan, S. (2016). Brand Architecture Strategy and Firm Value: How Leveraging, Separating, and Distancing the Corporate Brand Affects Risk and Returns. *Journal of the Academy of Marketing Science, 44*(2), 261–280.

Hung, K. (2000). Narrative Music in Congruent and Incongruent TV Advertising. *Journal of Advertising, 29*(1), 25–34.

Irmak, C., Block, L. G., & Fitzsimons, G. J. (2005). The Placebo Effect in Marketing: Sometimes You Just Have to Want it to Work. *Journal of Marketing Research, 42*(4), 406–409.

Janiszewski, C. (1993). Preattentive Mere Exposure Effects. *Journal of Consumer Research, 20*(3), 376–392.

Jiang, Y., Gorn, G. J., Galli, M., & Chattopadhyay, A. (2016). Does Your Company Have the Right Logo? How and Why Circular-and Angular-Logo Shapes Influence Brand Attribute Judgments. *Journal of Consumer Research, 42*(5), 709–726.

Kähr, A., Nyffenegger, B., Krohmer, H., & Hoyer, W. D. (2016). When Hostile Consumers Wreak Havoc on Your Brand: The Phenomenon of Consumer Brand Sabotage. *Journal of Marketing, 80*(3), 25–41.

Kao, D. T. (2015). Is Cinderella Resurging? The Impact of Consumers' Underdog Disposition on Brand Preferences: Underdog Brand Biography and Brand Status as Moderators. *Journal of Consumer Behaviour, 14*(5), 307–316.

Keller, K. L. (1993). Conceptualizing, Measuring, and Managing Customer-Based Brand Equity. *The Journal of Marketing, 57*, 1–22.

Kervyn, N., Chan, E., Malone, C., Korpusik, A., & Ybarra, O. (2014). Not All Disasters Are Equal in the Public's Eye: The Negativity Effect on Warmth in Brand Perception. *Social Cognition, 32*(3), 256–275.

Kervyn, N., Fiske, S. T., & Malone, C. (2012). Brands as Intentional Agents Framework: How Perceived Intentions and Ability Can Map Brand Perception. *Journal of Consumer Psychology: The Official Journal of the Society for Consumer Psychology, 22*(2), 166–176.

Kim, A. J., & Ko, E. (2012). Do Social Media Marketing Activities Enhance Customer Equity? An Empirical Study of Luxury Fashion Brand. *Journal of Business Research, 65*(10), 1480–1486.

Kim, H. C., & Kramer, T. (2015). Do Materialists Prefer the "Brand-as-Servant"? The Interactive Effect of Anthropomorphized Brand Roles and Materialism on Consumer Responses. *Journal of Consumer Research, 42*(2), 284–299.

Klink, R. R. (2001). Creating Meaningful New Brand Names: A Study of Semantics and Sound Symbolism. *Journal of Marketing Theory and Practice, 9*(2), 27–34.

Kohli, C. S., Harich, K. R., & Leuthesser, L. (2005). Creating Brand Identity: A Study of Evaluation of New Brand Names. *Journal of Business Research, 58*(11), 1506–1515.

Krishna, A., & Schwarz, N. (2014). Sensory Marketing, Embodiment, and Grounded Cognition: A Review and Introduction. *Journal of Consumer Psychology, 24*(2), 159–168.

Kwak, H., Puzakova, M., & Rocereto, J. F. (2015). Better Not Smile at the Price: The Differential Role of Brand Anthropomorphization on Perceived Price Fairness. *Journal of Marketing, 79*(4), 56–76.

Kwon, J., & Nayakankuppam, D. (2015). Strength Without Elaboration: The Role of Implicit Self-Theories in Forming and Accessing Attitudes. *Journal of Consumer Research, 42*(2), 316–339.

Labrecque, L. I. (2014). Fostering Consumer–Brand Relationships in Social Media Environments: The Role of Parasocial Interaction. *Journal of Interactive Marketing, 28*(2), 134–148.

Labroo, A. A., Dhar, R., & Schwarz, N. (2008). Of Frog Wines and Frowning Watches: Semantic Priming, Perceptual Fluency, and Brand Evaluation. *Journal of Consumer Research, 34*(6), 819–831.

Lambrecht, A., & Tucker, C. (2013). When Does Retargeting Work? Information Specificity in Online Advertising. *Journal of Marketing Research, 50*(5), 561–576.

Laroche, M., Habibi, M. R., & Richard, M.-O. (2013). To Be or Not To Be in Social Media: How Brand Loyalty is Affected by Social Media? *International Journal of Information Management, 33*(1), 76–82.

Lee, A. Y., & Labroo, A. A. (2004). The Effect of Conceptual and Perceptual Fluency on Brand Evaluation. *Journal of Marketing Research, 41*(2), 151–165.

Lovett, M. J., Peres, R., & Shachar, R. (2013). On Brands and Word of Mouth. *Journal of Marketing Research, 50*(4), 427–444.

Lowrey, T. M., & Shrum, L. J. (2007). Phonetic Symbolism and Brand Name Preference. *Journal of Consumer Research, 34*(3), 406–414.

Malär, L., Krohmer, H., Hoyer, W. D., & Nyffenegger, B. (2011). Emotional Brand Attachment and Brand Personality: The Relative Importance of the Actual and the Ideal Self. *Journal of Marketing, 75*(4), 35–52.

Mathur, P., Jain, S. P., & Maheswaran, D. (2012). Consumers' Implicit Theories about Personality Influence their Brand Personality Judgments. *Journal of Consumer Psychology, 22*(4), 545–557.

McQuarrie, E. F., & Mick, D. G. (2003). Visual and Verbal Rhetorical Figures Under Directed Processing Versus Incidental Exposure to Advertising. *Journal of Consumer Research, 29*(4), 579–587.

Mende, M., Bolton, R. N., & Bitner, M. J. (2013). Decoding Customer-Firm Relationships: How Attachment Styles Help Explain Customers' Preferences for Closeness, Repurchase Intentions, and Changes in Relationship Breadth. *Journal of Marketing Research, 50*(1), 125–142.

Melnyk, V., Klein, K., & Völckner, F. (2012). The Double-Edged Sword of Foreign Brand Names for Companies from Emerging Countries. *Journal of Marketing, 76*(6), 21–37.

Meyvis, T., Goldsmith, K., & Dhar, R. (2012). The Importance of the Context in Brand Extension: How Pictures and Comparisons Shift Consumers' Focus from Fit to Quality. *Journal of Marketing Research, 49*(2), 206–217.

Miller, F., Fournier, S., & Allen, C. (2012). Exploring Relationship Analogues in the Brand Space. *Consumer-brand Relationships: Theory and Practice* (pp. 30–56). New York: Routledge.

Monga, A. B., & John, D. R. (2010). What Makes Brands Elastic? The Influence of Brand Concept and Styles of Thinking on Brand Extension Evaluation. *Journal of Marketing, 74*(3), 80–92.

Mulyanegara, R. C., Tsarenko, Y., & Anderson, A. (2009). The Big Five and Brand Personality: Investigating the Impact of Consumer Personality on Preferences Towards Particular Brand Personality. *Journal of Brand Management, 16*(4), 234–247.

Muniz, A. M., & O'Guinn, T. C. (2001). Brand Community. *Journal of Consumer Research, 27*(4), 412–432.

Paharia, N., Avery, J., & Keinan, A. (2014). Positioning Brands Against Large Competitors to Increase Sales. *Journal of Marketing Research, 51*(6), 647–656.

Paharia, N., Keinan, A., Avery, J., & Schor, J. B. (2011). The Underdog Effect: The Marketing of Disadvantage and Determination Through Brand Biography. *Journal of Consumer Research, 37*(5), 775–790.

Park, C. W., Eisingerich, A. B., & Park, J. W. (2013). Attachment–Aversion (AA) Model of Customer–Brand Relationships. *Journal of Consumer Psychology, 23*(2), 229–248.

Park, C. W., MacInnis, D. J., Priester, J., Eisingerich, A. B., & Iacobucci, D. (2010). Brand Attachment and Brand Attitude Strength: Conceptual and Empirical Differentiation of Two Critical Brand Equity Drivers. *Journal of Marketing, 74*(6), 1–17.

Park, J. K., & John, D. R. (2010). Got to Get You into My Life: Do Brand Personalities Rub Off on Consumers? *Journal of Consumer Research, 37*(4), 655–669.

—— (2012). Capitalizing on Brand Personalities in Advertising: The Influence of Implicit Self-Theories on Ad Appeal Effectiveness. *Journal of Consumer Psychology, 22*(3), 424–432.

—— (2014). I Think I Can, I Think I Can: Brand Use, Self-Efficacy, and Performance. *Journal of Marketing Research, 51*(2), 233–247.

Pauwels, K., Aksehirli, Z., & Lackman, A. (2016). Like the Ad or the Brand? Marketing Stimulates Different Electronic Word-Of-Mouth Content to Drive Online and Offline Performance. *International Journal of Research in Marketing, 33*(3), 639–655.

Pavia, T. M., & Costa, J. A. (1993). The Winning Number: Consumer Perceptions of Alpha-Numeric Brand Names. *The Journal of Marketing, 57*(3), 85–98.

Perkins, A. W., & Forehand, M. R. (2012). Implicit Self-Referencing: The Effect of Nonvolitional Self-Association on Brand and Product Attitude. *Journal of Consumer Research, 39*(1), 142–156.

Plassmann, H., & Weber, B. (2015). Individual Differences in Marketing Placebo Effects: Evidence from Brain Imaging and Behavioral Experiments. *Journal of Marketing Research, 52*(4), 493–510.

Pozharliev, R., Verbeke, W. J., Van Strien, J. W., & Bagozzi, R. P. (2015). Merely Being with You Increases My Attention to Luxury Products: Using EEG to Understand Consumers' Emotional Experience with Luxury Branded Products. *Journal of Marketing Research, 52*(4), 546–558.

Price, L. L., & Arnould, E. (1999). Commercial Friendships: Service Provider-Client Relationships in Social Context. *Journal of Marketing, 63*(4), 38–56.

Puligadda, S., Ross Jr, W. T., & Grewal, R. (2012). Individual Differences in Brand Schematicity. *Journal of Marketing Research, 49*(1), 115–130.

Puzakova, M., Kwak, H., & Rocereto, J. F. (2013). When Humanizing Brands Goes Wrong: The Detrimental Effect of Brand Anthropomorphization Amid Product Wrongdoings. *Journal of Marketing, 77*(3), 81–100.

Rahinel, R., & Redden, J. P. (2013). Brands as Product Coordinators: Matching Brands Make Joint Consumption Experiences More Enjoyable. *Journal of Consumer Research, 39*(6), 1290–1299.

Rao, A. R., & Monroe, K. B. (1989). The Effect of Price, Brand Name, and Store Name on Buyers' Perceptions of Product Quality: An Integrative Review. *Journal of Marketing Research, 26*(3), 351–357.

Redker, C., Gibson, B., & Zimmerman, I. (2013). Liking of Movie Genre Alters the Effectiveness of Background Product Placements. *Basic and Applied Social Psychology, 35*(3), 249–255.

Rindfleisch, A., & Inman, J. (1998). Explaining the Familiarity-Liking Relationship: Mere Exposure, Information Availability, or Social Desirability? *Marketing Letters, 9*(1), 5–19.

Roggeveen, A. L., Grewal, D., Townsend, C., & Krishnan, R. (2015). The Impact of Dynamic Presentation Format on Consumer Preferences for Hedonic Products and Services. *Journal of Marketing, 79*(6), 34–49.

Romani, S., Grappi, S., Zarantonello, L., & Bagozzi, R. P. (2015). The Revenge of the Consumer! How Brand Moral Violations Lead to Consumer Anti-Brand Activism. *Journal of Brand Management, 22*(8), 658–672.

Russell, C. A., & Schau, H. J. (2014). When Narrative Brands End: The Impact of Narrative Closure and Consumption Sociality on Loss Accommodation. *Journal of Consumer Research, 40*(6), 1039–1062.

Schumann, J. H., von Wangenheim, F., & Groene, N. (2014). Targeted Online Advertising: Using Reciprocity Appeals to Increase Acceptance Among Users of Free Web Services. *Journal of Marketing, 78*(1), 59–75.

Sela, A., Wheeler, S. C., & Sarial-Abi, G. (2012). We Are Not the Same as You and I: Causal Effects of Minor Language Variations on Consumers' Attitudes Toward Brands. *Journal of Consumer Research, 39*(3), 644–661.

Shiv, B., Carmon, Z., & Ariely, D. (2005). Placebo Effects of Marketing Actions: Consumers May Get What They Pay For. *Journal of Marketing Research, 42*(4), 383–393.

Shrum, L., Lowrey, T. M., Luna, D., Lerman, D., & Liu, M. (2012). Sound Symbolism Effects Across Languages: Implications for Global Brand Names. *International Journal of Research in Marketing, 29*(3), 275–279.

Sood, S., & Keller, K. L. (2012). The Effects of Brand Name Structure on Brand Extension Evaluations and Parent Brand Dilution. *Journal of Marketing Research, 49*(3), 373–382.

Spiggle, S., Nguyen, H. T., & Caravella, M. (2012). More Than Fit: Brand Extension Authenticity. *Journal of Marketing Research, 49*(6), 967–983.

Srinivasan, S., Vanhuele, M., & Pauwels, K. (2010). Mind-Set Metrics in Market Response Models: An Integrative Approach. *Journal of Marketing Research, 47*(4), 672–684.

Stephen, A. T. (2016). The Role of Digital and Social Media Marketing in Consumer Behavior. *Current Opinion in Psychology, 10*, 17–21.

241

Strick, M., de Bruin, H. L., de Ruiter, L. C., & Jonkers, W. (2015). Striking the Right Chord: Moving Music Increases Psychological Transportation and Behavioral Intentions. *Journal of Experimental Psychology: Applied, 21*(1), 57–72.

Swaminathan, V., Stilley, K. M., & Ahluwalia, R. (2009). When Brand Personality Matters: The Moderating Role of Attachment Styles. *Journal of Consumer Research, 35*(6), 985–1002.

Sweldens, S., Van Osselaer, S. M., & Janiszewski, C. (2010). Evaluative Conditioning Procedures and the Resilience of Conditioned Brand Attitudes. *Journal of Consumer Research, 37*(3), 473–489.

Thomson, M., MacInnis, D. J., & Park, C. W. (2005). The Ties that Bind: Measuring the Strength of Consumers' Emotional Attachments to Brands. *Journal of Consumer Psychology, 15*(1), 77–91.

Thomson, M., Whelan, J., & Johnson, A. R. (2012). Why Brands Should Fear Fearful Consumers: How Attachment Style Predicts Retaliation. *Journal of Consumer Psychology, 22*(2), 289–298.

Touré-Tillery, M., & McGill, A. L. (2015). Who or What to Believe: Trust and the Differential Persuasiveness of Human and Anthropomorphized Messengers. *Journal of Marketing, 79*(4), 94–110.

Tucker, C. E. (2014). Social Networks, Personalized Advertising, and Privacy Controls. *Journal of Marketing Research, 51*(5), 546–562.

Walsh, M. F., Winterich, K. P., & Mittal, V. (2010). Do Logo Redesigns Help or Hurt Your Brand? The Role of Brand Commitment. *Journal of Product & Brand Management, 19*(2), 76–84.

White, K., & Dahl, D. W. (2007). Are All Out-Groups Created Equal? Consumer Identity and Dissociative Influence. *Journal of Consumer Research, 34*(4), 525–536.

Wittenbraker, J., Zeitoun, H., & Fournier, S. (2015). Using Relationship Metaphors to Understand and Track Brands. *Strong Brands, Strong Relationships* (360–375). Taylor & Francis.

Wright, P. (1986). Presidential Address Schemer Schema: Consumers' Intuitive Theories about Marketers' Influence Tactics. *NA-Advances in Consumer Research, 13*, 1–3.

Yang, L. W., Cutright, K. M., Chartrand, T. L., & Fitzsimons, G. J. (2014). Distinctively Different: Exposure to Multiple Brands in Low-Elaboration Settings. *Journal of Consumer Research, 40*(5), 973–992.

Yorkston, E., & Menon, G. (2004). A Sound Idea: Phonetic Effects of Brand Names on Consumer Judgments. *Journal of Consumer Research, 31*(1), 43–51.

Yorkston, E. A., Nunes, J. C., & Matta, S. (2010). The Malleable Brand: The Role of Implicit Theories in Evaluating Brand Extensions. *Journal of Marketing, 74*(1), 80–93.

Zayas, V., & Shoda, Y. (2014). Love You? Hate You? Maybe It's Both: Evidence That Significant Others Trigger Bivalent-Priming. *Social Psychological and Personality Science, 6*(1), 56–64.

16

BRAND ATTITUDE STRUCTURE

Frank R. Kardes, Ruth Pogacar, Roseann Hassey, and Ruomeng Wu

LINDNER COLLEGE OF BUSINESS AT THE UNIVERSITY
OF CINCINNATI, CINCINNATI, OH, USA

Brand attitudes have been and continue to be one of the most extensively studied topics in consumer research. A brand attitude is an evaluative judgment of a brand, and this chapter focuses on brand attitude structure. Like all attitudes, brand attitudes are influenced by cognitive responses (e.g., beliefs, knowledge), affective responses (e.g., feelings, moods, and emotions), and behavior (e.g., cognitive dissonance reduction following behavior, inferences from behavior). In addition to being influenced by cognition, affect, and behavior, brand attitudes also influence cognition, affect, and behavior (Zanna & Rempel, 1988). These reciprocal relationships explain how one attitudinal component can influence the other two, thereby increasing the predictive and explanatory power of brand attitudes.

Cognitive Influences on Brand Attitudes

Expectancy-Value Models

When consumers are willing and able to devote cognitive effort to brand considerations – usually in high involvement contexts – they may integrate information about many attributes to form evaluations. A person's brand attitude can be understood as their beliefs about the probability that a brand possesses certain attributes (Fishbein & Ajzen, 1975).

The expectancy-value model posits that brand attitudes can be modeled by multiplying a consumer's evaluations of each attribute by their expectations that the brand possesses each attribute (Baumgartner & Pieters, 2008; Bettman, Capon, & Lutz, 1975). For instance, imagine someone choosing between car A with low maintenance, good gas mileage, and reliability, and car B with quick acceleration, smooth handling, and a state-of-the-art sound system. A marketer might have the consumer evaluate each attribute from very bad (1) to very good (7), then rate the likelihood that each car actually possesses these attributes. The attribute ratings can then be multiplied by the likelihood ratings for each attribute, and each rating is then summed separately for car A and car B. This produces a measure of the consumer's attitude toward each car.

Mathematical models can be used to understand how consumers form attitudes by integrating multiple pieces of information. We describe two such expectancy-value models here: the theory of reasoned action, and information integration theory. One key difference between these models is that information integration theory is multiplicative (beliefs are averaged), whereas the theory of reasoned action is additive (beliefs about a brand are added to form brand attitudes).

Information Integration Theory

According to information integration theory, attitudes are formed and evolved as consumers receive, interpret, evaluate, and integrate brand attribute information. Thus, attitudes are formed by cognitive algebra, based on brand-related information stored in memory (Anderson, 1981). Information may be more or less likely to be integrated depending on its salience, the manner in which it is presented, and the degree of overall information integration, which may vary from one brand attitude to another (Schmitt, 2012). During the valuation stage, consumers evaluate the implication of each piece of information separately, and assign values to each. During the integration stage, values are multiplied to produce an integrated psychological impression. During the output stage, the brand attitude is represented by the participant's rating on a 0–100 scale (Anderson, 1981; Lynch, 1985)

This is a useful method of evaluation because consumers are often unable to explicitly tell researchers how important each attribute is to them. Information integration theory weights the importance of an attribute based on overall brand attitude ratings and individual attribute ratings following the formula: $A = \Sigma ws$, where

A = the attitude toward the brand
w = the importance weight of each individual attribute
s = the evaluation of each attribute.

These weights (w) must sum to one. According to information integration theory, marketers can change consumers' brand attitudes by targeting the importance they place on a given attribute (w), their evaluations of a given attribute (s), or both.

Theory of Reasoned Action

The additive model of reasoned action can be represented by the following formula:

A = Σbe, where
A = the attitude toward a brand or toward buying a particular brand
b = the belief that the brand possesses a given attribute
e = evaluation of each attribute, or the extent to which the consumer likes each attribute

Thus, multiple attributes are integrated to form brand attitudes. Based on this model, attitude favorability increases as the number of favorable beliefs increases (Fishbein & Ajzen, 1975). Attitudes are consequential because, according to the theory of reasoned action, attitudes determine intentions, which in turn lead to behavior (Ajzen, 2012). However, behavioral intentions are influenced by both attitudes and norms – the attitudes and beliefs of other people and society as a whole. Consequently, a person's intention to recommend the Starbucks brand is influenced both by the person's attitude toward Starbucks and their perception of other people's attitudes toward Starbucks.

The theory of reasoned action further posits that attitudes have two components: evaluation and strength of belief. Evaluation refers to the direction or valence of a belief. For instance, someone might evaluate the HBO brand positively or negatively. Strength of belief refers to how strongly a person holds their belief. For instance, one might have a very strong, positive attitude toward HBO, or just feel mildly good about HBO (Ajzen, 2012).

Strongly held beliefs tend to be more accessible (Fishbein, 1963), and highly accessible beliefs tend to correlate more strongly with independent measures of attitude than less accessible beliefs (Petkova, Ajzen, & Driver, 1995; Van der Pligt & Eiser, 1984). Multiattribute evaluation models are particularly useful for understanding judgments of new products and unfamiliar products, because consumers are more likely to evaluate each attribute independently (Wyer, 2004). For familiar products, on the other hand, schema-based judgment processes are more likely.

Comparing the Theory of Reasoned Action and Information Integration Theory

The formulation of attitudes based on beliefs and evaluations is an important difference between the theory of reasoned action and information integration theory. Another important difference is that, unlike the theory of reasoned action, which is additive, information integration suggests that simply adding more attributes does not necessarily guarantee better brand attitudes. This is because, in an averaging model like information integration, consumers must rate each new attribute as both important and positive to result in an increase in brand attitude. In other words, an addition-based model suggests that more is better, because brand attitudes increase as the number of favorable attributes increases. However, an averaging model suggests that less is more – marketers should focus consumers' attention only on the very best brand attributes because those with lower than average ratings pull the overall rating down.

Marketing Implications of Multiattribute Evaluation Models

Multiattribute evaluations are important because they have a profound impact on brand attitudes. Different attributes can influence brand attitudes in a number of ways. For instance, brand attitudes may be influenced by brand alliances (e.g., Starbucks and S'well) such that each brand, and the alliance itself, functions as an attribute in the evaluation of the other brand (Simonin & Ruth, 1998).

Consumers also integrate information from advertisements and product trials to form brand attitudes. The order in which information is received is important to this information integration process. Smith (1993) demonstrated this by manipulating information source (advertisement only, product trial only, or advertisement and product trial) and trial favorability (positive or negative), and varying whether the advertisement preceded product trial or product trial preceded the advertisement. Advertisements reduced the negative effects of unfavorable product trials on brand evaluations, particularly when the advertisement was viewed before trial. However, advertisements were not as influential on brand attitudes after product trial.

Affective Influences on Brand Attitudes

Evaluative Conditioning

Evaluative conditioning refers to attitude formation or change that occurs when a neutral object (the conditioned stimulus) is paired with a non-neutral object (the unconditioned stimulus; Jones, Olson, & Fazio, 2010). When consumers experience two objects at the same time, a cognitive association between the two may form, leading to a conditioned response. This process was illustrated by Staats and Staats (1958), who asked participants to remember lists of words in either a visual or auditory format. Participants were exposed visually to a set of nationality names, including the neutral stimuli Dutch and Swedish. The experimenter then announced a word that was neutral, positive, or negative. The positively or negatively valenced words were systematically paired with the two neutral stimuli such that one neutral stimuli always appeared with positive words and the other with negative words. Finally, the participants were asked to recall the words and then evaluate them. Participants rated the neutral stimuli that had been paired with the positive words (either Dutch or Swedish) as more pleasant than the one paired with the negative words.

Prior research shows that evaluative conditioning is mediated by multiple mechanisms, including Pavlovian conditioning (Zanna, Kiesler, & Pilkonis, 1970), inferential reasoning (Kim, Allen, & Kardes, 1996), and a new mechanism referred to as implicit misattribution (Jones, Fazio, & Olson, 2009). As eye gaze shifts increased between the conditioned stimulus and the unconditioned stimulus, source confusability increased, and evaluative conditioning increased.

Advertisers and marketers can use evaluative conditioning as a method to induce positive brand attitudes. Research shows that evaluative conditioning is particularly effective for unfamiliar brands (Shimp, Stuart, & Engle, 1991; Cacioppo, Marshall-Goodell, Tassinary, & Petty, 1992). However, evaluative conditioning may also influence attitudes toward mature brands (Gibson, 2008). In one experiment, participants were shown Coke images paired with negative pictures and words, and Pepsi images paired with positive pictures and words. This conditioning process influenced implicit, but not explicit, attitudes toward the mature brands such that participants without strong prior preferences were subsequently more likely to select Pepsi than Coke under cognitive load.

Mood Effects

Persuasion attempts are often accompanied by efforts to change people's moods (Schwarz, Bless, & Bohner, 1991). For example, children often say nice things to their parents before making a request, and advertising professionals use funny commercials to persuade consumers. Influencing people's moods for persuasion purposes is frequently effective due to misattribution or source confusability. That is, extraneous, favorable, affective responses tend to be misattributed to the target brand. Mood can be manipulated by music, videos, pictures, or recall of emotionally involving experiences (Cohen & Andrade, 2004). Experiences such as receiving an unexpected gift can also lead to positive mood, which triggers the norm of reciprocity (Kahn & Isen, 1993), and positive mood induced by a wrapped gift can enhance gift evaluation (Howard, 1992). Favorable affective responses also increase cognitive flexibility and efficiency (Isen, 2008; Kahn & Isen, 1993).

Fluency Effects

Feelings of fluency, or feelings concerning the ease or difficulty with which information can be processed, also influence brand attitudes (Schwarz, 2004; Schwarz, Song, & Xu, 2008). This is surprising because feelings of fluency can be influenced by a host of seemingly trivial variables, such as repetition, font readability, figure-ground contrast, priming, and stimulus duration. Regardless of how they are manipulated, feelings of fluency influence evaluation, familiarity, confidence, truth, risk, beauty, and the predicted amount of effort required to follow a set of directions.

In a classic early study of fluency effects on brand attitudes, Wånke, Bohner, and Jurkowitsch (1997) asked participants to list either one or ten reasons to choose a BMW over a Mercedes Benz. Because listing one reason is experienced as easy, participants inferred that there must be many reasons to prefer a BMW over a Mercedes. By contrast, because listing ten reasons is experienced as difficult, participants inferred that there must be few reasons to prefer a BMW over a Mercedes. As a result, the BMW was preferred more strongly when participants listed one reason to prefer a BMW than when they listed ten reasons to prefer a BMW. Hence, feelings of fluency can override objective information, because objectively, ten reasons are better than one.

Simple repetition increases fluency and increases the perceived validity of a product claim (the truth effect; Dechêne, Stahl, Hansen, & Wänke, 2010). However, the truth effect is observed only under low-involvement conditions (Hawkins & Hoch, 1992). Recent research also shows that the truth effect is observed only when the need for affect (Maio & Esses, 2001), or the reliance on feelings and intuitive responses, is high (Sundar, Kardes, & Wright, 2015).

Fluency effects are also moderated by the need for cognitive closure, or the preference for a definite answer or solution, any answer or solution, rather than confusion or ambiguity (Kruglanski, 1989; Kruglanski & Webster, 1996). This leads consumers to seize on information that is easy to process and that has immediate and obvious implications for action. Once a solution is rendered, people high in need for closure freeze on this solution and are unwilling to reevaluate the solution or to consider new information. Hence, the need for cognitive closure encourages consumers to oversimplify complex problems by focusing on the information that is easiest to process. When an answer or a solution is reached, epistemic freezing or closed-mindedness occurs.

Wu, Shah, and Kardes (2016) exposed participants to repeated information or non-repeated information about a product. Participants liked the product better and rated the information as more trustworthy after exposure to repeated information, but only if participants were high in need for cognitive closure. In a follow-up study, participants high in need for closure (or under high time pressure) rated a brand as well known and reputable, regardless of whether the product information was easy or difficult to process.

One way to debias fluency effects is by warning participants about the source of feelings of fluency before they are exposed to the product information. This was illustrated by Novemsky, Dhar, Schwarz, and Simonson (2007), who reduced the fluency effect by warning participants that the information they were about to see might be difficult to process. Wu et al. (2016) replicated this effect for participants low in the need for cognitive closure, but the effect backfired for participants high in the need for cognitive closure.

Marketing Implications of Affective Influences on Brand Attitudes

Many marketing communications and retail settings are specifically designed to influence feelings, and feelings have an important impact on brand attitudes. Humorous ads, pleasant music in ads and in retail outlets, salespeople who are pleasant to interact with, cobranding, and other marketing tactics produce positive affective responses and lead consumers to form favorable brand attitudes. Other types of feelings, such as feelings of fluency, also influence brand attitudes, brand attitude confidence, and the perceived validity of brand attitudes. Recent research has also shown that feelings of fluency can be used strategically to encourage pro-environmental behavior (Kidwell, Farmer, & Hardesty, 2013).

Behavioral Influences on Brand Attitudes

Attitudes can influence behavior; however, the reverse is also true – consumers' behavior can influence their brand attitudes. This was illustrated by Albarracin and Wyer (2000), who told participants they were testing a computer instrument that assessed implicit attitudes. Participants were told they were seeing a series of statements presented subliminally on a computer screen, and they pressed one of two keys to express their intuitive reaction to the statement. The computer then "interpreted" the responses. In reality, participants were randomly assigned to conditions in which they were told that they had responded either favorably or unfavorably toward instituting comprehensive exams at the university. Thus, the false feedback led participants to believe that their behavior had indicated either support or opposition to comprehensive exams. After the feedback task, participants reported their attitudes regarding an upcoming vote for comprehensive exams, and their voting intentions. Participants who believed their behavior indicated support for comprehensive exams reported higher intentions to vote in favor of instituting comprehensive exams; conversely, those who believed their behavior in the computer task indicated opposition reported higher intentions to vote against instituting comprehensive exams.

Cognitive Dissonance Theory

According to cognitive dissonance theory, people are motivated to maintain cognitive consistency between their attitudes and behaviors (Festinger, 1957). When there is an inconsistency, for instance if someone who dislikes the Microsoft brand is forced to use the Microsoft operating system on their work computer, this conflict between attitudes and behavior produces dissonance.

Dissonance is an aversive state; therefore, people may seek to eliminate it in one of three ways. One method is to change either the attitude or behavior. For instance, the person in the previous example might change their attitude about Microsoft to reduce the dissonance of having to use it at work, particularly if the behavior has already occurred and therefore cannot be changed. Alternatively, but probably less likely, they could change their behavior by quitting the job in order to avoid having to use a brand of operating system they dislike. Another way that dissonance may be reduced is by incorporating new information that supersedes the dissonant beliefs. For example, new information about how Microsoft is primarily useful for the workplace may reduce the dissonance that an Apple user feels in response to using Microsoft at work. Finally, people may decrease dissonance by reducing the importance of their attitudes. For instance, one could convince oneself that it is better to have a job than to be unbendingly loyal to a certain software brand. In this way, the person decreases the importance of the dissonant attitude that using Microsoft products is awful.

Festinger and Carlsmith (1959) demonstrated cognitive dissonance experimentally by asking participants to perform a dull task – turning pegs in a pegboard – for an hour. Participants' attitudes toward the task were very negative. However, they were paid either $1 or $20 to tell another participant that the task was interesting. When the participants who had lied about the task subsequently evaluated the experiment, those who were paid only $1 rated the tedious task as more fun and enjoyable than those who were paid $20. Festinger and Carlsmith propose that the dissonance caused by the conflicting cognitions – "I said the task was interesting" and "I actually believe it's boring" – was greater for those only paid $1, because $1 was too small an incentive to justify lying. To overcome the dissonance of having lied for only $1, these participants changed their attitudes toward the task by convincing themselves that it really was interesting and enjoyable. The participants paid $20, however, had a suffi-cient justification for their behavior, because $20 was sufficient incentive for lying, so they experienced less dissonance, and evaluated the task less highly.

Marketing Implications of Cognitive Dissonance

Cognitive dissonance theory has important implications for brand attitudes. The more con-sumers deliberate on a choice, for instance whether to buy a Honda or a Toyota, the more emotionally attached they become to each option. This leads to cognitive dissonance when one option is chosen, and the other forgone (Carmon, Wertenbroch, & Zeelenberg, 2003). To illustrate, in one experiment, participants were told they would receive one of the prod-ucts they evaluated. Participants then rated a number of products ranging from $15 to $30. Those in the low-dissonance condition chose between a desirable product and a much less desirable product. Those in the high-dissonance condition chose between two similarly desir-able products. In the control condition, participants were simply given one of the products. Then all participants rated all of the products again. Those in the high-dissonance condition, who were forced to choose between two similarly attractive products, rated the attractiveness of the chosen product much higher, and the attractiveness of the rejected product much lower, than low-dissonance or control participants, because they were more motivated to reduce the dissonance of having forgone an appealing option (Brehm, 1956).

Self-Perception Theory

Another way in which behavior can influence attitudes is via self-perception. Self-perception theory posits that people develop attitudes by observing their own behavior and concluding that they must hold an attitude that caused the behavior. This is likely to occur when the person does not have an existing attitude on the topic (Bem, 1972). For instance, if a con-sumer is ambivalent between Colgate and Crest toothpastes, and selects Crest at random, they may then conclude on the basis of their behavior that they must have a positive attitude toward the Crest brand.

To illustrate this effect, Bem (1972) instructed participants to answer questions truthfully when shown a green light, and to lie when shown a yellow light. Thus, participants were conditioned to believe their own statements when the light was green, and to disbelieve their own statements when the light was yellow. After being trained in this procedure, participants were asked to evaluate a series of cartoons that had been previously rated as neutral (neither funny nor unfunny) in the presence of the alternating colored lights. Participants were instructed to say either "this cartoon is very funny" or "this cartoon is very unfunny." Then they were asked to report their actual attitudes toward each cartoon. When participants had been instructed to say "this cartoon is very funny" in the presence of the green (truth) light, they subsequently reported more positive attitudes toward the cartoon than if they had been instructed to say it was funny in the presence of the yellow (lie) light.

Marketing Implications of Self-Perception

Self-perception theory has many marketing implications, including for sales techniques. For instance, the foot-in-the-door technique involves making a small request, such as answering a short questionnaire about a brand. Someone who grants a small request is subsequently more likely to comply with a larger, related request, such as buying a product made by that brand. This is because people observe their own behavior (e.g., complying with an initial request) and attribute the behavior to a positive attitude toward the brand (Snyder & Cunningham, 1975).

Goldstein and Cialdini (2007) extended self-perception theory by proposing that people sometimes infer their own attitudes by observing the behavior of others with whom they feel a sense of merged identity. Therefore, if a consumer feels a close sense of identity with their spouse, observing their spouse using a certain brand may lead them to form a positive attitude toward that brand.

Self-perception theory is also relevant for retail promotions. Consumers may be more likely to make a purchase when there is a promotion. However, the type of promotion determines the degree to which consumers develop positive brand attitudes and repeat purchase intentions. Price promotions lead consumers to ask themselves after purchasing whether they bought the brand because they like it, or because of the promotion. Since consumers are likely to conclude that they made the purchase due to the promotion, they may infer on the basis of their opportunistic behavior that they do not actually care for the brand very much. Conversely, non-price promotions, such as sampling, can have a positive influence on brand attitudes, because the consumer concludes on the basis of their behavior that they took the sample because they liked it, and therefore like the brand. Consequently, brand attitudes are higher after non-price promotion, or no promotion, than after price promotion purchases (Gedenk & Neslin, 2000).

Self-Perception versus Cognitive Dissonance

Fazio, Zanna, and Cooper (1977) explored the relationship between self-perception and cognitive dissonance and found the two theories to be complementary, with each governing a specific context. Specifically, in the context of small discrepancies between attitudes and behavior, self-perception theory holds, whereas in the context of large discrepancies, cognitive dissonance theory holds. These contexts are described as the "latitude of acceptance," in which attitude-congruent behavior leads to self-perception effects, and the "latitude of rejection," in which attitude-discrepant behavior leads to dissonance effects.

Brand Attitudinal Influences on Affect

Although the literature on affective influences on brand attitudes is quite large, relatively few studies have examined brand attitudinal influences on affect. This is surprising given the popularity of affect as a research topic, and suggests that this could be a fruitful area for future investigation. Indirect support for the idea that attitudes can influence affective responses is provided by Hoch's program of research on interpreting ambiguous product experiences (Ha & Hoch, 1989; Hoch, 2002; Hoch & Deighton, 1989; Hoch & Ha, 1986). Many product experiences are ambiguous, or open to multiple interpretations. In such cases, expectations and attitudes formed on the basis of advertising and other marketing communications guide the interpretation of ambiguous evidence. Selective information processing leads consumers to focus on the aspects of experience that are consistent with prior expectations and attitudes, and to neglect aspects that are inconsistent with these expectations and attitudes. Consequently, favorable brand attitudes frequently lead to favorable affective responses during product consumption. Consistent with the implications of research on transformative advertising, strong and favorable brand attitudes can make an automobile seem to handle and ride more smoothly, make clothes seem more comfortable and fashionable, and even make snack foods seem tastier. Privately consumed products seem more fun and enjoyable, and publicly consumed products seem more chic and sophisticated when brand attitudes guide affective responses.

Brand Attitudinal Influences on Cognition

Multiattribute judgment models suggest that cognitions influence attitudes. The reverse is also possible: attitudes influence cognitions via the halo effect and the placebo effect. The halo effect occurs when overall attitudes are used to draw inferences about the specific properties or characteristics of an attitude object. Favorable (unfavorable) attitudes lead to favorable (unfavorable) inferences, and these lead consumers to overestimate the benefits of products having favorable reputations (e.g., Chernev & Blair, 2015; Schuldt & Schwarz, 2010), and leads regulators to be more lenient toward firms having favorable reputations (e.g., Hong & Liskovich, 2014). Moreover, the halo effect is so powerful that it reduces the effect of perceived attribute variability on inferential beliefs (Sundar & Kardes, 2015). Despite these consequences, little is known about moderating variables. Prior research has shown that the halo effect increases over time (Sanbonmatsu, Kardes, & Sansone, 1991), but prior attempts to reduce the halo effect have failed completely despite the use of heavy-handed forewarning and introspection procedures (Wetzel, Wilson, & Kort 1981).

However, recent research has uncovered three new moderators of the halo effect (Sundar, Kardes, & Rabino, 2016). Individual differences in critical thinking skills reduce the magnitude of the halo effect because critical thinkers are motivated to process information in an even-handed or unbiased manner and are more likely to question assumptions and consider multiple interpretations of information (Halpern, 2003). Causal reasoning mindsets (Wyer & Xu, 2010), from cause to effect (predictive reasoning) or from effect to cause (diagnostic reasoning; Fernbach, Darlow, & Sloman, 2010), also increase critical thinking and decrease magnitude of the halo effect.

Finally, the paradoxical persuasion technique has also been shown to decrease the magnitude of the halo effect. According to self-verification theory (Swann 1987; Swann, Pelham, & Chidester, 1988), consumers rely heavily on stable and strongly held attitudes because such attitudes serve to organize experience, predict future events, and guide behavior. Because of the consequential nature of these attitudes, consumers resist direct persuasion attempts and resist endorsing statements that are misrepresentative. As a result, leading questions that are consistent with but more extreme than their true attitudes encourage consumers to adopt more moderate attitudinal positions, and this leads to more moderate inferential beliefs.

Research on the marketing placebo effect has shown that consumers form more favorable attitudes toward expensive (vs. inexpensive) products, and that these attitudes influence beliefs or expectations, which then influence behavior (Shiv, Carmon, & Ariely, 2005). Subjects consumed an expensive or an inexpensive energy drink, both purported to enhance mental acuity. Subjects indicated that they believed that the drink would be more effective in expensive (vs. inexpensive) experimental conditions. In addition, subjects solved a greater number of intellectual puzzles in expensive (vs. inexpensive) experimental conditions.

Follow-up research replicated these effects with price and demonstrated that these effects generalize to several non-price-related variables (Wright, da Costa Hernandez, Sundar, Dinsmore, & Kardes, 2013). Specifically, more favorable attitudes and beliefs, along with better performance on intellectual puzzles, occurred as set size, or the number of favorable attributes used to describe the product, increased. Scarcity, or limited shelf space availability, also lead to more favorable attitudes, beliefs, and performance. Because consumers believe that bad-tasting (vs. good-tasting) medicines are more powerful and effective, a bad-tasting energy drink increased beliefs about effectiveness, as well as actual memory performance. Finally, because consumers believe that medicines in typical (vs. atypical) packaging are less risky, an energy drink in a typical package led to more favorable beliefs and better memory performance.

Brand Attitudes Influence Behavior: MODE model

Many of our decisions are so routinized that we make them with little thought or effort. For example, consider the last time you went to the grocery store to replace the jar of mayonnaise you just finished. Now contrast this experience with the significant time and effort required when making your first car or home purchase. The more important the purchase decision, the more likely we are to carefully think through the attributes of different possible alternatives prior to making our purchase decision.

In 1990, Russell Fazio first introduced the MODE model of attitude-behavior relation as a means of explaining the wide range in effort that consumers expend when making judgments and decisions. According to this theory, **M**otivation and **O**pportunity to deliberate are key **DE**terminants of the two main processes that influence consumer choice, one involving a spontaneous reaction to perceptions of the situation at hand, while the other includes conscious deliberation prior to decision making (Fazio, 1990).

The spontaneous process focuses on how the strength of specific attitudes can guide behavior with no conscious awareness or reflection on the part of the consumer, working either through an immediate response or the activation of biases in attitudes toward the object's characteristics, while also being situationally triggered by time pressure. For example, research has shown that when the word flower is presented, for most individuals a positive attitude is automatically activated (Fazio, Sanbonmatsu, Powell, & Kardes, 1986). The deliberative process, by contrast, concerns when consumers take the time to analyze the pros and cons of a particular decision or behavior, carefully contemplating the costs and benefits of alternative choices in their consideration set (Ajzen, 1991; Ajzen & Fishbein, 1980).

Central to the MODE model, the occurrence of deliberative processing hinges on the consumer's motivation to engage in careful reflection prior to choosing a specific course of action. Central to this motivation is the consumer's fear of invalidity (Kruglanski, 1989), which focuses on the consumer's desire to avoid making a wrong decision due to both the importance of the decision and the potential for negative consequences, with a relevant research example including a student's decision regarding what college to attend (Sherman & Fazio, 1983). However, while motivation is a central tenet of deliberative processing, there must also be the opportunity for thoughtful reflection to occur. More specifically, either a lack of time or resource depletion on the part of the consumer may serve to undermine motivation.

The MODE model's assumptions of motivation and opportunity as central determinants of processing type were confirmed by a seminal research study involving consumer choice scenarios using two fictitious department stores (Sanbonmatsu & Fazio, 1990). In this study, consumers were presented with general information on these two department stores, one largely favorable (Smith's) when compared to the second (Brown's). However, details on the camera department reversed this preference, with Brown's being the preferred choice when purchasing a camera. When participants were asked to state where they would prefer to make a camera purchase, the conditions for decision making were manipulated both in terms of motivation and opportunity for reflection. Specifically, some consumers were motivated to make a correct decision by being told they would have to justify their store selection decision. Additionally, opportunity for thought was limited for a subset of participants by allowing them only 15 seconds in which to make their decision, while the remaining individuals did not have this time constraint. The results of this study were consistent with MODE model predictions, namely that research participants motivated to make the correct choice *and* having unlimited time chose to shop at Brown's department store, a decision reflective of deliberative processing due to the store's overall inferior reputation but superior camera department. Conversely, participants in the other three conditions' decision to shop at Smith's, despite its inferior camera department, was based on their overall general impressions of this department store and, thus, reflective of spontaneous (or general) processing.

Marketing Implications of the MODE Model

The MODE model suggests that brand attitude accessibility can be increased through multiple mechanisms, including direct trial of free product samples, repetitive advertising, curiosity-inducing advertising, and exposure to product surveys that encourage repeated attitude activation. Any procedure that increases attitude accessibility also increases the likelihood that the attitude will influence selective perception, and consumers' interpretation of a situation requiring a purchase decision or a product usage decision.

Returning to our initial examples of purchasing mayonnaise versus one's first car or home, and using the MODE model as our framework, we now understand that strong implicit attitudes toward the Hellmann's brand might be all that is necessary when deciding which mayonnaise to purchase. Conversely, consumers are much more likely to invest considerable time and thought when purchasing their first car or home, due to the significance of the purchase and the potential for long-term negative consequences resulting from making the wrong choice. Further research has been conducted, using the MODE model, in the areas of familiar versus unfamiliar products (Arvola, Lähteenmäki & Tuorila, 1999), loyalty to an existing brand despite the advantages of a newly introduced and seemingly superior product (for recent examples see Chaudhuri & Holbrook, 2001; Kim, Han, & Park, 2001), as well as a host of other marketing-related areas.

Controversies and Future Research Directions

Constructed versus Retrieved Brand Attitudes

Perhaps the greatest controversy in attitude research surrounds the question regarding whether attitudes are summary evaluations stored in memory for later retrieval and use, or whether attitudes are constructed whenever evaluations are needed, and are never retrieved from memory. Some researchers argue that automatic online attitude formation and storage in memory occurs whenever a consumer is exposed to an attitude object (Bargh, 2002; Ferguson & Zayas, 2009), whereas others argue that attitudes are merely constructed epiphenomena (Schwarz, Song, & Xu, 2008).

In one attempt to resolve this controversy, Cronley, Mantel, and Kardes (2010) employed a response-latency-based methodology to distinguish between the retrieval of previously formed brand attitudes versus newly constructed brand attitudes. Accuracy motivation was manipulated and the need to evaluate was measured (Jarvis & Petty, 1996). As the need to evaluate increases, consumers are more likely to form attitudes spontaneously and are more likely to possess a relatively large number of attitudes and opinions. Half of the subjects were induced to consolidate their attitudes via multiple, standard, paper-and-pencil attitude scales, and half were not. When attitudes are formed spontaneously and later retrieved from memory, this consolidation versus no-consolidation manipulation has no effect on response latencies to attitudinal inquiries. Conversely, when attitudes are constructed rather than retrieved, faster response latencies are observed in consolidation than in no-consolidation conditions. The results showed that consolidation had no effect when accuracy motivation or the need to evaluate was high. When accuracy motivation or the need to evaluate was low, however, faster response latencies were found in consolidation conditions. Hence, when consumers follow the central route to persuasion due to high accuracy motivation or due to a high need to evaluate, brand attitudes are formed spontaneously and are subsequently retrieved from memory relatively quickly when an attitudinal response is needed. However, when consumers follow the peripheral route to persuasion due to low accuracy motivation or due to a low need to evaluate, a relatively time-consuming brand attitude construction process occurred in no-consolidation conditions.

In a follow-up experiment (Cronley et al., 2010, experiment 1b), conceptually similar results were obtained using a cognitive load manipulation instead of an accuracy motivation manipulation. Again, when cognitive load was low, subjects were more likely to follow the central route to persuasion and form brand attitudes spontaneously. Conversely, when cognitive load was high, subjects were more likely to follow the peripheral route to persuasion and construct brand attitudes, on the spot, when asked to respond to attitudinal inquiries.

Attitude relevance, attitude accessibility, and incidental processing were manipulated in another follow-up experiment (Cronley et al., 2010, experiment 2). When the need to evaluate was high, consolidation had no effect on attitude latencies across conditions. However, when the need to evaluate was low, consolidation had a pronounced effect on attitude latencies in incidental processing conditions, a weaker effect in high attitude accessibility conditions, and no effect in high attitude relevance conditions. In a final experiment (Cronley et al., 2010, experiment 3), spontaneously formed brand attitudes had a larger effect on non-hypothetical brand choice, relative to constructed brand attitudes.

Additional evidence for the power and functionality of spontaneously formed attitudes was provided by Fazio and Powell (1997). Because accessible attitudes simplify everyday decision making, accessible attitudes serve to reduce stress and maintain mental and physical health, as assessed by the Hopkins Symptom Checklist, the Cohen–Hoberman Inventory of Physical Symptoms, and the Beck Depression Inventory. When initial health was poor, on the other hand, accessible attitudes facilitated recovery. These beneficial effects of accessible attitudes would not be observed if attitudes were merely constructed epiphenomena.

Singular versus Comparative Brand Attitudes

Even when many brands are available, consumers often simplify information processing by evaluating brands one at a time (singular evaluation), rather than by comparing two or more brands (comparative evaluation; Kardes, 2013). Because comparative processing is more effortful than singular processing, consumers often compare brands only when they are explicitly instructed to do so (Wang & Wyer, 2002). Furthermore, comparative processing is likely only when the motivation and the opportunity to process information carefully are high (Sanbonmatsu, Vanous, Hook, Posavac, & Kardes, 2011). Consumers are often cognitive misers, and this encourages the use of singular processing over comparative processing.

The conditions under which singular versus comparative processing are likely to occur can be investigated by orthogonally manipulating the valence of information about a focal target and the remaining alternatives. When singular processing occurs, the valence of the information about the alternatives has no influence on evaluation. When comparative processing occurs, the valence of the information about the alternatives influences evaluation. The valence of the information about the alternatives has no effect when accountability is low or when time pressure is high. In addition, the relative amount of time spent reading about the alternatives is low when time pressure is high (Sanbonmatsu et al., 2011).

The direction-of-comparison effect, or the tendency to weigh the unique features of the focal option more heavily than the unique features of the alternative option, also decreases when the singular processing is likely due to an impression set (i.e., instructions to form a global impression of each option; Sanbonmatsu, Kardes, & Gibson, 1991), or due to a low need for cognition, or due to the preference to think as little as possible (Mantel & Kardes, 1999). The direction-of-comparison effect is more pronounced when comparative processing is likely due to a memory set (e.g., instructions to memorize the specific features of each option) or due to a high need for cognition.

Research on the brand positivity effect, or the tendency to overvalue the first satisfactory brand that is encountered, shows that the brand positivity effect is a singular processing phenomenon, and that the effect is diminished when comparative processing occurs (Posavac, Kardes, Sanbonmatsu, & Fitzsimons, 2005; Posavac, Sanbonmatsu, Kardes, & Fitzsimons, 2004). Singular processing also encourages consumers to rate all brands as better than average, provided that the brands are moderately favorable (Klar & Giladi, 1997). The better-than-average effect disappears when comparative processing is likely.

Implicit versus Explicit Brand Attitudes

Traditional attitude scales ask consumers to evaluate objects on semantic differential or Likert scales. These scales are explicit attitude measures because consumers are well aware that an evaluative response is required. Recently, greater attention and interest has been allocated to implicit attitude measures, such as the Implicit Association Test (IAT; Greenwald, McGhee, & Schwartz, 1998; Perkins, Forehand, Greenwald, & Maison, 2008). This test assesses the strength of an association between a target object and an attribute dimension by measuring the latency with which subjects can press two response keys when each has been assigned a dual meaning. For example, one key could be assigned to two brands (e.g., Coke and Pepsi) and the other key could be assigned to two evaluative categories (e.g., good and bad). As the strength of the association between two concepts increases, response latency decreases. The procedure has been used to study stereotyping and other types of evaluative responses that participants often attempt to control or censor. Implicit attitudes can be consequential for branding; for instance, evidence suggests that nonconscious perceptions based on attributes like the sounds in a brand's name may influence brand performance in the marketplace (Pogacar, Plant, Rosulek, & Kouril, 2015).

Although advocates of the IAT and related priming procedures argue that the procedure assesses unconscious or implicit attitudes, others argue that it is unclear exactly what implicit measures actually assess (Fazio & Olson, 2003). It also is surprisingly difficult to predict patterns of correlation among explicit and implicit attitude measures, although the MODE model has provided some guidance on this issue. If the motivation or the opportunity to deliberate is low when an explicit measure is administered, explicit and implicit measures should be correlated. When motivation and opportunity to deliberate are high, explicit and implicit measures should diverge. Some evidence for this prediction has been obtained (Koole, Dijksterhuis & van Knippenberg, 2001). However, additional research is needed to shed light on the theoretical underpinnings and the appropriate interpretation of implicit and explicit attitude measures. Hence, brand attitude structure will continue to be an important topic of investigation for many years to come.

References

Ajzen, I. (1991). The theory of planned behavior. *Organizational Behavior and Human Decision Processes*, *50*, 179–211.

Ajzen, I. (2012). Attitudes and persuasion. In Deaux, K. & Snyder, M. (Eds.), *The Oxford handbook of personality and social psychology* (pp. 367–393). New York: Oxford University Press.

Ajzen, I., & Fishbein, M. (1980). *Understanding attitudes and predicting social behavior*. Englewood Cliffs, NJ: Prentice-Hall.

Arvola, A., Lähteenmäki, L., & Tuorila, H. (1999). Predicting the intent to purchase unfamiliar and familiar cheeses: The effects of attitudes, expected liking and food neophobia. *Appetite*, *32*, 113–126.

Albarracin, D., & Wyer Jr, R. S. (2000). The cognitive impact of past behavior: Influences on beliefs, attitudes, and future behavioral decisions. *Journal of Personality and Social Psychology*, *79*, 5–22.

Anderson, N. H. (1981). *Foundations of information integration theory*. New York: Academic Press.

Bargh, J. A. (2002). Losing consciousness: Automatic influences on consumer judgment, behavior, and motivation. *Journal of Consumer Research*, *29*, 280–285.

Baumgartner, H. and Pieters, R. (2008). Goal-directed consumer behavior: Motivation, volition, and affect. In C. P. Haugtvedt, P. M. Herr, & F. R. Kardes (Eds.), *Handbook of consumer psychology* (pp. 367–392). New York: Erlbaum.

Bem, D. J. (1972). Constructing cross-situational consistencies in behavior: Some thoughts on Alker's critique of Mischel. *Journal of Personality*, *40*, 17–26.

Bettman, J. R., Capon, N., & Lutz, R. J. (1975). Cognitive algebra in multi-attribute attitude models. *Journal of Marketing Research*, *12*, 151–164.

Brehm, J. W. (1956). Postdecision changes in the desirability of alternatives. *The Journal of Abnormal and Social Psychology*, *52*, 384–389.

Cacioppo, J. T., Marshall-Goodell, B. S., Tassinary, L. G., & Petty, R. E. (1992). Rudimentary determinants of attitudes: Classical conditioning is more effective when prior knowledge about the attitude stimulus is low than high. *Journal of Experimental Social Psychology*, *28*, 207–233.

Carmon, Z., Wertenbroch, K., & Zeelenberg, M. (2003). Option attachment: When deliberating makes choosing feel like losing. *Journal of Consumer Research*, *30*, 15–29.

Chaudhuri, A., & Holbrook, M. B. (2001). The chain of effects from brand trust and brand affect to brand performance: The role of brand loyalty. *Journal of Marketing*, *65*, 81–93.

Chernev, A., & Blair, S. (2015). Doing well by doing good: The benevolent halo of corporate social responsibility. *Journal of Consumer Research*, *41*, 1412–1425.

Cohen, J. B., & Andrade, E. B. (2004). Affective intuition and task-contingent affect regulation. *Journal of Consumer Research*, *31*, 358–367.

Cronley, M. L., Mantel, S. P., & Kardes, F. R. (2010). Effects of accuracy motivation and need to evaluate on mode of attitude formation and attitude–behavior consistency. *Journal of Consumer Psychology*, *20*, 274–281.

Dechêne, A., Stahl, C., Hansen, J., & Wänke, M. (2010). The truth about the truth: A meta-analytic review of the truth effect. *Personality and Social Psychology Review*, *14*, 238–257.

Fazio, R. H. (1990). Multiple processes by which attitudes guide behavior: The mode model as an integrative framework. *Advances in Experimental Social Psychology*, *23*, 75–109.

Fazio, R. H., & Olson, M. A. (2003). Implicit measures in social cognition research: Their meaning and use. *Annual Review of Psychology*, *54*, 297–327.

Fazio, R. H., & Powell, M. C. (1997). On the value of knowing one's likes and dislikes: Attitude accessibility, stress, and health in college. *Psychological Science*, *8*, 430–436.

Fazio, R. H., Sanbonmatsu, D. M., Powell, M. C., & Kardes, F. R. (1986). On the automatic activation of attitudes. *Journal of Personality and Social Psychology*, *50*, 229–238.

Fazio, R. H., Zanna, M. P., & Cooper, J. (1977). Dissonance and self-perception: An integrative view of each theory's proper domain of application. *Journal of Experimental Social Psychology*, *13*, 464–479.

Ferguson, M. J., & Zayas, V. (2009). Automatic evaluation. *Current Directions in Psychological Science, 18,* 362–366.

Fernbach, P. M., Darlow, A., & Sloman, S. A. (2010). Neglect of alternative causes in predictive but not diagnostic reasoning. *Psychological Science, 21,* 329–336.

Festinger, L. (1957). *A theory of cognitive dissonance.* Evanston, IL: Row, Peterson.

Festinger, L., & Carlsmith, J. M. (1959). Cognitive consequences of forced compliance. *The Journal of Abnormal and Social Psychology, 58,* 203–210.

Fishbein, M. (1963). An investigation of the relationships between beliefs about an object and the attitude toward that object. *Human Relations, 16,* 233–240.

Fishbein, M., & Ajzen, I. (1975). *Belief, attitude, intention and behavior: An introduction to theory and research.* Reading, MA: Addison-Wesley.

Gedenk, K., & Neslin, S. A. (2000). The role of retail promotion in determining future brand loyalty: Its effect on purchase event feedback. *Journal of Retailing, 75,* 433–459.

Gibson, B. (2008). Can evaluative conditioning change attitudes toward mature brands? New evidence from the Implicit Association Test. *Journal of Consumer Research, 35,* 178–188.

Goldstein, N. J., & Cialdini, R. B. (2007). The spyglass self: A model of vicarious self-perception. *Journal of Personality and Social Psychology, 92,* 402–417.

Greenwald, A. G., McGhee, D. E., & Schwartz, J. L. (1998). Measuring individual differences in implicit cognition: The implicit association test. *Journal of Personality and Social Psychology, 74,* 1464–1480.

Ha, Y. W., & Hoch, S. J. (1989). Ambiguity, processing strategy, and advertising-evidence interactions. *Journal of Consumer Research, 16,* 354–360.

Halpern, J. Y. (2003). *Reasoning about uncertainty.* Cambridge, MA: MIT Press.

Hawkins, S. A., & Hoch, S. J. (1992). Low-involvement learning: Memory without evaluation. *Journal of Consumer Research, 19,* 212–225.

Hoch, S. J. (2002). Product experience is seductive. *Journal of Consumer Research, 29,* 448–454.

Hoch, S. J., & Deighton, J. (1989). Managing what consumers learn from experience. *Journal of Marketing, 53,* 1–20.

Hoch, S. J., & Ha, Y. W. (1986). Consumer learning: Advertising and the ambiguity of product experience. *Journal of Consumer Research, 13,* 221–233.

Hong, H., & Liskovich, I. (2014). *Crime, punishment and the halo effect of corporate social responsibility.* Unpublished manuscript, Department of Economics, Princeton University, Princeton, NJ.

Howard, D. J. (1992). Gift-wrapping effects on product attitudes: A mood-biasing explanation. *Journal of Consumer Psychology, 1,* 197–223.

Isen, A. M. (2008). Some ways in which positive affect influences decision making and problem solving. *Handbook of Emotions, 3,* 548–573.

Jarvis, W. B. G., & Petty, R. E. (1996). The need to evaluate. *Journal of Personality and Social Psychology, 70,* 172–194.

Jones, C. R., Fazio, R. H., & Olson, M. A. (2009). Implicit misattribution as a mechanism underlying evaluative conditioning. *Journal of Personality and Social Psychology, 96,* 933–948.

Jones, C. R., Olson, M. A., & Fazio, R. H. (2010). Evaluative conditioning: the "how" question. In Mark P. Zanna and James M. Olson (eds.), *Advances in experimental social psychology, 43* (pp. 205–255). Elsevier.

Kahn, B. E., & Isen, A. M. (1993). The influence of positive affect on variety seeking among safe, enjoyable products. *Journal of Consumer Research, 20,* 257–270.

Kardes, F. R. (2013). Selective versus comparative processing. *Journal of Consumer Psychology, 23,* 150–153.

Kidwell, B., Farmer, A., & Hardesty, D. M. (2013). Getting liberals and conservatives to go green: Political ideology and congruent appeals. *Journal of Consumer Research, 40,* 350–367.

Kim, C. K., Han, D., & Park, S. B. (2001). The effect of brand personality and brand identification on brand loyalty: Applying the theory of social identification. *Japanese Psychological Research, 43,* 195–206.

Kim, J., Allen, C. T., & Kardes, F. R. (1996). An investigation of the mediational mechanisms underlying attitudinal conditioning. *Journal of Marketing Research, 33,* 318–328.

Klar, Y., & Giladi, E. E. (1997). No one in my group can be below the group's average: A robust positivity bias in favor of anonymous peers. *Journal of Personality and Social Psychology, 73,* 885–901.

Koole, S. L., Dijksterhuis, A., & van Knippenberg, A. (2001). What's in a name: implicit self-esteem and the automatic self. *Journal of Personality and Social Psychology, 80,* 669–685.

Kruglanski, A. W. (1989). *Lay epistemics and human knowledge: Cognitive and motivational bases.* New York: Penguin.

Kruglanski, A. W., & Webster, D. M. (1996). Motivated closing of the mind: "Seizing" and "freezing". *Psychological Review, 103*, 263–283.

Lynch Jr, J. G. (1985). Uniqueness issues in the decompositional modeling of multiattribute overall evaluations: An information integration perspective. *Journal of Marketing Research, 22*, 1–19.

Maio, G. R., & Esses, V. M. (2001). The need for affect: Individual differences in the motivation to approach or avoid emotions. *Journal of Personality, 69*, 583–614.

Mantel, S. P., & Kardes, F. R. (1999). The role of direction of comparison, attribute-based processing, and attitude-based processing in consumer preference. *Journal of Consumer Research, 25*, 335–352.

Novemsky, N., Dhar, R., Schwarz, N., & Simonson, I. (2007). Preference fluency in choice. *Journal of Marketing Research, 44*, 347–356.

Perkins, A., Forehand, M., Greenwald, A., & Maison, D. (2008). Measuring the nonconscious. In C. P. Haugtvedt, P. M. Herr, & F. R. Kardes (Eds.), *Handbook of consumer psychology* (pp. 461–475). New York: Erlbaum.

Petkova, K. G., Ajzen, I., & Driver, B. L. (1995). Salience of anti-abortion beliefs and commitment to an attitudinal position: On the strength, structure, and predictive validity of anti-abortion attitudes. *Journal of Applied Social Psychology, 25*, 463–483.

Pogacar, R., Plant, E., Rosulek, L. F., & Kouril, M. (2015). Sounds good: Phonetic sound patterns in top brand names. *Marketing Letters, 26*, 549–563.

Posavac, S. S., Kardes, F. R., Sanbonmatsu, D. M., & Fitzsimons, G. J. (2005). Blissful insularity: When brands are judged in isolation from competitors. *Marketing Letters, 16*, 87–97.

Posavac, S. S., Sanbonmatsu, D. M., Kardes, F. R., & Fitzsimons, G. J. (2004). The brand positivity effect: When evaluation confers preference. *Journal of Consumer Research, 31*, 643–651.

Sanbonmatsu, D. M., & Fazio, R. H. (1990). The role of attitudes in memory-based decision making. *Journal of Personality and Social Psychology, 59*, 614–622.

Sanbonmatsu, D. M., Kardes, F. R., & Gibson, B. D. (1991). The role of attribute knowledge and overall evaluations in comparative judgment. *Organizational Behavior and Human Decision Processes, 48*, 131–146.

Sanbonmatsu, D. M., Kardes, F. R., & Sansone, C. (1991). Remembering less and inferring more: Effects of time of judgment on inferences about unknown attributes. *Journal of Personality and Social Psychology, 61*, 546–554.

Sanbonmatsu, D. M., Vanous, S., Hook, C., Posavac, S. S., & Kardes, F. R. (2011). Whither the alternatives: Determinants and consequences of selective versus comparative judgemental processing. *Thinking & Reasoning, 17*, 367–386.

Schmitt, B. (2012). The consumer psychology of brands. *Journal of Consumer Psychology, 22*, 7–17.

Schuldt, J. P., & Schwarz, N. (2010). The "organic" path to obesity? Organic claims influence calorie judgments and exercise recommendations. *Judgment and Decision Making, 5*, 144–150.

Schwarz, N. (2004). Meta-cognitive experiences in consumer judgment and decision making. *Journal of Consumer Psychology, 14*, 332–348.

Schwarz, N., Bless, H., & Bohner, G. (1991). Mood and persuasion: Affective states influence the processing of persuasive communications. *Advances in Experimental Social Psychology, 24*, 161–199.

Schwarz, N., Song H., & Xu, J. (2008). When thinking is difficult: Metacognitive experiences as information. In: Wånke, M. (Ed.), *The social psychology of consumer behavior* (pp. 201–223). New York: Psychology Press.

Sherman, S. J., & Fazio, R. H. (1983). Parallels between attitudes and traits as predictors of behavior. *Journal of Personality, 51*, 308–345.

Shimp, T. A., Stuart, E. W., & Engle, R. W. (1991). A program of classical conditioning experiments testing variations in the conditioned stimulus and context. *Journal of Consumer Research, 18*, 1–12.

Shiv, B., Carmon, Z., & Ariely, D. (2005). Placebo effects of marketing actions: Consumers may get what they pay for. *Journal of Marketing Research, 42*, 383–393.

Simonin, B. L., & Ruth, J. A. (1998). Is a company known by the company it keeps? Assessing the spillover effects of brand alliances on consumer brand attitudes. *Journal of Marketing Research, 35*, 30–42.

Smith, R. E. (1993). Integrating information from advertising and trial: Processes and effects on consumer response to product information. *Journal of Marketing Research, 30*, 204–219.

Snyder, M., & Cunningham, M. R. (1975). To comply or not comply: testing the self-perception explanation of the "foot-in-the-door" phenomenon. *Journal of Personality and Social Psychology, 31*, 64–67.

Staats, A. W., & Staats, C. K. (1958). Attitudes established by classical conditioning. *The Journal of Abnormal and Social Psychology, 57*, 37–40.

Sundar, A., & Kardes, F. R. (2015). The role of perceived variability and the health halo effect in nutritional inference and consumption. *Psychology & Marketing, 32*, 512–521.

Sundar, A., Kardes, F. R. & Rabino, R. (2016). New moderators of the halo effect in consumer inference. Unpublished manuscript, Department of Marketing, University of Oregon, Eugene, OR.

Sundar, A., Kardes, F. R., & Wright, S. A. (2015). The influence of repetitive health messages and sensitivity to fluency on the truth effect in advertising. *Journal of Advertising, 44*, 375–387.

Swann, W. B. (1987). Identity negotiation: Where two roads meet. *Journal of Personality and Social Psychology, 53*, 1038–1051.

Swann, W. B., Pelham, B. W., & Chidester, T. R. (1988). Change through paradox: Using self-verification to alter beliefs. *Journal of Personality and Social Psychology, 54*, 268–273.

Van der Pligt, J., & Eiser, J. R. (1984). Dimensional salience, judgment, and attitudes. In *Attitudinal judgment* (pp. 161–177). New York: Springer-Verlag.

Wang, J., & Wyer Jr, R. S. (2002). Comparative judgment processes: The effects of task objectives and time delay on product evaluations. *Journal of Consumer Psychology, 12*, 327–340.

Wänke, M., Bohner, G., & Jurkowitsch, A. (1997). There are many reasons to drive a BMW: Does imagined ease of argument generation influence attitudes? *Journal of Consumer Research, 24*, 170–178.

Wetzel, C. G., Wilson, T. D., & Kort, J. (1981). The halo effect revisited: Forewarned is not forearmed. *Journal of Experimental Social Psychology, 17*, 427–439.

Wright, S. A., da Costa Hernandez, J. M., Sundar, A., Dinsmore, J., & Kardes, F. R. (2013). If it tastes bad it must be good: Consumer naïve theories and the marketing placebo effect. *International Journal of Research in Marketing, 30*, 197–198.

Wu, R., Shah, E. D., & Kardes, F. R. (2016). *Disfluency diminishes omission neglect.* Unpublished manuscript, Department of Marketing, University of Cincinnati, Cincinnati, OH.

Wyer, R. S. (2004). *Social comprehension and judgment: The role of situation models, narratives, and implicit theories.* Mahwah, NJ: Erlbaum.

Wyer, R. S., & Xu, A. J. (2010). The role of behavioral mind-sets in goal-directed activity: Conceptual underpinnings and empirical evidence. *Journal of Consumer Psychology, 20*, 107–125.

Zanna, M. P., Kiesler, C. A., & Pilkonis, P. A. (1970). Positive and negative attitudinal affect established by classical conditioning. *Journal of Personality and Social Psychology, 14*, 321–328.

Zanna, M. P., & Rempel, J. K. (1988). Attitudes: A new look at an old concept. In D. Bar-Tal & A.W. Kruglanski (Eds.), *The social psychology of knowledge* (pp. 315–334). Cambridge, UK: Cambridge University Press.

PART IX

Language

17

THE INFLUENCE OF MARKETING LANGUAGE ON BRAND ATTITUDES AND CHOICE

Ruth Pogacar,[1] Tina M. Lowrey,[2] and L. J. Shrum[2]

[1]LINDNER COLLEGE OF BUSINESS, UNIVERSITY OF CINCINNATI
[2]HEC PARIS, FRANCE

Marketers want to communicate with consumers for a variety of reasons, ranging from increasing brand awareness to persuading people to purchase products or services. In doing so, marketers have multiple means of communicating and persuading. For example, they may use emotional appeals, rational appeals, visual appeals, and so forth, which differ in terms of what is said. However, along with *what* is said (the content of the appeals), *how* it is said also makes a difference. That is, marketers may use linguistic devices to make their claims more persuasive.

In this chapter, we focus on *marketing language*. Language is a ubiquitous but often overlooked marketing tool. It facilitates brand communications in diverse modes and platforms, from print to digital, from personal sales to radio and television advertisements. By marketing language, we refer to various linguistic devices that are used to facilitate communication apart from the content of the communication. Examples include tropes (e.g., metaphors, puns, rhetorical questions), alliteration, rhyme, speech rate, and sound symbolism, just to name a few.

We explore these and other marketing linguistic devices that influence brand attitudes and choice in detail in the following sections. We also discuss the cross-modal interaction of marketing language devices with other sensory elements such as name font and logo, boundary conditions, and practical implications. Finally, we identify promising avenues for future research based on the reviewed literature.

Marketing Language Devices

Metaphor

Metaphor is a form of figurative speech in which a word or phrase that denotes a particular thing or concept is used to refer to another concept, thereby conveying similarities and linkages (e.g., "He is the black sheep of the family"). McQuarrie and Mick (1996) propose that metaphors increase elaboration and generate pleasure in consumers because their initial ambiguity stimulates interest, and resolving the ambiguity feels rewarding (cf. Berlyne, 1971; McQuarrie & Mick, 1992; Peracchio & Meyers-Levy, 1994).

Figurative language is often used in product reviews (e.g., "paradise disguised as a hotel"). Because hedonic experiences are more emotional than utilitarian experiences (Adaval, 2001; Babin, Darden, & Griffin, 1994; Dhar & Wertenbroch, 2000; Drolet, Williams, & Lau-Gesk, 2007; Kivetz & Simonson, 2002; Strahilevitz & Myers, 1998), and figurative language is a conversational norm for emotional communications, reviews containing more figurative language are more persuasive for hedonic than utilitarian products. Furthermore, reading a review with figurative language increases choice share of hedonic over utilitarian options. Perhaps intuiting this, consumers use more figurative language when sharing about hedonic than sharing about utilitarian products (Kronrod & Danziger, 2013). Thus, hedonic brands should benefit more from metaphorical marketing language than utilitarian brands.

Puns

A pun is a humorous play on words in which a word or phrase exploits the different possible meanings the same word might have or how two different words may sound alike but mean different things (e.g., "shoes with lasting soul"). Some research suggests that consumers prefer slogans with puns to slogans without puns (Van Mulken, van Enschot-van Dijk, & Hoeken, 2005) because the use of puns provides the pleasure of solving a mental puzzle. One way brand advertisements can leverage this preference is by incorporating verbal puns with visual imagery. For instance, in one study, participants who were shown hypothetical ads that either featured a verbal pun (e.g., for tea: "get yourself into a lot of hot water") or no verbal pun (e.g., "get yourself into a lot of hot tea") subsequently expressed more positive brand attitudes, attitudes toward the ad, and memory for the ad, in the pun condition than in the no-pun condition (McQuarrie & Mick, 1992). However, these effects are bounded by the degree of difficulty involved in comprehending the advertisement, because too much difficulty can have a negative impact, creating confusion rather than interest (McQuarrie & Mick, 1999). Similarly, participants prefer a hypothetical brand extension that is moderately incongruent with the parent brand (e.g., Coppertone book about Vitamin D) rather than very congruent (e.g., Coppertone book about healthy skin) or very incongruent (e.g., Coppertone book about grilling steak; Meyers-Levy, Louie, & Curren, 1994), because the increased elaboration that is stimulated by moderate incongruence and the pleasure of resolving the incongruity is limited to situations where resolving the incongruity is not too taxing (Berlyne, 1971; Eco, 1979; McQuarrie & Mick, 1992; Peracchio & Meyers-Levy, 1994).

Questions

Rhetorical questions (e.g., "Cheerios taste great, don't they?") may also stimulate elaboration and enhance message processing (Petty, Cacioppo, & Heesacker, 1981). Ahluwalia and Burnkrant (2004) found that rhetorical questions are not highly salient to un-savvy consumers (i.e., participants low in persuasion knowledge), and such participants are therefore unlikely to elaborate on a rhetorical question. However, rhetorical questions are salient to savvy consumers (i.e., participants high in persuasion knowledge), who are therefore more likely to elaborate on the question and try to infer why the communicator asked the question, which focuses attention on the communicator. Subsequently, for savvy consumers, rhetorical questions posed by positively perceived sources, such as socially responsible corporations, are deemed more open, less pressuring, and are more persuasive. Conversely, rhetorical questions posed by negatively perceived sources, such as corporations described as lacking concern for the environment, are deemed more pressuring and produce negative evaluations and brand attitudes.

Tag questions – short question phrases at the end of a statement, for example, "don't you think?" – may also increase or decrease persuasion, depending on source credibility (Blankenship & Craig, 2007; Holtgraves & Lasky, 1999). This subtype of rhetorical question can soften the impact of assertions (Lakoff, 1972), is associated with feminine speech patterns, (Mulac & Lundell, 1986), and has been found to produce negative perceptions of speakers' credibility and trustworthiness (Hosman, 1989). Furthermore, tag questions, along with hesitations (e.g., "um") and hedges (e.g., "sort of") are the three most common language markers of powerlessness (Ng & Bradac, 1993). Nevertheless, this linguistic device may sometimes be useful. For instance, tag questions can be persuasive when the speaker is highly credible (e.g., the dean of a university writing about the value of comprehensive exams). Under such conditions, communications with tag questions increase processing relative to communications without tag questions, and therefore strong arguments are more persuasive, but weak arguments are less persuasive. However, when the source is not credible (e.g., a high school student writing about the value of comprehensive exams), tag questions decrease persuasion regardless of argument strength (Blankenship & Craig, 2007).

Therefore, a highly credible brand spokesperson such as Steve Jobs could effectively ask a rhetorical question such as, "This iPhone is great, don't you think?" at a product launch where he also made many strong arguments for the iPhone's utility. However, many celebrity spokespeople should probably not use tag questions, particularly if they do not also present strong arguments.

Rate of Speech

Rate of speech may also be an important linguistic variable for brand spokespeople. In general, spoken communication can produce warmer listener attitudes than written communication (Novielli, de Rosis, & Mazzotta, 2010). However, rate of speech is an important factor because people with a faster rate of speech are perceived as more competent, credible, knowledgeable, and trustworthy than those with a slower rate of speech, a perception that can influence persuasion (Miller, Maruyama, Beaber, & Valone, 1976; Stewart & Ryan, 1982). In general, faster speakers are perceived more favorably than slower speakers, and younger speakers are perceived more favorably than older speakers. Similarly, using a synthetic speech system that passed for human speech, researchers found that low-pitched voices are generally evaluated more favorably than high-pitched voices, and slowing the rate of speech led participants to evaluate voices as less competent, whereas speeding up the rate of speech led participants to evaluate voices as less benevolent (Brown, Strong, & Rencher, 1973). However, when young people speak slowly this violates expectations, leading to especially negative attitudes toward speakers, whereas incongruent fast-speaking older people elicit mildly favorable attitudes (Stewart & Ryan, 1982).

Politeness

Politeness can be persuasive because matching the linguistic style of a request to the listener's expectations increases compliance (e.g., Brown & Levinson, 1987). Dispreferred markers are words or phrases, such as "I'll be honest," that allow speakers to downplay the negativity of their statements. Dispreferred markers function as a form of social etiquette by softening the delivery of criticism, which eases the social costs of negative (e.g., face-threatening) pronouncements for both communicators and listeners, for instance in product reviews. Consequently, dispreferred markers enhance attitudes toward communicators, perceptions of the product's personality, and consumers' willingness to pay. For example, when participants read a review with both positive and negative information, in which the negative information was preceded by the statement "I don't want to be mean, but . . .," they were willing to pay more for the product than when the negative information was not preceded by such a dispreferred marker (Hamilton, Vohs, & McGill, 2014). This finding has clear implications for brand spokespeople, salespeople, and online content managers.

Intensity

Language intensity refers to the degree to which words or phrases increase the extremity of a concept or proposition. Language intensity can increase brand message processing. Adverb intensifiers, such as "very," "really," or "extremely," increase the degree of intensity associated with a message, and intensity has been shown to influence attitudes (Hamilton, 1998), perceived credibility (Aune & Kikuchi, 1993; Hamilton, 1998), and behavior (Andersen & Blackburn, 2004; Buller, et al., 2000). For instance, e-mail messages featuring intense language increase survey response rates relative to the same messages without intense language (Andersen & Blackburn, 2004). Craig and Blankenship (2011) found that degree of processing led to enhanced attitudes toward comprehensive exams, and behavioral intentions to sign a petition in favor of comprehensive exams, for participants who read a message with intense language and strong arguments, relative to those who read the same message without intense language. Conversely, when intense language was used in conjunction with weak arguments, attitudes and behavioral intentions were reduced relative to strong argument conditions. However, for non-intense language, argument strength was not a significant factor. Marketing communications leveraging intense language in conjunction with strong arguments should therefore enhance brand attitudes, whereas communications with intense language and weak arguments risk undermining brand attitudes.

Explaining Language

Writing about why an experience happened, or why the experience was good or bad, can have a strong influence on people's evaluations and intentions to repeat or recommend products (Moore, 2012). Explaining language, such as "because . . ." statements, stimulate processing, which can help consumers understand their experiences better. This process of understanding subsequently dampens consumers' feelings about hedonic experiences (making positive experiences less positive, and negative experiences less negative in memory), but polarizes feelings about utilitarian experiences (making positive experiences more positive, and negative experiences more negative in memory). Thus, hedonic brands should not encourage consumers to think too analytically about their positive experiences. However, utilitarian brands may benefit from helping consumers explain and therefore understand their positive experiences.

Assertive Language

Assertive language (such as US Airway's slogan "Fly with us") is more persuasive in communications about hedonic products, and hedonically advertised utilitarian products, than non-assertive language (Kronrod, Grinstein, & Wathieu, 2012). Reference to hedonic consumption elevates positive mood (Chaudhuri & Holbrook, 2001), and listeners in a positive mood expect more assertive language (Bloch, 1996). Hence, assertive messages promoting hedonic consumption (e.g., Take a ride on a flying balloon!) are more congruent with expectations than nonassertive messages (e.g., Why not take a ride on a balloon?), and expectation-message congruence facilitates persuasion (Brown & Levinson, 1987; Burgoon & Aho, 1982; Kim, Rao, & Lee, 2009). Hedonic brands should therefore consider leveraging assertive language in marketing communications.

Sound Repetition and Alliteration

Sound repetition refers to multiple occurrences of the same sound within a word (e.g., *Pepsi*), whereas alliteration refers to occurrences of the same sound at the beginning of adjacent words (e.g., *Dunkin Donuts*). These phonetic devices can produce positive affect, which enhances brand evaluations, reactions to cross-selling, and product choices, particularly when the name is spoken aloud. For example, Argo, Popa, and Smith (2010) manipulated sound repetition by reading aloud to participants hypothetical brand names that either featured sound repetition (i.e., "sepsop" or "temasema") or did not (i.e., "sepfut" or "temafanu"), while varying whether participants were instructed to regulate or not regulate their emotions. In the natural (non-regulation) emotion condition, participants were told to be as natural as possible and to let their feelings flow. In the emotion suppression condition, participants were told to remain completely neutral, to try not to let any feelings show, and to suppress their internal reactions. The results showed that brand names with sound repetition were evaluated more favorably than those without in the natural emotion condition, but there were no differences in brand name evaluation in the emotion suppression condition. These findings suggest that emotion is an important mechanism by which marketing language influences consumers.

Rhyme

Brand names with sounds that are repeated to produce rhymes can be more memorable. The memory benefits of rhyme were illustrated by a study in which participants listened to recorded word lists that they were instructed to remember so they could subsequently recall and write down the words they had heard in the correct order. The words contained either rhyming suffixes (e.g., "pin – tin"), alliterative suffixes (e.g., "pin – pig"), or unrelated suffixes (e.g., "pin – mob"). Participants were better able to recall words with rhyming suffixes than words with alliterative suffixes, and better able to recall words with alliterative suffixes than unrelated suffixes. This effect was driven by enhanced recall for the final rhyming word in each list (Carr & Miles, 1997). These findings suggest that the initial and final syllables of a word are stored as separate entities in short-term acoustic memory (Treiman & Danis, 1988), leading to memory differences between alliteration, which is based on the first syllable, and traditional rhyme, which is based on the final syllable, because rhyme endings provide a retrieval cue that enhances recall (Tehan & Fallon, 1999).

Sound Symbolism

Sound symbolism refers to a non-arbitrary relation between the sound of a word and its meaning. More specifically, sound symbolism posits that the mere sound of a word, apart from its definition, conveys meaning. Sound symbolism is one of the most studied brand namings devices, possibly because it has been recognized as a phenomenon since antiquity (for a review, see Shrum & Lowrey, 2007). The notion that individual sounds convey meaning dates to Plato's *Cratylus*, in which Socrates suggests that although sound and meaning may sometimes be arbitrary, *good* words are those with sound and meaning that are congruent (Plato, 1892). Sound symbolic meaning can convey many attributes relevant to product branding (Lowrey & Shrum, 2007). For example, product names with front vowels seem smaller, lighter (relative to darker), milder, thinner, softer, faster, colder, more bitter, more feminine, friendlier, weaker, lighter (relative to heavier), and prettier than names with back vowels (Klink, 2000). Notably, the front vowel "eee" (as in *e*Bay), associated with the former group of concepts (small, fast, light, etc.), was found to be the most common vowel sound among top brand names (Pogacar, Plant, Rosulek, & Kouril, 2015).

Particles

Particles (including pronouns) are simple function words whose influence often goes unnoticed (Pennebaker, 2011), yet these function words can have profound influence. For instance, classifiers – which are particles, similar to "a" and "the" in English – are used in some languages to categorize objects. In Chinese, for instance, the words chopstick and pen share a classifier (zhi), which often accompanies the noun (e.g., "zhi chopsticks" or "zhi pens"), whereas the word bonsai is accompanied by a different classifier. For speakers of languages with classifiers, the valence associated with one object can influence the choice of a separate object that shares a common classifier. This phenomenon was demonstrated by Schmitt and Zhang (1998), who presented English and Chinese speaking participants with a gift-buying scenario and asked them to choose between two products. In the scenario, participants were asked to imagine that they had asked their friend's parents for guidance about what to buy for the friend's birthday, and learned that the friend would like two things (e.g., a pen or a bonsai), which are distinguished by different classifiers in Chinese. In the positive reference condition, the participants also learned that their friend would *most* like chopsticks, whereas in the negative reference condition the participants learned that their friend would *least* like chopsticks.

Importantly, as mentioned previously, chopsticks share a common classifier with pens in Chinese. In a control condition, no mention was made of chopsticks. Participants were then told that chopsticks were not available when they reached the store, and were asked to choose between buying their friend a pen or a bonsai. Chinese participants were more likely to choose the pen, which shares a classifier with chopsticks, in the positive reference condition, in which chopsticks were described as the most desirable gift, than in the control condition. Conversely, Chinese participants were less likely to choose the pen in the negative reference condition, in which chopsticks were described as an undesirable gift, than in the control condition. For English speakers, however, who did not perceive any classifier-based similarity between the pen and the chopsticks, there was no significant association between conditions and choice. These findings suggest that brand communications targeted at markets like China, with classifier systems, should be carefully crafted to make positive classifier associations.

Cross-Modal Sensory Interactions

Different elements of marketing language, such as the voice used to read a name and the font the name is written in, may interact with each other to influence consumer evaluations. Because the voice used to read the name is an audio element, and the font the name is written in is a visual element, this interaction can be termed cross-modal: it spans multiple modes of sensory perception. One illustration of such a cross-modal effect is provided by Pan and Schmitt (1996), who had Chinese and English speaking participants evaluate brand names in product categories that were either masculine (e.g., power tools) or feminine (e.g., lipstick). The brand names were written in either masculine or feminine fonts, or read by a male or female announcer. Thus, the design had four conditions: congruent font – congruent voice; congruent font – incongruent voice; incongruent font – congruent voice; and incongruent font – incongruent voice. All participants liked the brands best when both the font and voice matched the product category. However Chinese speakers liked brands more when the font matched the product category than when it did not, whereas English speakers' evaluations did not differ significantly based on font. Conversely, English speakers liked the brands better when the voice matched the product category than when it did not, whereas Chinese speakers' evaluations did not vary based on voice. These differences occur because Chinese features a logographic writing system, which emphasizes visual elements, whereas English uses an alphabetic system, which emphasizes phonetic (sound) elements.

Linguistic elements of brand name articulation may also interact with visual elements of the brand's logo to influence consumer perceptions of meaning. For instance, the sound symbolism in a brand name, as conveyed by front versus back vowels, can work together with the logo size, shape, and color to communicate brand meaning (Klink, 2003).

Boundary Conditions

Marketing language effects may differ as a function of contextual factors, individual differences, and consumers' bilingualism. We discuss these potential boundary conditions in the following sections.

Contextual Factors

Consumer Arousal. Consumers in a low state of arousal prefer extreme over moderate incongruity, because it creates curiosity (Noseworthy, Di Muro, & Murray, 2014). Thus, consumers in a low state of arousal should respond best to more complex marketing linguistic devices, which produce curiosity (e.g., via metaphor or pun) and pleasure through incongruence. Conversely, consumers in a high state of arousal prefer no incongruity, because it may be anxiety-producing (Noseworthy et al., 2014). It is therefore likely that consumers in a high state of arousal will respond best to simple marketing linguistic devices. Furthermore, high arousal reduces consumers' processing capacity, thereby increasing the influence of peripheral cues that require little processing capacity (Sanbonmatsu & Kardes, 1988). Consequently, simple marketing linguistic devices (e.g., sound symbolism or rhyme) are likely to have greater influence on brand attitudes when consumers are in a high, rather than moderate or low, state of arousal.

Involvement. High involvement contexts lend themselves more to complex language than do low-involvement contexts. For instance, Lowrey (1998) manipulated linguistic complexity by varying whether a claim for a bran cereal was written as a lower complexity, right-branching sentence ("BRAN-NEW is a healthy choice for breakfast, because it's high in fiber, and it's preservative-free"), or higher complexity, left-branching sentence ("Because it's high in fiber and contains no preservatives, BRAN-NEW is a healthy choice for breakfast"). For high involvement participants, complex syntax increased elaboration, was more persuasive than simple syntax, and enhanced attitudes toward products advertised with strong, rather than weak, arguments. However, complex syntax reduced low-involvement participants' motivation to process the information, suggesting that linguistic complexity is a potentially useful tool that may backfire if used in the wrong context. Simple marketing linguistic devices, such as rhyme and sound symbolism, may be more beneficial in low-involvement contexts.

Expectations are also an important variable in consumer preferences about brand communication. For example, consumers prefer that self/brand relationships are expressed using the closer "we," or more distant "you and I," depending on how close the consumer feels to the brand (Sela, Wheeler, & Sarial-Abi, 2012). Language congruent with consumer expectations of closeness can increase trust and brand evaluations, but only when consumers are able to devote processing effort to elaborating on the message.

Emotion. Consumers' abilities to experience emotion in a given situation is also an important variable in determining the degree to which marketing language may be effective. As mentioned previously, the benefits of sound repetition are limited when participants are told to regulate their emotions (Argo et al., 2010), suggesting that this device may be less effective in certain contexts, such as formal or professional settings (e.g., at the office), and more effective in casual or recreational settings (e.g., at an amusement park).

Emotional state may also lead to gender differences in language comprehension. Language congruent with one's emotional state is generally easier to comprehend. Women's reactivity to sad events facilitates faster comprehension of sentences about sad events, whereas men's reactivity to angry events facilitates faster comprehension of sentences about angry events. Switching between emotions slows comprehension, such that for women, reading a sad sentence slows subsequent reading of a happy sentence more than it does for men, whereas men are slower than women to read a happy sentence following an angry one (Glenberg et al., 2009).

Individual Differences

Individual differences in key personality traits also play an important role in how language affects consumer behavior. For example, participants high in tolerance for ambiguity like ads with mixed wordplay (i.e., both positive and negative elements) more than do participants low in tolerance for ambiguity (McQuarrie & Mick, 1992). Because tolerance for ambiguity is a component of need for closure (Webster & Kruglanski, 1994), it is likely that mixed wordplay will also appeal to those low in need for closure.

Sensory effects such as sound repetition and sound symbolism may be differentially influential depending on individual differences in sensory sensitivity. For example, the effect of sound repetition on preference and choice is moderated by individual differences in consumers' sensitivity to sound repetition (Argo et al., 2010).

People who are higher in need for cognition tend to generate more thoughtful analyses of written messages (Petty, Cacioppo, & Morris, 1983). Given that complex language requires ability and motivation to process (Lowrey, 1998), it is likely that high need for cognition increases appreciation for complex marketing language, such as metaphors and puns. Conversely, low need for cognition may decrease appreciation for such complex linguistic devices and increase preference for simple marketing linguistic devices such as rhymes.

Need for cognition also influences how people evaluate brand names. For example, consumers usually follow a "higher is better" rule of thumb when choosing among alphanumeric brand names (e.g., KP700 is considered better than KP300). However, consumers high in need for cognition are more likely than those low in need for cognition to process brand names systematically and form inferences about the product from the numbers imbedded in alphanumeric brand names. In contrast, low need for cognition consumers are more likely to choose products with higher-number alphanumeric brand names even when they are objectively inferior to alternatives (Gunasti & Ross, 2010).

Gender can also influence how consumers respond to some marketing linguistic devices. For instance, women prefer brand names with front vowels, such as "Trebbi," over names with back vowels, such as "Tròbbi," particularly when the masculinity/femininity of the product is considered important. Men, on the other hand, are less sensitive to brand name vowel sounds (Klink, 2009). This difference may emerge because women are more sensitive than men in most perceptual modalities (McGuinness, 1976).

Bilingualism

Research suggests that phonetic devices such as sound symbolism are effective across languages, because people from diverse linguistic backgrounds derive similar meaning from the sounds in names (Pogacar, Peterlin, Pokorn, & Pogacar, 2017), regardless of bilingualism or language fluency (Shrum, Lowrey, Luna, Lerman, & Liu, 2012). However, bilingualism, or cross-linguistic marketing environments, may also represent an important moderator of marketing linguistic effects. For example, advertisements are less well remembered when the text is in a consumer's second language rather than first language, because messages in one's second language are less likely to be processed at a conceptual level. However, including highly congruent imagery with second language text facilitates conceptual processing of second language messages, and increases memory among bilingual consumers (Luna & Peracchio, 2001).

Relatedly, bilingual consumers perceive text slogans using familiar words from their native language as more emotional than slogans in their non-native language. This effect occurs because, according to the encoding specificity principle (Tulving & Thomson, 1973), memories of experiences are stored together with the linguistic context. Consequently, because autobiographical memories are emotionally powerful (Bower, 1981) and likely to be stored in the context of one's native language, native language becomes a powerful emotional trigger (Puntoni, De Langhe, & Van Osselaer, 2009). Consistent with this reasoning, advertisements presented in consumers' native languages are more likely to stimulate self-referent thoughts about family, friends, home, or homeland, which can enhance attitudes and behavioral intentions toward the advertised product (Noriega & Blair, 2008). Indeed, findings from bilingual radio programs suggest that Spanish speakers use Spanish to talk about emotional topics and English to talk about work, finances, or politics (Pennebaker, Mehl, & Niederhoffer, 2003).

Code-switching refers to switching one or more words in a sentence from one language to another. Code-switching directs attention to the code-switched word(s) and activates language schemas associated with the switched-to language (e.g., high vs. low language status). This process leads to elaboration and processing of these associations, and the valence of the associations influences subsequent product evaluations (Luna & Peracchio, 2005). For instance, in the United States, English is commonly associated with affluence, whereas Spanish is associated with lower socioeconomic status, possibly triggering negative valence (Barker et al., 2001). Consequently, when advertisements switch from English to Spanish, which focuses attention on the Spanish language schema and associated valence, attitudes toward slogans are generally less favorable than when ads switch from Spanish to English, which focuses attention on the English language schema (e.g., "In my cocina I would never use any other coffeemaker" vs. "En mi kitchen nunca usaría ninguna otra cafetera"). However, when minority language associations are positive, this pattern is reversed and listeners prefer the slogan that directs their attention toward the minority language word (Luna & Peracchio, 2005).

The influence of pronouns may be particularly important in languages with formal and informal distinctions. For example, in Spanish, informally addressing consumers (e.g., "tu") elicits more positive reactions for warm brands, whereas formal address (e.g., "usted") elicits more positive reactions for competent brands (Lenoir, Puntoni, & van Osselaer, 2014).

Agenda for Future Research

Relatively little attention has been paid to many marketing language devices. Therefore, many open questions remain. For example, are different linguistic devices more appealing to consumers of different generations (e.g., millennials vs. baby boomers), levels of product adoption (e.g., innovators vs. laggards), or stages of the purchase process (e.g., information gathering vs. decision-making)? Future research should also address issues of measurement and stimuli, and the need for an integrated framework of marketing language.

Measurement and Stimuli

Most studies of marketing language fall into one of two categories: observational studies that measure the frequencies of different linguistic devices in the marketplace, and experimental studies that measure explicit reactions to (usually) hypothetical advertisements or brand names. One avenue for future research is to take different measurements of consumer responses to marketing language, such as neurological activation or response latency. A measurement method that shows promise is the implicit association test (IAT), which would be particularly appropriate for measuring implicit attitudes toward marketing language devices that are processed automatically and nonconsciously, like brand name phonetics (Klink, 2000; Lowrey & Shrum, 2007; Yorkston & Menon, 2004). One advantage of the IAT, relative to neurological measurement devices such as fMRI, is the availability of software that is free and user-friendly (Carpenter et al., 2016). This response latency approach would enable examination of whether different rhetorical devices are processed at equally implicit levels.

The degree to which different marketing language devices influence consumers when presented visually versus auditorially is another relevant topic for future research. It is interesting to note that whereas most wordplay and sound symbolism effects have been obtained using written experimental materials, which participants read and respond to (e.g., Lowrey & Shrum, 2007; McQuarrie & Mick, 1992), many sound repetition, alliteration, and rhyme effects have been studied using audio stimuli (e.g., Carr & Miles, 1997). Some researchers propose that the mode of brand name presentation (audio vs. visual) influences consumer responses (Argo et al., 2010), whereas others argue that this distinction is inconsequential, at least in the domain of sound symbolism (Brown & Nuttall, 1959; Klink & Athaide, 2012).

Organizing Framework for Marketing Language

Perhaps most importantly, future research should seek to synthesize marketing linguistic effects related to brand name articulation within a larger framework of marketing language that includes more complex communication devices like figurative and assertive language. Such an organizing theoretical framework may answer questions such as how simple and complex marketing linguistic devices interact to influence brand perceptions, and when a given device is more attention-getting or persuasive than others. Moreover, research should investigate when and how different marketing linguistic devices differentially influence consumer choices.

References

Adaval, R. (2001). Sometimes it just feels right: The differential weighting of affect-consistent and affect-inconsistent product information. *Journal of Consumer Research, 28*(1), 1–17.

Ahluwalia, R., & Burnkrant, R. E. (2004). Answering questions about questions: A persuasion knowledge perspective for understanding the effects of rhetorical questions. *Journal of Consumer Research, 31*(1), 26–42.

Andersen, P. A., & Blackburn, T. R. (2004). An experimental study of language intensity and response rate in e-mail surveys. *Communication Reports, 17*(2), 73–82.

Argo, J. J., Popa, M., & Smith, M. C. (2010). The sound of brands. *Journal of Marketing, 74*(4), 97–109.

Aune, R. K., & Kikuchi, T. (1993). Effects of language intensity similarity on perceptions of credibility relational attributions, and persuasion. *Journal of Language and Social Psychology, 12*(3), 224–238.

Babin, B. J., Darden, W. R., & Griffin, M. (1994). Work and/or fun: Measuring hedonic and utilitarian shopping value. *Journal of Consumer Research, 20*(4), 644–656.

Barker, V., Giles, H., Noels, K., Duck, J., Hecht, M. L., & Clement, R. (2001). The English-only movement: A communication analysis of changing perceptions of language vitality. *Journal of Communication, 51*(1), 3–37.

Berlyne, D. E. (1971). *Aesthetics and psychobiology (Vol. 336)*. New York: Appleton-Century-Crofts.

Blankenship, K. L., & Craig, T. Y. (2007). Language and persuasion: Tag questions as powerless speech or as interpreted in context. *Journal of Experimental Social Psychology, 43*(1), 112–118.

Bloch, C. (1996). Emotions and discourse. *Text-Interdisciplinary Journal for the Study of Discourse, 16*(3), 323–342.

Bower, G. H. (1981). Mood and memory. *American Psychologist, 36*(2), 129–148.

Brown, P., & Levinson, S. C. (1987). *Politeness: Some universals in language usage (Vol. 4)*. Cambridge University Press.

Brown, R., & Nuttall, R. (1959). Method in phonetic symbolism experiments. *The Journal of Abnormal and Social Psychology, 59*(3), 441–445.

Brown, B. L., Strong, W. J., & Rencher, A. C. (1973). Perceptions of personality from speech: Effects of manipulations of acoustical parameters. *The Journal of the Acoustical Society of America, 54*(1), 29–35.

Buller, D. B., Burgoon, M., Hall, J. R., Levine, N., Taylor, A. M., Beach, B. H., Melcher, C., Buller, M. K., Bowen, S. L., Hunsaker, F.G. & Bergen, A. (2000). Using language intensity to increase the success of a family intervention to protect children from ultraviolet radiation: Predictions from language expectancy theory. *Preventive Medicine, 30*(2), 103–113.

Burgoon, J. K., & Aho, L. (1982). Three field experiments on the effects of violations of conversational distance. *Communications Monographs, 49*(2), 71–88.

Carpenter, T. P., Pullig, C. P., Pogacar, R., LaBouff, J. P., Kouril, M., Isenberg, N., & Chakroff, A. (2016). *iatgen: A free, user-friendly package for implicit association tests in Qualtrics*. Paper presented at the annual meeting of the American Psychological Association, Denver, CO.

Carr, D., & Miles, C. (1997). Rhyme attenuates the auditory suffix effect: Alliteration does not. *The Quarterly Journal of Experimental Psychology: Section A, 50*(3), 518–527.

Chaudhuri, A., & Holbrook, M. B. (2001). The chain of effects from brand trust and brand affect to brand performance: The role of brand loyalty. *Journal of Marketing, 65*(2), 81–93.

Craig, T. Y., & Blankenship, K. L. (2011). Language and persuasion: Linguistic extremity influences message processing and behavioral intentions. *Journal of Language and Social Psychology, 30*(3), 290–310.

Dhar, R., & Wertenbroch, K. (2000). Consumer choice between hedonic and utilitarian goods. *Journal of Marketing Research, 37*(1), 60–71.

Drolet, A., Williams, P., & Lau-Gesk, L. (2007). Age-related differences in responses to affective vs. rational ads for hedonic vs. utilitarian products. *Marketing Letters, 18*(4), 211–221.

Eco, U. (1979). *The role of the reader*. Bloomington, IN: Indiana University Press.

Glenberg, A. M., Webster, B. J., Mouilso, E., Havas, D., & Lindeman, L. M. (2009). Gender, emotion, and the embodiment of language comprehension. *Emotion Review, 1*(2), 151–161.

Gunasti, K., & Ross, Jr, W. T. (2010). How and when alphanumeric brand names affect consumer preferences. *Journal of Marketing Research, 47*(6), 1177–1192.

Hamilton, M. A. (1998). Message variables that mediate and moderate the effect of equivocal language on source credibility. *Journal of Language and Social Psychology, 17*(1), 109–143.

Hamilton, R., Vohs, K. D., & McGill, A. L. (2014). We'll be honest, this won't be the best article you'll ever read: The use of dispreferred markers in word-of-mouth communication. *Journal of Consumer Research, 41*(1), 197–212.

Holtgraves, T., & Lasky, B. (1999). Linguistic power and persuasion. *Journal of Language and Social Psychology, 18*(2), 196–205.

Hosman, L. A. (1989). The evaluative consequences of hedges, hesitations, and intensifies powerful and powerless speech styles. *Human Communication Research, 15*(3), 383–406.

Kim, H., Rao, A. R., & Lee, A. Y. (2009). It's time to vote: The effect of matching message orientation and temporal frame on political persuasion. *Journal of Consumer Research, 35*(6), 877–889.

Kivetz, R., & Simonson, I. (2002). Earning the right to indulge: Effort as a determinant of customer preferences toward frequency program rewards. *Journal of Marketing Research, 39*(2), 155–170.

Klink, R. R. (2000). Creating brand names with meaning: The use of sound symbolism. *Marketing Letters, 11*(1), 5–20.

Klink, R. R. (2003). Creating meaningful brands: The relationship between brand name and brand mark. *Marketing Letters, 14*(3), 143–157.

Klink, R. R. (2009). Gender differences in new brand name response. *Marketing Letters, 20*(3), 313–326.

Klink, R. R., & Athaide, G. A. (2012). Creating brand personality with brand names. *Marketing Letters, 23*(1), 109–117.

Kronrod, A., & Danziger, S. (2013). "Wii will rock you!" The use and effect of figurative language in consumer reviews of hedonic and utilitarian consumption. *Journal of Consumer Research, 40*(4), 726–739.

Kronrod, A., Grinstein, A., & Wathieu, L. (2012). Enjoy! Hedonic consumption and compliance with assertive messages. *Journal of Consumer Research, 39*(1), 51–61.

Lakoff, R. (1972). Language in context. *Language, 48*, 907–927.

Lenoir, A. S. I., Puntoni, S., & van Osselaer, S. M. J. (2014). What shall I call thee? The impact of brand personality on consumer response to formal and informal address. In J. Cotte & S. Wood (Eds.), *NA-advances in consumer research* (Vol. 42, pp. 136–140). Duluth, MN: Association for Consumer Research.

Lowrey, T. M. (1998). The effects of syntactic complexity on advertising persuasiveness. *Journal of Consumer Psychology, 7*(2), 187–206.

Lowrey, T. M., & Shrum, L. J. (2007). Phonetic symbolism and brand name preference. *Journal of Consumer Research, 34*(3), 406–414.

Luna, D., & Peracchio, L. A. (2001). Moderators of language effects in advertising to bilinguals: A psycholinguistic approach. *Journal of Consumer Research, 28*(2), 284–295.

Luna, D., & Peracchio, L. A. (2005). Advertising to bilingual consumers: The impact of code-switching on persuasion. *Journal of Consumer Research, 31*(4), 760–765.

McGuinness, D. (1976). Sex differences in the organization of perception and cognition. In B. Lloyd & J. Archer (Eds.), *Exploring sex differences* (pp. 123–156). New York: Academic Press.

McQuarrie, E. F., & Mick, D. G. (1992). On resonance: A critical pluralistic inquiry into advertising rhetoric. *Journal of Consumer Research, 19*(2), 180–197.

McQuarrie, E. F., & Mick, D. G. (1996). Figures of rhetoric in advertising language. *Journal of Consumer Research, 22*(4), 424–438.

McQuarrie, E. F., & Mick, D. G. (1999). Visual rhetoric in advertising: Text-interpretive, experimental, and reader-response analyses. *Journal of Consumer Research, 26*(1), 37–54.

Meyers-Levy, J., Louie, T. A., & Curren, M. T. (1994). How does the congruity of brand names affect evaluations of brand name extensions? *Journal of Applied Psychology, 79*(1), 46–53.

Miller, N., Maruyama, G., Beaber, R. J., & Valone, K. (1976). Speed of speech and persuasion. *Journal of Personality and Social Psychology, 34*(4), 615–624.

Moore, S. G. (2012). Some things are better left unsaid: How word of mouth influences the storyteller. *Journal of Consumer Research, 38*(6), 1140–1154.

Mulac, A., & Lundell, T. L. (1986). Linguistic contributors to the gender-linked language effect. *Journal of Language and Social Psychology, 5*(2), 81–101.

Ng, S. H., & Bradac, J. J. (1993). *Power in language: Verbal communication and social influence*. Newbury Park: Sage Publications.

Noriega, J., & Blair, E. (2008). Advertising to bilinguals: Does the language of advertising influence the nature of thoughts?. *Journal of Marketing, 72*(5), 69–83.

Noseworthy, T. J., Di Muro, F., & Murray, K. B. (2014). The role of arousal in congruity-based product evaluation. *Journal of Consumer Research, 41*(4), 1108–1126.

Novielli, N., de Rosis, F., & Mazzotta, I. (2010). User attitude towards an embodied conversational agent: Effects of the interaction mode. *Journal of Pragmatics, 42*(9), 2385–2397.

Pan, Y., & Schmitt, B. (1996). Language and brand attitudes: Impact of script and sound matching in Chinese and English. *Journal of Consumer Psychology, 5*(3), 263–277.

Pennebaker, J. W. (2011). The secret life of pronouns. *New Scientist, 211*(2828), 42–45.

Pennebaker, J. W., Mehl, M. R., & Niederhoffer, K. G. (2003). Psychological aspects of natural language use: Our words, our selves. *Annual Review of Psychology, 54*(1), 547–577.

Peracchio, L. A., & Meyers-Levy, J. (1994). How ambiguous cropped objects in ad photos can affect product evaluations. *Journal of Consumer Research, 21*(1), 190–204.

Petty, R. E., Cacioppo, J. T., & Heesacker, M. (1981). Effects of rhetorical questions on persuasion: A cognitive response analysis. *Journal of Personality and Social Psychology, 40*(3), 432–440.

Petty, R. E., Cacioppo, J. T., & Morris, K. J. (1983). Effects of need for cognition on message evaluation, recall, and persuasion. *Journal of Personality and Social Psychology, 45*(4), 805–818.

Plato (1892), Cratylus. In *The dialogues of Plato* (B. Jowett, Trans.), (*Vol. 1*, pp. 253–289). Oxford: Clarendon.

Pogacar, R., Plant, E., Rosulek, L. F., & Kouril, M. (2015). Sounds good: Phonetic sound patterns in top brand names. *Marketing Letters, 26*(4), 549–563.

Pogacar, R., Peterlin, A. P., Pokorn, N. K., & Pogacar, T. (2017). Sound symbolism in translation: A case study of character names in Charles Dickens's Oliver Twist. *Translation and Interpreting Studies, 12*(1), 137–161.

Puntoni, S., De Langhe, B., & Van Osselaer, S. M. (2009). Bilingualism and the emotional intensity of advertising language. *Journal of Consumer Research, 35*(6), 1012–1025.

Sanbonmatsu, D. M., & Kardes, F. R. (1988). The effects of physiological arousal on information processing and persuasion. *Journal of Consumer Research, 15*(3), 379–385.

Schmitt, B. H., & Zhang, S. (1998). Language structure and categorization: A study of classifiers in consumer cognition, judgment, and choice. *Journal of Consumer Research, 25*(2), 108–122.

Sela, A., Wheeler, S. C., & Sarial-Abi, G. (2012). We are not the same as you and I: Causal effects of minor language variations on consumers' attitudes toward brands. *Journal of Consumer Research, 39*(3), 644–661.

Shrum, L. J., & Lowrey, T. M. (2007). Sounds convey meaning: The implications of phonetic symbolism for brand name construction. In T. M. Lowrey (Ed.), *Psycholinguistic phenomena in marketing communications* (pp. 39–58). Mahwah, NJ: Lawrence Erlbaum.

Shrum, L. J., Lowrey, T. M., Luna, D., Lerman, D. B., & Liu, M. (2012). Sound symbolism effects across languages: Implications for global brand names. *International Journal of Research in Marketing, 29*(3), 275–279.

Stewart, M. A., & Ryan, E. B. (1982). Attitudes toward younger and older adult speakers: Effects of varying speech rates. *Journal of Language and Social Psychology, 1*(2), 91–109.

Strahilevitz, M., & Myers, J. G. (1998). Donations to charity as purchase incentives: How well they work may depend on what you are trying to sell. *Journal of Consumer Research, 24*(4), 434–446.

Tehan, G., & Fallon, A. B. (1999). A connectionist model of short-term cued recall. In J. Wiles & T. Dartnall (Eds.), *Perspectives on cognitive science* (*Vol. 2*, pp. 221–237). Stamford, CT: Ablex.

Treiman, R., & Danis, C. (1988). Short-term memory errors for spoken syllables are affected by the linguistic structure of the syllables. *Journal of Experimental Psychology: Learning, Memory, and Cognition, 14*(1), 145–152.

Tulving, E., & Thomson, D. M. (1973). Encoding specificity and retrieval processes in episodic memory. *Psychological Review, 80*(5), 352–373.

Van Mulken, M., Van Enschot-van Dijk, R., & Hoeken, H. (2005). Puns, relevance and appreciation in advertisements. *Journal of Pragmatics, 37*(5), 707–721.

Webster, D. M., & Kruglanski, A. W. (1994). Individual differences in need for cognitive closure. *Journal of Personality and Social Psychology, 67*(6), 1049–1062.

Yorkston, E., & Menon, G. (2004). A sound idea: Phonetic effects of brand names on consumer judgments. *Journal of Consumer Research, 31*(1), 43–51.

18

ON THE SEARCH FOR THE PERFECT BRAND NAME

Sascha Topolinski

UNIVERSITY OF COLOGNE, COLOGNE, GERMANY

A brand name is a powerful tool for shaping consumers' attitudes toward a product (Brucks, Zeithaml, & Naylor, 2000; Rao & Monroe, 1989), particularly in the currently exploding ecommerce domain and in digital marketing (Degeratu, Rangaswamy, & Wu, 2000). For instance, Mazursky and Jacoby (1985) found that consumers use the brand name more frequently than any other information as a cue for judging the quality of a product, and the brand has been shown to be an even more important prompt for quality assessments than the price (Olson, 1976; Stokes, 1974).

Brand names are worth a lot because they have strong reputational associations. In actuality, most effects of the brand are due to reputation the brand has gained (De Chernatony, 1999; Selnes, 2013; Wheeler, 2003). But what about the initial encounter of a novel brand? Are there ways to prompt spontaneous favorable attitudes toward a name without prior experience or additional information? Exploring such name-specific sources of spontaneous attitudes is the purpose of this chapter. In this vein, the reviewed evidence will not only be limited to actual brand names, but will also deal in large parts with spontaneous attitudes toward person and company names. Still, since the underlying psychological principles in spontaneous attitude formation toward a word remain the same, research on the perception of person and company names also inform us about the principles of brand name perception.

Thus, the question of this chapter is whether we can shape (brand) names in a way that makes them initially more appealing in order to increase the likelihood that consumers would choose the bearer of that name. An obvious route to trigger positive attitudes toward a brand or product name at first sight is surely its semantic meaning: the name should contain or be similar to positive and product-relevant concepts. An insurance company might choose the name *Protective Life*, or a food processor *Triumph Foods* (these are all actual names of existing companies). However, in our world of ever newly arising digital companies and explosion of start-up foundings, the number of available meaningful names decreases everyday, for which reason more and more companies choose artificially created nonsense words as brand and product names.

There are indeed more subtle and indirect tools available to cue favorable attitudes at first sight or reading. And these routes lie in linguistically *superficial* features of names. What I mean here by superficial features, are the features of a word that are not semantically relevant, that is,

276

not at all structurally related to their meaning itself and thus arbitrary in the Saussurian notion of linguistics (de Saussure, 1916; for recent reviews, see Gasser, 2004; Levelt, Roelofs, & Meyer, 1999; Monaghan, Christiansen, & Fitneva, 2011). Such features are the length of a word, or its sound for instance: they do not have a structural correspondence with the meaning of the word. It is not the case that longer words denote longer things (e.g., YEAR vs. MILLISECOND), nor that soft things have soft-sounding names (e.g., SILK vs. BARBWIRE).

Recently, in various lines of research from different fields of psychology and consumer behavior analysis evidence has been accumuled that such superficial features of names do influence attitudes toward the name bearers, may these be companies, products, or persons. In this chapter, I will review these new developments starting with obvious superficial features, namely the complexity and the sound of a name. Then, a much larger part will be devoted to a more subtle feature of words, namely the mouth movements that are required for articulation, and how they shape spontaneous attitudes toward the name bearer. We can encounter (brand) names either visually, as for instance on the supermarket shelf or in internet ads, or auditorily, as for instance in radio commercials. And indeed, there is research on differences between reading or hearing a brand name (e.g., Bryce & Yalch, 1993; Topolinski, Lindner, & Freudenberg, 2014). However, most of the presently reviewed evidence stems from visual presentation of (brand) names, since, as we will learn, hearing a name spoken is not even necessary to evoke effects such as sound symbolism (see next).

Word Complexity

One important superficial feature of a word is its complexity, which is determined by features such as a word's length or pronounceability (Topolinski, Erle, & Bakhtiari, 2016). Whether a word is long or short has nothing to do with what it denotes, it is surely not the case that physically or temporally longer things bear longer words. Also, whether a word is easy or hard to pronounce should not show a systematic relation to its meaning. Still, recent results in experimental psychology have shown that these semantically irrelevant features do play a role in word perception and attitude generation, with complexity of brand or person names being a strong heuristic used in consumer decisions (Irmak, Vallen, & Robinson, 2011; Maheswaran, Mackie, & Chaiken, 1992; see Vanhuele, Laurent, & Dreze, 2006, for effect of verbal length of prices). These effects are reviewed in the following.

Effects of Mere Pronounceability

As one of the first demonstrations, Alter and Oppenheimer (2006) showed in real-world data that the pronounceability of the ticker codes of shares determines the price development of these shares, with easy-to-pronounce codes (such as KAR) leading to higher prices than hard-to-pronounce codes (such as KDR). Also, Song and Schwarz (2009) showed that ostensible food additives were rated as more harmful when they bore a relatively hard-to-pronounce name (such as HNEGRIPITROM) than a relatively easy-to-pronounce name (such as MAGNALROXATE). These effects are not constrained to company or product names, but also affect the social perception of target persons. Laham, Koval, and Alter (2012) found that target persons with easier-to-pronounce names are judged more positively (Experiments 1–4), and that even in real-world data people with easier-to-pronounce surnames occupy higher status positions in law firms. Also, Newman et al. (2014) found that claims made by target persons with easy-to-pronounce names are believed more likely than claims made by target persons with hard-to-pronounce names.

Pronounceability and Length of Digital Usernames

Most recently, Silva and Topolinski (2016b) explored the impact of word complexity in the digital consumer domain, using eBay as an example where superficial features of words, namely of the usernames of the sellers, play a role for consumer attitudes (cf., Irmak et al., 2011; Maheswaran et al., 1992). They presented participants with screenshots of ostensible eBay profiles of sellers and asked participants how trustworthy they feel the seller to be. Besides random information, these profiles contained the names of the sellers and their reputation, in the form of number of stars they had gained in recent ratings. Crucially, the name of the seller was either a simple (e.g., SIBU), moderate (e.g., PTONBIA), or complex (e.g., VLEGTIQCLAPL) name. Additionally and orthogonally to this name complexity manipulation, the sellers either had a good or bad reputation in the star reputation system. As a result of these manipulations, participants of course rated sellers with a good reputation as being more trustworthy than sellers with a bad reputation. However, in addition and independent of actual reputation, participants also rated sellers with simple names as being more trustworthy than sellers with moderate names, and the latter as being more trustworthy than sellers with complex names (Silva & Topolinski, 2016b, Experiments 1–2). This linear pattern of decreasing trustworthiness with increasing seller name complexity occured significantly for sellers with both high and low reputation.

Moreover, Silva and Topolinski (2016b, Experiments 3–7) isolated two independent determinants of word complexity, namely the length of a word, and its pronounceability, and manipulated these two factors independently from each other (see also Topolinski, Erle, & Bakhtiari, 2016). More specifically, they presented participants with ostensible eBay profiles with good and bad reputations and with usernames that were easy-to-pronounce and short (eg., BATREK), hard to pronounce and short (e.g., EAKRTB), easy-to-pronounce and long (e.g., FECHLIREN), and hard to pronounce and long (e.g., IECLHFRNE). As a result, each of these manipulations had its own independent main effect on trustworthiness ratings. Besides reputation of course, shorter names were trusted more than longer names, and easy-to-pronounce names were trusted more than hard-to-pronounce names, without any interaction between these factors.

These effects of word complexity even persisted when participants were made aware of the variations in word length and pronounceability and were explicitly instructed to ignore these features (Silva & Topolinski, 2016b, Experiment 4). Also, the impact of word complexity was not moderated by participants' beliefs about the sellers geographical background, since for both ostensible Polish and ostensible German sellers these effects occurred (Experiment 5); and they even occurred when participants received the information that not the sellers themselves, but an automatic username generation algorithm had compiled the usernames (Experiment 6). Also, participants' beliefs about the age of the seller account did not explain these effects, since for both ostensibly ten year and one year old accounts more complex usernames damaged trustworthiness (Experiment 7).

Besides the orthographic complexity of a word, there are more subtle features of words that nevertheless influence people's perception of the name bearer, which is reviewed in the following.

Sound Symbolism

Another superficial feature of words is their sound. That the sound of a word can play a role for the meaning or the perception of a word is already captured in the old idea of onomatopoeia

(Perniss, Thompson, & Vigliocco, 2010), meaning that words can sound similar to what they denote (e.g., "cuckoo"). Deriving from this notion, in his classic study Köhler (1929) predicted that people would like a match between sound features of a word and features of the object that word denotes. He showed participants a curvy and a spiky object together with two names, namely BALUMA and TAKETE, and found that participants preferred the soft-sounding name BALUMA for the round object, and the harsh-sounding name TAKETE for the spiky object (for related effects, see Westbury, 2005; for the related *kiki-bouba effect*, see Maurer, Pathman, & Mondloch, 2006; Ramachandran & Hubbard, 2001).

Such onomatopoeia effects are now a vividly explored phenomenon in the literature of *sound symbolism*, showing that matches between word sounds and denoted object features increase preference and consumer attitudes (e.g., Fitch, 1994; Hinton, Nichols, & Ohala, 2006; Klink, 2000; Kovic, Plunkett, & Westermann, 2010; Lowrey, Shrum, & Dubitsky, 2003; Shrum, Lowrey, Luna, Lerman, & Liu, 2012). I will only sketch one brief example here because this rich line of research is reviewed elsewhere in this volume (Chapter 17).

For instance, Lowrey and Shrum (2007) presented participants with word pairs that either featured front vowels, such as NILLEN or GIMMEL, which sound high-pitched and bear multi-modal associations with features such as small, fast, or sharp; or that featured back vowels, such as NALLEN or GOMMEL, which sound low-pitched and bear associations with features like large, slow, or dull. Participants were told that these words were brand names for certain products. These products, in turn, were either associated with the "high-pitched" features (i.e., small, fast, sharp), such as knife or a convertible, or with the "low-pitch" features (i.e., large, slow, dull), such as a hammer or a SUV. It turned out that participants preferred the front-vowel over the back-vowel brand names for the lighter and sharper products (knife, convertible), but the back-vowel over the front-vowel brand names for the heavier and slower products (hammer, SUV).

Thus, a word's sound can affect consumer attitudes and should therefore be considered an important factor when searching for the right brand or product name. However, there are more superficial non-semantic features of words that can shape a speaker or reader's attitude toward that word or its denoted object. An even more hidden feature is the mere mouth movements that are required to utter a word. Recent approaches have shown that also the form, biomechanical requirements, and patterns of these mouth movements have conse-quences on consumer behavior, which I will describe in detail in the following.

Mouth Movements

Although we execute them numerous times a day, the mere mouth movements that are required to utter a given word are rarely the object of our attention. Just utter the word MOUTH for yourself and observe what happens. First you press the lips together, then you open your mouth, form a round shape of your lips that gets smaller and smaller, and just before your lips would touch each other you stop and touch with the tip of your tongue your upper front teeth. Do this several times: isn't this a peculiar circus of actions running in your mouth, a carnival you are rarely aware of? As we will see in the following sections, these movements can have tremendous indirect influences on people's attitudes and moods, because they make people smile without them knowing (Rummer, Schweppe, Schlegelmilch, & Grice, 2014), they make things appear more or less distant (Maglio, Rabaglia, Feder, Krehm, & Trope, 2014), or they simulate swallowing or spitting movements and thereby induce positive and negative attitudes (Topolinski, Maschmann, Pecher, & Winkielman, 2014).

Importantly, such articulation movements already occur under silent reading. There is no need to utter words overtly to be affected by the mouth movements they require. This is because reading is so automatized that even during silent reading we covertly simulate articulation, in the form of so-called sub-vocalizations, as has been shown in experimental research (Stroop, 1935; Topolinski & Strack, 2009, 2010; see, for the more general notion of covert sensorimotor simulations, e.g., Barsalou, 1999; Foroni & Semin, 2009; Leder, Bär, & Topolinski, 2013; Sparenberg, Topolinski, Springer, & Prinz, 2012; Topolinski, 2010, 2012). Let's have a look now at what mouth movements can do.

Why You Have to Say "Cheese!"

Some of our orofacial muscles are tied to the expression of certain emotions, such as the zygomaticus muscle being responsible for smiling and thus being positively associated (Cacioppo, Petty, Losch, & Kim, 1986). In turn, some phonemes draw on the activity of those muscles during articulation. One prominent case is the phoneme /i:/, as the vowel sound in the English word CHEESE. It is by no surprise that the strategy to make folks smile while taking a picture is to ask them to say "Cheese!", because uttering this word activates the zygomaticus muscle, it literally makes people smile. Since the zygomaticus is in turn associated with positivity, it might be possible to induce positive feelings by uttering /i:/-containing words via facial feedback (Strack, Martin, & Stepper, 1988).

This hypothesis was the object of a recent experimental test by Rummer et al. (2014). They let participants read words containing either /i:/ vowels, which activate the zygomaticus muscle, or words containing /o:/ vowels, whose articulation inhibits activation of the zygomaticus muscle. It turned out that participants reported more positive mood after articulating /i:/-than /o:/-words (for an earlier related demonstration, see Zajonc, Murphy, & Inglehart, 1989). Thus, articulation movements can affect emotion-related muscles and thereby induce positive mood.

Voicedness and Gender Perception

Another muscle activity that is required in the articulation of some phonemes is activity of the vocal chord muscles, namely the feature whether a phoneme is voiced or not. For instance, while both letters require pressing the lips together, P is pronounced without voice, while B is pronounced with additionaly using your voice (to give other examples, T/K are unvoiced but D/hard G are voiced). This motor activity is not an actual mouth movement, but it is still a motor activity playing a role in articulation and being a superficial feature of words. Recently, Slepian and Galinsky (2016) demonstrated that the voicedness of the starting phoneme of names determines gender perception, with the pattern that voiced phonemes (which require vibration of the vocal cords, such as B or D) are more associated with male names, and unvoiced phonemes (which require no vibration of the vocal cords, such as P or T) are more associated with female names. This has strong implications for marketing and branding: if you want to activate male associations with a certain product, say a perfume, you should use voiced phonemes, while you should use unvoiced phonemes if the product shall radiate femaleness.

Close and Distant Letters and Concreteness of Mental Construal

Concerning vowels, some vowels require the tongue to lie back in the mouth, such as /o:/, they are called back vowels. On the other hand, other vowels require the tongue to be placed in the front of mouth, respectively, such as /i:/, they are called front vowels. Recently, Maglio et al. (2014) argued that front and back location of the tongue alters the psychological distance one adopts. Specifally, they argued that back vowels evoke abstract, high-level mental representations because they make the things we ponder seem more distant, while front vowels induce concrete, low-level mental representations because they make things seem closer. Supporting this claim, they found for instance that front vowels lead to higher precision in representing a fictitious city (Experiment 1). Participants received a map of a city, and this city bore a name either with front vowels (e.g., FLEEG) or with back vowels (e.g., FLOOG). After learning the name of the city, participants were asked to look over the map and to visually divide it into as many regions as made sense to them. It turned out that participants considering cities with names including front vowels divided their city into more regions than participants treating cities with back vowels, obviously because the former had a more concrete, low-level mental representation of the city than the latter. This highly fascinating finding shows that articulation movements can even influence the preciseness and concreteness of mental representations.

In a most recent line of different studies an even more hidden feature of articulation movements was explored. This currently emerging novel field has already accumulated so much evidence that I devote a whole section to it.

Oral Approach-Avoidance: Why EBOK is Better than EKOB

Speech production is not the only function of the mouth. The evolutionarily and also ontogenetically much earlier and more basic function of the mouth serves nutrition: the ingestion of foods and liquids and the expectoration of harmful substances (Duffy, 2007; Hejnol & Martindale, 2008; Rosenthal, 1999; Rozin, 1996). As we all know and experience numerous times every day, ingestion is done by moving desired nutritions from the lips over the tongue to the throat of the mouth to swallow them eventually. For instance, we take a sip from our coffee using our lips, let the coffee wander over our tongue to taste its aroma, and eventually move it with the back of our tongue down the throat. Obviously, these activities are muscle movements that systematically wander from the front to the back of the mouth, they *wander inwards* (Goyal & Mashimo, 2006). In contrast, expectoration takes the opposite way, it expels unwanted or even harmful substances from the throat or inner mouth over the tongue to the lips. For instance, we move a bitter substance with our tongue to the lips to spit it out. These expectorative activities *wander outwards* (Goyal & Mashimo, 2006). Given that ingestion obviously is more positive than expectoration (Rozin, 1996, 1999; Rozin & Fallon, 1987), one can assume that generally inward movements also feel more positive to individuals than outward movements. For instance, people would surely prefer swallowing movements over spitting movements.

And here comes the clue: such inward and outward movements can not only be triggered by real nutrition-related acts, but also more indirectly, namely via articulation. Consider the movements required for articulation and the spots where they take place. Particularly for consonants, every articulation takes place at a well-specified and narrow spot, using a very specific mouth movement (Ladefoged, 2001; Titze, 2008). For instance, for articulating P or B we press the lips together, and only the lips. Try to articulate P by using your lips *and* your front teeth, it will not work. Rather, this exercise will produce the consonant F. The consonant T is produced by tapping with the tip of your tongue against the front soft palate. If you, however, tap just a tiny bit more to the front, toward your front teeth, this will produce a TH instead of a T. As we see, every consonant has a very specified and narrowly located articulation spot (IPA, 1999).

When we map all the location spots of all consonants, we realize that they are located along the sagittal front-to-back axis of the mouth: while for instance B and P are produced in the front using only your lips, D, N, and T are produced in the middle using your front tongue, and K is produced in the back of the mouth by pressing the rear back of your tongue against the rear hard palate. What if we use this system to build words that actually feature consonant sequences whose articulation spots systematically wander inwards or outwards, respectively? For instance, for the word MENIKA the consonant articulation spots wander inward (lips, front tongue, back tongue), while for the word KENIMA they wander outward (back tongue, front tongue, lips). Because these articulation patterns resemble positive ingestive or negative expectorative mouth acts, respectively, would they induce good and bad feelings in a person articulating them?

This was tested recently by Topolinski et al. (2014) who construed such inward and outward words and asked participants to rate them for likeability. Note that this manipulation of inward vs. outward wanderings controls for any other features of the letters involved, the inward word MENIKA and its outward counterpart KENIMA consist of the same letters, only in reversed order. Also, note that this manipulation only pertained to consonants and not vowels, because consonants have those very specified muscle action spots, while vowels involve larger open mouth movements whose locations cannot be precisely assigned to front or back (IPA, 1999).

In several experiments using different stimulus pools, Topolinski and colleagues (2014) presented such inward and outward words to participants and asked them to rate them on likeability. It turned out that participants did indeed prefer inward over outward words. Importantly, these effects occurred already when the participants only silently read the words, no overt verbal utterance was necessary to evoke the effect. This is because already silent reading triggers subvocal articulation simulations (Topolinski, 2012; Topolinski & Strack, 2009, 2010). Relatedly, also the sound symbolism effects described earlier already occur under silent reading (e.g., Hinton et al., 2006; Klink, 2000; Kovic et al., 2010; Lowrey & Shrum, 2007).

Showing a more direct behavioral consequence, Topolinski et al. (2014; Experiment 7) told participants that they would enter an online chatroom and could choose a partner to chat with from two possible chatting partner's usernames. Unbeknownst to them, they always received an inward and an outward word as username. It turned out that participants chose inward names more often than outward names in this set-up.

This basic in-out effect has been replicated by independent research groups in English (Kronrod, Lowrey, & Ackerman, 2015) and Portuguese language (Godinho & Garrido, 2015). Moreover, yet another study realized even more complex movements. Specifically, Topolinski and Bakhtiari (2016) created sequential inward-outward movements within one stimulus word (e.g., in-out, FOLOKOLOF vs. out-in, KOLOFOLOK) and found that the ultimate movement of the word determines its likeability: Participants preferred words that wandered first outward and then inward over words that wandered first inward and then outward.

Moreover, Topolinski and Boecker (2016a) explored how little is necessary to evoke the in-out effect. They found that even only one jump within a word, using only two consonants, such as in EBUK versus EKUB, and even leaving out the vowel, such as in the letter pairs BK versus KB, does the trick (Experiments 1–4). Even only listening to a speaker uttering these words or letter pairs produced similar likeability gains for inward over outward stimuli (Experiment 2).

An alternative explanation for the in-out phenomenon might be the ease or fluency with which inward and outward words are being encoded. Generally, higher fluency elicits positive attitudes (e.g., Lee & Labroo, 2004; see articulation fluency, Alter & Oppenheimer, 2006; Topolinski, Erle, & Bakhtiari, 2016; for similar visual and motor fluency effects, see

Topolinski, 2010, 2013, 2014; Topolinski, Erle, & Reber, 2015; Topolinski, Likowski, Weyers, & Strack, 2009; Topolinski & Reber, 2010a, 2010b). However, in a research line exploring this possibility it has been found that processing fluency does not mediate the impact of articulation direction on liking (Bakhtiari, Körner, & Topolinski, 2016).

In sum, the articulation direction of words seems to be a robust determinant of the attractiveness of those words. The next section describes marketing and managerial consequences of this phenomenon.

Marketing Effects of Inward and Outward Articulation

Such laboratory findings on artificial words in dry experimental contexts provide interesting initial basic research evidence on the in-out effect. But does it also work in more applied contexts? Of course, the most obvious implication for applied issues is the use of inward and outward words for brand and product names, similar to work on sound symbolism (e.g., Lowrey & Shrum, 2007). In the following, several different lines of research exploring this are being reviewed.

Food palatability. In one line of research exploring the managerial implications of brand name articulation directions, Topolinski and Boecker (2016b, Experiment 2) presented participants with images of food items and asked how palatable participants felt the food to be. The items, for instance different pieces of cheese or different bottles of wines, bore either inward or outward names. As a result, participants rated food items bearing inward compared to outward names as being more palatable. This finding generalizes the in-out effect to consumers' assessments of foods, and informs food industry and also restaurant chefs on how to find an attractive name for their products. But the managerial consequences do not stop at edible products.

Product liking and willingness-to-pay. Another line of studies assessed the impact of articulation direction on consumer attitudes. In Topolinski, Zürn, and Schneider (2015) participants received inward and outward words and were told that these would be candidates for future brand names. When asked how much they liked each brand, participants reported higher liking for inward over outward words (Experiment 1). When asked how likely they would purchase a product with that brand name, they also reported higher purchase intentions for inward over outward brands (Experiment 2). Finally, when asked how much they would pay for a certain product, they accordingly reported higher willingness-to-pay for inward over outward brands (Experiments 3–4). This price gain due to articulation direction amounted to up to 13% of the average price participants reported to being willing to pay for a product. Also, this effect occurred for different kinds of products, may they be edible (e.g., chocolate bars) or not (e.g., antivirus software).

In these studies, however, participants received only the product name and no additional competitive information on the product. This stands in contrast to real-life situations, for instance being confronted with a shelf of many different wine brands, where also additional product information can be used to assess a product's value. Therefore, Topolinski, Zürn, and Schneider (2015) replicated the set-up using a chocolate bar as product adding a second factor orthogonally to articulation direction, namely the information whether the chocolate bar came from fair-trade production or not. As a result, participants reported higher willingness-to-pay for chocolate bars originating from fair-trade compared to non-fair-trade productions. Moreover, and more importantly, independently from whether the chocolate bar ostensibly originated from fair-trade or not, participants also reported higher willingness-to-pay for chocolate bars bearing inward than outward names. This shows that the in-out effect also persists in the presence of a much stronger price determinant and might therefore be an effective yet costless marketing strategy.

Trust in digital interactions. The ever-booming sector of ecommerce is a vast new field of consumer behavior worth exploring. The impersonal and anonymous character of such online environments renders trust being the crucial determinant of consumer choices (Beldad, De Jong, & Steehouder, 2010; Grabner-Kräuter & Kaluscha, 2003; Ridings, Gefen, & Arinze, 2002). To determine trustworthiness, however, users often have only a few cues available, namely most of the times only the names of the sellers and their respective ratings in the reputation systems (Metzger, Flanagin, & Medders, 2010). However, these reputation systems themselves are often perceived as being of questionable trustworthiness (Resnick, Zeckhauser, Swanson, & Lockwood, 2006), leaving often no other information than the name of a seller. The possible influence of articulation direction in such seller names for perceived trustworthiness was the target of studies by Silva and Topolinski (2016a), who used eBay as an example of digital consumer behavior (cf., Cabral & Hortacsu, 2010). They presented participants with screenshots of ostensible eBay seller profiles, containing seller names that featured either inward or outward articulation, and asked for spontaneous impressions of trustworthiness of the presented sellers. The result was that sellers with inward usernames were trusted more than sellers with outward usernames. This shows that articulation direction can also affect digital interactions.

Matching with product features. As we know from the literature on sound symbolism briefly reviewed in the beginning of this chapter, certain word features not always need to exert a main effect of their quality (e.g., high-pitch sounds are always better), but do meaningfully interact with features of the product denoted by those words. For instance, in Lowrey and Shrum (2007) participants preferred high and sharp word sounds over low and grave word sounds only when those names denoted products that should also be small or sharp (e.g., a knife), but showed reversed preferences for products that should be large and grave (e.g., a hammer).

It is thus possible that also articulation direction shows such interactions with features of the product (Topolinski, Boecker, Erle, Bakhtiari, & Pecher, 2015). While generally expectorative mouth acts are negatively associated, such as coughing or spitting, there are indeed products for which expectoration is part of its use, such as mouth rinse or chewing or tobacco. It might be possible that the general preference for inward over outward words disappears for products whose use includes such expectorative acts. To test this, Topolinski, Boecker et al. (2015, Experiment 6) gave participants a bubble gum and told them they would participate in a product test assessing the feature of this bubble gum and possible brand names for it. One half of the participants received the information that this gum was a chewing gum and that they should chew it and explore its taste for two minutes. We predicted that this taste test would induce ingestive mouth movements, chewing, but also sucking on the gum and swallowing the resulting liquid. The other half of the participants received the information that this gum was a bubble gum and that they should try to make bubbles with it for two minutes. We hypothesized that this exercise would result in more expectorative mouth movements, since making bubbles requires to press the gum against the lips and puff air into it, involving mouth movements similar to spitting.

After this exercise, participants were asked to spit out the chewing gum and were asked to rate possible brand names for it, which were again inward and outward words. It turned out that for chewing gums, participants did indeed again prefer inward over outward names, but for bubble gums this in-out effect disappeared. Apparently, this happened due to matching effects between the products' oral affordances and the articulation patterns: for the bubble gum requiring puffing expectorative mouth movements, inward words did not match as well as in the case of ingestion-associated chewing gum. Although this matching effect was not powerful enough to reverse the in-out effect, it did attenuate it.

In an even stronger manipulation of product features Topolinski, Boecker et al. (2015; Experiments 1–2) compared the impact of in-out branding between a positive, edible product, namely lemonade, and a negative, even harmful substance, namely a toxic chemical. It is obvious that the spontaneous mouth response to lemonade would be swallowing, while a toxic chemical would be spat out of course. In this more extreme comparison, participants preferred inward words over outward words as brand names for lemonade, but outward words over inward words as brand names for toxic chemicals, reversing the basic in-out effect. This line of research shows that also motorically relevant product features have to be taken into account when creating a brand name, particularly the mouth movements that are happening during the product's usage.

Conclusion on the In-Out Effect

As we can see from these various lines of research, articulation dynamics are an efficient and costless tool for marketing: Inward compared to outward articulation of a person's, company's, or product's name makes the person or company more likeable; it makes dishes seem more palatable, and it makes people being willing to pay more for products, and makes them want to chat with a bearer of an inward name. These demonstrations show that articulation dynamics should be carefully taken into account as a yet unknown determinant of attractiveness of brands, products, and persons.

Conclusion: Using Psychological Principles to Design the Perfect Brand Name

As we can see from these different lines of research, superficial features of names, such as their complexity, their sound symbolism, and the mouth movements their articulation requires, shape consumers' attitudes (e.g., Topolinski, Maschmann et al., 2014), their associations with the denoted product (e.g., Slepian & Galinsky, 2016), and even their mental representation (e.g., Maglio et al., 2014) – they can even make you happy (Rummer et al., 2014). They exert their influence already during silent reading, and, as far as this was tested experimentally, people cannot consciously correct for them (Silva & Topolinski, 2016a). Thus, these phenomena are a subtle yet effective cue to consumers' initial gut feelings.

The effects reviewed in this chapter suggest that such subtle features should be carefully taken into account when choosing a name: Make it short and easy, use inward articulation and /iː/ sounds, and carefully consider sound and motor matching with features of the denoted product or company. If you want to imply maleness, use voiced starting phonemes, and choose unvoiced phonemes if you want to imply femaleness. If you want to insinuate or prime preciseness, use front vowels; and if you want consumers to lie back and perceive things from a distance, use back vowels.

Future research will surely identify more of such covert influences of superficial name features. For instance, it is possible that the shape of the letters of a word (round as O or B vs. edged as K or Z), or their visual symmetry (full symmetry as in O, vertical symmetry as in A, or horizontal symmetry as in B) might influence name perception. Furthermore, the sheer position of a letter in the alphabet might work, with early letters being more positive than later letters, or the accordance of the sequence of letters in a name with the sequence these letters have in the alphabet. Let's wait for future surely intriguing developments, which will give brand and product name designers more and more effective tools to find the perfect name.

References

Alter, A. L., & Oppenheimer, D. M. (2006). Predicting short-term stock fluctuations by using processing fluency. *Proceedings of the National Academy of Sciences, 103*(24), 9369–9372.

Bakhtiari, G., Körner, A., & Topolinski, S. (2016). The role of fluency in preferences for inward over outward words. *Acta Psychologica, 171,* 110–117.

Barsalou, L. W. (1999). Perceptual symbol systems. *Behavioral and Brain Sciences, 22*(04), 577–660.

Beldad, A., De Jong, M., & Steehouder, M. (2010). How shall I trust the faceless and the intangible? A literature review on the antecedents of online trust. *Computers in Human Behavior, 26*(5), 857–869.

Brucks, M., Zeithaml, V. A., & Naylor, G. (2000). Price and brand name as indicators of quality dimensions for consumer durables. *Journal of the Academy of Marketing Science, 28*(3), 359–374.

Bryce, W. J., & Yalch, R. F. (1993). Hearing versus seeing: A comparison of consumer learning of spoken and pictorial information in television advertising. *Journal of Current Issues & Research in Advertising, 15*(1), 1–20.

Cabral, L., & Hortacsu, A. (2010). The dynamics of seller reputation: Evidence from eBay. *The Journal of Industrial Economics, 58*(1), 54–78.

Cacioppo, J. T., Petty, R. E., Losch, M. E., & Kim, H. S. (1986). Electromyographic activity over facial muscle regions can differentiate the valence and intensity of affective reactions. *Journal of Personality and Social Psychology, 50*(2), 260–268.

De Chernatony, L. (1999). Brand management through narrowing the gap between brand identity and brand reputation. *Journal of Marketing Management, 15*(1–3), 157–179.

De Saussure, F. (1916). Nature of the linguistic sign. Cours de linguistique générale. In *The critical tradition: Classic texts and contemporary trends.* Ed. David H. Richter. 2nd ed. [1988], 832–35. Boston: Bedford.

Degeratu, A. M., Rangaswamy, A., & Wu, J. (2000). Consumer choice behavior in online and traditional supermarkets: The effects of brand name, price, and other search attributes. *International Journal of Research in Marketing, 17*(1), 55–78.

Duffy, V. B. (2007). Oral sensation and nutrition. *Current Opinion in Gastroenterology, 23*(2), 171–177.

Fitch, W. T (1994). *Vocal tract length perception and the evolution of language* (Unpublished doctoral dissertation). Brown University, Providence, Rhode Island.

Foroni, F., & Semin, G. R. (2009). Language that puts you in touch with your bodily feelings: The multimodal responsiveness of affective expressions. *Psychological Science, 20*(8), 974–980.

Gasser, M. (2004). The origins of arbitrariness in language. In *Proceedings of the 26th Annual Conference of the Cognitive Science Society* (Vol. *26,* pp. 4–7). Cognitive Science Society.

Godinho, S., & Garrido, M. V. (2015). Oral approach-avoidance: A replication and extension for European–Portuguese phonation. *European Journal of Social Psychology, 46,* 260–264.

Goyal, R. K., & Mashimo, H. (2006). Physiology of oral, pharyngeal, and esophageal motility. *GI Motility online,* www.nature.com/gimo/contents/pt1/full/gimo1.html.

Grabner-Kräuter, S., & Kaluscha, E. A. (2003). Empirical research in on-line trust: A review and critical assessment. *International Journal of Human-Computer Studies, 58*(6), 783–812.

Hejnol, A., & Martindale, M. Q. (2008). Acoel development indicates the independent evolution of the bilaterian mouth and anus. *Nature, 456*(7220), 382–386.

Hinton, L., Nichols, J., & Ohala, J. J. (Eds.). (2006). *Sound symbolism.* Cambridge, UK: Cambridge University Press.

International Phonetic Association (Ed.). (IPA) (1999). *Handbook of the International Phonetic Association: A guide to the use of the International Phonetic Alphabet.* Cambridge, UK: Cambridge University Press.

Irmak, C., Vallen, B., & Robinson, S. R. (2011). The impact of product name on dieters' and nondieters' food evaluations and consumption. *Journal of Consumer Research, 38*(2), 390–405.

Klink, R. R. (2000). Creating brand names with meaning: The use of sound symbolism. *Marketing Letters, 11*(1), 5–20.

Köhler, W. (1929). *Gestalt psychology.* New York, USA: Liveright.

Kovic, V., Plunkett, K., & Westermann, G. (2010). The shape of words in the brain. *Cognition, 114*(1), 19–28.

Kronrod, A., Lowrey, T., & Ackerman, J. (2015). *The Effect of Phonetic Embodiment on Attitudes towards Brand Names.* Presentation at the Special Session on Language at the Society for Consumer Psychology International Conference. Miami, Florida.

Ladefoged, P. (2001). *Vowels and consonants: An introduction to the sounds of languages.* Oxford: Blackwell.

Laham, S. M., Koval, P., & Alter, A. L. (2012). The name-pronunciation effect: Why people like Mr. Smith more than Mr. Colquhoun. *Journal of Experimental Social Psychology, 48*(3), 752–756.

Leder, H., Bär, S., & Topolinski, S. (2013). Covert painting simulations influence aesthetic appreciation of artworks. *Psychological Science, 23*(12), 1479–1481.

Lee, A. Y., & Labroo, A. A. (2004). The effect of conceptual and perceptual fluency on brand evaluation. *Journal of Marketing Research, 41*(2), 151–165.

Levelt, W. J., Roelofs, A., & Meyer, A. S. (1999). A theory of lexical access in speech production. *Behavioral and Brain Sciences, 22*(01), 1–38.

Lowrey, T. M., & Shrum, L. J. (2007). Phonetic symbolism and brand name preference. *Journal of Consumer Research, 34*(3), 406–414.

Lowrey, T. M., Shrum, L. J., & Dubitsky, T. M. (2003). The relation between brand-name linguistic characteristics and brand-name memory. *Journal of Advertising, 32*(3), 7–17.

Maglio, S. J., Rabaglia, C. D., Feder, M. A., Krehm, M., & Trope, Y. (2014). Vowel sounds in words affect mental construal and shift preferences for targets. *Journal of Experimental Psychology: General, 143*(3), 1082–1096.

Maheswaran, D., Mackie, D. M., & Chaiken, S. (1992). Brand name as a heuristic cue: The effects of task importance and expectancy confirmation on consumer judgments. *Journal of Consumer Psychology, 1*(4), 317–336.

Maurer, D., Pathman, T., & Mondloch, C. J. (2006). The shape of boubas: Sound–shape correspondences in toddlers and adults. *Developmental Science, 9*(3), 316–322.

Mazursky, D., & Jacoby, J. (1985). Forming impressions of merchandise and service quality. *Perceived Quality,* 13–54.

Metzger, M. J., Flanagin, A. J., & Medders, R. B. (2010). Social and heuristic approaches to credibility evaluation online. *Journal of Communication, 60*(3), 413–439.

Monaghan, P., Christiansen, M. H., & Fitneva, S. A. (2011). The arbitrariness of the sign: Learning advantages from the structure of the vocabulary. *Journal of Experimental Psychology: General, 140*(3), 325–347.

Newman, E. J., Sanson, M., Miller, E. K., Quigley-McBride, A., Foster, J. L., Bernstein, D. M., & Garry, M. (2014). People with easier to pronounce names promote truthiness of claims. *PloS One, 9*(2), e88671.

Olson, J. C. (1976). *Price as an informational cue: Effects on product evaluations* (No. 43). College of Business Administration, Pennsylvania State University.

Perniss, P., Thompson, R., & Vigliocco, G. (2010). Iconicity as a general property of language: Evidence from spoken and signed languages. *Frontiers in Psychology, 1*(227), 1–15.

Rao, A. R., & Monroe, K. B. (1989). The effect of price, brand name, and store name on buyers' perceptions of product quality: An integrative review. *Journal of Marketing Research, 26*(3), 351–357.

Ramachandran, V. S., & Hubbard, E. M. (2001). Synaesthesia – a window into perception, thought and language. *Journal of Consciousness Studies, 8*(12), 3–34.

Resnick, P., Zeckhauser, R., Swanson, J., & Lockwood, K. (2006). The value of reputation on eBay: A controlled experiment. *Experimental Economics, 9*(2), 79–101.

Ridings, C. M., Gefen, D., & Arinze, B. (2002). Some antecedents and effects of trust in virtual communities. *The Journal of Strategic Information Systems, 11*(3), 271–295.

Rosenthal, A. J. (1999). *Food texture: Measurement and perception.* Maryland: Aspe.

Rozin, P. (1996). Towards a psychology of food and eating: From motivation to module to model to marker, morality, meaning, and metaphor. *Current Directions in Psychological Science, 5*(1), 18–24.

Rozin, P. (1999). Preadaptation and the puzzles and properties of pleasure. In D. Kahneman, E. Diener, & N. Schwarz (Eds.). *Well-being: The foundations of hedonic psychology,* 109–133. New York: Russell Sage Foundation.

Rozin, P., & Fallon, A. E. (1987). A perspective on disgust. *Psychological Review, 94*(1), 23–41.

Rummer, R., Schweppe, J., Schlegelmilch, R., & Grice, M. (2014). Mood is linked to vowel type: The role of articulatory movements. *Emotion, 14*(2), 246–250.

Selnes, F. (2013). An examination of the effect of product performance on brand reputation, satisfaction and loyalty. *European Journal of Marketing, 27*(9), 19–35. doi: 10.1108/03090569310043179.

Shrum, L. J., Lowrey, T. M., Luna, D., Lerman, D. B., & Liu, M. (2012). Sound symbolism effects across languages: Implications for global brand names. *International Journal of Research in Marketing, 29*(3), 275–279.

Silva, R. R., & Topolinski, S. (2016a). Is EBOG more trustworthy than EGOB? The influence of inwards versus outwards wandering usernames on judgments of online seller trustworthiness. *Submitted for publication.*

Silva, R. R., & Topolinski, S. (2016b). Make it short and easy! Username complexity determines trustworthiness above and beyond objective reputation. *Submitted for publication.*

Slepian, M. L., & Galinsky, A. D. (2016). The voiced pronunciation of initial phonemes predicts the gender of names. *Journal of Personality and Social Psychology, 110*(4), 509–527.

Song, H., & Schwarz, N. (2009). If it's difficult-to-pronounce, it must be risky: Fluency, familiarity, and risk perception. *Psychological Science, 20*(2), 135–138.

Sparenberg, P., Topolinski, S., Springer, A., & Prinz, W. (2012). Minimal mimicry: Mere effector matching induces preference. *Brain and Cognition, 80*(3), 291–300.

Strack, F., Martin, L. L., & Stepper, S. (1988). Inhibiting and facilitating conditions of the human smile: A nonobtrusive test of the facial feedback hypothesis. *Journal of Personality and Social Psychology, 54*(5), 768–777.

Stokes, R. C. (1974). *The effects of price, package design, and brand familiarity on perceived quality* (Doctoral dissertation, ProQuest Information & Learning).

Stroop, J. R. (1935). Studies of interference in serial verbal reactions. *Journal of Experimental Psychology, 18*, 643–662.

Titze, I. R. (2008). The human instrument. *Scientific American, 298*(1), 94–101.

Topolinski, S. (2010). Moving the eye of the beholder: Motor components in vision determine aesthetic preference. *Psychological Science, 21*(9), 1220–1224.

Topolinski, S. (2012). The sensorimotor contributions to implicit memory, familiarity, and recollection. *Journal of Experimental Psychology: General, 141*(2), 260–281.

Topolinski, S. (2013). The sources of fluency: Identifying the underlying mechanisms of fluency effects. In: C. Unkelbach & R. Greifeneder (Eds.), *The experience of thinking.* New York: Psychology Press.

Topolinski, S. (2014). A processing fluency-account of funniness: Running gags and spoiling punchlines. *Cognition and Emotion, 28*(5), 811–820.

Topolinski, S., & Bakhtiari, G. (2016). Sequential approach-avoidance movements. *Social Psychology, 47*(2), 98–117.

Topolinski, S., & Boecker, L. (2016a). Minimal conditions of motor inductions of approach-avoidance states: the case of oral movements. *Journal of Experimental Psychology: General, 145*(12), 1589–1603.

Topolinski, S., & Boecker, L. (2016b). Mouth-watering words: Articulatory inductions of eating-like mouth movements increase perceived food palatability. *Appetite, 99*, 112–120.

Topolinski, S., Boecker, L., Erle, T. M., Bakhtiari, G., & Pecher, D. (2015). Matching between oral inward–outward movements of object names and oral movements associated with denoted objects. *Cognition and Emotion*, 1–16.

Topolinski, S., Erle, T., & Bakhtiari, G. (2016). Can I cut the gordian tnok? The impact of pronounceability, actual solvability, and length on intuitive problem assessments of anagrams. *Cognition, 146*, 439–452.

Topolinski, S., Erle, T. M., & Reber, R. (2015). Necker's smile: Immediate affective consequences of early perceptual processes. *Cognition, 140*, 1–13.

Topolinski, S., Likowski, K. U., Weyers, P., & Strack, F. (2009). The face of fluency: Semantic coherence automatically elicits a specific pattern of facial muscle reactions. *Cognition and Emotion, 23*(2), 260–271.

Topolinski, S., Lindner, S., & Freudenberg, A. (2014). Popcorn in the cinema: Oral interference sabotages advertising effects. *Journal of Consumer Psychology, 24*(2), 169–176.

Topolinski, S., Maschmann, I. T., Pecher, D., & Winkielman, P. (2014). Oral approach–avoidance: Affective consequences of muscular articulation dynamics. *Journal of Personality and Social Psychology, 106*(6), 885–896.

Topolinski, S., & Reber, R. (2010a). Gaining insight into the "Aha"-experience. *Current Directions in Psychological Science, 19*(6), 402–405.

Topolinski, S., & Reber, R. (2010b). Immediate truth – Temporal contiguity between a cognitive problem and its solution determines experienced veracity of the solution. *Cognition, 114*(1), 117–122.

Topolinski, S., & Strack, F. (2009). Motormouth: Mere exposure depends on stimulus-specific motor simulations. *Journal of Experimental Psychology: Learning, Memory, and Cognition, 35*(2), 423–433.

Topolinski, S., & Strack, F. (2010). False fame prevented – avoiding fluency-effects without judgmental correction. *Journal of Personality and Social Psychology, 98*(5), 721–733.

Topolinski, S., Zürn, M., & Schneider, I. K. (2015). What's in and what's out in branding? A novel articulation effect for brand names. *Frontiers in Psychology, 6*, 585.

Vanhuele, M., Laurent, G., & Dreze, X. (2006). Consumers' immediate memory for prices. *Journal of Consumer Research, 33*(2), 163–172.

Wheeler, A. (2003). *Designing brand identity: A complete guide to creating, building, and maintaining strong brands.* Hoboken, NJ: John Wiley & Sons.

Westbury, C. (2005). Implicit sound symbolism in lexical access: Evidence from an interference task. *Brain and Language, 93*(1), 10–19.

Zajonc, R. B., Murphy, S. T., & Inglehart, M. (1989). Feeling and facial efference: implications of the vascular theory of emotion. *Psychological Review, 96*(3), 395–416.

PART X

Buying/Retailing/Services/Disposal

19

HOW RETAILING CUES INFLUENCE SHOPPING PERCEPTIONS AND BEHAVIOR

Dhruv Grewal, Anne L. Roggeveen, and
Lauren S. Beitelspacher

BABSON COLLEGE, BABSON PARK, MA, USA

Consumers use attribute cues, as established by retailers, to determine their evaluations of a product or a service (Grewal and Compeau 2006). Such cues can be embedded in the store environment, related to the merchandise, influenced by price and other retail tactics, or communicated through messages posted on websites, flyers, and circulars or in advertising. The cues help customers evaluate the available offerings and determine whether to make a purchase or search for more information. The volume of information provided by such cues also has exploded with the growth of the Internet and social media: Manufacturers steadily post offers on social media, and retailers share their own promotions as well as reiterating the manufacturer offers. Thus, cascading information cues (Rapp et al. 2013) can percolate among consumers, especially through social media, and affect their shopping perceptions and behavior.

Grewal and Compeau (2006, p. 112) highlight a difference between intrinsic and extrinsic cues, noting that

> Intrinsic cues are product attributes (e.g., color, nutrition content) that cannot be changed without physically altering the product, whereas extrinsic cues are external, product-related attributes that are not part of the physical product (e.g., price, brand name, and store name).

Retailers generally cannot change the intrinsic cues of the products they sell, such as the scent, nutritional value, or color of a product, but they can control the extrinsic cues, for which changes do not formally alter the offering (e.g., price, information). Among the nearly endless number of cues that a retailer can influence, as Figure 19.1 indicates, this chapter focuses on four types—store environment, merchandise, price, and communication cues—to explore how they affect shopping perceptions and behaviors.

For example, when a consumer enters a retail store maintained by Neiman-Marcus, he or she is exposed to a host of environmental cues: beautifully displayed merchandise on racks and

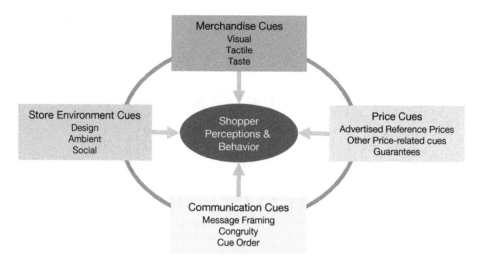

Figure 19.1   Retail cues and shopper behavior

mannequins, soft lighting, and well-dressed, well-trained sales personnel. These cues thus reflect the store design, ambiance, and social environment (Baker et al. 2002; Bitner 1992). A rich stream of research, building on work in environmental psychology (Mehrabian and Russell 1974), has examined and explored the roles of such in-store cues and how they shape the consumer decision process (for reviews, see Baker et al. 2002; Puccinelli et al. 2009).

These environmental cues often are closely related to the second type of cues, namely, merchandise cues. Retailers visually display their offerings with great care, and prior research sheds considerable insight into this domain (e.g., Nordfält et al. 2014). Beyond the visual element, merchandise cues involve tactile and taste factors.

Price-related cues are the third cue type we discuss. Understanding price and price-related cues goes back to work by Scitovszky (1945), who highlighted how increasing marketplace complexity prompted consumers to use various price cues to infer quality. Today, when consumers see an advertisement or look at merchandise displayed in a store, they also see numerous extrinsic, price-related cues, such as the price itself, advertised reference prices, and price-matching guarantees. The link between price information and other extrinsic cues also has attracted considerable research interest, as highlighted in reviews by Rao and Monroe (1989) and Monroe and Krishnan (1985).

Finally, the way cues get communicated can significantly influence consumer evaluations and choices. We focus on three communication factors: framing (e.g., positive or negative frames, semantic price cues, deal-saving frames), the congruity of the cues, and the order of cue presentation.

In each section in which we address these cues, we provide examples, as well as citations of previous research that explores these cues. We also highlight some avenues for further research in each domain.

Store Environment Cues

Retailers invest millions of dollars to ensure that their store atmosphere creates an appealing environment and encourages consumers to shop (Baker, Grewal, and Levy 1992), using elements that can be classified into three categories: design, ambiance, and social (Baker et al. 2002;

Bitner 1992). These cues determine the affect that a consumer feels (Mehrabian and Russell 1974), the level of stimulation (Lehrl et al. 2007), and the consumer's mood (Evans 2002), which in turn influence the consumption experience. Retailers need to understand how to manage these experiences (see Grewal, Levy, and Kumar 2009; Schmitt 1999), so they should address these cues, which likely influence consumer behavior in both brick-and-mortar and online settings. Prior research predominantly has examined these issues in a brick-and-mortar context.

Design Cues

Design cues pertain to visual merchandising elements, as well as store layout. The purpose of these cues is to attract customers and entice them to make a purchase (e.g., the maze layout in Ikea encourages more shopping). Visual merchandising highlights the ways that a retailer can showcase product features and merchandise. For many retailers, visual merchandising can be a source of competitive advantage and an effective tool for adding value to the retailer brand.

Creating an appealing physical environment also is an important objective, because customers are willing to pay more for merchandise that is curated in a more favorable environment. Customers form biases about merchandise quality, employee skills, and overall service based on the retail environment (Baker et al. 2002). Factors that contribute to overall in-store visual merchandising include the store organization, signage, and displays.

Signage is an important tool for communicating promotional messages to customers. Basic signage can influence customers' perceptions and facilitate purchases; it can also enhance a customer's approach or avoidance behavior. The goal of displays is to draw attention to certain products and ultimately increase their sales (Bemmaor and Mouchoux 1991). How signs are displayed also can cue different behaviors. Puccinelli et al. (2013) found that when prices appear in red, consumers perceive that they offer more value than if the same prices appear in black.

Signage can be printed or digital. In hypermarkets, digital signage encourages customers to browse more and search for new items, but it might threaten to hinder sales in smaller stores (e.g., supermarkets, convenience stores). In these smaller format stores, customers tend to be more task-oriented and respond less favorably to the additional stimuli represented by digital signage (Roggeveen, Nordfält, and Grewal 2016).

Ambient Cues

Ambient cues pertain to background conditions in the retail store, such as lighting, music, temperature, and odor (Baker, Grewal, and Levy 1992). They capture several sensory elements, including visual, auditory, and olfactory cues (Spence et al. 2014).

Retailers have long used auditory cues, such as music, to influence consumer behavior. These cues influence consumer perceptions of waiting time (e.g., Chebat, Gelinas-Chebat, and Filiatrault 1993). In an interesting field study in a wine store, Areni and Kim (1993) demonstrate that customers buy more expensive wine when they hear classical (vs. Top 40) music. These results reinforce the notion that music cues set the stage for shoppers to assess merchandise quality.

Olfactory cues relate to fragrances in the retail setting. Smells that consumers are not aware of have more impact on their purchase behavior than smells that consumers acknowledge (Li et al. 2007). Inserting a fresh smell in a retail aisle that displays shampoo for sale, for example, increases shoppers' moods, store evaluations, and unplanned purchases of the shampoo (Nordfält et al. 2014).

Visual cues can include the color, lighting, brightness, size, or structure of a retail space (Kotler 1974). Visual cues play an important role in the consumer's perceptions about a retail space. Color, as noted later, can affect the customer's emotional state and encourage or discourage store patronage. Lighting is also another critical visual stimulant that is often overlooked in the literature. Lighting can influence a consumer's ability to find things, how the consumer sees herself in the mirror in the fitting room, and the consumer's overall evaluation of the retail space. Many retailers invest heavily in lighting for their renovation efforts in the hopes of increasing spending and improving the consumer's evaluation of the retail space. Summers and Hebert (2001), for example, found that installing brighter lights led to customers spending more time in the store and more time inspecting merchandise. Visual cues can also be used in conjunction with olfactory cues and auditory cues to further enhance stimulation.

Social Cues

Social cues pertain to the presence of others in the environment, through some combination of employees and other customers. Research has demonstrated that if the facial expressions and behavior of salespeople match those of the customer, the customer responds more positively (Chartrand and Bargh 1999; Puccinelli et al. 2013). The social environment created by the retailer also can affect customers (Verhoef et al. 2009). For example, retailers recognize the need for compatibility management, which involves attracting similar customers (Martin and Pranter 1989), whose behaviors can affect others both directly and indirectly (Bitner 1992). In a socially connected world, communities of customers are increasingly important (Bagozzi and Dholakia 2002). Social interactions also might refer to exchanges with firms through social media or with avatars on websites.

Retail salespeople face a tougher selling arena though, because showrooming customers might use stores to learn more about the products, then turn to their mobile devices to purchase them online. The transformation of the store into a showroom has negative impacts on retail salespeople's self-efficacy and performance (Rapp et al. 2015). A possible way to counter such effects is through price-matching guarantees (as discussed in more detail subsequently).

Thus, design, ambiance, and social cues in the store environment affect shopper perceptions and behavior. Understanding their interactive effects also is important. Baker et al. (2002) report the results of two empirical tests of an extensive model that supports the impacts of these three store environment cues on consumers' evaluations and intentions. Baker, Grewal, and Parasuraman (1994) highlight how ambient and social cues also influence store images, an effect that is mediated by merchandise and store quality perceptions. Specifically, their study exposed participants to videos, filmed in a gift store in a mall, that presented eight different conditions that experimentally manipulated the design (high: green/peach color, brass trim on displays, open layout, neat organization vs. low: brown/white color, no brass trims on display, grid layout, messy organization of merchandise), ambiance (high: classical music, soft lighting vs. low: Top 40 music, bright lighting), and social factors (high: three salespersons, greeted the customer, wore an apron vs. one salesperson, did not greet the customer, did not wear an apron). Higher levels of the ambient and social cues enhanced perceptions of merchandise and service quality. Further research is needed to integrate affective components with cognitive components.

Merchandise Cues

Spence et al. (2014) provide an excellent framework that complements the design and ambient cues and depicts the role of sensory cues on shopping behavior. They highlight the role of visual, auditory, olfactory, tactile, and taste cues on affective and cognitive associations and ultimately behaviors. The merchandise presented can be influenced by all the sensory cues laid out by Spence et al. (2014), perhaps especially the visual, tactile, and taste forms.

Visual Cues

Where a product is visually and spatially located can cue information to a customer. For example, merchandise located to the left or bottom of a retail shelf is perceived as less expensive and of lower quality (Valenzuela and Raghubir 2015). When lower priced cereal appears in the middle of the aisle at eye level (versus bottom shelf), consumers perceive the entire aisle as more affordable (Nordfält et al. 2014). Even the organization of the merchandise in a display can cue different behaviors: When towels are displayed by color vertically (versus diagonally), more consumers look at, stop, and pick up the towels; for a beverage display, more consumers look at beverages displayed vertically versus horizontally (Nordfält et al. 2014).

Visual merchandise also can be displayed on digital screens or online, using static pictures or dynamic moving objects. Roggeveen et al. (2015) examine the impacts of these different displays of merchandise and find that dynamic video presentations enhance preferences for a more hedonic offer in a choice set. Building on vividness theory (Nisbett and Ross 1980), they articulate a process by which dynamic cues enhance hedonic preferences and reduce price sensitivity. Beyond the focus on visual cues, it would be interesting to understand whether these effects might be enhanced in the presence of other sensory cues (e.g., soothing music).

Another form of visual cues that can draw customer attention to the merchandise is store mannequins. Lindström et al. (2016) show that in brick-and-mortar stores, mannequins with human-like features, especially heads, enhance purchase intentions for the merchandise they display. However, in an online setting, mannequins without humanized heads increase purchase intentions among more fashion-savvy shoppers.

Tactile and Taste Cues

Tactile cues are communicated by how something feels, in terms of its softness, smoothness, or temperature (Kotler 1974). Retailers can make these cues more (or less) accessible to customers, as a function of how they display their merchandise. Taste cues are available if the retailer allows sampling of products. Only through the act of consumption can the consumer experience this cue. More details on tactile and taste cues are provided in a detailed review by Spence et al. (2014), who also highlight the need for additional studies in the area, especially research that addresses the role of multi-sensory cues (e.g., evaluation of ice cream based on visual, olfactory, and taste cues).

Price-Related Cues

In addition to store environment cues and merchandise cues, retailers must carefully consider how to present the price of their merchandise and services. In this section, we first discuss the impact of advertised reference prices as cues, then explore price and other extrinsic cues or tactics related to price. Finally, this section explores the impact of price-matching guarantees as cues that prompt consumer reactions.

Advertised Reference Price Cues

How consumers react to price cues depends on advertised reference prices and other methods used to communicate a discount (Biswas et al. 2013). An advertised reference price is a price comparison point, such that the product price gets compared with some other price (e.g., regular price, original price, manufacturer's suggested price), and the comparison suggests that consumers will save money. Advertisers often appeal to consumers' desire to get a deal by citing the offering price (e.g., sale price) together with some higher reference price (e.g., regular price), which makes the former more attractive. In a meta-analysis, Compeau and Grewal (1998) find that the advertised reference price (both its presence and its level) exerts a powerful influence on consumers' perceptions of value and reduces their likelihood of searching for lower prices.

The advertised reference price also influences internal reference price (IRP) perceptions. IRPs are held in a consumer's memory and used for comparison against other prices. If a price exceeds the consumer's IRP, he or she likely judges it as unacceptable and perhaps perceives that the product is unfairly priced. If the price is below the reference level, the consumer likely will accept the price and perceive additional value (savings) from purchasing the product. Thus, the IRP, which also can be influenced by the advertised reference price, determines the transaction value for customers (Grewal, Monroe, and Krishnan 1998).

Transaction value involves the trade-off between the consumers' IRP and their monetary sacrifice. How consumers assess a price promotion for a given item involves evaluating both the acquisition value and the transaction value for the item. Acquisition value reflects the trade-off between the sacrifice (i.e., how much time and money consumers must expend to acquire the product) and the quality of the product (Dodds, Monroe, and Grewal 1991; Monroe and Krishnan 1985; Zeithaml 1988). An intriguing insight is that the effects of advertised selling price on acquisition value are mediated by consumer perceptions of transaction value. Grewal, Monroe, and Krishnan (1998) develop and test a comprehensive framework, out-lining how selling price and advertised reference price influence quality, IRPs, sacrifice, value perceptions, and behavioral intentions. They also provide scales to assess acquisition value and transaction value.

Two important review articles, by Grewal and Compeau (1992) and Compeau and Grewal (1998), provide qualitative and quantitative insights into the role of advertised reference price cues in comparative price advertisements. They also highlight the important public policy implications. Comparative price advertising can be deceptive, leading the Federal Trade Commission to issue guidelines for determining when such advertising is deceptive. That is, "a comparative price advertisement can be construed as deceptive if it makes any representation, commits any omission of information, or involves any practice that may materially mislead a reasonable consumer" (Grewal and Compeau 1992, p. 52). Advertised reference prices have the potential to be informative if they are genuine reference prices (e.g., past prices, competitors' price), but in some cases, they function as fictitious references, and when discovered, they have prompted legal cases against various retailers (Friedman 2015).

Biswas et al. (2013) highlight that the visual presentation of advertised reference prices and sales prices also can influence consumer behavior, with more profound effects when the advertised reference price is to the left of the sales price. Such a presentation makes it easier for consumers to calculate the savings (i.e., easier to subtract the smaller sale price from the larger reference price). They also call for further research to address the effects of presenting a sale price below or above the reference price.

Price and Other Extrinsic Cues

Without preexisting knowledge of a product, consumers look to cues to determine its quality, value, and appeal. A widely researched topic thus pertains to the relationships of price with perceived quality or with perceived value (Grewal and Roggeveen 2011). Meta-analyses (Monroe and Krishnan 1985; Rao and Monroe 1989) support the price–perceived quality relationship, but beyond price, various other cues signal quality and value too. To reach a more comprehensive understanding of how multiple cues might influence consumer perceptions, several studies explore the joint effects of price and other cues (Miyazaki, Grewal, and Goodstein 2005).

For example, Dodds, Monroe, and Grewal (1991) consider the joint effects of price, brand name, and store name on consumers' perceptions of quality, value, and willingness to buy. With an intricate experimental design, they identify the individual effects of price, brand name, and store name on each of the dependent measures, as well as their joint effects. Price enhances perceived quality but reduces value perceptions and willingness to buy. Thus, price offers a signal of quality, and consumers trade-off this inferred quality against the sacrifice they must make, in the form of the price paid, to form value perceptions. Brand name and store name enhance all the dependent variables. In an extension of this study, Grewal et al. (1998) examine the effects of discount size, brand name, and store name on store image, perceived quality, IRPs, value, and purchase intentions. They also examine a potential moderating role of consumer knowledge and highlight the importance of (1) brand names for knowledgeable consumers but (2) discounts for less knowledgeable consumers.

Price-Matching Guarantee Cues

Another price-related cue that retailers can control is guarantees. These "low-scope" cues are easy to change, and their diagnosticity as a stand-alone signal of quality is relatively weaker than those of high-scope cues (Purohit and Srivastava 2001). In the pricing domain, retailers use two main types: price-matching guarantees (PMGs) and low price guarantees (LPGs). Their purpose is to provide consumers with confidence that the retail offers are fair and competitive, because if consumers find a lower price elsewhere, the retailer will refund the difference between the purchase price and the lower price. Thus, consumers can feel more comfortable, despite having limited knowledge of market prices (Dickson and Sawyer 1990; Monroe and Lee 1999).

PMGs influence people's perceptions while they make decisions about whether to purchase a product; they can also influence their evaluations after they have purchased the product (Estelami, Grewal, and Roggeveen 2007). For example, a refusal to honor PMGs, due to various restrictions, has strong negative effects on both price and service quality perceptions. Furthermore, PMGs can increase post-purchase price searches, though only among brick-and-mortar, not Internet, retailers (Kukar-Kinney and Grewal 2007).

Similarly, LPGs allow retailers to signal to consumers that they offer the lowest prices in town and will compensate customers if that information is not true. Many LPGs provide compensation that is greater than the difference between the sale price and the lowest price found. Thus, LPGs can serve both informative and protective functions. If the LPG signal turns out to be false though, it can harm perceptions of retailer credibility and repurchase intentions, even after the refund occurs (Dutta, Biswas, and Grewal 2007). Additional research is needed to specify how the effects of PMGs differ from those LPGs, as well as which underlying factors can determine when a retailer should offer a PMG versus an LPG.

Mobile phones make it easier for consumers to search for lower prices and take advantage of such guarantees. Therefore, we also need further research to understand how this function might be changing price perceptions and retail images. In the next section, we discuss how the presentation of these message cues can influence evaluations and behaviors.

Presentation of Message Cues

Beyond the actual, multiple cues that retailers can control, to influence how consumers respond to offers, the ways in which the cues are presented also may have effects. In this section, we explore three factors to consider when determining how to present a message-related cue: framing, congruity, and the order of presentation.

Framing Cues

Within the domain of price and product attribute cues, several framing and wording effects have been examined. We focus on positive and negative frames, the framing of semantic price cues, and whether a deal-saving cue is framed in dollar or percentage terms.

Positive versus Negative Frames. In this area of inquiry, Kahneman and Tversky's (1979) prospect theory provides a foundation for understanding why, in some studies, price cues influence perceptions of risk (e.g., Peterson and Wilson 1985), but in others they have minimal effects (e.g., Shimp and Bearden 1982). Grewal, Gotlieb, and Marmorstein (1994) demonstrate that message framing moderates the price–perceived performance risk relationship. In their study, they present a fictitious product with seven of eight attributes either positively framed (Hito rated superior to Toshiba) or negatively framed (Toshiba rated inferior to Hito). Their experimental results demonstrate that price exerts a greater impact in terms of reducing performance risk when the message is framed negatively. Roggeveen, Grewal, and Gotlieb (2006) extend these message framing effects to the domain of store reputation cues and performance risk. Positive framing results in more detailed processing, and the consistency among multiple cues matters; negative frames also result in increased use of extrinsic cues as heuristics. Building on such insights, Grewal and Lindsey-Mullikin (2006) demonstrate that message framing moderates the effect of price ranges for a given product on further search intentions. These results demonstrate that the effect of price range (another cue) on search intentions is more pronounced in a negative frame.

Between-Store versus Within-Store Price Comparisons. Another important area of inquiry pertains to the specific wording or semantic cue used to convey a price promotion. The specific wording might involve a within-store comparison/low consistency frame (e.g., regular price, sale price) or a between-store comparison/high consistency frame (e.g., compare at, sale price; Grewal, Marmorstein, and Sharma 1996; Lichtenstein, Burton, and Karson 1991). Past research offers inconsistent results about the effectiveness of various formats for advertised reference prices used to convey the deal.

Grewal, Marmorstein, and Sharma (1996) argue that the effectiveness of alternative semantic cues is contingent on the size of the discount and their viewing location. The effects of within-store cues are stronger if the customer sees them in a store, rather than at home, because they reduce the economic incentive to conduct further search, such that the consumer is more likely to accept confirming evidence. In contrast, between-store cues are more effective when viewed at home. Such subtle, semantic cues effects also are contingent on the discount being processed; the influences arise when the discount is of moderate size, which engenders greater processing of the cues, but not when the discount is small or very large. In this context as well, it would be useful to examine how mobile phone use influences the impacts of specific semantic cues, both in stores and at home.

The greater processing in the moderate discount condition is in line with information processing research that indicates that moderately discrepant conditions prompt greater processing than do low or high discrepant conditions (Ozanne, Brucks, and Grewal 1992). Grewal, Roggeveen, and Lindsey-Mullikin (2014) extend these results by demonstrating that the interaction effect of a semantic cue with its location is contingent on the consumer's shopping goal (hedonic or utilitarian). The interaction has a significant effect if the goal is utilitarian but not if it is hedonic in nature. Thus, we need further investigations to understand the role of various cues when consumers undertake more affective processing.

Percentage off versus Dollar off Deal Frames. The final area related to framing focuses on deal savings. Discounts can be communicated by providing the advertised reference price and the sale price, with the expectation that the customer can calculate the savings accurately. Alternatively, price savings can be communicated explicitly in the price promotion, as a percentage off or dollar off amount. With a series of studies, González et al. (2016) demonstrate the role of the *absolute number heuristic*, such that a format that communicates a larger number tends to be more effective. For deals under $100, a percentage off frame likely is more effective than a dollar off frame (i.e., 10% saving on $50 is more effective than $5 off), and the reverse holds for deals over $100 (i.e., 10% saving on $200 is less effective than $20 off).

Cue Congruity

An important area of inquiry considers how consumers integrate and interpret multiple cues. To understand this process, prior research has used various theories (e.g., information integration theory, Anderson 1981, 1986; congruity theory, Mandler 1982). Prior research emphasizes the importance of multiple cues, which can enhance product evaluations and purchase intentions (Dodds, Monroe, and Grewal 1991). Miyazaki, Grewal, and Goodstein (2005) also demonstrate that the consistency of multiple cues, such as a positive price cue matched with another positive cue (e.g., strong warranty, positive country of origin, strong brand), enhances evaluations. Even more interesting are insights into how these two cues influence evaluations when they are inconsistent. For example, a positive price cue and a weak brand results in a much lower product evaluation, implying overweighting of the negative cue.

Roggeveen, Goodstein, and Grewal (2014) apply Mandler's (1982) incongruity framework to examine the effects when a PMG cue is congruent or incongruent with the domain (e.g., offered by provider whose reputation is based on service, not pricing) or valence (e.g., offered by retailer known for carrying expensive merchandise). Consistently, across all their studies, they find that the best evaluations result when both cues are congruent. Under moderate congruity, if the valence is positive, the evaluations also improved.

At a broader level, retailers constantly face decisions about where to locate secondary displays of their merchandise (Roggeveen et al. 2016). For example, a grocery chain might display pasta on the end-cap of the pasta aisle, but it also could present it on the end-cap of the canned tomato sauce aisle or even set up a special display near the hamburger meat section. All such displays would be congruent with the broader category of pasta and meat sauce. However, locating the pasta in an unrelated aisle might be effective too, because pasta is a frequently purchased item, so the cue of its presence might prompt customers to purchase the pasta and then proceed to the sauce aisle and the meat aisle. End-caps that communicate information through both signage and location can create a sense of congruity surrounding the message, as a function of the location where the product is displayed. These findings also overlap with insights about merchandise-related cues.

Order of Cue Presentation

A final area of inquiry pertains to how the order of cues or information gets processed by consumers. Biswas, Grewal, and Roggeveen (2010) demonstrate that consumers prefer the second choice between two desirable options (recency effect) but the first option between two less desirable ones. Wilcox, Roggeveen, and Grewal (2011) build on prior sampling research (e.g., Biswas, Grewal, and Roggeveen 2010; Braun-LaTour and LaTour 2005) to understand how information cues presented prior to versus after an experience have differential impacts. As they show,

> when information is presented before consuming an experiential product, the information results in an assimilation effect such that consumers evaluate the same experience more positively when the product information is favorable compared to when it is unfavorable. More interestingly, when such information is presented after consuming an experiential product, it results in a contrast effect such that consumers evaluate the same experience more negatively when the product information is favorable compared to when it is unfavorable.
>
> (Wilcox, Roggeveen, and Grewal 2011, p. 763)

The effects of the spatial position of two cues in an ad or display also have been examined; Biswas et al. (2013) consider the influence when an advertised reference price is placed to the right or left of a sales price. They accordingly suggest a new principle, the subtraction principle, which indicates that it is easier to assess the difference between two numeric cues when the larger one is to the left of the smaller one. In a comparative price advertising context, a price reduction thus should be more effective when the larger advertised reference price is to the left of the smaller sales price. They confirm these results consistently for moderate discounts; however, the effects reverse when the discounts grow too small or too large.

Conclusions

In this article, we review our research on the role of retail cues and how they shape product evaluations and purchase behaviors. We focus on four types: store environment cues, merchandise cues, price cues, and communication cues. Store environment cues reveal the influence that design, ambient, and social cues exert on the consumer decision process. With our discussion of merchandise cues, we explore how visual, tactile, and taste cues affect consumers' perceptions and behavior. About price-related cues, we highlight the role of advertised reference prices and show how they further influence value through their influence on consumers' IRPs. We also introduce how price in combination with other extrinsic cues (e.g., brand name, store name, country of origin) influence consumers' perceptions of quality and value, as well as their purchase intentions and IRPs. Moreover, we consider PMGs and how they influence both purchase and search intentions. The final type of cue that we discuss herein is the presentation of message cues. In this section, we discuss how the framing of cues (e.g., positive and negative frames, semantic price cues, deal-saving frames), their congruity, and the order of cue presentation all can influence evaluations and behaviors. In turn, we hope this research serves as a helpful integration of retail-related cues and their impacts on shopper behavior, which also serves as a springboard for further research in this area.

References

Anderson, N. H. (1981), *Foundations of information integration theory*, New York, NY: Academic Press.

Anderson, N. H. (1986), *A functional theory of cognition*, Mahwah, NJ: Erlbaum.

Areni, C. S., & Kim, D. (1993), The influence of background music on shopping behavior: Classical versus top-forty music in a wine store, in *Advances in Consumer Research*, L. McAlister & M. L. Rothchild (eds.), Provo, UT: Association for Consumer Research, 336–340.

Bagozzi, R. P., & Dholakia, U. M. (2002), Intentional social action in virtual communities, *Journal of Interactive Marketing*, 16 (2), 2–21.

Baker, J., Grewal, D., & Levy, M. (1992), An experimental approach to making retail store environmental decisions, *Journal of Retailing*, 68 (Winter), 445–460.

Baker, J., Grewal, D., & Parasuraman, A. (1994), The influence of store environment on quality inferences and store image, *Journal of the Academy of Marketing Science*, 22 (4), 328–339.

Baker, J., Parasuraman, A., Grewal, D., & Voss, G. (2002), The influence of multiple store environment cues on perceived merchandise value and patronage intentions, *Journal of Marketing*, 66 (April), 120–141.

Bemmaor, A. C., & Mouchoux, D. (1991), Measuring the short-term effect of in-store promotion and retail advertising on brand sales: A factorial experiment, *Journal of Marketing Research*, 28 (2), 202–214.

Biswas, A., Bhowmick, S., Guha, A., & Grewal, D. (2013), Consumer evaluation of sale price: Role of the subtraction principle, *Journal of Marketing*, 77 (July), 49–66.

Biswas, D., Grewal, D., & Roggeveen, A. L. (2010), How the order of sampled experiential goods affects choice, *Journal of Marketing Research*, 47 (June), 508–519.

Bitner, M. J. (1992), Servicescapes: The impact of physical surroundings on customers and employees, *Journal of Marketing*, 56 (April), 57–71.

Braun-LaTour, K. A., & LaTour, M. S. (2005), Transforming consumer experience: When timing matters, *Journal of Advertising*, 34 (3), 19–30.

Chartrand, T. L., & Bargh, J. A. (1999), The chameleon effect: The perception-behavior link and social interaction, *Journal of Personality and Social Psychology*, 76 (6), 893–910.

Chebat, J. C., C. Gelinas-Chebat, & P. Filiatrault (1993), Interactive effects of musical and visual cues on time perception: An application to waiting lines in banks, *Perceptual and Motor Skills*, 77 (3), 995–1020.

Compeau, L. D., & Grewal, D. (1998), Comparative price advertising: An integrative review, *Journal of Public Policy & Marketing*, 17 (Fall), 257–274.

Dickson, P. R., & Sawyer, A. G. (1990), The price knowledge and search of supermarket shoppers, *Journal of Marketing* 54 (July), 42–53.

Dodds, W. B., Monroe, K. B., & Grewal, D. (1991), Effects of price, brand, and store information on buyers' product evaluations, *Journal of Marketing Research*, 28 (August), 307–319.

Dutta, S, Biswas, A., & Grewal, D. (2007), Low price signal default: An empirical investigation of its consequences, *Journal of the Academy of Marketing Science*, 35 (1), 76–88.

Estelami, H., Grewal, D., & Roggeveen, A. L. (2007), The negative effect of policy restrictions on consumers' post-purchase reactions to price-matching guarantees, *Journal of the Academy of Marketing Science*, 35 (2), 208–219.

Evans, D. (2002), *Emotion: The science of sentiment*, Oxford: Oxford University Press.

Friedman, D. A. (2015), Reconsidering fictitious pricing, *Minnesota Law Review*, 110 (March), 921–982.

González, E., Esteva, E., Roggeveen, A. L., & Grewal, D. (2016), Amount off versus percentage off: When does it matter? *Journal of Business Research*, 69 (March), 1022–1027.

Grewal, D., & Compeau, L. D. (1992), Comparative price advertising: Informative or deceptive? *Journal of Public Policy & Marketing*, 11 (Spring), 52–62.

Grewal, D., & Compeau, L. D. (2006), Consumer responses to price and its contextual information cues: A synthesis of past research, a conceptual framework, and avenues for further research, *Review of Marketing Research*, Volume 3, Naresh Malhotra (ed.), M.E. Sharpe, 109–131.

Grewal, D., Gotlieb, J., & Marmorstein, H. (1994), The moderating effects of message framing and source credibility on the price-perceived risk relationship, *Journal of Consumer Research*, 21 (June), 145–153.

Grewal, D., Krishnan, R., Baker, J., & Borin, N. (1998), The effect of store name, brand name and price discounts on consumers' evaluations and purchase intentions, *Journal of Retailing*, 74 (Fall), 331–353.

Grewal, D., Levy, M. & Kumar, V. (2009), Customer experience management: an organizing framework, *Journal of Retailing*, 85 (1), 1–14.

Grewal, D., & Lindsey-Mullikin, J. (2006), The moderating role of the price frame on the effects of price range and number of competitors on consumers' search intentions, *Journal of the Academy of Marketing Science*, 34 (1), 55–62.

Grewal, D., Marmorstein, H., & Sharma, A. (1996), Communicating price information through semantic cues: The moderating effects of situation and discount size, *Journal of Consumer Research*, 23 (September), 148–155.

Grewal, D., Monroe, K. B., & Krishnan, R. (1998), The effects of price comparison advertising on buyers' perceptions of acquisition value, transaction value and behavioral intentions, *Journal of Marketing*, 62 (April), 46–60.

Grewal, D., & Roggeveen, A. L. (2011), Decomposing the intricate role of price, quality, and value relationships, in *Legends in Marketing: Kent B. Monroe*, Grewal, D., & Roggeveen A. L. (eds.), Volume 3. Thousand Oaks, CA: Sage Publications.

Grewal, D., Roggeveen, A. L., & Lindsey-Mullikin, J. (2014), The contingent effects of semantic price cues, *Journal of Retailing*, 90 (2), 198–205.

Kahneman, D., & Tversky, A. (1979), Prospect theory: An analysis of decision under risk, *Econometrica*, 47 (March), 263–291.

Kotler, P. (1974), Atmospherics as a marketing tool, *Journal of Retailing*, 49 (Winter), 48–64.

Kukar-Kinney, M., & Grewal, D. (2007), Comparison of consumer reactions to price-matching guarantees in internet and bricks-and-mortar retail environments, *Journal of the Academy of Marketing Science*, 35 (2), 197–207.

Lehrl, S., Gerstmeyer, K., Jacob, J. H., Frieling, H., Henkel, A. W., Meyrer, R., Wiltfang, J., Kornhuber J., & Bleich, S. (2007), Blue light improves cognitive performance, *Journal of Neural Transmission*, 114 (4), 457–460.

Li, W., Moallem, I., Paller, K. A., & Gottfried, J. A. (2007), Subliminal smells can guide social preferences, *Psychological Science*, 18 (December), 1044–1049.

Lichtenstein, D. R., Burton, S., & Karson, E. J. (1991), The effect of semantic cues on consumer perceptions of reference price advertisements, *Journal of Consumer Research*, 18 (December), 380–391.

Lindström, A., Berg, H., Nordfält, J., Roggeveen, A. L., & Grewal, D. (2016), Does the presence of a mannequin head change shopping behavior? *Journal of Business Research*, 69 (February), 517–524.

Mandler, G. (1982), The structure of value: Accounting for taste, in *Affect and Cognition: The 17th Annual Carnegie Symposium*, Clark, M. S. & Fiske, T.S. (eds.), Hillsdale, NJ: Lawrence Erlbaum Associates, 3–36.

Martin, C. L., & Pranter, C. A., (1989), Compatibility management: Customer-to-customer relationships in service environments, *Journal of Services Marketing*, 3 (3), 5–15

Mehrabian, A., & Russell, J. (1974), *An approach to environmental psychology*, Cambridge, MA: MIT Press.

Miyazaki, A., Grewal, D., & Goodstein, R. C. (2005), The effect of multiple extrinsic cues on quality perceptions: A matter of consistency, *Journal of Consumer Research*, 32 (June), (14), 6–153.

Monroe, K., & Lee, A. Y. (1999), Remembering vs. knowing: Issues in buyers' processing of price information, *Journal of the Academy of Marketing Science*, 27 (Spring), 201–225.

Monroe, K. B., & Krishnan R. (1985), The effect of price on subjective product evaluations, in *Perceived quality: How consumers view stores and merchandise*, Jacoby, J. & Olson, J. C., (eds.), Lexington, MA: Lexington Books, 209–232.

Nisbett, R. E., & Ross, L. (1980), *Human inference: Strategies and shortcomings of social judgment*, Englewood Cliffs, NJ: Prentice-Hall.

Nordfält, J., Grewal, D., Roggeveen A. L., & Hill, K. (2014), Insights from in store experiments, *Review of Marketing Research*, Volume 12, Grewal, D., Roggeveen, A. L. & Nordfält, J. (eds.), 127–146.

Ozanne, J. L., Brucks, M., & Grewal, D. (1992), A study of information search behavior during the categorization of new products, *Journal of Consumer Research*, 18 (March), 452–463.

Peterson, R. A., & Wilson, W. R. (1985), Perceived risk and price reliance as price-perceived quality mediators, in *Perceived Quality: How Consumers View Stores and Merchandise*, Jacoby, J. & Olson, J. C. (eds.). Lexington, MA: Lexington Books, 247–267.

Puccinelli, N., Chandrashekeran, R., Grewal, D., & Suri, R. (2013), Are men seduced by red? The effect of red vs. black prices on price perceptions, *Journal of Retailing*, 89 (2), 115–25.

Puccinelli, N., Goodstein, R. C., Grewal, D., Price, R., Raghubir, P., & Stewart, D. (2009), Customer experience management in retailing: Understanding the buying process, *Journal of Retailing*, 85 (1), 15–30.

Purohit, D., & Srivastava, J. (2001), Effect of manufacturer reputation, retailer reputation, and product warranty on consumer judgments of product quality: A cue diagnosticity framework, *Journal of Consumer Psychology*, 10 (3), 123–134.

Rao, A., & Monroe, K.B. (1989), The effect of price, brand name and store name on buyers subjective product assessments: An integrative review, *Journal of Marketing Research*, 26 (August), 351–357.

Rapp, A., Baker, T. L., Bachrach, D. G., Ogilvie, J., & Beitelspacher L. S. (2015), Perceived customer showrooming behavior and the effect on retail salesperson self-efficacy and performance, *Journal of Retailing*, 91 (2), 358–369.

Rapp, A., Beitelspacher, L. S., Grewal, D., & Hughes, D. (2013), Understanding social media effects across seller, retailer, and customer interactions, *Journal of the Academy of Marketing Science*, (41), 547–566.

Roggeveen, A. L., Goodstein, R., & Grewal, D. (2014), Improving the effect of guarantees: The role of a retailer's reputation, *Journal of Retailing*, 90 (1), 27–39.

Roggeveen, A., Grewal, D., & Gotlieb, J. (2006), Does the frame of a comparative ad moderate the effectiveness of extrinsic information cues? *Journal of Consumer Research*, 33 (June), 115–122.

Roggeveen, A. L., Grewal, D., Nordfält, J., & Goodstein, R. (2016), The impact of congruency of a special display with its surroundings, *Academy of Marketing Science*, Orlando, Florida, May 2016.

Roggeveen, A. L., Grewal, D., Townsend, C., & Krishnan, R. (2015), The impact of dynamic presentation format on consumer preferences for hedonic products and services, *Journal of Marketing*, 79 (November), 34–49.

Roggeveen, A. L., Nordfält, J., & Grewal, D. (2016), Do digital displays enhance sales? Role of retail format and message content, *Journal of Retailing*, 92 (March), 122–131.

Schmitt, B. H. (1999), Experiential marketing. *Journal of Marketing Management*, 15, 53–67.

Scitovszky, T. (1945), Some consequences of the habit of judging quality by price, *Review of Economic Studies*, 12 (Winter), 100–105.

Shimp, T. A., & Bearden, W. O. (1982), Warranty and other extrinsic cue effects on consumers' risk perceptions, *Journal of Consumer Research*, 9 (June), 38–46.

Spence, C., Puccinelli, N. M., Grewal, D., & Roggeveen, A. (2014), Store atmospherics: A multisensory perspective, *Psychology & Marketing*, 31 (7), 472–488.

Summers, T.A., & Hebert, P.R. (2001), Shedding some light on store atmospherics: Influence of illumination on consumer behavior, *Journal of Business Research*, 54 (2), 145–150.

Valenzuela, A., & Raghubir, P. (2015), Are consumers aware of top-bottom but not of left-right inferences? Implications for shelf space positions, *Journal of Experimental Psychology: Applied*, 21 (September), 224–241.

Verhoef, P. C., Lemon, K. N., Parasuraman, A., Roggeveen, A. L., Tsiros, M., & Schlesinger, L. A. (2009), Customer experience creation: Determinants, dynamics and management strategies, *Journal of Retailing*, 85 (1), 31–41.

Wilcox, K., Roggeveen, A. L., & Grewal, D. (2011), Shall I tell you now or later? Assimilation and contrast in the evaluation of experiential products, *Journal of Consumer Research*, 38 (4), 763–773.

Zeithaml, V. A. (1988), Consumer perceptions of price, quality, and value: A means-end model and synthesis of evidence, *Journal of Marketing*, 52 (July), 2–22.

20

USING VISUAL DESIGN TO IMPROVE CUSTOMER PERCEPTIONS OF ONLINE ASSORTMENTS[1]

Barbara E. Kahn

THE WHARTON SCHOOL AT THE UNIVERSITY OF
PENNSYLVANIA, PHILADELPHIA, PA, USA

In the future, we expect the percentage of shopping done online will grow exponentially. That is not to say that physical stores will go away, but even when purchases are ultimately made in a physical store, the shopping process frequently will start online. In this omni-channel world, the smart phone will play an important role in making shopping connections. "It's essential to be there on mobile, yes," said Google director of marketing for performance ads, Matt Lawson, "But it's even more important to create rich and relevant experiences that connect your stores with shoppers in all of their micro-moments—and encourage those shoppers to come back again and again" (McDowell 2016).

There are two things worth noting about this predicted change in shopper behavior. First, when much of consumers' exposure to retail assortments comes through a digital interface, *visual design* decisions, both in how the overall assortment is depicted and in how the individual items within the assortment are shown, will become critical for influencing consumer reactions. While such stimulus-based judgments (Lynch and Srull 1982) are important in offline shopping, they will be particularly relevant in online shopping, because the focus is narrower (on a screen rather than at a multi-sensory physical store level), and online environments can be more attention demanding (Mosteller, Donthu and Eroglu 2014). Second, many critical perceptions can be formed in these "micro-moments" that occur throughout the consumer journey, impressions that are often made instantaneously and automatically. These can be decisive moments when preferences are shaped.

Paralleling this change in observed shopping behavior has come new research that helps us understand better what catches consumers' attention online, how consumers process stimuli, and how all of these influence perceptions. For example, by using sophisticated eye-tracking techniques we now have the capability to identify the exact stimuli that consumers fixate on when looking at assortments online, the sequence in which they fixate on these specific items, and the total time that consumers spend fixating on each item as well as on the assortment overall. With this knowledge, we can determine exactly:

1   What features of an assortment directs people's attention, and
2   What are the assortment variables that retailers can use to facilitate the ease of processing?

Consumer Attention

We know that visual search is not random but is guided by the salience of objects; salience, in turn, results from a combination of goal-directedness and stimulus-driven factors (Hutchinson, Lu, and Weingarten 2016). Sometimes bottom-up stimulus-related visual patterns can lead directly to choice, but more often top-down decisions, (e.g., involvement, pre-existing preferences, goals, expectations, memory) and marketing variables (e.g., price, sales support, delivery options) will interact in final choice process (Pieters and Wedel 2004, Pieters 2007). Even though goal-directed factors may exert a larger effect on purchase decisions, small stimulus-driven changes, to aspects of displays or packaging, or both, that capture consumers' attention are essential because they can result in increased brand familiarity, changes in perceptions and therefore ultimately affect choice (Chandon et al. 2007). Further, even mere attention to items in a category can in and of itself affect consumer purchases (Janiszewski 1998). Thus, isolating and understanding these bottom-up, stimulus-based, and frequently automatic effects is important, and will be the focus here. While aesthetic considerations are also important in building brand and store loyalty, the focus here is not on aesthetic desirability, but more specifically on design criteria that differentially affect consumer attention.

Processing Fluency

Once consumers pay attention to items within an assortment, they then have to make sense of it. Visual variables can influence the speed and accuracy of low-level processes (Schwarz 2015). This suggests that the design elements of an assortment can make it easier for consumers to process stimuli. Processing fluency is a term that encompasses all sources that facilitate processing in any form. Research shows that increasing fluency feels good and this mildly positive affect can serve as input into judgment. (Schwarz 2015). Fluency not only increases liking of a product but also decreases deferral (Novemsky et al. 2007). In addition, consumers hold lay theories of mental processes and the ease or difficulty of the experience causes them to form inferences. When fluency is high, consumers feel more confident and are more likely to form positive inferences and perceptions (Schwarz 2015). When processing is more difficult or more disfluent, processing styles shift from System 1 (automatic processing) to System 2 (more analytic processing) (Schwarz 2015).

Using this knowledge about processing fluency allows us to formulate three principles of design for online assortments:

1   Assortments that are designed to be easier to process will evoke positive affect and they will be liked more than those that are harder to process.
2   When assortments are easier to process, people will form positive inferences about the perceived variety that is included in the assortment (Deng et al. 2016).
3   When assortments are more complex, retailers need to provide tools or structure either to facilitate cognitive processing or to make the assortment less disfluent.

Finally, when shopping online, it is easy to drill down through the assortment and focus on an individual item. This type of scrutiny makes packaging decisions and product shape decisions more salient. Graphic product-level design issues will matter more here as well.

We begin with a discussion of what drives consumers' attention when scanning assortments. We then discuss the three principles of design for online assortments as stated before. Finally, we discuss some of the new findings in packaging design and product shape that affect consumers' perceptions at the individual item level (see Figure 20.1).

Patterns of Attention

Today we can accurately measure attention using sophisticated eye-tracking techniques capable of recording fixations and saccades. Saccades are rapid jumps of the eyes (they last 20–40 milliseconds) during which no useful information is acquired. Fixations are moments between the saccades when the eyes are relatively still and a person is focusing on a specific stimulus. Fixations are necessary for object identification. Scan paths are a sequence of fixations and saccades that track the order in which stimuli are viewed (Rayner 1998, Lin and Yang 2014). Using eye-tracking techniques, we can identify which stimulus a viewer sees first, last, and in between, the duration of time fixated on each, as well as the total duration of the episode. What people pay attention to is a function of what the brain assesses as most important, and the assessment can either come from "top-down" (i.e., based on previously fixated information, prior knowledge, goals or expectations) or be "bottom-up" (based on the salient attributes of the environmental stimuli: Hutchinson, Lu, and Weingarten 2016).

Attention is Correlated with Consideration

Using an experimental online assortment of novel brands that consumers had never seen before, researchers were able to remove "top-down" motivations and focus only on "bottom-up" or stimulus-based patterns of attention (Chandon et al. 2009). Consumers were then engaged in choice tasks and attention was measured using eye-tracking technology. Attention, as measured by the number of fixations, is weakly correlated with recall, but strongly correlated with brands identified to be in the consumers' consideration sets. This suggests that attention is important in and of itself, and that self-reported memory measures are not a valid proxy for it. Individuals cannot always tell you why they buy or do not buy a specific product, and when asked, they often provide cognitive explanations based on post choice attributions (Nisbett and Wilson 1977). These explanations can be biased, because once a person has made a choice, it can influence their subsequent preferences or inferences (e.g., cognitive dissonance reduction, Festinger 1957).

Attention can either be involuntary or voluntary (i.e., self-directed). Involuntary attention is a function of the visual properties of the assortment. Self-directed attention may be driven by top-down considerations such as goals or cognitive expectations (which we are not focusing on here), but research has also shown that self-directed attention can influence subsequent inferences *without* extensive decision-making because it results in some brands being noticed while other are ignored.

Visual Features of the Assortment Influence Involuntary Attention

Involuntary attention is influenced by visual properties of the assortment. These properties include relative salience of objects within the assortment, location effects of those items on a screen, and number of facings and display size. Retailers can also use techniques like color blocking to direct involuntary attention.

Attention to items within online assortments is not random; Attention is correlated with choice consideration

Involuntary Attention
- Salience
- Location effects
- Number of facings
- Color blocking

Self-direction Attention
- Selectively attended items more likely to be chosen in the future
- Selectively avoided items less likely to be chosen later

Principles of Online Retail Assortment Design

Assortments that are easy to process are liked more
- Reduce the size
- Reduce information intensity
- Reduce the friction between the item and the background

Assortments that are easy to process will result in higher perceived variety inferences
- Horizontal vs vertical depiction
- Visual vs. verbal depiction
- Increasing the fluency of processing complex alternatives

When assortments are large retailers need to provide tools to facilitate processing
- Organizational structure
- Visual vs. verbal cues
- Categorization and filtering

Graphic Decisions for Packaging and Product Shape

Location of product image on the package

Product shape

Figure 20.1 Visual design decisions that influence online assortments

Visual Salience Bias

Studies conducted by Milosavljevic et al. (2012) have shown that attention to a brand is a function of its salience within the assortment and this visual salience can affect not only consideration as mentioned above but also choice. Even at rapid decision speeds, items that are more visually salient (due, for example, to brightness or color) "pop-out" of an assortment and lead to automatic attention toward those items, which can be measured through eye-tracking by increases in the duration of fixations toward those items.

In a unique experimental design that eliminated other explanations, Milosavljevic et al. (2012) found that higher liking ratings were given to stimuli at the time of choice as a function of the amount of attention that they received during the decision-making process (similar to the Chandon et al. 2009). In this study, however, consumers had previous experiences with some of the brands. When consumers had strong preferences for a particular brand, they were good at choosing that brand in rapid decision-making tasks and presumably paid more attention to those brands—perhaps not surprising. But when preferences were weak, consumers were more influenced by the visual features of the stimuli. Milosavljevic et al. (2012) found that when brands were relatively similar, consumers ended up choosing items that were visually prominent at least 40% of the time, even when these choices were inconsistent with prior preferences.

This suggests that more visually salient options are more likely to be chosen because of the way the visual information is processed. This visual salience bias is long lasting and can influence choice more than changes in preferences do, especially when preferences are relatively weak. The visual salience bias is even stronger in the presence of cognitive load, which mimics the frequent state of a busy shopper. Although these experiments were conducted using rapid decision-making tasks, these are not unusual circumstances. For example, one study found that participants could make accurate choices in less than 3 seconds in displays that included 16 items (Reutskaja et al. 2010). In these studies, the magnitude of the visual saliency bias was small, less than a 1-point increase on liking scale, yet this could still have a sizable effect on the bottom line.

Other studies in the advertising context have shown that another factor that affects the attention or relative salience of an item is the visual clutter surrounding the brand (Pieters, Wedel, and Batra 2010). Although their results were only tested in an advertising context, it seems reasonable to expect they will extend to attention paid to items within an online assortment. Pieters et al.'s (2010) results show that when the background is homogeneous (regardless of color), when the brand is larger relative to the others in the assortment, and when the contrast between the brand and background is large, then the brand is easier to identify. This suggests that when attention resources are limited, such as in the case of the "micro-moments" discussed earlier or when consumers are otherwise time pressured in their shopping, it is important to make sure a brand can be easily identified from its background (or from the assortment) or else consumers will pay less attention to it and be less likely to choose it.

Finally, other studies have shown that the number of objects in a display can affect the salience of individual objects in the set (Rosenholtz, Li, and Nakano 2007). The larger the number of items in an assortment, the less salient any individual item is. This is because viewer attention allocation is a function not only of the focal object but also of other stimuli within the field of vision (Lu and Itti 2005). One way to increase the salience of individual objects in a large assortment is to increase the number of facings or increase the size of the object. Using online displays, Chandon et al. (2009) found that the number of facings had strong positive effects on both noting and re-examination. They conclude that shelf facings strongly influence visual attention and through attention modestly affect brand evaluation. Other eye-tracking studies find that display size is one of the most reliable drivers of attention (Wedel and Pieters 2008).

Location Effects within an Online Assortment

Previous research in physical stores has shown that the location of an item on the shelf can affect choice and quality inferences. For example, Drieze, Hoch, and Purk (1994) found the better location for product choice in a physical store was near eye level and the worst location was on the lowest shelf. Raghubir and Valenzuela (2006) also found shelf position effects and suggested these were motivated by quality inferences as measured by memory recall. Raghubir and Valenzuela (2008) found that consumers believed that retailers placed the expensive, high-quality brands on the top shelves and the cheaper brands on the bottom, but had no pre-conceived beliefs about horizontal positioning. Valenzuela and Raghubir (2015) show that all else equal, people judge products at the bottom or on the left as being of lower quality and less expensive.

While some of these effects may hold for online assortments as well, much of the new research in this domain has focused on how various locations of items within an online assortment affect the patterns of attention paid to that item and how those gaze patterns affected subsequent recall and evaluation. For example, Chandon et al. (2007) found that brands located near the center of the scene of online displays were the first to be fixated on and were noted (and re-examined) more often, but that this did not affect recall. Being on the left or right side made no difference to attention or evaluation. Further, Chandon et al. (2009) showed that at point of purchase the brand's horizontal centrality had a strong positive effect on choice.

Similarly, Atalay et al. (2012) find that the brand in the center of an online display benefits from a disproportionally more prominent gaze cascade, which they call the "central gaze cascade effect." The "central gaze cascade effect" builds on previous research by Shimojo et al. (2003) who found using eye-tracking that the role of attention on preference is rapid and concentrated in the final few seconds of the choice task. Just prior to choosing, the observer's gaze is increasingly more likely to be directed toward the chosen stimulus; Shimojo et al. call this the "gaze cascade effect." The gaze pattern is iteratively connected with preference formation in that the more individuals look at a stimulus the more they like it, and the more they like it the more they look at it. Atalay et al.'s (2012) result builds on this idea by describing the effects of location on gaze cascade effects. They point to a center fixation bias (Tatler 2007) defined as a strong inclination to look first at the center of the scene.

Two theories exist suggesting why this happens: (1) consumers expect that there will be more information in this location (even when there is not) and (2) physically the pupils are positioned to look straight ahead. These factors in turn stimulate a re-centering bias whenever people look away. Atalay et al. (2012) found when setting a planogram of unfamiliar brands online and then asking participants to study the assortment and then make a choice, there was a significant effect of horizontal centrality on visual attention captured by eye-tracking and on choice, but *not* on the brand inferences or memory-based measures. Brands in the horizontal center received more frequent eye fixations, longer durations, and were chosen more often. In addition, they found there was a higher tendency to fixate on the central located brand in the first few and the last few seconds of the gaze duration, but only fixations observed in the last few seconds increased the likelihood of choosing a brand in the center (results supported by mediation analyses). This is a recency, rather than a primacy effect. Although individuals have been shown to forget what they attend to (Milosavljevic and Cerf 2008), attention can nonetheless affect choice. Further, this centrality bias is related to the center of the planogram, not the center of the screen.

Retailer-Directed Salience Effects

These results describe natural gaze patterns that are at least partially motivated by physical features of eyes that naturally look straight ahead. But retailers can also help direct gaze patterns by making specific items within the assortment more salient. Preliminary evidence shows that color blocking can affect how people scan an assortment. Specifically, people looked at more SKUs in regions that had sharper color blocks. Although these effects were measured in a physical store by having shoppers wear eye-tracking goggles, follow-up studies indicate that these results are likely to hold in online assortments as well (Weingarten, Kahn, and Hutchinson (in process)). It is hypothesized that the color blocking affects attention because of possible mechanisms: (1) the visual contrast of sharper color blocks increase salience of the individual items—If items are connected to each other through this color blocking the overall category is larger and more salient, and (2) color blocking can help people efficiently find what they are looking for, and when this happens they are more likely to fixate for a longer time within the color block.

These preliminary results suggest that in the future, retailers can create "eye catching regions" of an online (or offline) display that include items that people are likely to want. If the items in these regions make it easier for people to find what they like, that is, to match their preferences, they are likely to think more highly of the store. Retailers could also fill these "eye catching regions" with highly aesthetic or desirable products to create a positive store image, similarly to the way that high-end grocery stores have typically led with beautiful produce or sweet smelling bakery items (Kahn and McAlister 1997).

Self-Directed Attention Effects on Subsequent Choice

Even when top-down motivations are affecting attention patterns, there can still be unanticipated influence on subsequent choice. Janiszewski, Kuo, and Tavassoli (2013) showed that even self-directed selective attention can influence choice independently, without extensive decision-making. They suggest that when viewing an assortment, consumers may selectively attend to some items while ignoring others due to top-down motivations (e.g., goals, expectations). Since the visual cortex is limited as to the amount of information that can be processed at any one time, the brain efficiently directs attention to the situational information most relevant to ongoing behavior. This results in enhanced neural responses to selectively attended items and inhibited neural responses to ignored items.

The directed attention (and related avoidance) functions are enhanced where there is more competition (or assortment) in the visual field that makes looking at just one item more difficult. These neural responses influence the perception of stimuli when they are seen at a later time. So, items that were looked at in the past are more likely to be chosen in the future than they would have been had they not initially received attention, and items that were neglected in the past are less likely to be chosen later than they would have been if inhibition had not initially drawn attention away from them. If the stimuli in the assortment are very familiar, there will not be advantages for those items from selective attention, but the targeted neglect effects will still hold.

Speculatively, these observed patterns could occur for several reasons, including: (1) attentional blindness, where consumers see what they had seen before and just don't see what is not familiar; (2) increased salience, such that things you have seen before "pop-out" of the display more easily, so these are considered first and that gives it an advantage; or (3) priming, such that selective attention energizes cognitive processes that are instrumental in choice. Note these attention effects are different from "mere exposure effects" (Zajonc 1968), because all alternatives were presented the same number of times.

Summary

Recent advances in sophisticated eye-tracking technology have allowed us to explore the patterns of attention that consumers exhibit when viewing assortments. Attention, in and of itself, can influence consideration and subsequent choice. Involuntary attention is influenced by the visual aspects of an assortment. One key aspect of the assortment that influences attention is the salience within the assortment. Items that are more visually salient due to brightness, color, size, number of facings, cause items to "pop out" of the display, leading to automatic attention toward those items, which increases the duration of fixations and can affect subsequent preferences. There are also location effects within an assortment that affect attention. Items located near the center of online displays are noted and re-examined more often. Retailers can proactively affect involuntary attention by using graphic techniques, such as color blocking, that increases the salience of individual objects or regions of an assortment. Finally, even self-directed attention can differently affect future choice because items that are not paid attention to are less likely to be attended to in the future.

Online Assortments Must Be Easy to Process

After consumers pay attention to items within an assortment, they then have to "make sense" of those items. Reber, Schwarz, and Winkielman (2004) distinguish between perceptual fluency, which relates to the high speed, low-resource-demand processing, and conceptual fluency, or the ease of interpretation in relation to semantic knowledge structures (which is moderated by expectation and attribution). However, it has been difficult empirically to separate between these two sources of fluency, so researchers have recently turned to the more generic term of "processing fluency." Processing fluency is defined as the ease of perceiving, encoding and comprehending a stimulus. Schwarz (2004) showed that processing fluency could affect preference for an option independently of benefits the option confers. This has been labeled "preference from process" rather than "preference from information" (Janiszewski et al. 2013). Reber and colleagues (2004) show that processing fluency also affects the attractiveness of the stimulus. This could happen for several reasons, such as (1) it results in successful recognition of the stimulus, (2) the knowledge needed to interpret the stimulus is readily available (Carver and Scheier 1990), or (3) because it signals that the stimulus is familiar (Zajonc 1968). (See Schwarz (2010) for a review of these effects.)

Thus, higher fluency increases positive affect, decreases choice deferral (Novemsky, et al. 2007), and creates positive inferences (Schwarz 2015). When processing is difficult or more disfluent, consumers no longer process automatically, but rather shift to more analytic processing (Schwarz 2015). These findings about processing fluency lead us to formulate three principles specifically related to the design for online assortments:

1   Assortments that are easy to process will be liked more.
2   Assortments that are easy to process will result in higher perceived variety inferences.
3   When assortments are very large they are more difficult to process, retailers need to provide tools or structure to facilitate cognitive processing or make large assortments less disfluent.

Given these principles, the next sections outline tactics that online retailers can use to maximize the likelihood that their online assortments are well received.

Principle One: Assortments that are Easy to Process are Liked More

More fluent processing triggers positive affect, which in turn increases attractiveness and liking (Winkielman et al. 2003). There are a few key concepts that help make an assortment easier to process: (1) reduce the size of the assortment, (2) reduce information intensity and increase familiarity, and (3) reduce the friction between the item and the background.

Reduce the Size of the Assortment

The harder it is to pay attention to any particular item within the assortment, the less fluent the overall assortment is (Janiszewski and Meyvis 2001). Therefore, one way to make an assortment more fluent is to reduce the number of items, which increases the salience of each individual object (Rosenholtz, Li, and Nakano 2007) and makes it easier to process. In addition to reducing the number of objects in displays, retailers can make the processing of each item easier by decreasing the dissimilarities among objects presented together and decreasing the numbers of colors and contrasts. Even if assortments are relatively small, if it is hard to grasp the differences and complexities among the items, the assortment could still be difficult to process. Offline, this trend is playing out in luxury stores where operators present merchandise in simple, even "Spartan" displays so as not to detract from key items.

Related to this idea of "less is more," Pracejus, Olsen, and O'Guinn (2006) showed "white space" can lead to more positive brand attitudes. Although this was shown in advertisement contexts, their findings should extend to assortment displays as well. They found that white space conveys prestige and upscale meaning. More white space gives the perception of higher quality, prestige, trust and leadership, and lower risk.

Reduce Information Intensity

Mosteller, Donthu, and Eroglu (2014) show information intensity is negatively related to processing fluency because more visual attentive effort is required. Therefore, anything that makes it easier to process information will increase fluency.

One way to deliver information easily is through the use of pictures. Images are highly effective, attention-grabbing elements of web design (Katerattanakul 2002) because they are more quickly processed than text and require less cognitive effort (Luna and Peracchio 2003, Lam, Chau, and Wong 2007). There is also evidence that some image processing is automatic and unconscious, such that people may not even realize why they find some things pleasurable. It is also faster to search for an image than for words (Paivio 1974), and it arouses more pleasure and sensory curiosity, so that it also leads to further search (Lee, Amir, and Ariely 2009). There can be technical downsides to using too many images, however, in that it can slow down the loading speed of a page (Lynch and Horton 2001).

If text is used, the clarity or easiness of reading the text is important, as is the background color contrast with the text font. Both of these factors would affect the cognitive and affective evaluation of information processed (Mosteller, Donthu, and Eroglu 2014). Labroo, Dhar, and Schwarz (2008) show that simply making the text easier to read reduces information overload because it reduces cognitive effort. This is especially relevant when consumers have to view multiple pages of information, which will become more and more common as consumers do more online shopping.

Positive judgments are also higher the less information people have to extract from a stimulus to perceive it, so if there is high redundancy in the stimulus, people like it more because it is easier to grasp quickly (Garner 1974). This is consistent with the people's preference for symmetry because information can be grasped more quickly than for irregular or asymmetric shapes. Royer (1981), using reaction times, showed that vertical symmetry is easier to detect than horizontal symmetry, which is easier than diagonal symmetry.

Consistent with this idea of reducing information intensity to increase fluency, Im, Lennon, and Stoel (2010) found that consumers liked websites more when they were familiar with the stimuli, when the stimuli were more prototypic and more symmetric. They also showed that the online retail websites were easier to process and thus liked more when they included bigger photos, sans serif type fonts (e.g., Arial), and more symmetric images and had less information intensity. Websites designed using these features were evaluated more highly on aesthetics and pleasure, but pleasure was positively correlated both with re-patronage and purchase intent, while positive aesthetic evaluation was correlated only with re-patronage intent.

Relationship of Item to Assortment Context

Another factor that affects the processing fluency of items within an assortment, and hence the overall impression of the assortment as a whole, is the relationship between the individual items and the assortment context. Orth and Crouch (2014) studied how visual complexity of a retail context affects fluency and perceived attractiveness of a specific item within it. In order to assess how easy it is to process a specific item (e.g., the packaging or the product itself), the retail context in which the product is contained needs to be considered as well, and that context should also facilitate processing fluency. Orth and Crouch (2014) show that a target design will be evaluated as more attractive when it is presented in a context that is low, rather than high in visual complexity—and, further, that this effect is more important for items high in inherent appeal. (For low inherent appeal products, context complexity is less important.)

Related to this idea is the observation that people are sensitive to changes in their subjective experience. Fluency effects are more pronounced in within-subject designs (where fluent and disfluent targets are mixed) than in between-subjects designs (where everything is fluent or disfluent). Dechene, Stahl, Hansen, and Wanke (2010) show that in heterogeneous contexts where there is variability in processing fluency, people notice the differences and are more likely to use that information as a heuristic cue to inform judgment. This would suggest an all-fluent store environment might be less advantageous than an environment where the product of interest is presented in more fluent ways than others.

In offline retail, product variety is the third most important factor in choosing a physical store (behind location and price) (Arnold et al. 1983, Louviere and Gaeth, 1987). In online environments, where physical constraints are not as limiting, the variety of an assortment may be an even more important differentiating factor in determining website satisfaction and store loyalty (Bansal et al. 2004). How much actual variety to include in an assortment is obviously important but would be a function of product characteristics, supply chain issues, logistics, and so on. Here, the focus is on how visual design decisions may affect decision-making, and thus the variable of interest is the perceived variety of the assortment holding actual variety of an assortment (i.e., the number of distinct SKUs) constant. Even for the same actual variety in an assortment, perceptions of variety (or how those SKUs are processed), can vary. Increasing perceived variety is generally beneficial (Kahn et al. 2013), until it becomes too complex and results in choice overload (Iyengar and Lepper 2000). More perceived variety offers consumers more perceived flexibility (Kahn and Lehmann 1991) and more opportunity to choose different options over time (McAlister 1982, Kahn 1998).

Several studies have shown how visual design features of an assortment can affect the perceived variety. Specifically, it has been shown that (1) whether displays are oriented horizontally or vertically, (2) whether information about the alternatives within an assortment are depicted visually or verbally, and (3) whether the information about complex alternatives within an assortment is displayed by alternative or by attribute will all influence processing fluency and will affect inferences about the perceived variety of the overall assortment.

Horizontal versus Vertical Displays

Deng et al. (2016) found that whether items are displayed horizontally or vertically affects the ease of processing or processing fluency. Since horizontal displays match the horizontal or binocular vision field, information can be processed more efficiently than if the items were arrayed in vertical displays. That the human perceptual span is wider in the horizontal direction facilitates horizontal (vs. vertical) eye movement (Shi, Wedel, and Pieters 2013). Vertical stimuli also frequently require additional head movement. Thus, horizontal should be more fluent than vertical scanning and should allow more options to be viewed quickly, which in turn increases the perceptual variety. These differences in processing fluency occur in very short time periods (less than 3 seconds). Although this efficiency is easily overcome with more time, the initial variety perceptions persist and result in more variety and higher quantities purchased downstream (Kahn and Wansink 2004).

The results also have implications for designing "scrolling" mechanisms. Although this was not directly tested, these results suggest that when more than one item is likely to be purchased, the retailers should direct the consumers to scroll horizontally to view the items within the assortment. Whereas if the assumption is that only one item is to be purchased, then the scrolling direction should be vertical. These results also suggest that when the task is to choose among different product categories, the categories should be viewed vertically. However, when the task is to choose items within a product category assortment, and ideally, more than one might be chosen, the viewing direction should be horizontal. When the whole assortment can be viewed on one screen (or a few), marketers can use horizontal versus vertical design or color blocking or packaging design to visually direct customers' eye movements (DuPuis and Silva 2008).

Visual versus Textual Depiction Can Affect Perceived Variety

In addition to the affective differences in processing visual versus textual depictions of objects described earlier there are also differences in the way information is interpreted. Words are processed sequentially or in a piecemeal manner, whereas an image is processed all at once (Hart 1997). This makes the information shown visually easier to process. But in addition, Townsend and Kahn (2014) showed that holding information constant, images made it easier for consumers to recognize the interactions between the attributes within an option and this increased inferences or perceptions of how much variety existed in the assortment overall.

Fluency of Processing Individual Items Can Affect Perceived Variety

Although perceived variety was not explicitly measured, Huffman and Kahn (1998) showed that the overall variety of an assortment is affected by the complexity of the products themselves (e.g., multi-attribute structure of choice alternatives, complexity of their technical specifications, degree of similarity or differences among items). This research was also conducted before online shopping was as popular as it is today; however, the studies were done online and actually mimicked the way online shopping is now executed. They found that the assortment variety where the options themselves are very complex could be processed more easily as a function of the way the information about the options was presented. Holding actual assortment variety constant, they found that the consumers were able to process more fully and were more satisfied, when the information about the products within the assortment was presented in an attribute- vs alternative-based approach. These results were specifically relevant for complex choices and would not hold in general for less difficult to process product alternatives.

In the advertising context, Pieters et al. (2010) differentiate between different types of complexity that cause different effects. They show when "design complexity" is greater, more attention is paid, and this increases liking. They identify six general principles of design complexity: (1) number of objects, (2) irregularity of objects, (3) dissimilarity of objects, (4) detail of objects (more is more complex), (5) asymmetry of object arrangement, and (6) irregularity of object arrangement. This kind of "design complexity" can have a positive aesthetic quality and can be engaging. However, "feature complexity" is related to "clutter" and reduces liking. If it is difficult to identify the brand, then people react negatively. "Feature complexity" is related to more detail, more color luminance and edges are more complex—visual clutter. This is measured online by the pixels in the photo and the more computer memory that is needed to store the image. Although they do not discuss their findings with regard to the online retailing context or to perceived variety, it would seem that as long as the assortments are small enough to process easily, design complexity at the individual stimulus level could be positive given people have the time and inclination to pay attention. However, "feature complexity" or "clutter" at the assortment level, or anything that makes processing the assortment difficult, is not good. (Note: discussion of how these features apply to large assortments follows in the next section.)

Advantages of Disfluency

Counter-intuitively, Huang and Kwong (2015) argue that sometimes if design features make processing too easy, variety perceptions can decrease. Manipulating difficulty of fluency by hard-to-read fonts, Huang and Kwong (2015) find that as consumers experience more subjective difficulty they confuse this difficulty in reading about the options with the subjective difficulty of making a choice (Schwarz 2004). When people infer the choice is more difficult, they assume there is more variety in the assortment. This is because consumers know large assortments result in choice difficulty and discomfort (Jacoby et al. 1974). This effect is stronger when people have a strong lay belief that links high variety assortments with choice difficulty. Although these results are interesting, they should probably be taken with a grain of salt, as decreasing perceptual fluency can result in less pleasure that could result in consumer disengagement.

Similarly, others found that disfluency can make a single object seem more complex, special and unique (Pocheptsova, Labroo, and Dhar 2010). This could be valuable for "special occasions" or for instances when the product is being marketed as "exclusive," or "limited edition" because in these circumstances the lay belief is that the choice should be difficult, and hence disfluency will result in higher perceptions of quality.

Principle 3: When Assortments are Very Large, Retailers Need to Provide Tools to Facilitate Processing

One of the advantages of online retailing is that assortment size can get very large, because it is not limited by physical showroom space. Clearly, all things equal, larger assortments should be better than smaller assortments because they allow more choice flexibility, optimization, variety, and so on (Chernev et al. 2015). In fact, unsurprisingly, bigger assortments can lead to more online sales (Borle et al. 2005).

But to the degree that large assortments increase choice overload, require greater cognitive effort (i.e., move consumers to System 2 processing) delay decision-making, etc.: Iyengar and Lepper 2000), they are detrimental. This is a well-covered area in the literature. Chernev et al. (2015) conducted a meta-analysis that identified four key factors, (1) choice set complexity, (2) decision task difficulty, (3) preference uncertainty, and (4) decision goal, as moderators of the impact of assortment size on choice overload. Other moderators, which are more top-down and cognitive in nature and can clearly have an effect later in the choice process, include expectations (Diehl and Poynor 2010), articulated ideal point (Chernev 2003), individual differences (Iyengar, Wells, and Schwartz 2006), construal level (Goodman and Malkoc 2012), and expertise (Mogilner, Rudnick, and Iyengar 2008).

But, here the focus is on stimulus–driven visual design features that can assist the consumer in processing large assortments. The research discussed below specifically considers the size of the assortment as an important moderator. When the assortment gets large, visual design features can be used either to reduce the disfluency of the assortment or to provide tools that can help consumers parse the information and appreciate the variety of the assortment.

Specifically, the following structural elements affect processing fluency for large assortments: (1) organizational structure, (2) visual versus verbal depiction, and (3) categorization and filtering. These tools can affect consumers' affective reactions to both the assortments as well as the perceived variety. On the flip side, when the assortment is smaller and thus disfluency is significantly reduced, these same structural variables can be used, in reverse (e.g., random vs. organized) to increase perceived variety and affect.

Organizational Structure

In thinking about how consumers process assortments, Hoch, Bradlow, and Wansink (1999) considered two types of processing style: analytic and holistic. Holistic, or superficial processing is more automatic and requires fewer attentional resources: this is more similar to System 1 processing (Kahnmean 2011). Analytic processing requires deeper consideration of underlying dimensions of stimuli, and focuses on diagnostic criteria; this is more similar to System 2 processing (Kahnmean 2011). Hoch et al. (1999) found that when people engage in analytic processing, organized displays offer more perceived variety, and when processing is holistic, random displays offer more perceived variety. But Kahn and Wansink (2004) found that the size of the assortment was an important moderator of this effect. They found that when assortments were large, organized displays offered more perceived variety, but when assortments were small, random displays offered more perceived variety. This suggests that small assortments are easier to process holistically, or automatically. However, as the assortment becomes larger, more systematic processing is required to make sense of the perceived variety; here the organizational structure of the assortment in essence helps the consumer parse the complexity; essentially the organizational structure facilitates analytic processing in large assortments.

In addition to organized versus random, Kahn and Wansink (2004) found another organizational structure that affected processing: entropy, or the relative symmetry in frequencies of items within assortments (Young and Wasserman 2001). Kahn and Wansink found that as assortment sizes became larger and more complex, asymmetric distributions (less entropy) were easier to process than symmetric distributions (more entropy). They speculated that this was because in asymmetric assortments, there is a natural processing order in which dominant items are processed and appreciated first, after which remaining items can then be identified. When the assortment is symmetrically distributed, there is no easy heuristic for processing the variety. (Note that related to this method of evaluating assortments, Broniarczyk et al. (1998) and Boatwright and Nunes (2001) found that for physical assortments when highly preferred items were cut, perceptions of assortment variety decreased regardless of how much variety was actually present.) When the set is small and thus easy to process, the increased complexity offered by a symmetric distribution could increase perceived variety. This is similar to the "design complexity" discussed above and as predicted by Pieters et al. (2010). But the advantages of "design complexity" should only hold for small assortments; for large assortments, the overall complexity would be too great.

Kahn and Wansink (2004) did not consider perceptual fluency in designing their studies, but it seems post hoc as though perceptual fluency related to the organizational structure of the assortment is driving their results. Although they did not take perceptual fluency measures, they did measure "anticipated consumption utility," which measures the pleasure derived from the assortment, and this has been shown to be a consequence of more fluent assortments (Reber et al. 2004). They found that when assortments were small and where parsing different elements was easy, scrambled, symmetric assortments were more pleasant and offered more perceived variety. When assortments were large, organized and asymmetric assortments offered more perceived variety and pleasure and together, the results from these two studies (Hoch et al. 1999; Kahn and Wansink 2004) suggest that, for larger assortments, design features (such as organization, reduced entropy) that help consumers to process assortments systematically increase pleasure and perceptions of variety. In contrast, when assortments are small and easily or automatically processed, more interesting organizational structures, such as randomization or high entropy, increase pleasure and perceptions of variety. Kahn and Wansink (2004) measured aesthetic factors as well and found that these criteria did not affect assortment variety perceptions.

Visual versus Textual Depiction

One type of online product assortment display that is often used in online retail sites is the use of "thumbnails," or miniature product images that are typically hyperlinked to other pages on the site (Lam et al. 2007). Such images typically have text titles and often price information as well. Thumbnails are typically shown in a rectangular array. Using eye-tracking technology (in the context of advertisements, but with results that should generalize to online product assortments), Pieters and Wedel (2004) show that pictorial aspects capture the most baseline attention, which is attention directed to a stimulus independent of surface size and related to the visual pop-out-ness of the element. Text captures the most incremental attention, which is attention beyond the baseline, and could be due to factors such as size that demand attention. Image perception is more peripheral and pre-attentive, more automatic and parallel, faster, and less effortful. Text perception is more attention focused, slower, and more effortful. Text requires more eye fixations to be understood.

Because of these differences in the processing of visual versus textual material, Townsend and Kahn (2014) hypothesized and found a "visual preference heuristic" such that when asked how consumers would prefer to see assortments of products depicted, they indicated they would prefer visual to verbal depiction of the information, holding all other elements constant. Further, as noted in Principle 2, graphic depictions of product assortments were shown to produce greater perceptions of assortment variety, regardless of assortment size. However, consistent with the organization structure results described just above, when assortment size is large and preferences unknown or unstable, assortments composed only of visual stimuli are very difficult to process and would result in overload, causing consumers to delay making a choice.

Again, similar to conclusions drawn about the use of organizational structure, consumers could use graphic devices to help them process the complexity of these large assortments. Townsend and Kahn (2014) found that textual material served this function. Holding assortment size and information contained within the assortment constant, eye-tracking results showed that assortments with stimuli only described in text resulted in slower, more systematic processing, and fewer items ignored, which is consistent with the analytic, or piecemeal processing discussed above. Eye-tracking also showed that assortments composed of graphical stimuli tended to be processed more holistically, in gestalt-like fashion, and faster, with more haphazard scanning, resulting in more items ignored. Thus, for large assortments, when stimuli were shown only graphically, there was more choice deferral and perceived complexity than when large assortments were shown with items described only textually. Townsend and Kahn found that both perceived complexity and time taken mediated the effect of depiction method on choice deferral, such that large textual assortments were perceived to be less complex, but took more time to scan than assortments with graphic stimuli, and this resulted in less choice deferral.

Lam et al. (2007) also studied thumbnail online displays and found that consumers process information in the middle and left regions and hypothesized that consumers were essentially "reading" these displays that had photos and text, even though they could be scanned randomly and there was no particular benefit to using a "reading" style.

To test this reading hypothesis, they used thumbnail displays where the text captions were written in Chinese characters. Participants in the experiment were divided into two groups, those who grew up in mainland China and those who grew up in Hong Kong. This grouping was particularly meaningful because students in mainland China typically read Chinese from left to right (as English is read), whereas Hong Kong students read Chinese from right to left, as well as from left to right (both groups read from top to bottom). As indicated by the first fixation points, both the local and mainland participants initially looked at the upper middle region of the thumbnail array. Then they typically looked left and then right. Differences began to arise from the fourth fixation onward; Hong Kong students tended to look vertically down and then right to left; whereas mainland students moved toward the lower left region and moved from left to right and downwards, differences that were consistent with the participants' dominant reading direction. The regions to which consumers first paid attention were processed more than the regions to which they attended later. Although in the initial scanning the students seemed to "read" the display, this became less true later in the session.

Taken together, these studies suggest that for large, complicated assortments, retailers should use graphic techniques that help consumers parse complexity. Use of text, which inspires a systematic processing similar to reading and organizational structure, can help consumers appreciate the variety in large assortments and avoid overload. When assortments are smaller, consumers process holistically, and in these cases visual depiction and more random assortment structure increases the interesting-ness of assortments and engages the consumer, which makes choice deferral less likely.

Categorizing and Filtering Decisions

Another way to help consumers parse through the complexity of large assortments is through the use of categorization and filtering tabs. Although these devices are designed to put more structure into large assortments, there are many ways they can be employed, and studies have been run in order to gain critical insights in the optimal implementation techniques.

One critical insight is that retailers should first determine how consumers themselves categorize the items within these large assortments, and then organize the shelf accordingly. Morales et al. (2005) found that for familiar categories, congruency between a consumer's internal categorization structure and external store layout leads to higher perceptions of variety and higher satisfaction with product choices. For example, if consumers think about wines by grape varieties and the website organizes them by brand name, consumers will experience less satisfaction with the choice process and take more time to process. When the two organization structures are incongruent, consumers become confused and overwhelmed by large assortments and are unable to perceive the full extent of the variety offered. These conclusions are consistent with eye-tracking research, which has found that when consumers can easily find an item within an assortment they experience positive affect and shopping enjoyment. If the product category is unfamiliar, and consumers do not have a well-defined categorization scheme for it, organizing the assortment in a manner consistent with shopping goals has the same effect.

Morales et al. (2005) suggest a caveat to this matching process however. The results noted before relate to category organization, not filtering. If the retailer chooses to use filtering methodologies (in which consumers click on tabs that then lead directly to the items they want to scan) rather than showing the whole assortment at once, then consumers are able to sort through an assortment very quickly to find their desired option. While filtering methods are efficient, consumers are less likely to appreciate the variety of the assortment. Although consumers will be able to find their desired option easily with efficient filtering mechanisms, they will be less likely to appreciate the whole range of options available in the assortment and will make fewer unplanned purchases. Thus, sorting filters allow consumers to get to the objects they want quickly and easily, but because of limited visualization of assortments they may inhibit browsing and future purchasing.

Poynor and Wood (2010) found results similar to those of Morales et al. (2005), but through a different mechanism that does not require knowledge of consumers' internal categorization structures. Rather than relying on internal categorization structures, Poyner and Wood (2010) show that consumers learn the structure of a category by exposure to it. Then when they are re-exposed to the category, if the categorization scheme remains as they expect (congruent), low knowledge consumers are more satisfied than when the scheme is unexpected (incongruent). This is not true, however, for consumers who have high category knowledge. Instead, unexpected categorization of assortments dispels complacency and leads to greater satisfaction with the shopping experience.

Mogilner, Rudnick, and Iyengar (2008) show that the mere presence of categories within large assortments can positively increase satisfaction with an assortment for consumers who are unfamiliar with a category. They show that the more categories that are present, the higher the perceived variety of the assortment, which in turns allows for the perception that there are more likely to be options available that meet one's needs. These categories can even be vague or not particularly descriptive, and the effect will still hold. They label this the "mere categorization effect." This effect does not hold for consumers who are familiar with the items within assortment.

Looking specifically at filtering schemes, rather than categorization of product assortments, Chang (2011) suggests that retailers need to think strategically about the number of levels to build into hierarchical filtering schemes. She finds that keeping the overall number of SKUs in an assortment constant (at 90 in her experiment), but changing the number of subcategories (3, 9, 18), affects perceptions of variety. Specifically, she finds an inverted U-shape pattern, such that products sorted into a "moderate" number of categories (9 here, although this could vary by product class) generates the optimal effect, and that this works through ease of navigation and shopping pleasure. More subcategory levels led to higher perceptions of product variety, but choice uncertainty moderated the effects. For low uncertainty, 18 was best for ease of navigating (utilitarian motive). For shopping pleasure (hedonic motive), online store attitudes, and purchase intensions, the means followed an inverted U-shaped pattern, such that the moderate number generated the most favorable ratings. With high choice uncertainty, consumers were unaffected by the number of subcategories. There were no differences between browsing and buying goals.

Summary

Once consumers have been exposed to and paid attention to assortments they must be able to make sense of them. In this section, we have identified three goals of online retail assortment. First, retailers want consumers to like their assortments (react with positive emotion), and therefore design properties should be used to make assortments attractive. Assortments that are easy to process are liked more. Factors that influence the ease of processing include making the assortments smaller, reducing the information intensity and reducing the friction between the items within the assortment and the background. Second, retailers would like consumers to form inferences about the flexibility and variety offered within the assortment. Again, assortments that are easier to process will result in higher inferences or perceptions of variety and flexibility. Here research has shown that horizontal (as opposed to vertical) and visual (as opposed to textual) depictions of the assortments facilitates higher perceptual fluency and leads to inferences of more variety within the assortment. The perceived variety is also lessened if the individual items within the assortment are complex, making it difficult to understand all of the trade-offs. Here presenting the attributes of the complex stimuli attribute-by-attribute (versus by alternative) facilitates processing and increases perceived variety and lessens perceived complexity.

Finally, one of the advantages of online assortments is that they can offer large set sizes, but large assortments can be complex and move consumers from System 1 type to System 2 processing. This requires design features that would help with more elaborate cognitive processing. Here retailers can either use structural features of an assortment, such as organization or textual labels, to reduce complexity of large assortments, and thus move customers back to more System 1 type processing. Or they can provide categorization and filtering options, that help with the System 2 type processing. When the assortment sets are smaller, disfluency is not an issue, and then the opposite recommendations hold. For example, for small assortments, random organization, visual depiction and other instances of "design complexity" often results in higher perceptions of variety and more consumer satisfaction.

Visual Display Decisions: Specific Items within the Assortment

We now address visual display decisions that are relevant on the item (rather than on the assortment level). Certainly, in online retailing in the future, it will be easy for the consumer to drill down and focus at the individual item level. When consumers click down through the assortment, and focus on the stimulus at the item level the packaging and product shape decisions are influential in deciding "whether to purchase" and "how much to purchase." Here, we focus on the attention-getting aspects of the packaging. Research has shown that small differences can have significant impact on attention and perceptions and subsequently on consideration.

Location of Product Image on Packages

It is well-known that packaging can have strong influences on attention, perceptions, and purchase. Rather than review that extensive literature, the focus here will be on a few observations that parallel some of the other conclusions drawn earlier. As noted previously, any marketing activity that attracts attention is generally beneficial. The more a package design differs from existing expectations, the more attention it is likely to get. Vivid information maintains consumer attention (McGill and Anand 1989).

We also know that visual imagery significantly attracts attention quickly, which is critical in the "micro-moments" that will define future online shopping. Product images on packages are apt to be particularly attention-getting since they can induce imagery processing (Paivio 1986) and serve as a cue to communicate information about the product inside. Deng and Kahn (2009) show that location of the product image on a package façade (either top vs. bottom or left versus right) influences perceptions of the visual heaviness of the product, and these perceptions can influence choice and quantity decisions.

Predicated on principles in design (Arnheim 1974) the bottom and the right sides of a visual field are perceived to be the "heavy" sides paralleling physical forces. Bottom-heaviness occurs because of gravitational pull and right-heaviness occurs because of the lever effect. We are used to seeing light things float up and heavy things weighed down. Left and right positions are a little less intuitive but right-heaviness follows from the lever principle that states that the greater the distance on the lever from fulcrum position that an object is placed, the heavier it is perceived to be. Since people tend to "read" items on a screen from left to right (as discussed above), objects on the right side are on the far side of the lever. Right-heaviness perception is also supported for physical reasons. People have a stronger physiological preference for one eye over the other, and Porac and Coren (1976) report that approximately 65% of the population favor their right eye. Objects seen on the same side of the dominant eye are often overestimated, thus for a majority of consumers, items on the right will be perceived as heavier.

Deng and Kahn (2009) show that when product images are placed on the bottom or right side of the package, consumers perceive those products to be heavier than packages where the images are on the top or left. When perceived heaviness is an asset, for example when it is associated with "more" or "higher quality," consumers prefer packages with the product image placed at heavy locations. The opposite is true when perceived heaviness is a liability, for example, for healthy or diet snacks. Further, when consumers perceived objects to be "lighter" they may choose larger quantities.

Product Shape

Product shape also influences preferences, and volume and quantity estimates. For example, Krider, Raghubir and Krishna (2001) suggest that consumers judge the area of a shape by comparing across the most salient (most attention-getting) linear dimension, weighing that dimension more heavily than the second dimension and that those differential weights lead to a systematic bias in volume perceptions. Folkes and Matta (2004) amend this idea to suggest that visual attention tends to be directed toward objects as a whole rather than to simple dimensions, and that any package shape that attracts more attention (e.g., an asymmetric versus a symmetric one,) will be perceived as larger.

In addition to attention-getting principles, consumers can use product shape characteristics to form impressions about the product. For example, Sevilla and Kahn (2014) show that the degree of "completeness" of the shape serves as a heuristic determining how large a serving should be, and ultimately how much product to consume. Without taking actual size into consideration, consumers assume that a "complete" unit contains more quantity than one that is incomplete. What constitutes a complete unit depends on the notion of unity or the "congruity among the elements of the design of an item, such that they look as though they belong together or as though there is some visual connection beyond mere chance that has caused them to come together" (Veryzer and Hutchinson 1998, p. 374). What constitutes a complete unit can also depend on previous experience and prior expectations.

In summary, similarly to how perceptions are formed about assortments, perceptions about individual items are a function of which stimulus gets the most attention, and how easy it is to process the information about the stimulus. Those items that receive more attention and can be processed fluently have consistent advantages in both affective response and consideration. Here we have specifically shown how these graphical decisions can also affect inferences, such as perceived heaviness or size of serving, and this can ultimately affect choice and quantity decisions.

Conclusions

In the future, more shopping will be online. This will not eliminate the importance of the physical store, but it will change how consumers shop. Even if a shopper buys in a physical store, likely some part of the shopping process will be online. Since the online environment is essentially visual, in the future it will be more important for retailers to understand how various design decisions can affect consumer perceptions. Particularly as consumers move more of their shopping journey to mobile devices, consumers' attention to these retailer visual stimuli can be very quick and perceptions form almost automatically without cognitive intervention. Understanding the fundamental psychology of attention, perception, and automatic inference is critical.

Although obviously, top-down factors like expectations, familiarity, expertise, and goals will moderate these effects, here the focus is on stimulus-driven effects, or bottom-up reactions to design decisions. Perceptions form as a function of what stimuli consumers are exposed to, how often and in what manner they pay attention to those specific stimuli, and how they interpret what they see. In the future, retailers should use design elements to direct attention and to increase the perceptual fluency, or ease of processing of the stimuli. This suggests in general, that to increase positive feelings toward their assortments retailers will find that "less is more," at least at the initial interface with the consumer. Thus, small assortments and assortments with less information intensity (and more white space) are liked more.

Prioritizing on key items will also be very important, and such prioritization can make the overall assortment easier to process. Design elements, such as visual salience, can direct attention to specific items. Also, where items are placed within the assortment can affect attention. Consumers naturally gaze initially at the center of the assortment, and even as they scan other aspects of the assortment, they frequently return their gaze to the center. This natural central gaze effect gives advantage to items that are placed in this location. Attention can also be directed by using color blocking within the assortment.

After the consumer has been exposed to the assortment and has paid attention, then being able to easily process the information offered will affect the perceived attractiveness of the assortment. This ease of processing is also influenced by design factors. For example, whether the stimuli within the assortment are arrayed horizontally or vertically can affect the perceived variety of the assortment; items displayed horizontally yield higher perceptions of variety and will result in more variety-seeking behavior. Further, the ease with which one can identify a brand as a function of the complexity of the background can also affect the perceived attractiveness of the items within the assortment.

However, online assortments also offer the advantage of providing large variety relatively easily, resulting in very large assortments. These types of assortments shift the processing styles from easy, holistic automatic processing as described before into a more analytic or cognitive type of processing. In these cases, retailers can still use design factors to affect the perceived variety of the assortment and the likelihood to consider, choose or consume specific items within the assortment.

Since too much variety can cause choice overload and delaying purchase or choosing not to purchase at all, retailers must use the design features to reduce the perceived complexity of large assortments. Design features such as organization, strategic use of text, helping consumers learn preferences easily, categorization, and filtering can affect likelihood to choose. While small assortments can be processed holistically, larger assortments require more systematic processing. Organization that is consistent with consumers' internal categorizations and text-based information can help promote more systematic processing.

Finally, when consumers delve deeper into the assortment and start to look at the individual level then packaging and product shape decisions can affect the perceived attractiveness of specific items, and the likelihood they will be considered and chosen. For example, design criteria that make the item easier to process, such as symmetry and redundancy of information will make the item seem more attractive. In some situations, disfluency can be an advantage—in choice situations where complexity at the individual item level is preferred, such as special occasions or situations where novelty is especially valued—then design complexity at the item level might be a plus. Location of the product image on the package can affect the perceived heaviness or lightness of the product; product shape can influence size and volume perceptions. Consequently, design criteria in product packaging, labeling and product shapes also influence perceptions and will affect the likelihood of choice as well as decisions about how much to consume.

Future Research

The research reviewed helps us understand the automatic reactions consumers have to stimulus-based design features of assortments and individual level stimuli. Given advances in measurement techniques, for example eye-tracking measurement, we can ascertain actual patterns of attention that are not based on individual's recall—which is known to be biased. Now that we have accumulated a solid knowledge base of how these design features affect perceptions, we can layer upon this foundation the moderating effects of top-down, cognitive influences such as expertise, familiarity, goals, and individual differences. We know that these top-down factors are very important as consumers get closer to the purchase process and can overpower the stimulus-based bottom-up factors described here. However, it is likely that these top-down factors do not overpower and cancel out the bottom-up criteria, but rather interact with them. Understanding how all of these factors work together will help the retailer target offerings even more precisely to various consumers.

Many of the results described in this chapter came from scientific laboratory experiments that were designed to isolate certain factors so that we could understand the underlying consumer processes and establish causality. To that effect, they are quite useful and help us to develop comprehensive theory. However, effects that work in the laboratory may work differently in the field. Hopefully the ideas presented here can be tested using A/B experiments on retailers' websites to see if there are moderating influences that should be noted.

Note

1   This chapter was also published in the *Journal of Retailing*, Volume 93, Issue 1, March 2017, pages 29–42.

References

Arnheim, R. (1974), *Art and Visual Perception: A Psychology of the Creative Eye*. Berkeley, CA: University of California Press.

Arnold, S. J., T. H. Oum, and D. J. Tigert. (1983), Determinant Attributes in Retail Patronage: Seasonal, Temporal, Regional and International Comparisons. *Journal of Marketing Research*, 20 (May), 149–157.

Atalay, A. S., H. O. Bodur, and D. Rasolofoarison (2012), Shining in the Center: Central Gaze Cascade Effect on Product Choice. *Journal of Consumer Research*, 39 (December), 848–866.

Bansal, H. S., G. H. G. McDougall, S. S. Dikolli, and K. L. Sedatole (2004), Relating E-Satisfaction to Behavioral Outcomes: An Empirical Study, *Journal of Services Marketing*, 18 (4), 290–302.

Boatwright, P., and J. C. Nunes (2001), Reducing assortment: An attribute-based approach. *Journal of Marketing*, 65 (3), 50–63.

Borle, S., P. Boatwright, J. B. Kadane, J. C. Nunes, and G. Shmueli (2005), The Effect of Product Assortment Changes on Consumer Retention, *Marketing Science*, 24, 4, 616–22.

Broniarczyk, S. M., W. D. Hoyer, and L. McAlister (1998), Consumers' Perceptions of the Assortment Offered in a Grocery Category: The Impact of Item Reduction. *Journal of Marketing Research*, 35, 166–176.

Carver, C. S. and M. F. Scheier (1990), Origins and Functions of Positive and Negative Affect: A Control-Process View, *Psychological Review*, 97 (1), Jan 1990, 19–35.

Chandon, P., J. W. Hutchinson, E. T. Bradlow, and, S. Young (2007), Measuring the Value of Point-of-Purchase Marketing with Commercial Eye-Tracking Data, in *Visual Marketing: From Attention to Action*, M. Wedel and R. Pieters (Eds.), 225–258, Mahwah, NJ: Lawrence Erlbaum Associates.

Chandon, P., J. W. Hutchinson, E. T. Bradlow, and S. H. Young (2009), Does In-Store Marketing Work? Effects of the Number and Position of Shelf Facings on Brand Attention and Evaluation at the Point of Purchase, *Journal of Marketing*, 73 (6, Nov), 1–17.

Chang, C. (2011), The Effect of the Number of Product Subcategories on Perceived Variety and Shopping Experience in an Online Store, *Journal of Interactive Marketing*, 25 (May), 159–168.

Chernev, A. (2003), When More is Less and Less is More: The Role of Ideal Point Availability and Assortment in Consumer Choice, *Journal of Consumer Research*, 30 (September), 170–183.

Chernev, A., U. Bockenhhold, and J. Goodman (2015), Choice Overload: A Conceptual Review and Meta-Analysis, *Journal of Consumer Psychology*, 25 (2), 333–358.

Dechene, A., Stahl, C., J. Hansen, and M. Wanke (2010), The Truth about the Truth: A Meta-Analytic Review of the Truth Effect, *Personality and Social Psychology Review*, 14(2), 238–257.

Deng, X. and B. E. Kahn (2009), Is Your Product on the Right Side? The "Location Effect" on Perceived Product Heaviness and Package Evaluation, *Journal of Marketing Research*, (December), 46(6), 725–738.

Deng, X., B. E. Kahn, R. Unnava, and H. Lee (2016), A "Wide" Variety: The Effects of Horizontal vs. Vertical Product Display, *Journal of Marketing Research*, 53(5), 682–698.

Diehl, K., and C. Poynor (2010), Great Expectations?! Assortment Size, Expectations and Satisfaction, *Journal of Marketing Research*, 47 (April), 312–322.

DuPuis, S. and J. Silva (2008), *Package Design Workbook: The Art and Science of Successful Packaging*, Rockport Publishers.

Drieze, X., S. J. Hoch, and M. E. Purk (1994), Shelf Management and Space Elasticity, *Journal of Retailing*, 70 (4), 301–326.

Festinger, L. (1957), *A Theory of Cognitive Dissonance*, Evanston, IL: Row & Peterson.

Folkes, V., and S. Matta (2004), The Effect of Package Shape on Consumers' Judgments of Product Volume: Attention as a Mental Contaminant, *Journal of Consumer Research*, 31 (2), 390–401.

Garner, W. R. (1974), *The Processing of Information Structure*, Potomac, MD: Lawrence Erlbaum Associates, Inc.

Goodman, J., and, S. Malkoc (2012), Choosing Here and Now versus There and Later: The Moderating Role of Psychological Distance on Assortment Size Preferences, *Journal of Consumer Research*, 39 (December), 751–768.

Hart, R. P. (1997), Analyzing Media, in *Modern Rhetorical Criticism*, R. Hart and S. Daughton (Eds.), 177–208, 2nd ed. Boston: Allyn & Bacon.

Hoch, S. J., E. T. Bradlow, and B. Wansink (1999), The Variety of an Assortment, *Marketing Science*, 18 (4), 527–546.

Huang, Z., and J. Y. Y. Kwong, (2015), Illusion of Variety: Lower Readability Enhances Perceived Variety, *International Journal of Research in Marketing*, http://dx.doi.org/10.1016/j.ijresmar.2015.11.006.

Huffman, C. and B. E. Kahn (1998), Variety for Sale: Mass Customization or Mass Confusion? *Journal of Retailing*, 74 (4, Winter), 491–513.

Hutchinson, J. W., Lu, J. and Weingarten, E. (2016), Visual Attention in Consumer Settings, University of Pennsylvania working paper.

Iyengar, S. S., and M. R. Lepper (2000), When Choice is Demotivating: Can One Desire Too Much of a Good Thing? *Journal of Personality and Social Psychology*, 79 (December), 995–1006.

Iyengar, S. S., R. E. Wells, and B. Schwartz (2006), Doing Better but Feeling Worse, *Psychological Science*, 17 (February), 143–150.

Im, H., S. J. Lennon and L. Stoel (2010), The Perceptual Fluency Effect on Pleasurable Online Shopping Experience, *Journal of Research in Interactive Marketing*, 4 (4), 280–295.

Jacoby, J., D. E. Speller, and C. A. Kohn (1974), Brand Choice Behavior as a Function of Information Load. *Journal of Marketing Research*, 11 (1), 63–69.

Janiszewski, C. (1998). The Influence of Display Characteristics on Visual Exploratory Search Behavior. *Journal of Consumer Research*, 25, 290–301.

Janiszewski, C. and T. Meyvis (2001), Effects of Brand Logo Complexity, Repetition, and Spacing on Processing Fluency and Judgment, *Journal of Consumer Research*, 28, 18–32.

Janiszewski, C., A. Kuo, N. T. Tavassoli (2013), The Influence of Selective Attention and Inattention to Products on Subsequent Choice, *Journal of Consumer Research* 39 (April), 1258–1274.

Kahn, B. E. (1998), Dynamic Relationships with Customers: High-Variety Strategies, *Journal of the Academy of Marketing Science*, 26 (Winter), 45–53.

Kahn, B. E. and L. McAlister (1997), *Grocery Revolution: The New Focus on the Consumer*, Reading, MA: Addison Wesley, Longman.

Kahn, B. E., and D. R. Lehmann (1991), Modeling Choice Among Assortment, *Journal of Retailing*, 67 (Fall), 274–299.

Kahn, B. E. and B. Wansink (2004), The Influence of Assortment Structure on Perceived Variety and Consumption Quantities, *Journal of Consumer Research*, 30 (4, March), 519–534.

Kahn, B. E., E. Weingarten and C. Townsend (2013), Assortment Variety: Too Much of a Good Thing? *Review of Marketing Research (RMR)*, 10, 1–23.

Kahnmean, D. (2011), *Thinking, Fast and Slow*, New York: Farrar, Straus and Giroux.

Katerattanakul, P. (2002), Framework of Effective Web Site Design for Business-to-Consumer Internet Commerce. *INFOR*, 40 (1), 57–70.

Krider, R. E., P. Raghubir, and A. Krishna (2001), Pizzas: p or Square? Psychophysical Biases in Area Comparisons, *Marketing Science*, 20 (4), 405–425.

Labroo, A. A., R. Dhar, and N. Schwarz (2008), Of Frog Wines and Frowning Watches: Semantic Priming, Perceptual Fluency and Brand Evaluation, *Journal of Consumer Research*, 34, 819–831.

Lam, S. Y., A. W-L. Chau and T. J. Wong (2007), Thumbnails as Online Product Displays: How Consumers Process Them, *Journal of Interactive Marketing*, 21 (1, Winter), 36–50.

Lee, L., O. Amir, and D. Ariely (2009), In Search of Homo Economicus: Cognitive Noise and the Role of Emotion in Preference Consistency, *Journal of Consumer Research*, 36, 173–187.

Lin, H-H. and S.-F. Yang (2014), An Eye Movement Study of Attribute Framing in Online Shopping, *Journal of Marketing Analytics*, 2 (2), 72–80.

Louviere, J. J. and G. Gaeth, (1987), Decomposing the Determinants of Retail Facility Choice Using the Method Hierarchical Information Integration: A Supermarket Illustration. *Journal of Retailing*, 63 (Spring), 25–49.

Lu, J. and L. Itti (2005), Perceptual Consequences of Feature-Based Attention, *Journal of Vision*, 5 (7), 2–32.

Luna, D. and L. A. Peracchio (2003), Visual and Linguistic Processing of Ads by Bilingual Consumers, in *Persuasive Imagery: A Consumer Response Perspective*, L. Scott and R. Batra (Eds.), 153–174, Mahwah, NJ: Lawrence Erlbaum.

Lynch, P. J., and Horton, S. (2001), *Web Style Guide: Basic Design Principles for Creating Web Sites* (2nd ed.). New Haven, CT: Yale University Press.

Lynch, J. G., and T. K. Srull (1982), Memory and Attentional Factors in Consumer Choice: Concepts and Research Methods, *Journal of Consumer Research*, 9, 18–37.

McAlister, L. (1982), A Dynamic Attribute Satiation Model of Variety Seeking Behavior, *Journal of Consumer Research*, 9 (September), 141–150.

McDowell, M. (2016), Google: Mobile Shoppers are Valuable to Physical Stores, *WWD Retail News*, (February 8), online.

McGill, A., and P. Anand (1989), The Effect of Imagery on Information Processing Strategy in a Multiattribute Choice Task, *Marketing Letters*, 1 (1), 7–16.

Milosavljevic, M., and M. Cerf (2008), First Attention, Then Intention: Insights from Computational Neuroscience of Vision, *International Journal of Advertising*, 27 (3), 381–398.

Milosavljevic, M., V. Navalpakkam, C. Koch, and A. Rangel (2012), Relative Visual Salience Differences Induce Sizable Bias in Consumer Choice, *Journal of Consumer Psychology*, 22 (1), 67–74.

Mogilner, C., T. Rudnick, and S. S. Iyengar (2008), The Mere Categorization Effect: How the Mere Presence of Categories Increases Consumers' Perceptions of Assortment Variety and Outcome Satisfaction, *Journal of Consumer Research*, 35 (August), 202–215.

Morales, A., B. E. Kahn, L. McAlister, and S. M. Broniarczyk (2005), Perceptions of Assortment Variety: The Effects of Congruency Between Consumers' Internal and Retailers' External Organization, *Journal of Retailing*, 81, 159–169.

Mosteller, J., N. Donthu and S. Eroglu (2014), The Fluent Online Shopping Experience, *Journal of Business Research*, 67 (March) 2486–2493.

Nisbett, R. E., and T. D. Wilson (1977), Telling More Than We Can Know: Verbal Reports on Mental Processes, *Psychological Review*, 84 (March), 231–259.

Novemsky, N., R. Dahr, N. Schwarz and I. Simonson (2007), Preference Fluency in Choice, *Journal of Marketing Research*, Vol XLIV (August) 347–356.

Orth, U. and R. C. Crouch (2014), Is Beauty in the Aisles of the Retailer? Packaging Processing in Visually Complex Contexts, *Journal of Retailing*, 90 (4), 524–537.

Paivio, A. (1974), Pictures and Words in Visual Search, *Memory & Cognition*, 2(3), 515–521.

Paivio, A. (1986), *Mental Representations: A Dual-Coding Approach*, New York: Oxford University Press.

Pieters, R. (2007), A Review of Eye-tracking Research in Marketing, *Review of Marketing Research* 4, 123–147.

Pieters, R. and, M. Wedel (2004), Attention Capture and Transfer in Advertising, Brand, Pictorial and Text-Size Effects, *Journal of Marketing*, 68 (2, April), 36–50.

Pieters, R., M. Wedel, and R. Batra (2010), The Stopping Power of Advertising: Measures and Effects of Visual Complexity, *Journal of Marketing*, 74 (5, September), 48–60.

Pocheptsova, A., A. A. Labroo, and R. Dhar (2010), Making Products Feel Special: When Metacognitive Difficulty Enhances Evaluation, *Journal of Marketing Research*, 47 (6), 1059–1069.

Porac, C., and S. Coren (1976), The Dominant Eye, *Psychological Bulletin*, 83 (5), 880–897.

Poynor, C. and S. Wood (2010), Smart Subcategories: How Assortment Formats Influence Consumer Learning and Satisfaction, *Journal of Consumer Research*, 37 (June), 159–175.

Pracejus, J. W., G. D. Olsen, and T. C. O'Guinn (2006), How Nothing Became Something: White Space, Rhetoric, History, and Meaning, *Journal of Consumer Research*, 33 (June), 82–90.

Raghubir, P. and A. Valenzuela (2006), Center-of Inattention: Position Biases in Decision-Making, *Organizational Behavior and Human Decision Processes*, 99 (1), 66–80.

Raghubir, P. and A. Valenzuela (2008), Center of Orientation: Effect of Vertical and Horizontal Shelf Space Product Position, working paper, Baruch College, City University of New York.

Rayner, K. (1998), Eye Movements in Reading and Information Processing: 20 Years of Research, *Psychological Bulletin*, 124 (November), 372–422.

Reber, R., N. Schwarz, and P. Winkielman (2004), Processing Fluency and Aesthetic Pleasure: Is Beauty in the Perceiver's Processing Experience?, *Personality and Social Psychology Review*, 8, 364–382.

Reutskaja, E., R. M. Nagel, C. Camerer, and A. Rangel (2010), Search Dynamics in Consumer Choice Under Time Pressure: An Eye-tracking Study, *American Economic Review*, 101, 900–906.

Rosenholtz, R., Y. Li, and L. Nakano (2007), Measuring Visual Clutter, *Journal of Vision*, 7 (2), 1–22.

Royer, F. (1981), Detection of Symmetry, *Journal of Experimental Psychology: Human Perception and Performance*, 7, 1186–1210.

Schwarz, N. (2004), Metacognitive Experiences in Consumer Judgment and Decision Making. *Journal of Consumer Psychology*, 14 (4), 332–348.

Schwarz, N. (2010), Meaning in Context: Metacognitive Experiences, in B. Mesquita, L. F. Barrett, and E. R. Smith (Eds), *The Mind in Context*, 105–125, New York: Guilford.

Schwarz, N. (2015), Metacognition, in *APA Handbook of Personality and Social Psychology: Vol. 1 Attitudes and Social Cognition*, M. Mikulincer and P. R. Shaver (Editors-in-Chief), American Psychological Association.

Sevilla, J. and B. E. Kahn (2014), The Effect of Product Shape Completeness on Size Perceptions, Preference and Consumption, *Journal of Marketing Research*, LI (February), 57–68.

Shi, S. W., M. Wedel, and F. G. M. Pieters (2013), Information Acquisition During Online Decision Making: A Model-based Exploration Using Eye-tracking Data, *Management Science* 59 (5), 1009–1026.

Shimojo, S., C. Simion, E. Shimojo, and C. Scheier (2003), Gaze Bias Both Reflects and Influences Preference, *Nature Neuroscience*, 6 (December), 1317–1322.

Tatler, B. W. (2007), The Central Fixation Bias in Scene Viewing: Selecting an Optimal Viewing Position Independently of Motor Biases and Image Feature Distributions, *Journal of Vision*, 7 (November), 1–17.

Townsend, C., and B. E. Kahn (2014), The Visual Preference Heuristic: The Influence of Visual versus Verbal Depiction on Assortment Processing, Perceived Variety, and Choice Overload. *Journal of Consumer Research*, 40 (5), 993–1015.

Valenzuela, A. and P. Raghubir (2015), Are Consumers Aware of Top-Bottom but Not of Left-Right Inferences? Implications for Shelf Space Positions, *Journal of Experimental Psychology: Applied* 21 (3), 224–241.

Veryzer, R. W. and J. W. Hutchinson (1998), The Influence of Unity and Prototypicality on Aesthetic Responses to New Product Design, *Journal of Consumer Research*, 24 (4), 374–385.

Wedel, M. and R. Pieters (2008), A Review of Eye-Tracking Research in Marketing, in *Review of Marketing Research*, 4, N. K. Malhotra (Ed.), 123–147, Armonk, NY: M.E. Sharpe.

Weingarten, E., B. E. Kahn and W. Hutchinson (in process), research in process, The Wharton School, University of Pennsylvania, Philadelphia, PA.

Winkielman, P., N. Schwarz, T. A. Fazendeiro and R. Reber (2003), The Hedonic Marking of Processing Fluency: Implications for Evaluative Judgment, in *The Psychology of Evaluation*, M. Jochen and K. C. Klauer (Eds.), 189–217, Mahwah, NJ: Lawrence Erlbaum.

Young, M. E. and E. A. Wasserman (2001), Entropy and Variability Discrimination. *Journal of Experimental Psychology: Learning, Memory, and Cognition*, 27, 278–293.

Zajonc, R. B. (1968), Attitudinal Effects of Mere Exposure, *Journal of Personality and Social Psychology*, 9 (2, Pt. 2, June), 1–27.

PART XI

Family

21

POWER AND GENDER DYNAMICS IN CONTEMPORARY FAMILIES

Gokcen Coskuner-Balli[1] *and Samantha N. N. Cross*[2]
(Author names are in alphabetical order. Both authors contributed equally to this chapter)

[1]ARGYROS SCHOOL OF BUSINESS AND ECONOMICS, CHAPMAN UNIVERSITY, ORANGE, CA, USA
[2]COLLEGE OF BUSINESS AT IOWA STATE UNIVERSITY, AMES, IA, USA

> . . . in order to exist and persist, and to function as a *body*, the family always tends to function as a *field*, with its physical, economic and above all, symbolic power relations (linked, for example, to the volume and structure of the capital possessed by each member), its struggles for conservation and transformation of these power relations . . . The forces of *fusion* must endlessly counteract the forces of *fission*.
>
> On The Family as a Realized Category, Bourdieu (1996, p. 22)

In his essay, Bourdieu (1996) defines the family as a set of individuals, living under the same roof, linked together by some affiliation such as marriage, or kinship. Bourdieu sees the family as an arena, where the "forces of fusion" (that unite the interests of the individual with that of the collective), compete against the "forces of fission" (the differing, sometimes competing "selfish" interests of the various family members) (Bourdieu 1996, p. 23). Hence, Bourdieu (1996) argues that it is futile to discuss the family (and we argue, family decision-making) without examining "the structure of power relations" and "the effects of male domination." We agree, and in this chapter, we take a moment to reflect and discuss two underlying forces that have shaped, and continue to permeate, the rich body of family decision-making literature to date – power and gender dynamics. Our review starts over 50 years ago, as we critically explore the manifestation, effects and implications of power and gender dynamics, from the earliest work in family decision-making (FDM) to more recent research on contemporary, non-traditional families.

Early Research on Power and Gender Dynamics and Myths in Family Decision-Making

Power and Gender Dynamics in Family Decision-Making

Research in FDM or household decision-making (HDM) has typically focused on the family member or partner that has the most influence in making the decision of what, when and where to purchase or consume a particular good or service. The emphasis has been on the underlying factors contributing to disparate influence levels and the changes in those factors over the years. In other words, the literature has typically focused on power structures and the shift in those structures of power within the home as gender roles have morphed and evolved since the 1950s.

Wolfe (1959) conducted a series of structured interviews with 731 wives, examining the characteristics of different family authority structures. He studied the link between the type of family authority structure – husband dominant, wife dominant, and joint (both autonomic and syncratic) – and the wife's level of marital satisfaction. In essence, Wolfe (1959) was investigating the effects of differing power sources in the spousal relationship. He concluded that when power was more equally balanced between genders in the home, that is, in households with joint syncratic decision-making, wives were generally well satisfied, as opposed to wives in households with other family authority structures.

As a result of this focus on power structure and gender roles, several theories evolved to explain the bases of influence and power in the home. Social psychologists, French and Raven (1959) defined five theoretical bases of social power – referent, expert, reward, coercive, and legitimate. During the same time frame, Blood and Wolfe (1960) proposed resource theory, which argues that an individual's relative personal resources form the basis for conjugal power in the home, for example, income, education, social status, and available time. Thus, as women became more educated and contributed more income post World War I, decision-making processes also became more egalitarian. Rodman (1972) later extended resource theory and contended that cultural norms and influences moderated the relationship between resources and power.

Davis and Rigaux (1974) and Putnam and Davidson (1987) later built on Wolfe's study, using survey data collected in Belgium and the U.S. respectively, to show how the shift in decision-making between the spouses has influenced the decision-making stages over the years. These researchers reveal a greater number of shared or joint decisions in more recent years, with wives playing a greater role in the decision-making process for items that had been traditionally husband dominant. Thus, applying French and Raven's (1959) earlier social power theory perspective to the family decision-making literature, Raven, Centers, and Rodrigues (1975) identified six bases of conjugal power: coercive, reward, legitimate, referent, informational, and expert power.

Whether the stated focus was on power structure or gender roles, the findings are similar. Looking at changing sex roles in product contexts where few joint decisions were traditionally made, Qualls (1982) concluded that husbands and wives in the U.S. were exerting greater influence in areas that had traditionally been the other's domain. Spiro (1983) examined conflict situations and identified six influence strategies (expert, legitimate, bargaining, reward/referent, emotional, impression management) and six influence strategy mixes used by husbands and wives to resolve purchase disagreements of furniture or heavy durables. She identified wife employment and wife income as significant determinants of greater women influence in household decisions. Hence, in Corfman and Lehmann's (1987) study of the group decision-making processes of 77 couples in conflict situations, the researchers found that while other factors were still important determinants of relative influence, such as relative preference intensity and decision history, the conflict resolution process was predominantly cooperative. Yet, this balancing of power and gender roles was still a U.S phenomenon at the time, as Ford, LaTour, and Henthorne (1995), in a cross–cultural comparative study between China and the U.S., found a prevalence of husband-dominant decision-making and little wife role specialization or joint decision-making in patriarchal societies. At the turn of the century, Belch and Willis (2002) conducted a survey of 242 households in the southwestern U.S. and also noted a growing wife influence or greater balance of power between genders, due to the greater expertise, as well as the greater resources of women in the home.

More recently, Commuri and Gentry (2005) demonstrated that one of the basic assumptions of resource theory – the pooling of resources for household use – was not applicable when women were the chief wage earners. Commuri and Gentry's (2005) study showed that, in that context, there were often multiple resource pools and multiple areas of decision-making control.

Two other interesting power theories were introduced, however, neither of these were empirically substantiated in later studies. Ideology theory argues that the particular cultural characteristics of the society determines the behavior of the individual and the type of decision-making prevalent in households. Thus, the more patriarchal the society, the more husband-dominant decision-making prevails in the home (Webster 2000). Least-interested partner theory argues that since the least-interested partner has less to lose from the dissolution of the relationship, that partner ultimately wields more power in the relationship (Waller 1938; Waller and Hill 1951).

Instead, the literature seemed to support a series of more role-based theories. For example, one of the more popular ones developed conceptual models focusing on category-based role behavior. These models suggest that within particular purchase categories, marital roles differ depending on (1) the product characteristic selected – store, brand, color, price, and so on (Davis 1970), (2) the different phases in the decision-making process, and (3) by consumption category (Davis and Rigaux 1974). Researchers also focused on changes in marital roles between different phases of the decision process, rather than just static decision roles (Davis and Rigaux 1974, Putnam and Davidson 1987). Davis and Rigaux (1974) and Putnam and Davidson (1987) identified three phases: problem recognition, information search, and the final decision, and concluded that most role specialization occurred in the information search phase.

In addition to category-based role behavior, as previously noted, gender-based role behavior was also a popular underlying theme, implying a clear separation of the roles of husbands and wives, with little or no joint decision-making activity (Webster 2000). However, this supposition was contradicted by several researchers. Qualls (1987) examined the impact of sex role orientation on household decision-making and concluded that, rather than being viewed as a series of static independent actions, family decision-making should be perceived as a network of household relationships. Engel, Blackwell, and Miniard (1990) later introduced the concept of prescribed role behavior, which implied uniformity across families, through an identification of prescribed roles. They argued that family members perform five roles within the decision-making process: gatekeeper, influencer, decision-maker, buyer, and user, but this concept was not empirically supported in later studies.

Thus, in the last three decades, researchers documented significant shifts in gender roles due to the influence of urbanization (Pleck and Pleck 1980), the increase of women in the paid workforce (Crosby and Jaskar 1993), the women's movement, and gay liberation movement (Kimmel 1987) and the increasing percentage of women who earn more than their spouses (Commuri and Gentry 2000). However, although gender roles have been shifting, research suggests that myths such as breadwinner father or the homemaker mother, and gender discourses of care still underlie how men and women navigate the marketplace while they engage in everyday practices to construct their family.

Gender Myths and Narratives in Family Decision-Making

The separation of spheres of activities has served to naturalize the home and the tasks (caring and tending for the children, taking care of household chores) as feminine, whereas the role of breadwinning became the inherent responsibility of men (Coltrane 1996, Ehrenreich and English 1989, Firat 1994). With greater specialization and mass distribution, production increasingly became delegated to the public domain. In the new market economy, increasing numbers of fathers left their farms to become breadwinners, leaving their wives to run the household and look after the children (Griswold 1993). As men increasingly left the home to work for wages, the cult of domesticity glorified motherhood and reassured women that their natural place was in the home.

Maternal responsibility for home and children was further promoted by the rise of scientific mothering and the home economics movement. The ideal of separate spheres strongly encouraged women to bear children, especially if they were white and middle class. Motherhood for these women was elevated to a revered status, and wives' homemaking came to be seen as a calling and a worthy profession. The field of home economics blossomed during this time and the domestic science movement taught women efficient housewifery based on time management techniques (Griswold 1993). With the separation of spheres, fathers' responsibilities became primarily defined by their abilities to compete in the marketplace for income and social status, whereas the role of mothers became increasingly defined as being the primary custodians and caretakers of children (Gillis 1996, Griswold 1993, LaRossa 1988, Rotundo 1993).

Because mothers had come to symbolize the home, male domesticity became problematic: "Too intimate a relationship with one's children had become unmanly, likely to call into question not only a fellow's masculinity but also his maturity" (Gillis 1996, p. 193). Carving out specifically male modes of domesticity, such as after-work "fun dads", allowed early 20th century fathers to be involved in their families while maintaining their ground as real men. Throughout the 20th century, there have been waves of attention to fatherhood in U.S. family politics. In magazines, films and advice literature, fathers' family involvement has been carved out in terms of breadwinning, discipline, play, "role modeling," and "protection," in complementary relationships to notions of motherhood and femininity (Weiss 2000).

Researchers also note that even in Western societies, the occupation of the private domain by women and the public domain by men was largely mythical, especially in the experiences of working class families (Firat 1994). This myth was reinforced in the examples of women being forced into the home following the Industrial Revolution in England and following the two World Wars in the United States, and still has implications on how the spheres of consumption and production are viewed. For example, although women are encouraged to go to college and pursue their careers as never before, they are still held accountable for what was once called "women's work." If their houses are a mess, or if their children are unkempt, women are still the objects of blame (Hochschild 1989).

Thus, through the separation of spheres, devotion and care became associated with notions of femininity and have been viewed as inherent characteristics of motherhood. In *Feeding the Family*, DeVault (1991) finds that her informants would not view the activity of shopping and feeding as work, but constantly referred back to an ideology that instituted devotion as the sole legitimate grounds and criteria by which work is done. Along similar lines, Miller's (1998) ethnography of North London housewives discusses how shopping acts as an expression of devotional love. He asserts that having become sanctified through her agency in the self-sacrifice of thrift, the housewife returns with the blessing of love to her family.

Studying the consumption practices of professional mothers, Thompson (1996) also shows how the lifestyles of these jugglers are linked to the broad array of sociological meanings that have structured cultural conceptions of femininity and ideals of motherhood. He suggests

that cultural meanings and ideals related to motherhood are realized within the field of consumption and the way women use market resources in their everyday lives. The self-conceptions
and consumption experiences of working women are embedded in the gendered notion of a
caring orientation (Chodorow 1999). As such, women employ products and services that aid
them in their projects of holding the family together and creating ideal family settings.
Thompson (1996) concludes that for these women everyday consumer tasks evoke emotionally charged meanings grounded in a historical legacy of cultural ideals pertaining to motherhood, and that these women perform their gender.

The common theme repeated in these studies is the voluntary embrace of this ideal by
women and the reluctance to relinquish control to the male members in the family. In his
ethnography, Miller (1998) confirms the basic asymmetry of housework and the exploitation
of female labor; however, this labor is woven into an ideology of love and care and women
take part in reproducing this discourse. Miller provides an anecdote that is an interesting
example of this phenomenon. In one shopping expedition to the supermarket with his infor-
mant and her husband, he observes that the wife constantly criticizes her husband, thereby
affirming that as a man, although he may shop, he is not a natural shopper. Miller discusses
how the husband takes such criticism actually as praise for his natural manliness (Miller 1998,
p. 25).

The distinction of spheres and discourses of care have important implications for family
decision-making and who does what in the household, and how. As household studies have
shown, women remain the main caregivers and laborers in the household. Even among
families where men participate more fully in housework, women are still responsible for
organizing and managing the tasks and they undertake more repetitive and mundane tasks
such as cleaning, ironing, and laundry. In contrast, men do more stereotypically masculine
tasks such as mowing the lawn or playing with children. The ideology of separate spheres
also exerts an influence on the work lives of men and women. Employers are ambivalent
about men's desires to be at home instead of at work. When they take advantage of parental
leave or part-time work, they are often considered unreliable or not serious (Coltrane 1996,
Pleck 1993). By definition, a man's job is supposed to be more important than a woman's
job, and most people are uncomfortable if a wife makes more money than her husband
(Commuri and Gentry 2005, Coltrane 1996, La Rossa 1988). For example, Commuri and
Gentry (2005) showed that women earning more than their spouses creates tensions in the
household, and that these couples jointly construct a number of compensatory strategies to
minimize the identity threat that husbands experience when they are not the primary wage
earner.

In their review of the literature in family decision-making, while highlighting the important
research developments in the literature, Commuri and Gentry (2000) also point out that the
focus in FDM has been relatively limited, emphasizing the "who" and the resultant decision
outcomes (Belch and Willis 2002, Corfman and Lehmann 1987, Ford, LaTour, and Henthorne
1995, Putnam and Davidson 1987, Qualls 1982, Spiro 1983, Wolfe 1959), rather than the
"how" and the corresponding decision processes (Davis and Rigaux 1974, Putnam and
Davidson 1987, Qualls 1987), echoing the earlier assertions of Olson and Cromwell (1975)
and Olson et al. (1975). In addition, Commuri and Gentry (2000) argue that in studying the
domains of relative influence, power and gender in the home, not only should researchers
examine the characteristics of individual members and their impact but also the characteristics
of the family and household as an entity in itself. They assert that it is important to understand
how the family itself functions and exerts power as a unit or group (Commuri and Gentry
2000). More contemporary research in family decision-making addresses these issues.

Contemporary Research on Power and Gender
Dynamics in Family Decision-Making

Bourdieu's (1996) earlier definition of the family remains valid, that is, a set of individuals living under the same roof linked together by some affiliation. However, as families have mutated and changed over the past 20 years, defying the traditional assumptions of what constitutes "a family", researchers need to delve deeper to better understand (1) who comprises the individuals living under the same roof?; (2) does that roof have to be in the same physical space or can that roof encompass different locales and even countries? and (3) what exactly is the nature of those actual and perceived links and affiliations that bind family members together? Thus, for research on contemporary families, it is important, as Commuri and Gentry (2000) argue, to think more broadly and to encompass factors such as family composition, family identity, non-traditional family structures including same gender partners, cross-cultural (between and within country) comparisons, family myths, and a wider range of research methodologies. In their study on family identity and consumption practices, Epp and Price (2008) also consider non-traditional contemporary family forms, including divorced couples. Power and gender dynamics in contemporary families have become even more complex, as gender roles have morphed and the power bases have become more fluid. In the following sections, we focus on power and gender roles and dynamics in two non-traditional types of contemporary families that have become prevalent as our society has become increasingly global, with larger numbers of women in the workforce – (1) culturally diverse families, focusing on bi-national and bi-cultural families, and (2) structurally diverse families, focusing on families with stay-at-home fathers and single fathers.

Culturally Diverse Families – Gender Dynamics
and Power in the Household

Data show that the foreign-born population in the U.S. has been growing rapidly: from 9.6 million in 1970, to 31.1 million in 2000 (triple the 1970 figure), to 37.4 million in 2006 (a 20% increase over 2000). As a result of this increased contact between immigrants and natives, the rate of intermarriage has also increased in the U.S. According to the Pew Research Center, one in seven new marriages in 2010 was between partners of different ethnicities or races, that is, 15% of new marriages, compared to 6.7% of new marriages in 1980. Yet, despite this growth in immigration and in bi-cultural partnerships, there have been relatively limited studies examining cross-cultural interactions in the early consumer behavior literature on family decision-making (Ford, Latour, Henthorne 1995, Green, Leonardi et al. 1983, Peñaloza and Gilly 1986, 1999, Wallendorf and Reilly 1983, Webster 2000). This section focuses on the dynamics of power and gender in the home in post-2000 studies on culturally diverse families, with a specific focus on bi-national families.

Cross and Gilly (2013, 107) defined the bi-national family as a family where the partners are "born and raised in different countries of origin." They point out that, in bi-national families, not only is at least one of the partners bi-cultural, that is, able to navigate life, and familiar with the language and customs, in two different cultural contexts (Lau-Gesk 2003, Luna, Ringberg, and Peracchio 2008), but these families may also be bi-ethnic and bi-racial as well (Cross and Gilly 2013). The authors argue that these characteristics of bi-national families denote their unique role in society, as partners in bi-national families and the bi-national family itself "provide a conjugal and communal link between different cultural norms and perspectives" (Cross and Gilly 2013, p. 108). Lauth Bacas (2002) refers to this as the gatekeeper role; a role performed by partners in cross-border marriages. In playing the role of bridge, broker, boundary spanner (Cross and Gilly 2013) or gatekeeper (Lauth Bacas 2002) between the immigrant partner and the wider culture of residence, the native partner provides cultural access and knowledge, and becomes a source of expertise and ultimately power to the immigrant partner (Cross and Gilly 2014a). Meng and Gregory (2005) refer to this as an "intermarriage premium" where the immigrant spouse gains an economic advantage and greater economic societal power through intermarriage to the native spouse. Yet, even as the immigrant spouse gains, so too does the native spouse, as he/she is able to exert a unique source of power within the home.

Wamwara-Mbugua (2007) concluded that even when it conflicted with traditional gender roles, Kenyan immigrant couples delegated initial decision-making to the spouse who had been in the U.S. longer and thus had more knowledge of U.S. norms and customs. In the context of bi-national families, Cross and Gilly (2014a) explored this natural advantageous influence of the spouse with greater familiarity of the culture of residence; that is, the native spouse. They argue that relative cultural competence in the home (i.e. knowledge and familiarity with the social norms, expectations, traditions, language, and markets in the culture of residence) is a source of cultural capital and ultimately a source of expert power, irrespective of traditional gender roles in each spouse's country of origin. Cross and Gilly (2014a) expand the construct of expert power, demonstrating that, while expertise is still a valid base of conjugal power (Raven, Centers, and Rodrigues 1975), expert power has several dimensions: "expertise due to vocation, expertise arising from experience, expertise based on related roles and responsibilities, and expertise resulting from cultural competence" (Cross and Gilly 2014a, 134). Cross and Gilly (2014a) also argue that it is important to view family decision-making as an interconnected process, whereby decisions made in the formative stages of the home, have a residual impact on later spheres of decision-making spousal influence. Thus, in the context of bi-national families, cultural compensatory mechanisms come into play. The native spouse, who possesses a relative source of locational power and advantage – cultural competence in the culture of residence – compensates by relinquishing power over decisions related to vacations, children's education and food to his/her immigrant spouse. Thus, the less culturally competent spouse also has a source of power based not on location, but on his/her decision to relocate during the early stages of the union (Cross and Gilly 2014a).

By studying decision-making processes within culturally diverse families, using a non-traditional mixed-method approach, Cross and Gilly's (2014a) findings reveal a source of conjugal power – cultural competence, that is perhaps only manifested clearly when an individual in the family is outside her or his customary cultural context (Cross and Gilly 2014a). This has implications for expatriate and other displaced families. Yet, the very formation of a union where one partner is outside of his or her cultural comfort zone, invites trade-offs and compromises, a phenomenon explored further by the authors in another study. Cross and Gilly (2014b) discuss the consumption compromises in bi-national families, and the negotiation and accommodation given by one spouse to the other, in an effort to acknowledge and embrace the differences in the spousal consumption preferences. Cross and Gilly (2014b) show an ongoing effort by the partners to balance the relative spheres of power in the home across decisions and over time, rather than subjugate or dominate one partner's preferences by the other partner's influence. For example, preferred food products and brands for the immigrant spouse (often difficult to acquire in the U.S.) are avidly stockpiled by both spouses when purchased, such as the South African brands Bovril and Five Roses Tea (Cross and Gilly 2014b). Vacations can also be less of an escape or retreat in the conventional sense, but a "going-home," back to Mexico, South Africa, or China, for the immigrant spouse (Cross and Gilly 2014a).

This accommodation of, and compromise between, spousal preferences in culturally diverse unions is also supported by Nelson and Deshpande (2004), who examine the wedding planning decision-making of bi-national couples. Thus, they study decision-making at the formative stage of the bi-national family. Their findings show that bi-national couples try to accommodate different ritual audiences (parents and friends from both cultures) and therefore modify wedding rituals in an effort to integrate multiple cultural elements into one ceremony. Nelson and Otnes' (2005) also demonstrate the use of compromise to cope with conflicts in the postings of bi-national couples on wedding message boards. They highlight the complexity of the conflicts, given the two cultures involved, to explain the wide range of coping mechanisms of cross-cultural brides. Again, this need to bridge cultural differences in Greek-German bi-national unions (Lauth Bacas 2002), forces the bi-national partners to develop coping strategies and mechanisms to deal with disparate family networks, cultural consumption preferences and conjugal power struggles.

It is undisputed that early research in family decision-making laid an invaluable base for more contemporary research, even as the prior focus seemed limited to gender roles and who dominates in a particular purchase decision. This snapshot of more recent studies (Cross and Gilly 2013, Cross and Gilly 2014a, 2014b, Lauth Bacas 2002, Nelson and Deshpande 2004, Nelson and Otnes 2005) examines the impact of power and gender dynamics on consumption in culturally diverse families, families that deviate from the cultural norm. Studying these deviations in contemporary families enriches the family decision-making literature, adding another level of complexity to earlier conceptualizations of conjugal power and gender roles in prior family decision-making research.

Structurally Diverse Families – Gender Dynamics and Consumption in the Household

Although the notion of care has been traditionally associated with women, more contemporary gender narratives concerning egalitarian marriages and the ideology of the new male suggest that men embrace more nurturing father roles (Coltrane 1996, Pleck and Pleck 1997). As women's participation in the labor market has increased throughout the industrialized world, and as welfare states seek to reconcile work and care, fathers' involvement in care has become a hot societal topic. Recent U.S. discourses on fatherhood may be situated as part of similar tendencies and mobilizations across western welfare states focusing on men's financial, social, and moral obligations in families (Hobson and Morgan 2002). Fathers' rights groups are primarily concerned with legislation within a legal system that they believe discriminates against men in divorce and child custody issues (Messner 1997).

The new discourse that encourages men to get in touch with their emotions highlights the therapeutic benefits of fatherhood. This perspective maintains that men, like women, are victims of patriarchy: women for obvious reasons, and men because patriarchal assumptions prevent them from "getting in touch with their feelings" (Griswold 1993). In books, newspaper articles, newsletters, radio, and television programs, and classes for expectant or new fathers, the message is more or less the same: the new, liberated father is a nurturing man. This nurture is not only good for the child but also beneficial to the psychological well-being of fathers. Freidan (1981) describes the new freedom of one man who quit his advertising job to write a novel: "I go over to the dock with the kids and their bikes after they get home from the camp. I look forward to putting them to bed every night. I go to bed tingling all over" (p. 153).

The Father Responsibility Movement shares a concern with fathers' rights in wanting to remove barriers to father involvement within the child support system. There are numerous fatherhood organizations that seek recognition for the indispensability of fathers to families. According to the leading representatives of the father responsibility movement, parenting has been feminized by becoming synonymous with motherhood (Blankenhorn 1995). Promoting responsible fatherhood through constituting masculine versions of parenthood leads to a dilemma. On one hand, fatherhood must domesticate masculinity, which is perceived as innately aggressive, but on the other hand, fatherhood needs to be masculinized through, for instance, sport, religion, or other "manly" activities and discourses to not appear domesticated: that is, feminized or "sissified" (Blankenhorn 1995, p. 225). When the father responsibility movement urges men to get more involved with their kids, it also insists on making fatherhood into a man thing, asserting that dads shouldn't be like moms but rather keep wearing the pants in the family and be real men (Gavanas 2004).

Within consumer research, a handful of research stands out as investigating family compositions that deviate from traditional perceptions of the family structure. In an ethnographic study of the emergence of at-home fathers, Coskuner-Balli and Thompson (2013) explored how these men perform and attempt to legitimate an alternative fatherhood model. While dual career families have become a more general phenomenon, stay-at home fathers still remain a statistically small and stigmatized portion of the population. According to the 2004 U.S. census report, there are 98,000 men who are stay-at-home dads as opposed to 5.4 million stay-at-home moms (Daly 2006). However, stay-at-home fathers are fighting against their stigmatized masculine position by forming support groups; a social activity that has historically been associated with various factions of the women's movement. These stay-at-home fathers organize local meetings, play groups and post blogs on the internet. In addition, they meet at yearly conventions where they can get together with other at-home fathers and discuss issues such as reactions from their family and friends, the isolation they face, exchange ideas on child care and housekeeping. Stay-at-home fathers do housework, are familiar with domestic technologies, take care of the children all of which are traditionally thought as "women's work." Yet, they refuse the cultural epithet "Mr. Mom" and the emasculating connotations it carries.

Coskuner-Balli and Thompson (2013) argue that as socio-historic conditions have rendered domesticity as both a cultural province of femininity and a devalued form of cultural capital, stay-at-home fathers' decision-making is oriented towards increasing the conversion rate of their acquisitions of domestic cultural capital and attaining greater cultural legitimacy for their alternative performances of fatherhood and masculinity. While having made willing identity investments in a subordinate form of cultural capital, their participants' habituated predispositions as members of a dominant gender and class group make it difficult for them to accept being placed in a marginalized social position. Accordingly, stay-at-home fathers undertake a series of capitalizing practices that seek to enhance the status value of their domesticated cultural capital by converting it into more valued forms of economic, social, and symbolic capital.

For example, to acquire economic capital, stay-at-home fathers use a combination of thrift and entrepreneurial practices. As they lack the conventional income stream, stay-at-home fathers embrace the idea that they are providing economic value to the household by being thrifty shoppers who scour the marketplace for good deals whether for toys or daily groceries. As reflected in the name of the webpage "rebeldad" that hosts numerous stay-at-home father blogs, at-home fathers adopt a rebel-trickster (Holt and Thompson 2004) subtext that treats the marketplace as a network of free or very low cost recreational facilities and ludic playscapes

(Sherry et al. 2004). In this sense, visiting Home Depot or PetSmart become daily excursions with one's children which playfully appropriates these retail spaces into their new fatherhood performance.

The authors also report that the dominant gender roles lead to routine confrontations in maternally oriented marketplaces where stay-at-home fathers are confronted by questions about their competence and trustworthiness as primary care givers (Petroski and Edley 2006 and Rochlen, McKelley, and Whittaker 2010). To cope with these ostracizing encounters and stigma in the marketplace, these participants sought social capital by forming at-home father playgroups (Coskuner-Balli 2008). The strategy of participating in all-dad playgroups allowed stay-at-home fathers to claim public parenting spaces as legitimate stages for performing their unconventional gender identity and reciprocally, their manifest displays of social capital help to buffer stigmatizing reactions. In addition to local playgroups, stay-at-home fathers mobilized the internet to build social capital and further allay their feelings of social isolation by engaging in social media interactions with other stay-at-home fathers. These web-based forums such as rebeldad.com, fatherneed.com, and stayathomedad.org provide informational resources, social networking opportunities, and a means to exchange stories, ideas, and solutions to common problems. The stay-at-home father convention is also a forum where these men can express frustrations over their lack of recognition by the commercial marketplace and discuss strategies for combating the prevailing marketing assumption that mothers are the primary caregivers (and shoppers for the household). From difficulties in finding an appropriately masculine diaper bag, to reading parental magazines that address the audience as mothers only, to changing diapers in public parks where men's restrooms lack baby care stations, stay-at-home fathers share a myriad of examples where they felt marginalized by media, advertising, and major manufacturers who offered few childcare products designed for male caregivers.

To fight the stigma emanating from the feminizing (and hence emasculating) associations conventionally invoked by their full-time commitment to the domestic realm, stay-at-home fathers furthermore adopted more direct capitalizing practices, all serving the goal of masculinizing domesticity. As Coskuner-Balli and Thompson (2013) explain, these masculinizing practices involved (1) re-situating their domestic responsibilities in the public sphere; (2) altering the cultural connotations of domesticity through an emphasis on technological acumen and D.I.Y. projects; and (3) outsourcing their responsibilities for meal preparation to the commercial marketplace, thereby, disassociating their identities from connotations of domestic drudgery and maternal duty. For example, stay-at-home fathers' third strategy for masculinizing their domesticated cultural capital ideologically frames meal provision (and by implication provisional shopping) as a mere necessity that is secondary to their primary caregiving responsibilities and, hence, a tertiary aspect of their collective identity. In the manner of a self-perpetuating family myth (Hochschild 1989), participants often use their activity dense, on-the-go style of parenting as a ready-made justification for outsourcing their cooking responsibilities to the market.

In another study of a contemporary family structure, Harrison, Gentry and Commuri (2012) looked at single fathers and how they construct a caring fatherhood model within the cultural background of traditional gender roles. Like stay-at-home fathers, Harrison, Gentry and Commuri (2012) reported that single fathers developed distanced relationships to domesticity and household tasks. For example, while cooking has been central to the social construction of motherhood (Matthews 1987, Strasser 1982), it is not central to the social construction of fatherhood. The fathers often looked to food projects to make meal preparation quick and easy. In their daily experiences, conforming to the ideals of traditional masculinity while they took on feminine roles created tensions which they resolved through a set of reprioritization strategies.

Most notably with their new-found role, single fathers re-casted their commitment to work and de-emphasized the traditional masculine values such as achievement and competition while placing more value on involved parenting.

Conclusion and Future Research

Building on Epp and Price's (2008, 62) call for "investigation of how families construct and manage tensions, synergies, and commitments among individual, relational, and family identities that get constituted in consumers' selection and experience of activities," we encourage consumer researchers to explore how shifting cultural conditions, power dynamics and changing perspectives on gender structure the lives of families from different social classes and mediate these familial tensions.

As social conditions are in constant flux, so are family structures and identities. Whether to stay at home or outsource child care, how to mobilize the marketplace resources to feed and care for one's family, which extracurricular activities to send one's children, where to go on a vacation, are the kinds of consumption decisions families entertain and take to "do" their family. As families construct their identity, they face competing interests and demands oftentimes due to the countervailing set of ideals (Communi and Gentry 2005, Cross and Gilly 2013, 2014b, Epp and Price 2008). In this chapter, we highlighted specific sets of tensions families navigate, and discussed the set of strategies they adopt.

We contend that adopting a power and gender lens to explore rituals, narratives, everyday practices, in which families constitute and manage identity has further potential to understand family decision-making. While we have focused on how cultural capital and masculine gender capital influence family decision-making, there is much more to be learned in further exploring how gender fits into Bourdieu's theory. The types of embodied dispositions of masculinity and femininity can be used as a resource for both the individual and the family. For example, the gendered dispositions of women can be mobilized to mount up economic, cultural, and social capital for their families. The Kabyle women in Algeria, for example, engage in husbanding (cultural housekeeping) by displaying cultural taste and investing in social ties with kin as capital accumulation strategies for their family (Bourdieu 1998). Furthermore, the way in which gendered dispositions impact family life can vary by class. One exemplary study explores the roles of working class women who experience greater difficulty than middle class women in transferring their care and attention to educational achievement for their children, as they are more typically hampered by poverty and lack of knowledge (Reay 2004). Another ongoing study examines the manner in which families transfer and utilize family cultural and symbolic capital, as the authors examine the dynamics and tensions that support intergenerational family continuity (Schill, Godefroit-Winkel, and Bonsu 2016). The authors argue that the tensions and conflicts occurring within families are "necessary in managing a family capital within and over generations." We suggest that looking at these intergenerational dynamics through a power and gender lens would also provide additional insights for the family decision-making literature.

Exploring how gender is constructed within the family can also help gain important insights on family decision-making. Judith Butler (2004) states, femininity and masculinity are socially constructed through practices that are constrained in culturally accepted conceptions and that are embedded in interpersonal relations. One important domain in which gender roles are constructed is the family. Becker (1965) labels family a "small factory" that produces commodities (children, health, leisure, etc.) of value to the family. Risman (1998) suggests that a household is a gender factory. West and Zimmerman (1987), along similar lines, suggest that "doing gender" consists of interacting with others in such a way that people will perceive one's actions as expressions of an underlying masculine or feminine nature. Thus, one is not automatically classified as a man or woman on the basis of biological sex, but on the basis of appearance and behavior in everyday social interaction. Family work offers people a prime opportunity to "do gender" because of our cultural prescriptions about the appropriateness of men and women performing certain chores. Doing household chores or caring for children allows people to reaffirm their gendered relation to work and to the world. Thus, women can create and sustain their identities as women through cooking and cleaning the house and men can sustain their identities as men by *not* cooking and *not* cleaning house. As Butler argues, gender then gets reinstituted/constructed/challenged through these repetitive performances. These performances by which gendering occur are set within constraints of the past and the future that mark at once the limits of agency and its most enabling conditions. So, the performances in the household – cooking, cleaning, taking care of the children – are shaped within the embodying norms of society, one's personal history, and social class positioning. Future research can continue to explore how hegemonic masculinities/femininities are created, how traditional norms of gender and family are challenged and how these performances underlie family decision-making.

References

Becker, Gary S. (1965), "A theory of the allocation of time," *Economics Journal* 76 (299): 493–517.

Belch, Michael A. and Laura A. Willis (2002), "Family decision at the turn of the century: Has the changing structure of households impacted the family decision-making process?" *Journal of Consumer Behaviour*, 2(2), 111–124.

Blankenhorn, David (1995), *Fatherless America: Confronting Our Most Urgent Social Problem*, New York: Basic Books.

Blood, Robert O. and Donald Wolfe (1960), *Husbands and Wives*, New York, NY: Free Press.

Bourdieu, Pierre (1998), *Masculine Domination*, Stanford: Stanford University Press.

—— (1996), "On the family as a realized category," *Theory, Culture & Society*, 13(3), 19–26.

Butler, Judith (2004), *Undoing Gender*, New York: Routledge.

Chodorow, Nancy J. (1999), *The Reproduction of Mothering*, Berkeley: University of California Press.

Coltrane, Scott (1996), *Family Man: Fatherhood, Housework and Gender Equity*, New York: Oxford University Press.

Commuri, Suraj and James W. Gentry (2000), "Opportunities for family research in marketing," *Academy of Marketing Science Review*, 8, www.amsreview.org/articles/commuri08–00.pdf

—— (2005), "Resource allocation in households with women as chief wage earners," *Journal of Consumer Research*, 32 (September), 185–195.

Corfman, Kim P. and Donald R. Lehmann (1987), "Models of cooperative group decision-making and relative influence: An experimental investigation of family purchase decisions," *Journal of Consumer Research*, 14(1), 1–13.

Coskuner-Balli, Gokcen (2008), "Stay-at-home dads unite: Coping with stigma and isolation (18:38)", in NA – *Advances in Consumer Research* Volume 35. Eds. Angela Y. Lee and Dilip Soman, Duluth, MN: Association for Consumer Research, p. 878.

Coskuner-Balli, Gokcen and Thompson, Craig J. (2013), "The status costs of subordinate cultural capital: At-home fathers' collective pursuit of cultural legitimacy through capitalizing consumption practices," *Journal of Consumer Research*, 40(June), 19–41.

Crosby, Faye J. and Jaskar, Karen L. (1993), "Women and men at home and at work: Realities and illusions," in *Gender Issues in Contemporary Society*. Eds. S. Oskamp and M. Costanzo, Newbury Park: Sage Publications, 143–171.

Cross, S. N. N. and M. C. Gilly (2013), "Bridging cultural divides: The role and impact of bi-national families," *Journal of Public Policy and Marketing*, 32, 106–111.

—— (2014a), "Cultural competence and cultural compensatory mechanisms in bi-national households," *Journal of Marketing*, 78(3), 121–139.

—— (2014b), "Consumption compromises: Negotiation and unification within contemporary families," *Journal of Business Research*, 67, 449–456.

Daly, Ian (2006), "Stay home dads, unite!," *Details*, (January/February): 118–120.

Davis, H. L. (1970), "Dimensions of marital roles in consumer decision making," *Journal of Marketing Research*, 7(2), 168–177.

Davis, H. L. and B. P. Rigaux (1974), "Perception of marital roles in decision processes," *Journal of Consumer Research*, 1(1), 51–62.

DeVault, Marjorie (1991), *Feeding the Family*, Chicago, IL: University of Chicago Press.

Ehrenreich, Barbara and Deirdre English (1989), *For Her Own Good: 150 Years of the Experts' Advice to Women*, New York: Anchor Books.

Engel, James E., Roger D. Blackwell, and Paul W. Miniard (1990), *Consumer Behavior*, Orlando, FL: The Dryden Press, International Edition.

Epp, Amber M. and Linda L. Price (2008), "Family identity: A framework of identity interplay in consumption practices," *Journal of Consumer Research*, 35(June), 50–70.

Firat, Fuat A. (1994), "Gender and consumption: Transcending the feminine?" in *Gender Issues and Consumer Behavior*. Ed. Janeen Arnold Costa, Thousand Oaks, CA: Sage Publications, 205–228.

Ford, John B., Michael S. LaTour, and Tony L. Henthorne (1995), "Perception of marital roles in purchase decision processes: A cross-cultural study," *Journal of the Academy of Marketing Science*, 23(2), 120–131.

Freidan, Betty (1981), *The Second Stage*, New York: Summit Books.

French, John and Bertram H. Raven (1959), "The bases of social power," In *Studies in Social Power*. Ed. D. Cartwright. Ann Arbor: MI: Institute for Social Research, 150–167.

Gavanas, Anna (2004), "Domesticating masculinity and masculinizing domesticity in contemporary U.S. fatherhood politics," *Social Politics*, 11 (Summer), 247–266.

Gillis, John (1996), *A World of Their Own Making: Myth, Ritual, and the Quest for Family Values*, New York: Basic Books.

Green, Robert T., Jean-Paul Leonardi, Jean-Louis Chandon, Isabella C. M. Cunningham, Bronis Verhage, and Alain Strazzieri (1983), "Societal development and family purchasing roles: A cross-national study," *Journal of Consumer Research*, 9(4), 436–442.

Griswold, Robert L. (1993), *Fatherhood in America: A History*, New York: Basic Book.

Harrison, Robert, James W., Gentry and Suraj Commuri (2012), "A grounded theory of transition to involved parenting: The role of household production and consumption in the lives of single fathers," in *Gender, Culture and Consumer Behavior*. Eds. Cele C. Otnes and Linda Tuncay Zayer. New York: Routledge.

Hobson, Barbara and David Morgan (2002), "Making men into fathers," in *Making Men into Fathers: Men, Masculinities and Social Politics of Fatherhood*. Ed. Barbara Hobson. London: Cambridge University Press.

Hochschild, Arlie (1989), *The Second Shift*, New York: Avon Books.

Holt, Douglas B. and Craig J. Thompson (2004), "Man-of-action heroes: The pursuit of heroic masculinity in everyday consumption," *Journal of Consumer Research*, 31 (September), 425–440.

Kimmel, Micheal (1987), "Rethinking Masculinity: New Directions in Research" in *Changing Men: New Directions in Research on Men and Masculinity*. Ed. Micheal Kimmel. NewBury Park, CA: Sage, 9–24.

La Rossa, Ralph (1988), "Fatherhood and social change," *Family Relations*, 37, 431–457.

Lau-Gesk, Loraine G. (2003), "Activating culture through persuasion appeals: An examination of the bicultural consumer," *Journal of Consumer Psychology*, 13(3), 301–315.

Lauth Bacas, Jutta (2002), "Cross-border marriages and the formation of transnational. families: A case study of Greek-German couples in Athens," www.transcomm.ox.ac.uk/working%20papers/WPTC-02–10%20Bacas.pdf

Luna, David, Torsten Ringberg and Laura A. Peracchio (2008), "One individual, two identities: Frame switching among biculturals," *Journal of Consumer Research*, 35(2), 279–293.

Matthews, Glenna (1987), *Just a Housewife*, New York: Oxford University Press.

Meng, Xin and Robert G. Gregory (2005), "Intermarriage and the economic assimilation of immigrants," *Journal of Labor Economics*, 23(1), 135–175.

Messner, Michael A. (1997), *Politics of Masculinities: Men in Movements*. University of Southern California: Sage.

Miller, Daniel (1998), *A Theory of Shopping*, New York: Cornell University Press.

Nelson, Michelle R. and Sameer Deshpande (2004), "Love without borders: An examination of cross-cultural wedding rituals," in *Contemporary Consumption Rituals: A Research Anthology*. Ed. Cele C. Otnes and Tina M. Lowrey. Mahwah, NJ: Lawrence Erlbaum Associates, Publishers, 125–148.

Nelson, Michelle R. and Cele Otnes (2005), "Exploring cross-cultural ambivalence: A netnography of intercultural wedding message boards," *Journal of Business Research*, 58, 89–95.

Olson, David H. and Ronald E. Cromwell (1975), "Methodological issues in family power," in *Power in Families*, ed. Ronald E. Cromwell and David H. Olson, New York, NY: Sage Publications Inc., 131–50.

Olson, David H., Ronald E. Cromwell, and David M. Klein (1975), "Beyond family power," in *Power in Families*, Ed. Ronald E. Cromwell and David H. Olson, New York, NY: Sage Publications Inc., 235–240.

Peñaloza, Lisa N. and Gilly Mary C. (1986), "The Hispanic family – Consumer research issues," *Psychology & Marketing*, 3(4), 291–304.

—— (1999), "Marketer acculturation: The changer and the changed," *Journal of Marketing*, 63 (3), 84–104.

Petroski, David John, and Paige P. Edley (2006), "Stay-at-home fathers: Masculinity, family, work, and gender stereotypes," *Electronic Journal of Communication*, 16 (3/4), www.cios.org/EJCPUBLIC/016/3/01634. HTML.

Pleck H., Elizabeth and Joseph H. Pleck (1997), "Fatherhood ideals in the United States: Historical dimensions," in *The Role of the Father in Child Development*. Ed. M. E. Lamb, Wiley & Sons: New York, 33–48.

—— (1980), *The American Man*, Englewood Cliffs, NJ: Prentice Hall.

Pleck, Joseph H. (1993), "Are family supportive employer policies relevant to men?" in *Men, Work and Family*. Ed. Jane C. Hood, Newbury Park: Sage, 217–237.

Putnam, M. and W. R. Davidson (1987), "Family purchasing behavior: II family roles by product category, in The RIS Consumer Focus Series," Dublin, OH: Management Horizons, A Division of Price Waterhouse.

Qualls, W. J. (1982), "Changing sex roles, its impact upon family decision making," *Advances in Consumer Research*, 267–270.

Qualls, William J. (1987), "Household decision behavior: The impact of husbands' and wives' sex role orientation," *Journal of Consumer Research*, 14(2), 264–279.

Raven, B. H., R. Centers, and A. Rodrigues (1975), "The bases of conjugal power," in *Power in Families*, ed. Ronald E. Cromwell and David. H. Olson, New York, NY: Sage Publications Inc., 217–232.

Reay, Diane (2004), "Gendering Bourdieu's Concepts of Capitals? Emotional Capital, Women and Social Class," in *Feminism After Bourdieu*. Ed. Lisa Adkins and Beverley Skeggs. Malden: Blackwell Publishing.

Risman, Barbara J. (1998), *Gender Vertigo: American Families in Transition*, New Haven, CT: Yale University Press.

Rochlen, Aaron B., Ryan A. McKelley, and Tiffany A. Whittaker (2010), "Stay-at-home fathers' reasons for entering the role and stigma experiences: A preliminary report," *Psychology of Men and Masculinity*, 11 (October), 279–285.

Rodman, H. (1972), "Marital power and the theory of resources in a cultural context," *Journal of Comparative Family Studies*, 3(1), 50.

Rotundo, Anthony (1993), *American Manhood: Transformations in Masculinity from the Revolution to the Modern Era*, NY: Basic Books.

Schill M., D. Godefroit-Winkel and S. K. Bonsu (2016), "Cultural (re)production across generations: Family heritage and the market" (working paper).

Sherry, John F., Jr., Robert V. Kozinets, Adam Duhachek, Benét DeBerry-Spence, Krittinee Nuttavuthisit, and Diana Storm (2004), "Gendered behavior in a male preserve: Role playing at ESPN zone Chicago," *Journal of Consumer Psychology* 14 (1/2), 151–158.

Spiro, R. L. (1983), "Persuasion in family decision-making," *Journal of Consumer Research*, 9 (4), 393–402.

Strasser, Susan (1982), *Never Done: A History of American Housework*, New York: Pantheon.

Thompson, Craig J. (1996), "Caring consumers: Gendered consumption meanings and the juggling lifestyle," *Journal of Consumer Research*, 22 (March), 388–407.

Wallendorf, M. and M. D. Reilly (1983), "Ethnic migration, assimilation, and consumption," *Journal of Consumer Research*, 10 (3), 292–302.

Waller, Willard (1938), *The Family: A Dynamic Interpretation*, New York: Dryden.

Waller, Willard and Reuben Hill (1951), *The Family: A Dynamic Interpretation*, New York: Dryden (revision).

Wamwara-Mbugua, L. Wakiuru (2007), "An investigation of household decision making among immigrants," *Advances in Consumer Research*, 34, 180–186.

Webster, Cynthia (2000), "Is spousal decision making a culturally situated phenomenon?" *Psychology & Marketing*, 17(12), 1035–1058.

Weiss, Jessica (2000), *To Have and to Hold: Marriage, Baby Boom and Social Change*, Chicago: University of Chicago Press.

West, Candace and Don H. Zimmerman (1987), "Doing gender," *Gender and Society*, (1), 125–151.

Wolfe, D. M. (1959), "Power and authority in the family," in *Studies in Social Power*. Ed. Dorwin Cartwright. Ann Arbor, MI: Research Center for Group Dynamics, Institute for Social Research, The University of Michigan, 99–117.

22

CONDUCTING INTERNATIONAL CONSUMER RESEARCH WITH CHILDREN: CHALLENGES AND POTENTIAL SOLUTIONS

Tina M. Lowrey,[1] Lan Nguyen Chaplin,[2] Agnes Nairn,[3]
Aysen Bakir,[4] Verolien Cauberghe,[5] Elodie Gentina,[6]
Liselot Hudders,[5] Hua Li,[7] Fiona Spotswood,[8]
and Anna Maria Zawadzka[9]

[1]HEC PARIS, JOUY-EN-JOSAS, FRANCE
[2]UNIVERSITY OF ILLINOIS-CHICAGO, CHICAGO, IL, USA
[3]HULT INTERNATIONAL BUSINESS SCHOOL, LONDON, UK
[4]ILLINOIS STATE UNIVERSITY, NORMAL, IL, USA
[5]FACULTY OF POLITICAL AND SOCIAL SCIENCES, GHENT UNIVERSITY, GHENT, BELGIUM
[6]IESEG SCHOOL OF MANAGEMENT, LEM-CNRS (UMR 9221), LILLE, FRANCE
[7]EMLYON BUSINESS SCHOOL, ECULLY, FRANCE
[8]BRISTOL BUSINESS SCHOOL, UNIVERSITY OF THE WEST OF ENGLAND, BRISTOL, UK
[9]INSTITUTE OF PSYCHOLOGY, UNIVERSITY OF GDANSK, GDANSK, POLAND

Marketing to children remains firmly in focus for public policy makers, be it in relation to advertising High Salt Sugar and Fat (HSSF) food and drink (Moore 2007), the effects of internet advertising and advergames (Nairn and Hang 2012; Panic et al. 2013), or corporate use of children as brand ambassadors selling to their friends (Nairn and Mayo 2009). Recent years have seen the UK government banning advertising of HSSF products in and around TV programs of particular appeal to children; the Advertising Association banning members from using children as brand ambassadors; and food and drink companies in the US and Europe producing voluntary codes to restrain the advertising of less healthy products to children (CFBAI 2015; EU Pledge 2015). These issues are not only important for national governments and industry groups but are increasingly within the remit of the biggest global NGOs who provide internationally aligned impetus for regulation change. For example, the WHO (2010) recently provided strong recommendations to all nation states on food and drink marketing to children, and the United Nations (2014) has recommended that its member states "prohibit all forms of advertising to children under 12 years of age, regardless of the medium, support or means used, with the possible extension of such prohibition to children under 16 years of age" (p. 23).

Marketing research with children is thus paramount and pivotal in informing public policy at a global level. Yet, international research projects with children are fraught with difficulties which must be overcome if the marketing research community is to provide timely and reliable evidence to policy makers. At the most fundamental level research with children is not the same as research with adults as children occupy a favored social position across the world. This has been formally recognized in the United Nations Convention on the Rights of the Child (UNCRC 1990). As researchers, we have to acknowledge that "Children are not small adults; they have an additional, unique set of interests" (McIntosh 2000, p. 177).

The aim of this chapter, therefore, is to describe specific challenges faced when doing international public policy research with children (aged 12 and younger) and adolescents (aged 13–17), and to provide suggested solutions to these challenges. Throughout, we suggest possible solutions, given that we do not think there is one "right" way to "do" research design, ethics, and data collection, or any definitive solutions on how to involve children in research. The inspiration for this chapter stems from an international public policy research project underway by the current authors in multiple countries (Belgium, China, France, Poland, the UK, and the US). The general approach taken here is to present and describe a particular challenge, followed by a possible solution, followed by another challenge and possible solution, and so on. Thus, the chapter is a handbook of sorts, to be consulted by those engaged in similar public policy research projects.

We present a time-line of challenges faced by international research teams working with children. The first challenge is to gain ethical approval from different institutions across the world. Second, an internationally comparable sample frame must be drawn up. Third, sampling equivalence must be established. Fourth, data collection must be standardized and, fifth and finally, the methodological challenges of working across cultures must be addressed.

Challenges and Possible Solutions

Challenge #1: The Research Approval Process

The first challenge when conducting international projects involving children and adolescents is the difference both between and within countries with respect to gaining permission from University Ethics Committees (Markham and Buchanan 2012; Tsaliki and Chronaki 2013). This process is often referred to as the "ethics approval process." The process ranges from extremely demanding and restrictive constraints in many US institutions to no process at all, such as in some French business schools. There appears to be little international agreement across higher education institutions as to either the content or process of ethics approval for research with children and adolescents. This can lead to difficulties in collecting matched national samples. Five important issues are described here:

1   Most universities in the US have an Institutional Review Board (IRB) comprised of a group of professors who approve or reject research projects on ethical grounds. Institutions might establish specific branches (i.e. The Office of Research Ethics and Compliance) to administer university-wide compliance with federal, state, and university policies regarding the conduct of ethical research. In Poland, researchers comply with the Polish Academy of Science code of ethics. This is a government institution covering all of Poland (rather than institution-specific, as in the US). Similar to the US, however, before conducting research on children and adolescents in Poland, researchers have to apply for permission to their own University Research Ethics Committee (appointed by the

Council of the Faculty), consisting of faculty with extensive research experience. The application must include a description of the research purpose, its participants, methods, tools, procedures, and parental consent forms (as in the US). Contrast this with many French universities, which have no IRB or ethics approval process whatsoever.

2   Directly tied to the IRB process just described, there are a limited number of experts on research with children and adolescents, which can lead to difficulties in getting such research approved. It can also lead to later difficulties during the review process as projects move towards publication. During these later stages, researchers might find it difficult to meet reviewers' concerns, given a lack of understanding regarding the difficulties of working with children, particularly in an international context. While conducting our study, at the initial stage, the researchers went through significantly different experiences. Tables 22.1 and 22.2 summarize these differences in terms of the ethics review process across countries.

3   There is difficulty encountered in obtaining consent and assent. As stated by the CITI Program (2015), which guides many review processes in the US, the consent process starts with recruitment, since it covers information about the study itself. All recruitment materials, including e-mails, fliers, and so on, must be approved by IRBs (in many countries) before their usage. Local regulations in many countries require IRBs to guarantee that appropriate practices are employed to protect the rights and welfare of vulnerable subjects (such as children and adolescents) from coercion and undue influence during the consent process. Appropriate practices include assessing the decision-making capacity of participants, gaining consent from both parents (rather than just one parent for some studies), and assuring that incentives are not coercive, among other things. Another aspect related to informed consent is child/adolescent assent to participating. Hicks (2015) defines assent as "a child's affirmative agreement to participate" and states that "the absence of

Table 22.1 Ethics review process across countries

	Need permission from Ethics Committee?	Personal interview or correspondence?	Length of process?	Committee demands changes in process?	Child experts on board?
US	Y	Personal/email	Relatively lengthy	Y	N
France	N	–	–	N	–
UK	Y	Email	Variable	Y	N
Belgium	Y	Email			N
China	N	–	Relatively lengthy	N	–
Poland	Y	Personal/email	Relatively short	N	N

Table 22.2 Research approval process practices across countries

	Ethics training	Parental consent	Child consent/assent	School permission	Additional permission for school access (i.e. district office)
US	Yes	Yes	Yes	Yes	Yes
France	No			Yes	No
UK	No	Yes	Yes	Yes	No
Belgium	No			Yes	No
China	No			Yes	No
Poland	No	Yes	No	Yes	No

dissent should not be construed as assent when the child is old enough that assent is meaningful. Generally, parental permission can only override a child's dissent when the health of the child is at stake." Several factors should be considered in the development of the assent procedures, such as the type of research activity as well as the age and maturity of the participants involved. In fact, the assent process with children should be similar to the informed consent process with adolescents, whose abilities are similar to those of adults. In the ongoing global research that inspired this chapter, we had to apply the consent and assent processes differently, depending on the country in which data were collected. The general process in the US is as follows: The researcher sends consent forms to the parents. Once parental consent is obtained, the researcher may initiate interaction with the participants. However, before initiating actual data collection, the researcher must obtain the child's assent. If the child does not give assent, the child should still be given a prize for doing the study, in an effort to avoid coercing children to participate for a prize. In France, however, the researcher does not need to go through the same lengthy process with multiple checkpoints. French schools require only parental consent. In the UK, it depends on the ethics committee in a particular university.

4 Gaining access to schools to collect data from children and adolescents presents substantial differences in processes across countries. For example, in the US, after IRB approval, gaining permission from schools can differ within the country. Gatekeepers that provide school access have different expectations and procedures to follow, even though they may work under similar guidelines and policies. Schools belong to specific districts in their town or city. In order to gain school access, researchers are often expected to get permission from the district first, followed by permission from the principal in each school. Thus, a researcher might not be able to collect data at all schools in a district, even though district-level permission was obtained (the opposite can also occur, where a researcher can get permission from a school principal, but the district will not grant permission). In other cases, a school district may require permission from the principals prior to granting district-level permission. In Poland and the UK, only school permission is required (i.e. no district-level permission is necessary).

5 Finally, individual researchers are often required to undergo ethics training. However, there is no uniform process in place within or across countries. Universities in the US appear to use one or more of the following training providers: The Collaborative Institutional Training Initiative (CITI Program), the National Institutes of Health (NIH), and/or the course offered by Public Responsibility in Medicine and Research (PRIM&R). The CITI Program offers a substantial amount of web-based training, and is available in Canada, India, Japan, Korea, and Latin America. However, it is a commercial program purchased at the discretion of each University, and is therefore not uniformly applied across the US. Furthermore, it also appears to be less popular outside the US, where different countries have more or less rigorous processes, often not requiring training for individual researchers.

Possible Solution: More transparent communication across University Ethics Committees is needed, particularly with respect to approving research involving children and adolescents. In addition, a universally shared international process would be invaluable. This could enhance the probability of obtaining comparable international samples, increase transparency (and, thus, lead to higher standards), and provide IRBs with objective guidance. Such a process would also provide for greater protections of children and adolescents, and potentially enhance the reputation of academic research involving children and adolescents.

However, which process should be chosen? Looking at the history helps us to understand how some codes of conduct were established. For example, the United Nations Convention on the Rights of the Child (UNCRC) established children's rights to participation (Article 12) in 1989 (Nairn and Clarke 2012) in issues that involve them, and there now exists a growing body of research on children stemming from anthropology, psychology, and sociology, among others (Nairn and Clarke 2012; Powell and Smith 2009). This has led to the introduction of new government policies. For example, in the UK, the Children's Act 2004 specifically commands the Children's Commissioner to consult with children – in other words ask their opinions through research (Section 2:4). Children's participation is an important component in the areas of education, health policies, and social care (Nairn and Clarke 2012; Prout 2005). Equally important to children's participation is children's protection. The UNCRC yields the coexisting right to be protected (Article 3; Nairn and Clarke 2012). The challenge to find the right balance between children's active participation and protection was at the center of intense debates in the mid-1990s (Morrow and Richards 1996; Nairn and Clarke 2012), and continues to date. One answer to this difficult issue may lie in the Market Research Society (MRS) code of conduct. This is already used by commercial and social researchers outside the University environment, and might usefully be adopted internationally by academic researchers. It rests on three core principles: wellbeing, voluntary informed consent, and confidentiality. The child's wellbeing must be the overriding concern, both physically and emotionally. Voluntary informed consent implies that children are able to understand the purpose and scope of the study, which may require age-related adaptations. Confidentiality should always be maintained, as in most research practice. In summary, a standardized international process for conducting research with children and adolescents is highly recommended.

Challenge #2: Defining an Internationally Comparable Sample

Having gained permission to carry out research with children from the university, the school, the parents, and the children, the next step is to establish a sample that is internationally comparable. Of interest to a great deal of consumer and marketing research with children is socioeconomic status (SES), as purchasing power is closely related to disposable income and social position. A popular definition of SES describes it as a relative position of an individual or family within a given social structure, reflecting access to economic and social resources (Mueller and Parcel 1981). SES calculations typically include measures such as parental education level, parental occupational prestige, and household income. However, countries can differ enormously in the levels of wealth and living conditions provided for residents. Thus, SES comparability may be difficult to assess.

The average level of education is a case in point. In our study, the percentage of adults who have completed secondary education ranges from a high of 90% in Poland to a low of 72% in Belgium (see Table 22.3; OECD 2015). Similarly, the average length of time spent in higher education ranges from 18.9 years in Belgium down to 16.4 years in France and the UK. It is also important to describe the problems that arise from studying children who are exposed to different educational systems and as a result, develop different kinds and levels of knowledge proficiencies. Table 22.3 details several factors that differ cross-nationally, including age at which school begins, levels of education (with associated ages for each level), age at which compulsory education ends, total years in the system, and proficiency levels in mathematics, reading, and science literacy. For example, knowledge proficiencies range from a high of 521 in Poland to a low of 492 in the US (OECD 2015). Such educational

Table 22.3 Differences in educational systems across the six countries

Education system	Belgium[1]	China[2]	France	Poland	UK	US[3]
Age, school starts	6	6–7	6	6	5	5–7[4]
Levels of education	3	3	4	3	4	3
Age, compulsory education ends	18	15–16	16	18	17	16–18
Total years in the system	12	9	10	12	11	10–13[4]

[1] Compulsory Education in Europe 2014/2015, www.eacea.edu.en; The structure of the European Education Systems 2014/15, Nov. 2014; http://eacea.ec.europa.en/education/eurydice/facts and figures.en.php#diagrams
[2] Education in China, Oct, 2010, KPMG, Hong Kong; kpmg.com/cn; Compulsory education Law of the People's Republic of China; www.moe.edu.cn
[3] Structure of U.S. Education; www2.ed.gov/about/offices/list/ous/international/usnei/us/edlite-structure-us.html; Education commission of the state free and compulsory school age requirements in the United States, Jun, 2015; www.ecs.org/clearinghouse/01/18/68/11868.pdf
[4] Depending on the state.

Table 22.4 Differences in socioeconomic status across the six countries (OECD, 2015)

SES	Belgium	China	France	Poland	UK	US
Percentage of adults (aged 25–65) who have completed secondary education	72	–	75	90	78	89
Average length of time spent in higher education	18.9	–	16.4	18.4	16.4	17.2
Average household income	28,307.00	–	28,799.00	17,852.00	27,029.00	41,355.00

differences may lead to differences in understanding assent forms and study instructions, and interpretation of stimuli, among others. Thus, they imply a need for careful selection of grade levels across countries.

Occupational prestige also varies across countries, particularly with respect to agriculture and services (Treiman 1977). Finally, differences in household income are particularly problematic to address, ranging from USD 41,355.00 on average in the US down to USD 17,852.00 on average in Poland (see Table 22.4).

Possible Solution: Data must be harmonized to compare cross-nationally, and there are two strategies for this: (1) input harmonization (i.e. harmonized concepts included in questionnaires); and (2) output harmonization (i.e. using pre-existing regional data, and amending them to harmonized format). For input harmonization, the International Social Survey Programme Database (ISSP; www.issp.org; Braun and Uher 2003) is a program of collaboration on important topics in the social sciences across countries. Researchers from the ISSP pay special attention to the development of reliable tools. They develop relevant and meaningful questionnaires for all countries involved through extensive pretesting, a reliable way to construct good questionnaires. For output harmonization, original questionnaires are used to find matches within index categories in available databases.

There are many resources to help gain a better understanding of cultural and socioeconomic differences across countries. The World Values Survey dataset (WVS 2015; www.worldvaluessurvey.org/wvs.jsp) indicates value orientations among adults across countries. The aim of this database is to study and monitor changes in values and attitudes in

Table 22.5 Resources to help gain better understanding of cultural and socioeconomic differences across the countries

No.	Sources	Type of information	Countries
1	Survey Programme Database (ISSP)	important topics in social sciences	worldwide
2	WVS the world Value Survey	value orientation	worldwide
3	ESS European Social Survey	education, family, identity, income, living conditions, religion	EU countries
4	ISCO-8 the Internal Standards Classification of Occupations	occupation	worldwide
5	SILC the EU Statistics on Income and Living Conditions	income and living conditions	EU countries
6	ISCED-12 the UNESCO International Standard Classification of Education	education concept, education mapping program	worldwide
7	HBSC: the Health Behavior in School-Aged Children	children's health, well-being, living conditions	worldwide

socioeconomic, sociopolitical, sociopsychological, and sociogeographical domains in the lives of people from all over the world. Good sources of cultural values differences for Europe include the European Social Survey (ESS; www.europeansocialsurvey.org; Kolsrud and Skjåk 2005) and the European Value Survey (see Table 22.5). These are academically managed databases, giving comparable information for all EU countries on education, families, identities, income levels, living conditions, and religion. For occupational prestige, harmonized measures can be found in the Internal Standards Classification of Occupations (ISCO-8; www.ilo.org/public/english/stat/isco/index.htm; International Family of Economic and Social Classification). ISCO-8 can serve as a good basis for comparisons of statistical data about occupations across countries. For income differences in the EU, the EU Statistics on Income and Living Conditions (SILC; www.eui.en/Research/Library/Researchbuilds/Economics/Statistics/DataPortal/En-SILC.aspx) includes harmonized data on income distribution, living conditions, and poverty. A good source of information about educational differences is the UNESCO International Standard Classification of Education (ISCED), part of the International Family of Economic and Social Classification. ISCED 2012 includes internationally-agreed-upon concepts of education, and education mapping programs across countries. One final resource is the Health Behavior in School-Aged Children (HBSC) dataset, which includes a Family Affluence Scale (Batista-Foguet et al. 2004). Finally, researchers must standardize assent forms, instructions, and stimuli to ensure that same-age participants, regardless of reading levels or knowledge proficiencies, can understand and respond in comparable ways.

Challenge #3: Sampling Equivalence

Samples across countries need to be comparable. There are seven important sampling equivalence issues:

1   In cross-cultural research, in general, researchers can take an etic (context-free) or emic (context-bound) approach (Buil et al. 2012). The etic approach uses standardized measures and a standardized approach across samples. The emic approach, conversely, develops specific measures for each unit of analysis (which can compromise data equivalence).

Possible Solution: An alternative described by Douglas and Craig (cited in Buil et al. 2012, p. 227) is the adaptation of the etic approach so culturally specific differences can be taken into account and incorporated in the general measurement instrument, or the adaptation of the emic approach so specific differences in each culture are summed and combined to become a general measurement instrument. In the global study that inspired this chapter, we took the adapted etic approach, constructing a standardized measurement instrument that took cultural differences into account that was used in all countries. For example, when assessing levels of social media usage, we altered the type of social media (e.g. Facebook, Instagram, Twitter) to correspond to the most popular methods in a particular country.

2   Selecting the unit of analysis needs to be carefully considered. In much cross-cultural research, countries are often considered the unit of analysis. Yet culture can be conceptualized at different levels, including national, regional, or ethnic (Engelen and Brettel 2011). Because members of a nation share a common history, language, political/legal, and educational environment, they are believed to possess a distinct "national character"; that is, a distinct and stable pattern of behavior, personality characteristics, and values (Clark 1990; Luna and Gupta 2001). Some marketing studies have empirically shown the predominance of national culture over other cultural levels (regional, age, education) or subcultures (ethnic groups) (Singh et al. 2003). For instance, in a study conducted in 13 countries, Schwartz and Ros (1995) found that national culture explained three times more variance than within-country determinants (age and education). More recently, Trompenaars and Hampden-Turner (2004) also concluded that national culture was the level of culture that exhibited the strongest heterogeneity in major values.

Possible Solution: When countries must be the unit of analysis, it is important that they are comparable on factors that might impact the research topic (e.g. the topic should be equally important in all countries), or mediating and moderating factors should be taken into account.

3   When aiming at sampling equivalence, researchers encounter conflicting aims: comparability versus generalizability (Buil et al. 2012). To make comparisons across countries (and, thus, samples), it is important to obtain sample comparability. This implies that samples are homogeneous in terms of relevant factors in the context of the research topic. However, homogeneity may have negative implications for the representativeness of the sample. Representativeness implies that statements can be generalized to the population from which the sample was taken.

Possible Solution: Balancing comparability and generalizability is a dilemma in cross-cultural research, and has major implications for the sampling method used. To obtain generalizability, researchers should use probabilistic sampling methods, while non-probabilistic sampling methods lead to greater comparability. Which methods are ultimately used should be guided by the goals of the research project.

4   If probabilistic sampling is used to enhance generalizability, random sampling is required. However, a number of issues may arise in the context of cross-cultural research, such as sampling frame, sampling method, and sample size (Ólafsson et al. 2013).

Possible Solution: A list of potential participants should be made available, from which participants can be selected in a random manner. Since such lists are not readily available, particularly across countries, a frequently used method is cluster sampling. With this method, natural groups of children are used as selection units, and within these units, a random sample is recruited. For example, a list of schools available in each participating country can be used for random selection of schools (representative for region, educational level, etc.), followed by random selection of individual participants from the schools selected.

5   If non-probabilistic sampling is used to enhance comparability, quota sampling may be required, which involves obtaining comparable samples in terms of relevant variables (Buil et al. 2012).

   Possible Solution: The Buil et al. (2012) method was used in the global study that inspired this chapter – children with comparable socio-demographic backgrounds in terms of age and SES were included. However, such a method does not allow for gener-alizations from the sample to the general population. As previously stated, the ultimate goals of the research project must be considered to determine whether to emphasize comparability or generalizability. Another method for enhancing comparability (but not generalizability) is to use online, international panel data, which allows for screening on initially determined characteristics (e.g. SES). Online questionnaires are not suitable, of course, for all topics or for younger children. For young children, taking a questionnaire online can be difficult, due to limited reading and writing skills.

6   Researchers need to consider how to improve participation rates from schools (or other organizations). It is important to stimulate approval from such entities, by explaining the importance and implications of the study (not only for scientific value, but also for society). The ability to place the research project in a larger context may increase partici-pation rates. However, at the same time, there may be some risk associated with such a strategy. For example, in the ongoing global study that inspired this chapter, for the data collection in China, decision-makers were concerned with the implications of the study. We were measuring materialism levels, and they were wary of the possibility of comparisons between countries regarding children's materialism levels. Thus, researchers should be aware of positive, but also potentially negative consequences of cross–country comparisons.

   Possible Solution: It is important to emphasize that no statements will be made about the results from individual participants, nor about the results within one school/organization. It is also important to recognize the limitations of the study, and not to over-emphasize the implications of the study (Laws and Mann 2004). In addition, donating something in return for participation may increase participation rates. For example, researchers can promise the school/organization to return after data analysis and present the results, or to give a short educational training to participants on the research topic. Schools appreciate this, and this stimulates their willingness to participate in the study. Additionally, it is important to maintain a strict schedule, and communicate this clearly. This increases the chance that schools will contact the researcher if there is a problem involving data col-lection. It is also a good idea to send frequent reminders.

7   Researchers need to consider how to improve parental consent rates. Researchers must explain the value of the study thoroughly, so parents can appreciate why their children are being asked to participate. Finally, researchers need to consider how to improve assent rates from the participants themselves. Incentives can be used to stimulate assent from child and adolescent participants (although they should not be coercive). For many studies, participants spend large amounts of time on the study that they could have spent in other ways (Laws and Mann 2004). Thus, it is important to consider compensating participants for the time spent on the research. In addition, incentives can greatly increase participation levels. Incentives can be either financial or non-financial. However, giving financial com-pensation can have negative implications (Ólafsson et al. 2013). For one, financial incen-tives can change the relationship, as participation is no longer fully voluntary, thus forcing participants to complete the study even if they no longer feel comfortable doing so.

Participants can more easily withdraw from a study when receiving no compensation (although our experience with very young children indicates that they don't really expect any sort of reward, but still enjoy participating). Financial incentives may also cause participants to comply with what they think the researcher is wanting from them (i.e. socially desirable responding or demand characteristics; Laws and Mann 2004). Incentives could also negatively impact data quality if children are no longer, or at least less, intrinsically motivated to respond (Collins et al. 2008; Ólafsson et al. 2013). They may complete the study more quickly, and with less consideration, than when receiving no compensation. Further, financial incentives may bias the sample, as those who need the money more may be more likely to participate than those who do not. However, the opposite can also happen – that is, if no compensation is offered, those who need money may choose not to participate, thinking that their time will be better spent in other activities (Laws and Mann 2004). All of these issues, of course, are within the remit of the IRB and are thus linked with our recommendations for finding an internationally agreed set of guidelines.

Possible Solutions: Researchers should send parents an individual letter where the purpose of the study is clearly explained. In addition, positive attitudes of the school principal and the teacher towards the study can help convince parents of the value of the study and the importance of their child's participation. Researchers should also consider the distinction between seeking active versus passive parental consent. With active consent, the researcher explicitly asks parents to return the letter to indicate their approval of their child participating in the study. With passive consent, parents only need to return the letter if they do not consent to their child's participation. Research has shown that participation rates increase dramatically when using the passive consent method (Kristjansson et al. 2013). Finally, regarding children's assent, an alternative to individual compensation is compensation to the school/organization. If using this approach, compensation should be independent of the number of participants, and the researcher should emphasize that participation is completely voluntary, and that participants have the right to withdraw from the study at any time. Cross-cultural study complications may arise when compensation levels are different across countries. Researchers should be very sensitive about establishing compensation equivalence. Non-financial incentives may provide a good solution for many of the previously mentioned issues, particularly in cross-cultural research. Giving a small gift (e.g. a neat pencil or a small toy) can give children the feeling that their participation is highly valued, and they are being thanked for their work. In addition, it can stimulate participation while not being overly coercive. However, children who choose not to participate should be given the same gift to avoid any negative consequences.

Challenge #4: Data Collection Equivalence

To be able to compare data across countries, it is not only important to use rigorous sampling methods, but also to carefully control the data collection process. It is important to have a standardized procedure to collect the data in the different participating countries. A written procedure is indispensable in this case, especially given the necessity of obtaining ethical approval for the study, as it can guarantee that participants across countries included in the study are treated equivalently.

Depending on the modalities of the research, different settings can be used for the study: a home, school, clinic, or online research context. These settings have implications for participant recruitment, and all have both advantages and disadvantages. When recruiting participants, it may be easier to gain access by working with larger institutions (e.g. schools, youth organizations, etc.). The setting in which the study will be conducted can strongly impact the results, and should be equivalent across countries (Buil et al. 2012). Questions to consider include whether participants will take part in the study individually or in a group setting, and the timing of the data collection (e.g. time of day vs. week vs. year). Differences in holiday and exam schedules should be considered when making final decisions in this regard. Further, given that school systems differ across countries, such differences should be taken into account to obtain both data and sample equivalence (as addressed previously). Other important factors include selecting a setting where participants are comfortable (Ólafsson et al. 2013), and one that provides the necessary facilities (e.g. are computers necessary? Are certain media required? Is interaction between research and participant required? How much privacy is required?).

Possible Solution: In all cases, the procedure should be as identical as possible across countries and samples, as differences in research settings can strongly impact research quality. Any discrepancies should be duly noted in the resulting manuscript and/or report.

Challenge #5: Methodological Challenges

Our view is that the methodological challenges for conducting research with children cross-culturally are similar to general methodological challenges researchers face when conducting research with children within a single country, only the difficulties are even more pronounced cross-culturally:

1   Measuring children's attitudes, beliefs, and values can be more difficult than measuring those of adults for a number of reasons. Young children have short attention spans as well as limited reading, writing, and verbal skills, making it difficult to use common methods such as surveys, focus groups, and interviews. Although adolescents have the attention span, reading, writing, and verbal skills to answer survey questions or to sit through an interview, they pose a different challenge entirely – adolescents often have little desire to talk to or to reveal personal information to researchers. Therefore, it can be challenging to track developmental changes across a wide age range. Although documenting developmental trends in behavior and values is important to any field of study, there are few studies that sample a wide age range (e.g. age 3–17), given the difficulty of developing appropriate and engaging measures for use with very young children, tweens, and older teens in a single study. Stimuli selection requires months of pretesting since the interests of children can be so different from those of tweens and teens. Yet, researchers must aim for stimuli equivalences for age-related analyses.

Possible Solution: Although retrospective methodologies show promise for identifying developmental patterns of consumer behavior (Braun-LaTour and LaTour 2004; Connell et al. 2014; Ellis et al. 2010; Richins and Chaplin 2015), these may not be suitable for investigating what is currently happening among 21st-century children, which might require more engaging methods than typical surveys.

There is a shortage of novel and engaging methods to bring out thoughtful responses from a wide age range of youth participants (Chaplin and Connell 2015). Tasks that are fun, engaging, and rely less on reading, writing, and verbal skills (e.g. "drawing what comes to mind when you think of X," building collages, sorting, and reaction time methods) are likely to work well with a wide age range because the researcher can test a wide range of stimuli, and can study thoughts and behaviors of young children and tweens, as well as older teenagers, while minimizing socially desirable responding. Thus, we suggest administering game-like tasks or art projects over traditional rating scales or interviews typically used with adult samples. The downsides of developing and utilizing tasks akin to games or projects – requiring one-on-one interviews with children (see Chaplin and John 2007; Chaplin and Lowrey 2010) – make it difficult to run studies with large sample sizes.

Often, using validated rating scales is preferred and/or is more efficient. When validated rating scales are preferred, we echo Chaplin and Connell's (2015) suggestion to follow Chaplin and John's (2005) sorting method to administer surveys to children, where they printed each survey question on a small card and had children sort the cards into four piles representing the rating scale (e.g. disagree a lot: agree a lot). This way, researchers are able to administer a validated scale in a way that helps keep children attentive, and elicits thoughtful responses.

Although interviews are not ideal for young children who lack developed verbal skills, they do have the benefit of allowing children to describe their attitudes, beliefs, and values in their own words, unprompted. When researchers prefer interviews, we recommend the following (adapted from Chaplin and Connell 2015): (1) Gauge your participants' verbal abilities by first discussing a fun and familiar topic. If they have difficulty discussing this topic (e.g. their birthday or what they like to do with their parents), it is unlikely they will be successful at handling your study interview questions. This initial test will allow you to determine whether you need to study an older age or change your research method entirely; (2) Conduct interviews with young children at locations that are comfortable and familiar to them (e.g. unused classroom at school, camp); (3) Study non-sensitive topics to avoid children feeling embarrassed or judged by an adult; (4) Keep interviews brief and focused (e.g. to measure materialistic values, Chaplin and John (2007) asked: "What makes you happy?"); (5) To arm children with confidence, avoid questions with a right or wrong answer and be clear to children that there are no right or wrong answers; and (6) Finally, ask questions that allow children to feel as if they are teaching the researcher something, rather than being evaluated by an adult. A little encouragement from the experimenter, such as asking: "Really? Why?" or "Really? How?" goes a long way to show you are interested in what children have to teach you, which will encourage them to be more verbal and thoughtful in their responses.

2   These methodological challenges are more evident when recruiting children cross-nationally. Stimuli development for projective measures, such as collages or sorting games, become even more challenging when sampling children who are exposed to different products, brands, and experiences. Furthermore, certain measures may pass research ethics approval in some countries with less stringent guidelines for conducting research with children (e.g. France and Poland) and researchers would be ready to run the study, but when it comes to approval in the US (IRB), it likely would need to go through multiple rounds of full board review before obtaining approval. Ultimately, cross-cultural studies with children will be limited to the methods and research procedures that receive research approval from the US since the approval process is the most rigorous in the US.

Possible Solution: If American children will be recruited, researchers should begin by developing study materials and methods that will be approved by the IRB committee in the US, as it will be the country that determines whether the study can move ahead, given its rigorous Research Approval Process. It is only after the US IRB has given approval that researchers should move forward to collect data in other countries, which likely have less rigorous ethics approval processes. If researchers proceed in the opposite direction (e.g. starting in a country with a lenient approval process, such as France), the necessary methods and procedure equivalences may render any data collected unusable if the US IRB committee does not approve the study materials and/or procedure.

When developing stimuli for more engaging tasks such as collages or sorting games for cross-cultural studies with children, it is important to pretest a range of products, brands, and experiences for familiarity, salience, and interest across cultures. Researchers should interview children to record what sort of things they like and to note any commonalities across cultures. From there, researchers should develop a comprehensive list of stimuli to be used in a cross-national sample.

General Discussion

The relation between children and the commercial world is likely to remain on the global political agenda, particularly as obesity levels rise, costing governments enormous amounts of money in health care, and as concerns about children's use of technology and their levels of materialism continue to grow. It is thus crucial that consumer and marketing researchers work together internationally to ensure a steady stream of relevant and timely evidence to inform policy. Yet, we see too little cross-cultural research on children. This is not because of a lack of need or interest in this demographic, but a function of how difficult it is to develop clean studies for young children, for wide age ranges, across cultures. It is also difficult to get ethics approval, to get schools to participate, to get parental consent, and to get children's assent. This chapter was inspired by an ongoing global study being conducted by a subset of the current authors, as they struggled to overcome the many challenges of studying children's materialism in six countries spanning three continents.

Our chapter has provided a handbook of sorts for those embarking on policy research with children; a list of challenges and solutions. We have discussed five critical challenges to conducting cross-national research with children and offered some recommendations: (1) Differences in the Research Approval Process; (2) Internationally Comparable Sample Frames; (3) Sampling Equivalence; (4) Standardized Data Collection; and (5) Methodological Challenges. Although this chapter does not cover every possible solution for each challenge, we hope that what we have shared, given our experiences in our project, will be of assistance (and encouragement) to others considering conducting public policy research with children and/or in an international setting.

References

Batista-Foguet, J.M., Fortiana, J., Currie, C. & Villalbi, J.R. (2004). Socio-economic Indexes in Surveys for Comparisons Between Countries. *Social Indicators Research, 67* (3), 315–32.

Braun-LaTour, K.A. & LaTour, M.S. (2004). Assessing the Long-term Impact of a Consistent Advertising Campaign on Consumer Memory. *Journal of Advertising, 33* (2), 49–61.

Braun, M. & Uher, R. (2003). The ISSP and its Approach to Background Variables. In J.H. P. Hoffmeyer-Zlotnik & C. Wolf (Eds.), *Advances in Cross-National Comparison. A European Working Book for Demographic and Socio-economic Variables.* New York, NY: Kluwer Academic/Plenum Publishers.

Buil, I., de Chernatony, L. & Martínez, E. (2012). Methodological Issues in Cross-cultural Research: An Overview and Recommendations. *Journal of Targeting, Measurement and Analysis for Marketing, 20* (3), 223–34.

CFBAI (2015). *Children's Food & Beverage Advertising Initiative.* Retrieved from www.bbb.org/council/the-national-partner-program/national-advertising-review-services/childrens-food-and-beverage-advertising-initiative/.

Chaplin, L.N. & Connell, P.M. (2015). Developmental Consumer Psychology. In M.I. Norton, D.D. Rucker, and C. Lamberton (Eds.), *The Cambridge Handbook of Consumer Psychology*. Cambridge: Cambridge University Press.

Chaplin, L.N. & Lowrey, T.M. (2010). The Development of Consumer-based Consumption Constellations in Children. *Journal of Consumer Research, 36* (5), 757–77.

Chaplin, L.N. & John, D.R. (2005). The Development of Self-brand Connections in Children and Adolescents. *Journal of Consumer Research, 32* (1), 119–29.

Chaplin, L.N. & John, D.R. (2007). Growing up in a Material World: Age Differences in Materialism in Children and Adolescents. *Journal of Consumer Research, 34* (4), 480–93.

CITI (2015). *Informed Consent*. Retrieved from www.citiprogram.org/members/index.cfm?pageID=665&ce=1.

Clark, T. (1990). International Marketing and National Character: A review and Proposal for an Integrative Theory. *The Journal of Marketing, 54* (4), 66–79.

Collins, A., Bronte-Tinkew, J. & Burkhauser, M. (2008). *Using Incentives to Increase Participation in Out-of-school Time Programs*. Washington, DC: Child Trends.

Connell, P.M., Brucks, M. & Nielsen, J.H. (2014). How Childhood Advertising Exposure can Create Biased Product Evaluations that Persist into Adulthood. *Journal of Consumer Research, 41* (1), 119–34.

Ellis, A.W., Holmes, S.J. & Wright, R.L. (2010). Age of Acquisition and the Recognition of Brand Names: On the Importance of Being Early. *Journal of Consumer Psychology, 20* (1), 43–52.

Engelen, A. & Brettel, M. (2011). Assessing Cross-cultural Marketing Theory and Research: Reply to Craig and Douglas' Commentary. *Journal of Business Research, 64*, 782–784.

EU Pledge (2015). Retrieved from www.eu-pledge.eu/.

Hicks, L. (2015). *Research with Children – SBE*. Retrieved from www.citiprogram.org/members/index.cfm?pageID=665&ce=1.

Kolsrud, K. & Skjåk, K.K. (2005). Harmonising Background Variables in the European Social Survey. In J.H. Hoffmeyer-Zlotnik and J.A. Harkness (Eds.) *Methodological Aspects in Cross-National Research*. Mahwan, NJ: Lawrence Erlbaum Associate.

Kristjansson, A.L., Sigfusson, J., Sigfusdottir, I.D. & Allegrante, J.P. (2013). Data Collection Procedures for School-based Surveys among Adolescents: The Youth in Europe Study. *Journal of School Health, 83* (9), 662–67.

Laws, S. & Mann, G. (2004). *So You Want to Involve Children in Research?: A Toolkit Supporting Children's Meaningful and Ethical Participation in Research Relating to Violence Against Children*, Save the Children Sweden Retrieved from http://images.savethechildren.it/f/download/Policies/st/strumenti.pdf.

Luna, D. & Gupta, S.F. (2001) An Integrative Framework for Cross-cultural Consumer Behavior. *International Marketing Review*, 18 (1), 45–69.

McIntosh, N. (2000). Guidelines for the ethical conduct of medical research involving children. *Archives of Diseases of Childhood, 82*, 177–82.

Markham, A. & Buchanan, E. (2012). *Final Draft: Ethical Decision-making and Internet Research: Recommendations from the AOIR Ethics Committee*. Retrieved from http://aoir.org/reports/ethics2.pdf.

Moore, E.S. (2007). Perspectives on Food Marketing and Childhood Obesity. *Journal of Public Policy & Marketing, 26* (2), 157–61.

Morrow, V. & Richards, M. (1996). The Ethics of Social Research with Children: An Overview. *Children & Society, 10* (2), 90–105.

Mueller, C.W. & Parcel, T.L. (1981). Measures of Socioeconomic Status: Alternatives and Recommendations. *Child Development, 52* (1), 13–30.

Nairn, A. & Clarke, B. (2012). Researching Children: Are We Getting It Right, *International Journal of Market Research, 54* (2), 177–98.

Nairn, A., & Hang, H. (2012). *Advergames: Its Not Childs Play: A Review of Research*. London: Family & Parenting Institute.

Nairn, A. & Mayo, E. (2009). *Consumer Kids*. London: Constable Robinson.

OECD (2015). Better Life Index. Retrieved from www.oecdbetterlifeindex.org.

Ólafsson, K., Livingstone, S. & Haddon, L. (2013). *How to Research Children and Online Technologies?: Frequently Asked Questions and Best Practice*. London: EU Kids Online, LSE.

Panic, K., Cauberghe, V. & De Pelsmacker, P. (2013). Comparing TV Ads and Advergames Targeting Children: The Impact of Persuasion Knowledge on Behavioral Responses. *Journal of Advertising, 42* (2–3), 264–73.

Powell, M.A. & Smith, A.B. (2009). Children's Participation Rights in Research, *Childhood, 16* (1), 124–42.

Prout, A. (2005). *The Future of Childhood*. London: Routledge-Falmer.

Richins, M.L. & Chaplin, L.N. (2015). Material Parenting: How the Use of Goods in Parenting Fosters Materialism in the Next Generation. *Journal of Consumer Research, 41* (6), 1333–57.

Schwartz, S.H. & Ros, M. (1995). Value Priorities in West European Nations: A Cross-Cultural Perspective. *World Psychology, 1*, 99–122.

Singh, N., Kwon, I-K. & Pereira, A. (2003). Cross-cultural Consumer Socialization: An Exploratory Study of Socialization Influences Across Three Ethnic Groups. *Psychology & Marketing, 20* (10), 867–81.

Treiman, D.J. (1977). *Occupational Prestige in Comparative Perspective*. New York, NY: Academic Press.

Trompenaars, F. & Hampden-Turner, C. (2004). *Managing People Across Cultures*. Chichester: Capstone.

Tsaliki, L. & Chronaki, D. (2013). Introduction to Ethical Aspects in Researching Children and Their Internet Use. In M. Barbovschi, L. Green, and S. Vandoninck (Eds.) *Innovative Approaches for Investigating How Children Understand Risk in New Media. Dealing with Methodological and Ethical Challenges*. London: EU Kids Online, London School of Economics and Political Science.

United Nations (2014). *Report of the Special Rapporteur in the Field of Cultural Rights*. Sixty-ninth session Item 69 (b) of the provisional agenda. Retrieved from www.ohchr.org/EN/Issues/CulturalRights/Pages/impactofadvertisingandmarketing.aspx.

UNCRC (1990). *Convention on the Rights of the Child*. Retrieved from www.ohchr.org/en/professionalinterest/pages/crc.aspx.

WHO (2010). *Set of Recommendations on the Marketing of Foods and Non-alcoholic Beverages to Children*. Retrieved from http://whqlibdoc.who.int/publications/2007/9789241595247_eng.pdf.

WVS (2015). *World Value Survey 1981–2015 Official Aggregate WVS*. World Value Survey Association.

PART XII

Groups/Social Media

23

SOCIAL MEDIA

Ashlee Humphreys

MEDILL SCHOOL OF JOURNALISM, MEDIA, AND INTEGRATED
MARKETING COMMUNICATION, NORTHWESTERN UNIVERSITY,
EVANSTON, IL, USA

Introduction

What is social media? Twenty years ago, the term did not exist. Emerging only around 2006 to describe social networking platforms such as Facebook and Twitter, social media has come to encompass the growing number of ways that people communicate—with each other and occasionally with companies—in a mediated environment. Yet, when we look back we also find a legacy of research about phenomena that we would now call social media. Social media is "a set of practices for communicating, usually collaboratively, and usually so that it is visible to more than one person" (Humphreys 2016, p. 7). As a set of practices, social media lies between forms of mass media communication such as television, radio, and film and inter-personal forms of communication such as the telephone or a face-to-face conversation (Humphreys 2016; Webster 2014). Although these practices have become more common as digital communication platforms have emerged, we can trace the origins of social media to letters to the editor, radio call-in shows, and by-mail fan clubs, all ways in which consumers communicated collaboratively through previous forms of media.

This chapter first outlines the conceptual foundations of social media and then provides an overview of consumer behavior pertaining to social media, exploring how social media informs studies of the self, social influence, and consumer communities.

The Conceptual Foundations of Social Media as a Mode of "Communications"

Social media has some traits associated with interpersonal communication, yet it also shares other traits with mass communication. Direct discussions like one has on the telephone or face to face can now be potentially observed by millions of people—and those people can contribute to, circulate, or reframe the message. Large organizations like companies can now talk directly to consumers, and consumers can talk back, sharing complaints, innovating on existing products and services, and sharing experiences with others.

Social media usually, although not necessarily, involves the use of digital technology to facilitate this kind of public or semi-public communication (see also Miller 2013). We can see social media in previous genres such as radio call-in shows, letters to the editor, by-mail fantasy baseball leagues, and fan clubs. Yet digital technology has also changed the pace, cost, and prevalence of these media practices. The conceptual foundations of social media stem primarily from Communications (e.g. Baym 2015). However, scholars in consumer research have long studied the ways in which social media relates to communities, social influence, and the self. And while consumer behavior research on digital technology preceded the term social media (e.g. Giesler 2006; Kozinets 2002; Muñiz Jr and Schau 2005; Schau and Gilly 2003), it has integrated this term into what is a thriving and theoretical area of inquiry.

Communication Model

Relative to previous forms of media, social media have three key properties. First, in social media information flows are bi-directional in the sense that the "audience" receives messages, but it also produces them. Users are active rather than passive in producing content (Jenkins 2004, 2006; Jenkins et al. 2013), and this implies, consequently, that value can be created through these networks of collaborative communication (Benkler 2006).

Secondly, audiences are more narrowly targeted in social media than in traditional media. When messages are produced and sent, they can be and usually are targeted at a very particular audience. For example, when crafting a Facebook message, the intended audience, or public, is bounded by your network of friends or connections. This means that one's audience size will vary with one's social capital; a celebrity like Taylor Swift has a much larger audience than a typical consumer. Yet consumers can themselves vary in the size of their audience, and the possibility exists for their messages to spread quickly and broadly through the media system (see Jenkins et al. 2013 for a discussion of diffusion). Likewise, when companies target ads on social media, they are able to purchase online ad space based on a very narrow set of criteria such as having previously visited a certain site or being in a very small demographic group rather than the broader niches that characterize advertising sales of broadcast or even cable television.

Thirdly, users potentially have more control or ownership over the means of communication (Benkler 2006; Jenkins 2004). In traditional media, large organizations like the *New York Times* or *Time Magazine* have had a strong influence in agenda setting and framing issues of the day (McCombs and Shaw 1972). Although these organizations are still influential (Meraz 2009), new social media networks and practices mean that it is now possible for frames and issues to arise from the "bottom-up," grabbing national attention and translation in the mainstream press (Meraz 2009; Weber and Monge 2011). For example, #blacklivesmatter, "we are the 99%," and #yesallwomen are frames that emerged from social media. Social issues like ALS, Kony 2012, and #bringbackourgirls can also leap onto the national agenda through this same "viral" or bottom-up process. Some argue that the decreasing costs of the material technology for creating and transmitting media such as videos, songs, and text has led to a "democratization" of media more generally (Jenkins 2004; Sunstein 2006). However, others contend that traditional modes of power like state power (Tufekci and Wilson 2012), digital literacy (Hargittai 2008; Hargittai and Hinnant 2008), and cultural and social capital (Selwyn 2004) play a critical role in the degree to which technology can have a democratizing influence. Further, social media platforms like Facebook and Twitter own the data circulated on them in the sense that they can control what is posted and can resell it to advertisers and others.

While the traditional mass communication model is linear, primarily one-directional, and involves two parties (Figure 23.1a), social media is more often conceptualized as a network (Figure 23.1b). Consequently, marketing and consumer behavior scholars studying digital media have shifted focus from a model of mass media of communication where digital networks are

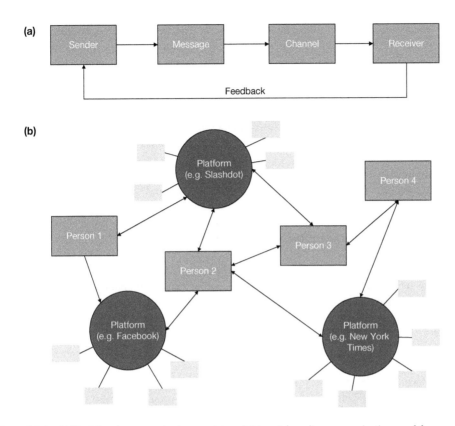

Figure 23.1   (a) Traditional communication model, and (b) social media communication model

conceptualized as another channel of company-to-consumer communication (e.g. Hoffman and Novak 1996) to a networked model that sees communication as triadic or rhizomal—from consumer to consumer, and sometimes consumer-to-company (e.g. Arvidsson and Caliandro 2016; Giesler 2006). This means that when studying social influence, for example, a network of peers has come to supplant two-step flow models that preceded them. Nonetheless, opinion leaders, or those with social and cultural capital, remain critical in studies of social influence (Arsel and Bean 2013; McQuarrie et al. 2013), as they are nodes in the network with many ties and significant cultural influence.

Aspects and Affordances of Social Media

Although we can categorize a group of practices, tools, and platforms as having commonalities that we label social media, different genres of social media have different attributes that give them different affordances. Affordances are aspects of a particular social media platform that enable some behaviors and constrain others (Gibson 1977). For example, Twitter has the affordance of sending messages that are a maximum of 140 characters. This enables tweets to be used for quick dispatches in times of crisis (Jin et al. 2014; Mendoza et al. 2010), but constrains them from being used to express an elaborate argument or narrative (for that, perhaps a blog post has better affordances). Some social networking sites like Match.com have affordances for making new connections, while others, like Facebook, have affordances for maintaining social connections (Piskorski 2014).

To systematically study affordances, researchers have outlined six attributes of social media: social presence, temporal structure (synchronic or asynchronic), media richness, permanence, replicability, and mobility (Baym 2010). Genres of social media vary on these attributes. For example, Skype group video chat can be rich in social presence and media richness, but low in permanence. A blog is likely low in richness, but high in permanence. The differences in these types of modality potentially influence word of mouth communication and other aspects of consumer use. For example, Berger and Iyengar (2013) find that the asynchronicity of writing produces more interesting content than a synchronous mode like spoken communication.

Yet the attributes and affordances of social media can change over time. Consumers innovate, changing the tools to meet their needs and goals, and sometimes these innovations are integrated with the product. For example, although Twitter began as a micro-blogging platform to share personal updates, user practices of circulating news via Twitter have changed the platform over time as features aligned with these practices (e.g. "Moments") have been incorporated.

Other times, product attributes are introduced that shape consumer use. For example, Facebook adopted its newsfeed feature amidst protest, but it is now a taken for granted—and much used—part of the platform. For example, the affordance of tweeting "what's happening" right now, as the platform requests, orients the messages toward immediacy and often self-related content.

Social Media and Consumer Behavior

To consider the role of social media in consumer behavior, one may want to think for a moment about media's influence on consumer behavior more generally. The study of the relationship between the media and consumer behavior goes back to at least Adorno and Horkheimer's theory of mass culture (Adorno and Horkheimer 1955/1997) in which they argued that media such as movies, advertisements, and television stoke consumer desire and manipulate naïve consumers into purchasing products they do not need. Although this line of social critique is still an important and thriving tradition (Fuchs 2013), more recent perspectives have studied media as something consumers use and, in many cases, control (Fiske 1989/2010; Jenkins 2004) and have looked at media itself as a product of consumption (e.g. Parmentier and Fischer 2015). How and when media shapes consumer behavior in general is largely still an open question (Humphreys 2010; Humphreys and Latour 2013; Humphreys and Thompson 2014; Zhao and Belk 2008). While initial perspectives on social media veered toward the utopian, the incorporation of social media into business models and hot button issues like trolling and fake news have prompted scholars to be less sanguine.

Nonetheless, the emergence of social media has increased investigation of the mediated lives of consumers. The study of social media in consumer behavior research has been based on strong prior theoretical concepts such as community, self, and social influence, and over time, this work has been integrated with these foundational topics.

Online/Offline Communities

Communities share three traits: consciousness of kind, rituals and traditions, and a sense of moral obligations (Durkheim 1912/2008; Muñiz and O'Guinn 2001). Consumer research has investigated online communities as groups of consumers who share these traits, often using the tool of netnography (Kozinets 2002). Research on virtual communities (Rheingold 1993) has found that online groupings can indeed share properties of more traditional, offline communities. Muñiz Jr. and Schau (2005), for instance, find that the online community is bound together by tales of persecution and survival that shape their collective identity. In the Harry Potter Alliance, an online site devoted to Harry Potter fan fiction, Jenkins (2015) observes shared rituals and traditions of the House Cup competition and "sorting" rituals that create and maintain social bonds. In a study of a peer-to-peer sharing community, Mathwick et al. (2008) find that moral obligations indeed motivate participation for users with high experience and social capital. Thomas, Price, and Schau (2013) note that consciousness of kind can be challenged by heterogeneity of the group—which is expressed via the formation of different online groups. In their study of online and offline running communities, they find that sharing economic and social resources continue to bind the group together. Parmentier and Fischer (2015) further find that dynamics in the group such as reframing, remixing, and rejection result in the dissolution of online communities altogether.

Status and social roles in these online communities have been other important topics of research. Status can be built from: subcultural capital (Thornton 1996; Williams 2006) in the form of extensive product expertise, knowledge of group norms, rituals, and codes; from social capital in the form of extensive connections in the group; or from longevity in membership, which is positively correlated with these two types of capital (Mathwick et al. 2008). Hierarchies develop and can be signaled formally through textual or symbolic markers or informally through language and tacit knowledge. Social roles in communities include lurkers (Nonnecke and Preece 2000), information seekers, gatekeepers, and trolls (Phillips 2015).

Information seekers bring information from outside of the community to the group (c.f. Jenkins 2006), while gatekeepers like moderators decide who is authorized to speak and enforce rules and norms of discourse. Trolling usually refers to "disruptive or otherwise annoying speech and behavior online," (Phillips 2013), and while some have argued that these practices constitute social vandalism, others have made finer distinctions between cyber-bullying and trolling aimed at critique or fun (Coleman 2014; Phillips 2015). Finally, lurkers are those who do not interact with the community, but merely read or watch without engaging in open discussion. Across studies the estimated percentage of lurkers in online communities ranges from 80 to 90%, although it can vary dramatically by group (Bagozzi and Dholakia 2002; Mathwick et al. 2008; Nonnecke and Preece 2000).

Online communities come in a variety of forms. Communities of practice, for instance, are groups that share a common task or goal, and will often co-create content (Wenger 2000). Audience communities gather around a particular media product such as a film, television show, or band. Subcultures can form taste communities that innovate new fashion practices (Dolbec and Fischer 2015) and reinforce taste regimes (Arsel and Bean 2013). Sometimes these groupings constitute market subgroups that take on a social movement ethos to fight for under-represented needs in the market (Scaraboto and Fischer 2013). In therapeutic communities consumers use information technology such as message boards and virtual reality games to cope with the trauma of personal illness, to find social support for physical and mental health, and to seek information from others (Eysenbach et al. 2004; Tian et al. 2014). In contrast to mass media, in which journalists, doctors, and academics are perceived as elite, social media enables sufferers to feel understood and cared for (Tian et al. 2014).

Publics

Publics are different from communities in that they are based on a shared focus rather than interpersonal connections, are structured by affect rather than discussion and deliberation, and are driven by a logic of visibility and publicity rather than identity (Arvidsson and Caliandro 2016;

de Tarde 1898; Warner 2002). They are "organized media space kept together by continuity of practices of mediation," (Arvidsson and Caliandro 2016). For example, when users tweet about a product like Dom Perignon, it is not to interact extensively with others or to discuss anything of great substance in the content of their message (Rokka 2015). Rather, the point of tweeting a picture of Dom Perignon with a hashtag like #goodlife is to express affiliation with the brand that is affective or phatic rather than discursive (here also see the role of phatic communication: Marwick and Boyd 2011; Miller 2008; Papacharissi 2015; Papacharissi and de Fatima Oliveira 2012). When taken together, the appearance and linking of these words help form a public that is not focused on a particular identity, but rather bring together the many contexts of use. Through play and performance people express private, sometimes strongly held emotion, bringing these thoughts to public visibility. When these outpourings are negative and cascading, they are often called firestorms (Pfeffer et al. 2014). With publics, communal bonds do not form, but rather a searchable database of discourse emerges through the use of hashtags. Note here how the hashtag affordance of a feed like Twitter creates a public whereas an affordance of a message board like a thread may instead facilitate community (Baym 2010).

Networks

Consumer discourse online can also be understood using the model of a social network (Monge and Contractor 2003). As Figueiredo and Scaraboto (2016) show, networked communication can occur without the attendant communal bonds that come with online community. Rather, a network can facilitate information sharing and other goal-directed communication with other consumers that produces value. The perspective of "networked individualism" offered by Wellman and Rainie (2012) is the perspective that social capital can lie dormant, only become active when needed by an individual. For example, when one becomes sick, needs a job, or solicits advice online, one is often met with a cascade of well wishes, leads, or responses. Networked individualism claims that rather than being socially isolated, as some have claimed (Putnam 1995), we are surrounded by social ties that can be activated for support.

Social capital (Bourdieu 2011) is an important topic in the study of networks in social media. There are two kinds of social capital commonly studied in social media: strong and weak ties. Strong ties are those that provide close social support, and weak ties are based on less frequent and less intimate connections (Granovetter 1973). As the classic research in the area shows, weak ties can have significant value because they bring us new information that is not held by others who constitute our stronger ties (Granovetter 1973). Studies of social capital in social media have found that social media is used to build both strong and weak ties (Ellison et al. 2007; Steinfield et al. 2008). For example, Ellison et al. (2007) find that college students who maintained high school connections using Facebook had higher self-esteem, and this effect carried over at least a year (Steinfield et al. 2008). Facebook use was particularly effective for students with lower self-esteem in maintaining weak ties. Social capital also means that nodes—people or organizations—can have different types of influence in a network. Hubs, those with many connections, play a pivotal role in distributing information while bridges fill structural holes in the network. Without these kinds of bridges, information would not travel between clusters in the network (Burt 2001).

Co-Creation

The interaction and collaboration of consumers within communities or networks can sometimes create value (Figueiredo and Scaraboto 2016; Schau, Muñiz Jr, and Arnould 2009).

Co-creation describes "situations in which consumers collaborate with companies or with other consumers to produce things of value," (Humphreys and Grayson 2008). Co-creation has been observed in industries ranging from computers to consumer package goods (Prahalad and Ramaswamy 2004; Schau et al. 2009). As Schau et al. (2009) show, practices such as badging, where users provide tokens of experience, and customizing, where users modify existing products, increase value for consumers beyond what the firm directly offers.

User-generated content is a type of co-creation, usually when media content such as advertising, text, or other media product is produced rather than a material product or thing. For example, Muñiz Jr. and Schau (2005) observe that consumer groups devoted to Firefox, Jones Soda, and Apple Newton who create advertising become part of evangelical efforts to spread brand messages. Social media platforms, in fact, are almost entirely constituted by user-generated content. Although co-creation can produce objects and content of value, the equity of how this value is allocated between consumers and companies has been a topic of intense debate (Cova, Dalli, and Zwick 2011; Humphreys and Grayson 2008).

One well known example of co-creation in online communities is the Linux communities of the early 1990s (Hemetsberger and Reinhardt 2009). Working mostly through message boards and other early forms of social media, users created an open-source operating system and related components to compete with commercially produced products such as Windows. Groups co-create not only software, which can be shared virtually, but also physical tools. For example, the Apple Newton community, a group devoted to one of the first, now discontinued personal digital assistants, created code, and a user support group that continued long after the devices were supported by Apple. Likewise, the mini-moto community, enthusiasts for adapting miniature motorcycles to adult bodies, worked together to create an online and offline market for parts and supplies to modify bikes, largely outside the scope of major companies like Honda (Martin and Schouten 2014).

The Self

Social media has also had an impact on how we view individual consumer behavior. People use social media for a variety of reasons: to create and maintain social ties, to learn new things, for self-expression, or any other number of uses as various as consumer goals (Bonds-Raacke and Raacke 2010). The emergence of digital technology has many complex implications for the way we define and represent ourselves (Belk 2013). Concepts of ideal and actual self, social comparison, and performativity all have a place in the study of social media. The self— the illusory core of who we perceive ourselves to be—is represented in our physical possessions (Belk 1988), but also online in digital objects such as photographs, playlists, and comments (Belk 2013; Boyle and Johnson 2010; Dobson 2008; Drenten 2012; Ellison, Heino, and Gibbs 2006; Papacharissi 2011, 2012). Yet people are more likely to share positive information about the self online, and quite clearly curate a public self through their personal pages (Barasch and Berger 2014; Ellison et al. 2006; Hogan 2010; Schau and Gilly 2003).

Performance of the Self

The selfie is one common example of self-presentation, commonly of an idealized self. A selfie is a self-portrait taken with a digital camera or webcam, usually by oneself and usually close up, and has been a focus of study as a type of performance (Iqani and Schroeder 2016; Kedzior et al. 2015). Through selfies, consumers can play with self performance and share experiences. The performance of gender, for example has been one area of selfie study

(Marwick 2013a; Murray 2015). For example, a study of profile photos on Facebook finds that men tend to portray themselves as dominant and agentic while women emphasize traits of dependence and attractiveness (Rose et al. 2012).

Consumers quite literally create a self-image when they create an avatar—a digital recreation of a physical body—but this also extends to the ways in which we curate self by selecting a profile picture, including certain quotations, interests, and preferences on a profile page. Early research indicated that people selected avatars (Denegri–Knott and Molesworth 2010; Turkle 1995/2011)—and maintained several of them—in order to experiment with different identities, playing at what Lisa Nakamura calls "identity tourism," (Nakamura 2002/2013). Men can be women online; women can be men (although as Herring and Stoerger 2013 find, linguistic cues will often betray the performance). However, much of this identity play has declined as affordances of mainstream social networking sites shape practices toward expressing identities more tied to offline personas (Herring 2004; Marwick 2005). Some have suggested that this trend is due in part to the commercial practices of selling advertising to users in measurable, recognizable demographics, which require offline identities (Fuchs 2012).

More mundanely, people can maintain multiple social roles online (Marwick 2005; Marwick and Boyd 2011). One might be a professional self on LinkedIn, a family self on Facebook, and a fun or playful self on Snapchat. Yet digital space does not prevent these identities from crossing as different audiences mix in digital space, a phenomena Marwick and Boyd (2011) call "context collapse." Digital selves, once created, can even outlive their creator and must be dealt with by surviving friends and family (Marwick and Ellison 2012).

Co-Creation of Self

Digital selves are not created alone, but rather are co-constructed with feedback from others (Drenten 2012; Ito et al. 2008; Papacharissi 2011). For example, young girls will often post pictures of themselves wearing new outfits and trying on new poses and adjust performances according to the social feedback received (e.g. Livingstone 2008), and reciprocation in these comments is often expected (boyd 2014). Here, symbolic interactionism, the idea that we form a sense of self through interaction with the social world, has been used to understand this co-construction process.

Social connections are another way to signify the self. As Donath and Boyd argue (2004), they "warrant" trust by demonstrating to others that you are trusted by others. Social connections online provide evidence for trust by communicating to others who we are through our relationships with others (Donath and Boyd 2004). Likewise, messages, which are visible to an audience beyond the sender and receiver, may be exchanged for their phatic function to maintain and display social ties, not to convey semantic content (Marwick and Boyd 2011).

The Positive and Negative Effects of Social Media on the Self

How does social media use affect self-esteem? Findings on the relationship between social media use and self-esteem are mixed. At least two studies find that social media use is associated with decreases in self-esteem, and explain this using social comparison (Kross et al. 2013; Zuo 2014). That is, as we know, people perform ideal selves online which creates a false standard of comparison. Other studies have found that social media use increases self-esteem (Wilcox and Stephen 2013), particularly when people focus on the social media content of strong ties.

Communication scholars have pointed out the role of affordances reinforcing self-related goals such as achievement. As Marwick (2013b) argues, many tools like Facebook were created by people who value status, and she further shows how cultural or subcultural values such as achievement can be encoded into the affordances of tools we use, and thus come to structure consumer practices.

Research has also investigated the more pernicious effects of social media use. While it may increase self-esteem in some contexts, it can also lead to a decrease in self-control (Wilcox and Stephen 2013). And although it can be a virtual space of escapism and relaxation particularly for those who have trouble forming offline relationships (Turkle 1995/2011), it can also be addictive and used to express aggression (Song et al. 2004; Suler 2004a; Wan and Chiou 2006).

Anonymity, the absence of identity cues, and pseudonymity, the separation between online and offline identity, have both been found to affect online behavior in systematic ways. Anonymity or pseudonymity can lead to depersonalization of others and disinhibition of the self (Lapidot-Lefler and Barak 2012; Suler 2004b), which can, in turn, lead to aggression. In the absence of interpersonal cues such as eye-contact and physical proximity, individuals who are anonymous and who interact with others who are relatively anonymous behave more aggressively (Lapidot-Lefler and Barak 2012). Anti-social behavior online such as cyber-bullying or trolling has been attributed to some of these effects of mediation.

Yet the lack of identity cues can also increase self-disclosure. People disclose personal thoughts and feelings more quickly online due to the removal of other interpersonal cues (Qian and Scott 2007; Tidwell and Walther 2002). Social media is often a space where people feel they can be their "true selves," and seek social support amongst like-minded others. For example, young gay men and women report that communities such as Planet Out, and Gay.com played an important role in their coming out (Gray 2009).

Social Influence and Word of Mouth

Social influence is an enduring area of research in both communications and consumer behavior (Dahl 2013; Katz and Lazarsfeld 1970). Traditionally, social influence in consumer behavior has been conceptualized as "word of mouth" communication, Reviews, ratings, ratings of ratings, and comments all constitute a social shopping system (Stephen and Toubia 2010) that may move well beyond what we traditionally think of as word of mouth (Lamberton and Stephen 2016). The shift from studying offline word of mouth to online word of mouth prompts reconsideration of several central aspects. The effects of anonymity, the multiplicity of different sources, and quantification of recommendations in terms of valence, volume, and velocity emerge when word of mouth is considered in the digital context.

Antecedents. There are many potential motives for sharing online word of mouth. Self-enhancement—the self-esteem that comes from being thought to be an expert or knowledgeable friend—is one common motive (Angelis et al. 2012; Hennig-Thurau et al. 2004). Perhaps for this reason, consumers tend to share things that are more interesting (Berger and Milkman 2012; Berger and Schwartz 2011). Issues of self-presentation and self-image mentioned previously play a role in motivations for producing word of mouth communication as well. When broadcasting to many others, versus one person, people will avoid sharing information that makes them look bad (Barasch and Berger 2014). Further, self-enhancement, or "boasting," in online word of mouth has effects on the persuasiveness of the message. When trust is low, boasting can increase vigilance in the receiver of word of mouth communication; however, when trust is high boasting has the opposite effect, increasing the receiver's confidence in the source due to perceptions of expertise (Packard et al. 2016).

Consequences. Social media produces about 3.3 billion brand impressions every day (Keller and Libai 2009). It can affect sales (Babić Rosario et al. 2016; Chevalier and Mayzlin 2006; Chintagunta, Gopinath, and Venkataraman 2010; Floyd et al. 2014; Godes and Mayzlin 2004; Luca 2011; Moe and Trusov 2011) and stock price (Moe and Schweidel, 2012; Tirunillai and Tellis, 2012). Word of mouth is more influential than mass media messages, and consumers trust reviews from other customers more than advertising. Scholars find that this is because consumers perceive the source to be more like themselves and they trust an individual with little apparent self-interest (Brown and Reingen 1987; Money, Gilly, and Graham 1998). Non-anonymous reviews are more influential than anonymous ones (Forman, Ghose, and Wiesenfeld 2008). Despite the influence of online word of mouth, ratings do not predict product quality, as represented by Consumer Report rating or resale price (De Langhe, Fernbach, and Lichtenstein 2015). Instead, online word of mouth is influenced by experience, which can be highly heterogeneous, by price, and by brand image (De Langhe et al. 2015). Nonetheless, reviews may capture aspects of products that are important to users, but not technical experts (Simonson 2016; Winer and Fader 2016).

Properties. Most scholars see online word of mouth as being defined by valence, variance, and volume (Dellarocas, Gao, and Narayan 2010). Valence and volume have the strongest effect on purchase (Chevalier and Mayzlin 2006), but variance can also be influential when products are complex or when consumers believe that tastes on the product can widely vary. In terms of valence, reviews will tend to become more negative over time (Godes and Mayzlin 2004; Moe and Trusov 2011), and complaints will often be structured by identity, injustice, and agency frames (Ward and Ostrom 2006). One study of complaint websites found that consumer complaints were structured like civic protests—along lines of unfairness and asserting certain "rights" as consumers (Ward and Ostrom 2006).

More broadly, social media provide a way for consumers to share experiences—trips and meals over Instagram, family and friend gatherings over Facebook, and fleeting funny occurrences over Snapchat. Seen this way, social media is simply a set of practices that are a part of consumers' daily lives and not necessarily strategic attempts at self-presentation, self-aggrandizement, or statement-making.

The Social Media Future

Embeddedness

As social media becomes more embedded in consumers lives, it presents a distinct set of new phenomena for study. Social media makes possible the quantification and sharing performance on tasks like running. However, research shows that this may ultimately decrease the enjoyment of such activities (Etkin 2016). Augmented reality games like *Pokemon Go* change the way consumers experience the physical world and present companies with new opportunities for engagement (Scholz and Smith 2016). Augmented consumer life has opened several new areas of study. For instance, instantly accessible information such as calorie counts or product information may change aspects of the decision process. The ability to instantly produce and share product information may change market power. The ease of participating in political and social causes online might increase awareness, but results of how this actually affects political action are complex

(Earl and Kimport 2011). For instance, one study of slacktivism (Rotman et al. 2011) shows that token participation in a cause on social media dampens offline volunteering, but only if the token participation is public. If made privately, these forms of token participation lead to volunteering, likely to provide a social impression they were not able to achieve by signaling support online.

Platforms and Privacy

The other emerging area of interest involves the capacity of social media to connect buyers and sellers in new ways, thus creating new kinds of markets. Uber, Airbnb, and Taskrabbit provide platforms that coordinate service providers (e.g. drivers) with consumers (e.g. riders). Yet they do so without the attendant institutional assurance that legal corporations provide. Mechanisms for signaling trust, insuring against risk, and coordinating consumption all merit investigation. Sharing both material (Botsman and Rogers 2010; Ozanne and Ballantine 2010) and virtual (Belk 2013) objects through social media platforms is another burgeoning area of interest with similar issues of trust, equality, heterogeneity, and distribution being key areas of investigation. Although technological innovations have enabled us to coordinate quickly and easily, social and cultural barriers are not as easily reconciled in sharing systems. Yet some speculate that sharing resources can help mitigate issues like consumer waste (Ozanne and Ballantine 2010).

Lastly, how consumers respond to having their behavior measured and tracked by either a company or other consumers are future areas of interest. Humans have long lived in communities where their personal information was limited to close acquaintances and was relatively impermanent. Now, however, most of us grow up in a sea of documentation in the form of photographs, records, and archived communication. We can set our phones so that friends and family can track where we are at any moment. We are able to maintain social ties with people we knew when we were five long into adulthood. How will this affect our conception of self and our social relationships? How will the ability of others to track us change our relationship with our friends and family and shape the nature of our commercial interactions? While some studies show that consumers are willing to trade off their personal information for service or customization, the long-terms effects of these attitudes could change depending on data security and shifting norms of surveillance. Research has shown that although people do try to erect social boundaries around different parts of their digital identities, these can be undermined, both intentionally and unintentionally (boyd 2014). How will we continue to swim in this sea of socially mediated communication?

Conclusion

In sum, consumer lives and practices are increasingly mediated by digital technology. This embeddedness has prompted adapting enduring areas of study in communities, self, and social influence to account for these new realities. These shifts have also brought together phenomena and new areas of consumer behavior research such as brand publics (Arvidsson and Caliandro 2016), the role of documentation and quantification in experience (Diehl et al. 2016; Etkin 2016), and the investigation of how platforms structure markets. Importantly, we see how the conceptual and methodological tools for studying consumer life are readily adaptable to understand consumers in this brave new mediated world.

References

Adorno, Theodor W and Max Horkheimer (1955/1997), *Dialectic of Enlightenment*, Vol. 15. Verso.

Angelis, Matteo De, Andrea Bonezzi, Alessandro M Peluso, Derek D Rucker, and Michele Costabile (2012), "On Braggarts and Gossips: A Self-Enhancement Account of Word-of-Mouth Generation and Transmission," *Journal of Marketing Research*, 49 (4), 551–63.

Arsel, Zeynep and Jonathan Bean (2013), "Taste Regimes and Market-Mediated Practice," *Journal of Consumer Research*, 39 (5), 899–917.

Arvidsson, Adam and Alessandro Caliandro (2016), "Brand Public," *Journal of Consumer Research*, 42 (5), 727–48.

Babić Rosario, Ana, Francesca Sotgiu, Kristine De Valck, and Tammo HA Bijmolt (2016), "The Effect of Electronic Word of Mouth on Sales: A Meta-Analytic Review of Platform, Product, and Metric Factors," *Journal of Marketing Research*, 53 (3), 297–318.

Bagozzi, Richard P and Utpal M Dholakia (2002), "Intentional Social Action in Virtual Communities," *Journal of Interactive Marketing*, 16 (2), 2–21.

Barasch, Alixandra and Jonah Berger (2014), "Broadcasting and Narrowcasting: How Audience Size Affects What People Share," *Journal of Marketing Research*, 51 (3), 286–99.

Baym, Nancy K (2010), *Personal Connections in the Digital Age*. Cambridge, UK; Malden, MA: Polity.

Baym, Nancy K (2015), *Personal Connections in the Digital Age*. Hoboken, NJ: John Wiley & Sons.

Belk, Russell (1988), "Possessions and the Extended Self," *Journal of Consumer Research*, 15 (2), 139–68.

Belk, Russell W (2013), "Extended Self in a Digital World," *Journal of Consumer Research*, 40 (3), 477–500.

Benkler, Yochai (2006), *The Wealth of Networks: How Social Production Transforms Markets and Freedom*. Yale University Press.

Berger, Jonah and Raghuram Iyengar (2013), "Communication Channels and Word of Mouth: How the Medium Shapes the Message," *Journal of Consumer Research*, 40 (3), 567–79.

Berger, Jonah and Katherine L Milkman (2012), "What Makes Online Content Viral?," *Journal of Marketing Research*, 49 (2), 192–205.

Berger, Jonah and Eric M Schwartz (2011), "What Drives Immediate and Ongoing Word of Mouth?," *Journal of Marketing Research*, 48 (5), 869–80.

Bonds-Raacke, Jennifer and John Raacke (2010), "MySpace and Facebook: Identifying Dimensions of Uses and Gratifications for Friend Networking Sites," *Individual Differences Research*, 8 (1), 27–33.

Botsman, Rachel and Roo Rogers (2010), "What's Mine Is Yours," *The Rise of Collaborative Consumption*.

Bourdieu, Pierre (2011), "The Forms of Capital (1986)," in *Cultural Theory: An Anthology*, eds Imre Szeman and Timothy Kaposy, 81–93. Wiley–Blackwell.

boyd, danah (2014), *It's Complicated: The Social Lives of Networked Teens*. New Haven: Yale University Press.

Boyle, Kris and Thomas J Johnson (2010), "MySpace Is Your Space? Examining Self-Presentation of Myspace Users," *Computers in Human Behavior*, 26 (6), 1392–99.

Brown, Jacqueline Johnson and Peter H Reingen (1987), "Social Ties and Word-of-Mouth Referral Behavior," *Journal of Consumer Research*, 14 (3), 350–62.

Burt, Ronald S (2001), "Structural Holes Versus Network Closure as Social Capital," *Social Capital: Theory and Research*, 31–56.

Chevalier, Judith A and Dina Mayzlin (2006), "The Effect of Word of Mouth on Sales: Online Book Reviews," *Journal of Marketing Research*, 43 (3), 345–54.

Chintagunta, Pradeep K, Shyam Gopinath, and Sriram Venkataraman (2010), "The Effects of Online User Reviews on Movie Box Office Performance: Accounting for Sequential Rollout and Aggregation across Local Markets," *Marketing Science*, 29 (5), 944–57.

Coleman, Gabriella (2014), *Hacker, Hoaxer, Whistleblower, Spy: The Many Faces of Anonymous*. Verso Books.

Cova, Bernard, Daniele Dalli, and Detlev Zwick (2011), "Critical Perspectives on Consumers' Role as 'Producers': Broadening the Debate on Value Co-Creation in Marketing Processes," *Marketing Theory*, 11 (3), 231–41.

Dahl, Darren (2013), "Social Influence and Consumer Behavior," *Journal of Consumer Research*, 40 (2).

De Langhe, Bart, Philip M Fernbach, and Donald R Lichtenstein (2015), "Navigating by the Stars: Investigating the Actual and Perceived Validity of Online User Ratings," *Journal of Consumer Research*, ucv047.

de Tarde, Gabriel (1898), *Études De Psychologie Sociale*, Vol. 14. V. Giard & E. Brière.

Dellarocas, Chrysanthos, Guodong Gao, and Ritu Narayan (2010), "Are Consumers More Likely to Contribute Online Reviews for Hit or Niche Products?," *Journal of Management Information Systems*, 27 (2), 127–58.

Denegri-Knott, Janice and Mike Molesworth (2010), "Concepts and Practices of Digital Virtual Consumption," *Consumption, Markets and Culture*, 13 (2), 109–32.

Diehl, Kristin, Gal Zauberman, and Alixandra Barasch (2016), "How Taking Photos Increases Enjoyment of Experiences."

Dobson, Amy Shields (2008), "The 'Grotesque Body'in Young Women's Self Presentation on Myspace," in *Australian Sociological Association Conference*. Re-Imagining Society, Melbourne.

Dolbec, Pierre-Yann and Eileen Fischer (2015), "Refashioning a Field? Connected Consumers and Institutional Dynamics in Markets," *Journal of Consumer Research*, 41 (6), 1447–68.

Donath, Judith and Danah Boyd (2004), "Public Displays of Connection," *BT Technology Journal*, 22 (4), 71–82.

Drenten, Jenna (2012), "Snapshots of the Self," in *Online Consumer Behavior: Theory and Research in Social Media, Advertising, and E-tail*, Angeline Close (ed), 3–34. Routledge.

Durkheim, Emile (1912/2008), *The Elementary Forms of the Religious Life*. Courier Corporation.

Earl, Jennifer and Katrina Kimport (2011), *Digitally Enabled Social Change: Activism in the Internet Age*. MIT Press.

Ellison, Nicole B, Charles Steinfield, and Cliff Lampe (2007), "The Benefits of Facebook "Friends:" Social Capital and College Students' Use of Online Social Network Sites," *Journal of Computer-Mediated Communication*, 12 (4), 1143–68.

Ellison, Nicole, Rebecca Heino, and Jennifer Gibbs (2006), "Managing Impressions Online: Self-Presentation Processes in the Online Dating Environment," *Journal of Computer-Mediated Communication*, 11 (2), 415–41.

Etkin, Jordan (2016), "The Hidden Cost of Personal Quantification," *Journal of Consumer Research*, 42 (6), 967–84.

Eysenbach, Gunther, John Powell, Marina Englesakis, Carlos Rizo, and Anita Stern (2004), "Health Related Virtual Communities and Electronic Support Groups: Systematic Review of the Effects of Online Peer to Peer Interactions," *BMJ*, 328 (7449), 1166.

Figueiredo, Bernardo and Daiane Scaraboto (2016), "The Systemic Creation of Value through Circulation in Collaborative Consumer Networks," *Journal of Consumer Research*, ucw038.

Fiske, John (1989/2010), *Understanding Popular Culture*. Routledge.

Floyd, Kristopher, Ryan Freling, Saad Alhoqail, Hyun Young Cho, and Traci Freling (2014), "How Online Product Reviews Affect Retail Sales: A Meta-Analysis," *Journal of Retailing*, 90 (2), 217–32.

Forman, Chris, Anindya Ghose, and Batia Wiesenfeld (2008), "Examining the Relationship between Reviews and Sales: The Role of Reviewer Identity Disclosure in Electronic Markets," *Information Systems Research*, 19 (3), 291–313.

Fuchs, Christian (2012), "The Political Economy of Privacy on Facebook," *Television & New Media*, 13 (2), 139–59.

—— (2013), *Social Media: A Critical Introduction*. Sage.

Gibson, James J (1977), *The Theory of Affordances*. Lawrence Erlbaum.

Giesler, Markus (2006), "Consumer Gift Systems," *Journal of Consumer Research*, 33 (2), 283–90.

Godes, David and Dina Mayzlin (2004), "Using Online Conversations to Study Word-of-Mouth Communication," *Marketing Science*, 23 (4), 545–60.

Granovetter, Mark (1973), "The Strength of Weak Ties," *American Journal of Sociology*, 78 (6), 1360–80.

Gray, Mary L (2009), "Negotiating Identities/Queering Desires: Coming Out Online and the Remediation of the Coming-Out Story," *Journal of Computer-Mediated Communication*, 14 (4), 1162–89.

Hargittai, Eszter (2008), "The Digital Reproduction on Inequality." in *Social Stratification*, ed. David Grusky. Boulder, CO: Westview Press, 936–44.

Hargittai, Eszter and Amanda Hinnant (2008), "Digital Inequality: Differences in Young Adults' Use of the Internet," *Communication Research*, 35 (5), 602–21.

Hemetsberger, Andrea and Christian Reinhardt (2009), "Collective Development in Open-Source Communities: An Activity Theoretical Perspective on Successful Online Collaboration," *Organization Studies*, 30 (9), 987–1008.

Hennig-Thurau, Thorsten, Kevin P Gwinner, Gianfranco Walsh, and Dwayne D Gremler (2004), "Electronic Word-of-Mouth Via Consumer-Opinion Platforms: What Motivates Consumers to Articulate Themselves on the Internet?," *Journal of Interactive Marketing*, 18 (1), 38–52.

Herring, Susan C (2004), "Slouching toward the Ordinary: Current Trends in Computer-Mediated Communication," *New Media and Society*, 6, 26–36.

Herring, Susan C and Sharon Stoerger (2013), "Gender and (A)Nonymity in Computer-Mediated Communication," *Handbook of Language, Gender, and Sexuality*. 2nd ed. Hoboken, NJ: Wiley-Blackwell Publishing, 567–86.

Hoffman, Donna L, and Thomas P Novak. (1996), "Marketing in Hypermedia Computer-mediated Environments: Conceptual Foundations." *The Journal of Marketing* 60 (3), 50–68.

Hogan, Bernie (2010), "The Presentation of Self in the Age of Social Media: Distinguishing Performances and Exhibitions Online," *Bulletin of Science, Technology & Society*, 0270467610385893.

Humphreys, Ashlee (2010), "Megamarketing: The Creation of Markets as a Social Process," *Journal of Marketing*, 74 (2), 1–19.

—— (2016), *Social Media: Enduring Principles*. Oxford University Press.

Humphreys, Ashlee and Kent Grayson (2008), "The Intersecting Roles of Consumer and Producer: A Critical Perspective on Co-Production, Co-Creation and Prosumption," *Sociology Compass*, 2 (3), 963–80.

Humphreys, Ashlee and Kathryn A Latour (2013), "Framing the Game: Assessing the Impact of Cultural Representations on Consumer Perceptions of Legitimacy," *Journal of Consumer Research*, 40 (4), 773–95.

Humphreys, Ashlee and Craig J Thompson (2014), "Branding Disaster: Reestablishing Trust Through the Ideological Containment of Systemic Risk Anxieties," *Journal of Consumer Research*, 41 (4), 877–910.

Iqani, Mehita and Jonathan E Schroeder (2016), "#Selfie: Digital Self-Portraits as Commodity Form and Consumption Practice," *Consumption Markets & Culture*, 19 (5), 405–15.

Ito, Mizuko, Heather Horst, Matteo Bittanti, Danah Boyd, Becky Herr-Stephenson, Patricia G Lange, CJ Pascoe, and Laura Robinson (2008), "Living and Learning with New Media: Summary of Findings from the Digital Youth Project," The MIT Press.

Jenkins, Henry (2004), "The Cultural Logic of Media Convergence," *International Journal of Cultural Studies*, 7 (1), 33–43.

—— (2006), *Convergence Culture: Where Old and New Media Collide*. NYU Press.

—— (2015), ""Cultural Acupuncture": Fan Activism and the Harry Potter Alliance," in Lincoln Geraghty (ed), *Popular Media Cultures*. Springer, 206–29.

Jenkins, Henry, Sam Ford, and Joshua Green (2013), *Spreadable Media: Creating Value and Meaning in a Networked Culture*. NYU Press.

Jin, Fang, Wei Wang, Liang Zhao, Edward Dougherty, Yang Cao, Chang-Tien Lu, and Naren Ramakrishnan (2014), "Misinformation Propagation in the Age of Twitter," *Computer*, 47 (12), 90–94.

Katz, Elihu and Paul Felix Lazarsfeld (1970), *Personal Influence, the Part Played by People in the Flow of Mass Communications*. Transaction Publishers.

Kedzior, Richard, D Allen, and J Schroeder (2015), "The Selfie Phenomenon–Consumer Identities in the Social Media Marketplace," *European Journal of Marketing* (Special issue), 50 (9/10), 1767–2.

Keller, Ed and Barak Libai (2009), "A Holistic Approach to the Measurement of Wom. Its Impact on Consumer's. Part 5/the Power of Social Media. Wm3-Worldwide Multi Media Measurement 2009," in ESOMAR Worldwide Media Measurement Conference, Stockholm, 4–6.

Kozinets, Robert V (2002), "The Field Behind the Screen: Using Netnography for Marketing Research in Online Communities," *Journal of Marketing Research*, 39 (February), 61–72.

Kross, Ethan, Philippe Verduyn, Emre Demiralp, Jiyoung Park, David Seungjae Lee, Natalie Lin, Holly Shablack, John Jonides, and Oscar Ybarra (2013), "Facebook Use Predicts Declines in Subjective Well-Being in Young Adults," *PloS One*, 8 (8), e69841.

Lamberton, Cait and Andrew T Stephen (2016), "A Thematic Exploration of Digital, Social Media, and Mobile Marketing Research's Evolution from 2000 to 2015 and an Agenda for Future Research," *Journal of Marketing*, DOI: 10.1509/jm.15.0415.

Lapidot-Lefler, Noam and Azy Barak (2012), "Effects of Anonymity, Invisibility, and Lack of Eye-Contact on Toxic Online Disinhibition," *Computers in Human Behavior*, 28 (2), 434–43.

Livingstone, Sonia (2008), "Taking Risky Opportunities in Youthful Content Creation: Teenagers' Use of Social Networking Sites for Intimacy, Privacy and Self-Expression," *New Media & Society*, 10 (3), 393–411.

Luca, Michael (2011), "Reviews, Reputation, and Revenue: The Case of Yelp. Com," *Com (September 16, 2011). Harvard Business School NOM Unit Working Paper* (12–016).

Martin, Diane M and John W Schouten (2014), "Consumption-Driven Market Emergence," *Journal of Consumer Research*, 40 (5), 855–70.

Marwick, Alice (2005), "'I'm a Lot More Interesting Than a Friendster Profile': Identity Presentation, Authenticity and Power in Social Networking Services," *Association of Internet Researchers*, 6.

—— (2013a), "Gender, Sexuality, and Social Media," in *The Social Media Handbook*, eds. Jeremy Hunsinger and Theresa M Senft. Routledge.

Marwick, Alice E (2013b), *Status Update: Celebrity, Publicity, and Branding in the Social Media Age*. Yale University Press.

Marwick, Alice E and Danah Boyd (2011), "I Tweet Honestly, I Tweet Passionately: Twitter Users, Context Collapse, and the Imagined Audience," *New Media & Society*, 13 (1), 114–33.

Marwick, Alice and Nicole B Ellison (2012), ""There Isn't Wifi in Heaven!" Negotiating Visibility on Facebook Memorial Pages," *Journal of Broadcasting & Electronic Media*, 56 (3), 378–400.

Mathwick, Charla, Caroline Wiertz, and Ko De Ruyter (2008), "Social Capital Production in a Virtual P3 Community," *Journal of Consumer Research*, 34 (6), 832–49.

McCombs, Maxwell E and Donald L Shaw (1972), "The Agenda-Setting Function of Mass Media," *Public Opinion Quarterly*, 36 (2), 176–87.

McQuarrie, Edward F, Jessica Miller, and Barbara J Phillips (2013), "The Megaphone Effect: Taste and Audience in Fashion Blogging," *Journal of Consumer Research*, 40 (1), 136–58.

Mendoza, Marcelo, Barbara Poblete, and Carlos Castillo (2010), "Twitter under Crisis: Can We Trust What We RT?," in *Proceedings of the first workshop on social media analytics*: ACM, 71–9.

Meraz, Sharon (2009), "Is There an Elite Hold? Traditional Media to Social Media Agenda Setting Influence in Blog Networks," *Journal of Computer–Mediated Communication*, 14 (3), 682–707.

Miller, Daniel (2013), "'What Is Social Media?' – a Definition," in *Global Social Media Impact Study Blog*, Vol. 2013, UCL Social networking Sites & Social Science Research Project: University College London.

Miller, Vincent (2008), "New Media, Networking and Phatic Culture," *Convergence: The International Journal of Research into New Media Technologies*, 14 (4), 387–400.

Moe, Wendy W and Michael Trusov (2011), "The Value of Social Dynamics in Online Product Ratings Forums," *Journal of Marketing Research*, 48 (3), 444–56.

Moe, Wendy W and David A Schweidel (2012), "Online Product Opinions: Incidence, Evaluation, and Evolution," *Marketing Science* 31 (3), 372–86.

Money, R Bruce, Mary C Gilly, and John L Graham (1998), "Explorations of National Culture and Word-of-Mouth Referral Behavior in the Purchase of Industrial Services in the United States and Japan," *The Journal of Marketing*, 62 (4), 76–87.

Monge, Peter R and Noshir S Contractor (2003), *Theories of Communication Networks*. New York: Oxford University Press.

Muñiz Jr, Albert M, and Thomas C O'Guinn (2001), "Brand Community," *Journal of Consumer Research*, 27 (4), 412–32.

Muñiz Jr, Albert M and Hope Jensen Schau (2005), "Religiosity in the Abandoned Apple Newton Brand Community," *Journal of Consumer Research*, 31 (4), 737–47.

Murray, Derek Conrad (2015), "Notes to Self: The Visual Culture of Selfies in the Age of Social Media," *Consumption Markets & Culture*, 18 (6), 490–516.

Nakamura, Lisa (2002/2013), *Cybertypes: Race, Ethnicity, and Identity on the Internet*. Routledge.

Nonnecke, Blair and Jenny Preece (2000), "Lurker Demographics: Counting the Silent," in *Proceedings of the SIGCHI conference on Human Factors in Computing Systems: ACM*, 73–80.

Ozanne, Lucie K and Paul W Ballantine (2010), "Sharing as a Form of Anti-Consumption? An Examination of Toy Library Users," *Journal of Consumer Behaviour*, 9 (6), 485–98.

Packard, Grant, Andrew D Gershoff, and David B Wooten, (2016), "When Boastful Word of Mouth Helps Versus Hurts Social Perceptions and Persuasion," *Journal of Consumer Research* 43 (1), 26–43.

Papacharissi, Zizi (2011), *A Networked Self: Identity, Community and Culture on Social Network Sites*. Taylor & Francis.

—— (2012), "Without You, I'm Nothing: Performances of the Self on Twitter," *International Journal of Communication*, 6 (2012), 1–18.

—— (2015), *Affective Publics: Sentiment, Technology, and Politics*. Oxford University Press.

Papacharissi, Zizi and Maria de Fatima Oliveira (2012), "Affective News and Networked Publics: The Rhythms of News Storytelling on# Egypt," *Journal of Communication*, 62 (2), 266–82.

Parmentier, Marie-Agnès and Eileen Fischer (2015), "Things Fall Apart: The Dynamics of Brand Audience Dissipation," *Journal of Consumer Research*, 41 (5), 1228–51.

Pfeffer, Jürgen, Thomas Zorbach, and Kathleen M Carley (2014), "Understanding Online Firestorms: Negative Word-of-Mouth Dynamics in Social Media Networks," *Journal of Marketing Communications*, 20 (1–2), 117–28.

Phillips, Whitney (2013), "A Brief History of Trolls," *The Daily Dot*, www.dailydot.com/via/phillips-brief-history-of-trolls/.

——, (2015), "This Is Why We Can't Have Nice Things: The Origins, Evolution and Cultural Embeddedness of Online Trolling." MIT Press.

Piskorski, Mikolaj Jan (2014), *A Social Strategy: How We Profit from Social Media*. Princeton University Press.

Prahalad, Coimbatore K and Venkat Ramaswamy (2004), "Co-Creation Experiences: The Next Practice in Value Creation," *Journal of Interactive Marketing*, 18 (3), 5–14.

Putnam, Robert D (1995), "Bowling Alone: America's Declining Social Capital," *Journal of Democracy*, 6 (1), 65–78.

Qian, Hua and Craig R Scott (2007), "Anonymity and Self-Disclosure on Weblogs," *Journal of Computer-Mediated Communication*, 12 (4), 1428–51.

Rheingold, Howard (1993), *The Virtual Community: Homesteading on the Electronic Frontier*. Basic Books.

Rokka, Joonas (2015), "Self-Transformation and Performativity of Social Media Images," *NA-Advances in Consumer Research Volume 43*, eds. Kristin Diehl and Carolyn Yoon. Duluth, MN: Association for Consumer Research, 111–116.

Rotman, D, Vieweg, S, Yardi, S, Chi, E, Preece, J, Shneiderman, B, . . . Glaisyer, T (2011), *From slacktivism to activism: participatory culture in the age of social media*. Paper presented at the CHI'11 Extended Abstracts on Human Factors in Computing Systems.

Rose, Jessica, Susan Mackey-Kallis, Len Shyles, Kelly Barry, Danielle Biagini, Colleen Hart, and Lauren Jack (2012), "Face It: The Impact of Gender on Social Media Images," *Communication Quarterly*, 60 (5), 588–607.

Scaraboto, Daiane and Eileen Fischer (2013), "Frustrated Fatshionistas: An Institutional Theory Perspective on Consumer Quests for Greater Choice in Mainstream Markets," *Journal of Consumer Research*, 39 (6), 1234–57.

Schau, Hope Jensen and Mary C Gilly (2003), "We Are What We Post? Self-Presentation in Personal Web Space," *Journal of Consumer Research*, 30 (3), 385–404.

Schau, Hope Jensen, Albert M Muñiz Jr, and Eric J Arnould (2009), "How Brand Community Practices Create Value," *Journal of Marketing*, 73 (5), 30–51.

Scholz, Joachim and Andrew N Smith (2016), "Augmented Reality: Designing Immersive Experiences That Maximize Consumer Engagement," *Business Horizons*, 59 (2), 149–61.

Selwyn, Neil (2004), "Reconsidering Political and Popular Understandings of the Digital Divide," *New Media & Society*, 6 (3), 341–62.

Simonson, Itamar (2016), "Imperfect Progress: An Objective Quality Assessment of the Role of User Reviews in Consumer Decision Making, a Commentary on De Langhe, Fernbach, and Lichtenstein," *Journal of Consumer Research*, 42 (6), 840–45.

Song, Indeok, Robert Larose, Matthew S Eastin, and Carolyn A Lin (2004), "Internet Gratifications and Internet Addiction: On the Uses and Abuses of New Media," *CyberPsychology & Behavior*, 7 (4), 384–94.

Steinfield, Charles, Nicole B Ellison, and Cliff Lampe (2008), "Social Capital, Self-Esteem, and Use of Online Social Network Sites: A Longitudinal Analysis," *Journal of Applied Developmental Psychology*, 29 (6), 434–45.

Stephen, Andrew T and Olivier Toubia (2010), "Deriving Value from Social Commerce Networks," *Journal of Marketing Research*, 47 (2), 215–28.

Suler, John (2004a), "Computer and Cyberspace "Addiction"," *International Journal of Applied Psychoanalytic Studies*, 1 (4), 359–62.

—— (2004b), "The Online Disinhibition Effect," *CyberPsychology & Behavior*, 7 (3), 321–26.

Sunstein, Cass R (2006), *Infotopia: How Many Minds Produce Knowledge*. Oxford University Press.

Thomas, Tandy Chalmers, Linda L Price, and Hope Jensen Schau (2013), "When Differences Unite: Resource Dependence in Heterogeneous Consumption Communities," *Journal of Consumer Research*, 39 (5), 1010–33.

Thornton, Sarah (1996), *Club Cultures: Music, Media, and Subcultural Capital*. Wesleyan University Press.

Tian, Kelly, Pookie Sautter, Derek Fisher, Sarah Fischbach, Cuauhtemoc Luna-Nevarez, Kevin Boberg, Jim Kroger, and Richard Vann (2014), "Transforming Health Care: Empowering Therapeutic Communities through Technology-Enhanced Narratives," *Journal of Consumer Research*, 41 (2), 237–60.

Tidwell, Lisa Collins and Joseph B Walther (2002), "Computer-Mediated Communication Effects on Disclosure, Impressions, and Interpersonal Evaluations: Getting to Know One Another a Bit at a Time," *Human Communication Research*, 28 (3), 317–48.

Tirunillai, Seshadri, and Gerard J Tellis (2012), "Does Chatter Really Matter? Dynamics of User-Generated Content and Stock Performance," *Marketing Science*, 31 (2), 198–215.

Tufekci, Zeynep and Christopher Wilson (2012), "Social Media and the Decision to Participate in Political Protest: Observations from Tahrir Square," *Journal of Communication*, 62 (2), 363–79.

Turkle, Sherry (1995/2011), *Life on the Screen*. Simon and Schuster.

Wan, Chin-Sheng and Wen-Bin Chiou (2006), "Psychological Motives and Online Games Addiction: Atest of Flow Theory and Humanistic Needs Theory for Taiwanese Adolescents," *CyberPsychology & Behavior*, 9 (3), 317–24.

Ward, James C and Amy L Ostrom (2006), "Complaining to the Masses: The Role of Protest Framing in Customer-Created Complaint Web Sites," *Journal of Consumer Research*, 33 (2), 220–30.

Warner, Michael (2002), "Publics and Counterpublics," *Public Culture*, 14 (1), 49–90.

Weber, Matthew S and Peter Monge (2011), "The Flow of Digital News in a Network of Sources, Authorities, and Hubs," *Journal of Communication*, 61 (6), 1062–81.

Webster, James G (2014), *The Marketplace of Attention: How Audiences Take Shape in a Digital Age*. MIT Press.

Wellman, Barry and Lee Rainie (2012), "Networked: The New Social Operating System," The MIT Press.

Wenger, Etienne (2000), "Communities of Practice and Social Learning Systems," *Organization*, 7 (2), 225–46.

Wilcox, Keith and Andrew T Stephen (2013), "Are Close Friends the Enemy? Online Social Networks, Self-Esteem, and Self-Control," *Journal of Consumer Research*, 40 (1), 90–103.

Williams, J Patrick (2006), "Authentic Identities: Straightedge Subculture, Music, and the Internet," *Journal of Contemporary Ethnography*, 35 (2), 173–200.

Winer, Russell S and Peter S Fader (2016), "Objective Vs. Online Ratings: Are Low Correlations Unexpected and Does It Matter? A Commentary on De Langhe, Fernbach, and Lichtenstein," *Journal of Consumer Research*, 42 (6), 846–49.

Zhao, Xin and Russell W Belk (2008), "Politicizing Consumer Culture: Advertising's Appropriation of Political Ideology in China's Social Transition," *Journal of Consumer Research*, 35 (2), 231–44.

Zuo, Angie (2014), "Measuring Up: Social Comparisons on Facebook and Contributions to Self-Esteem and Mental Health." Dissertation. Ann Arbor, MI: University of Michigan.

24

SEGMENTED CLUSTERS VERSUS SOCIAL GROUPINGS AND STATUS GAMES: THE CHANGING LANDSCAPE OF LUXURY CONSUMERS

Laurel Steinfield

BENTLEY UNIVERSITY, WALTHAM, MA, USA

Introduction

By definition, luxury has value due to a perception of scarcity (Kapferer, 2015) and the prestigious sign-value (Baudrillard, 1998) it elicits. As Shukla (2011) delineates, luxury products are "conducive to pleasure and comfort, are difficult to obtain, and bring the owner esteem, apart from functional utility" (p. 243). They are products that allow consumers to capture their dreams and that hold psychological benefits such as social recognition and self-esteem (Chandon, Laurent, & Valette-Florence, 2016). They include goods, services, and experiences that Berry (1994) classifies into four categories: substance (e.g. food and drink), shelter (e.g. hotels), clothing and accessories (e.g. haut couture fashions, jewelry, perfume), and leisure (e.g. travel, entertainment, prestigious sports, and events). However, how one separates luxury products from ordinary items is difficult, and perhaps best viewed on a continuum (Tynan, McKechnie, & Chhuon, 2010). Luxury is thus a subjective, relative and dynamic concept, especially in today's consumer landscape. Products that were once considered luxury are now becoming readily available as the market expands through mass produced prestige products (masstige), counterfeit products, brand extensions, growth in emerging economies, and an increased involvement of consumers in procuring luxury sales (prosumerism). A hyper-connected market is eroding the key attribute of luxury—exclusivity. Digital, online channels are expanding access to goods. Fashion bloggers are spreading awareness and acculturating masses on how luxury should be consumed. The sharing economy is eroding the ability of price points to constrict acquisition. Luxury has become democratized (Chandon et al., 2016; Kapferer, 2015). What Veblen (2009) once ascribed to be the exclusive right of the leisure class, Goffman (1951) labeled as a status symbol, and Bourdieu (1984) positioned as the visible enactments of the elite's symbolic and cultural capital, is now available to consumers across socioeconomic categories. Luxury is being shaped by an iterative interplay between producers and an increasingly empowered base of consumers. Consequently, luxury is a function not only of a brand manager's ability to adopt "abundant rarity" strategies (Kapferer, 2015), and to align and deliver high-quality, aesthetically and hedonically pleasing products to predetermined, segmented consumer groups; it is also a concept influenced by consumers' co-creation of value and desire to reshape value propositions for their own expressive purposes (Tynan et al., 2010).

This chapter will summarize these changes. It will start with a brief overview of how scholars have historically conceptualized luxury and luxury consumers. It will explore how, against the backdrop of a changing marketscape, academics redefined who could be considered a luxury consumer by creating consumer segments based on consumers' perceptions of luxury brands and extrinsic and intrinsic motives. It will review the more recent literature that shifts consumers from objects to be segmented to subjects with agency who (although influenced by social structures) use luxury—conspicuously or inconspicuously—for hedonic and sensory purposes, to express dreamed identities, and to maintain distinctions and a sense of group affiliation. It will conclude with a consideration of how more recent technological disruptions and consumer movements—such as demands for sustainability, the rise of social media and prosumption, and the transition of luxury to experiences vested in a sharing economy—are shifting luxury from a system based on clearly delineated socioeconomic levels to a system built around desired lifestyles and sociocultural preferences.

Luxury Consumers: Then and Now

In 1889, Thorstein Veblen adapted an evolutionary perspective to describe a society that was increasingly evolving along class-based stratifications. In his *Theory of the Leisure Class*, he argued that the leisure classes' status was not conferred through the mere accumulation of wealth, but by wealth as evidence of excessive leisure time and an abstention from labor. These conditions were represented through what he called conspicuous consumption, that is, the wasteful exhibition of wealth for the purpose of conferring prestige. The leisure class exhibited conspicuous consumption through acquiring fine silverware, hand-painted china, and the latest fashion wear. The purpose of these goods was not vested in their ability to convey food or to cover the body, as this could be achieved with less expensive substitutes, but in their ability to denote that the leisure class had sufficient wealth to afford such unproductive goods. Veblen (2009) accordingly demarcated consumption of "luxuries and the comforts of life [to] belong to the leisure class" (p. 50). Given that the proliferation of goods allowed luxuries to be consumed by lower classes, Veblen further stressed whom the "rightful" consumers of luxury entailed. He categorized the conspicuous consumption of the higher, leisure class as "invidious consumption"—consumption used to convey and legitimize one's "relative worth or value" and to dissociate from lower classes (p. 27). The consumption of the lower class was deemed as "pecuniary emulation"—competitive consumption used to associate with higher classes. Accordingly, from Veblen's theory emerged a segmentation of luxury consumers in which income-related dimensions were perceived to shape motivations.

Although prior to Veblen, philosophers and academics had noted the (often negative) sociocultural effects and (often positive) economic underpinnings of luxury and its affiliation with a life of "ease, pleasure and pomp" (Barbon 1905, p. 14), it was Veblen's theory of conspicuous consumption that became synonymous with modern day theories about luxury (see Mason (1993) and Berry (1994) for historical overviews). This was, in part, brought about by fellow sociologists, Simmel ([1904] 1957), Goffman (1951), and Bourdieu (1984), reinforcing a perspective of legitimate versus illegitimate consumers of luxury.

Simmel (1957), for example, denoted that it was the "upper classes" who had to protect their symbols of status and demarcation (in this case fashion) from the "charm of imitation," that is, the belief amongst the lower classes that they could achieve group affiliation with upper society through imitating their fashions (p. 542, p. 545). This threat led to an incessant change in fashion: as the masses imitated the elites, the elites abandoned the fashion for a newer mode to maintain their distinctions from the lower classes; the masses would then seek to imitate the new style and the cycle would begin anew. Goffman (1951) built upon the themes of "fraudulent" imitation and "conspicuous consumption," arguing that class-based status symbols hold expressive purposes (they express the cultural values, lifestyles, privileges, or duties a person holds) and categorical purposes (they visibly divide the social world) (p. 296). As a consequence, classes attempt to protect status symbols through the enactment of restrictive devices (e.g. moral restrictions such as a cultural disdain or societal proprieties, or intrinsic restrictions such as sufficient means of wealth). Bourdieu (1984), in turn, expanded upon the ways class-based distinctions and the "legitimate" owners of luxury were maintained through agentic forces (similar to Veblen, Simmel and Goffman) *and* structural forces, or what he termed modes of capital. Bourdieu argued that varying levels of capital—which included economic (e.g. income), social (e.g. networks), cultural (e.g. education), and symbolic (e.g. conferred prestige)—determine a class's position within the social hierarchy and shaped class-based distinctions. Groups maintain their social distinctions through reproducing acculturated, shared and embodied lifestyles, values, norms, and tastes (or a person's appreciation and atheistic orientation for things such as music, art and food). Distinguishing between various sources and levels of capital allowed Bourdieu to break apart the grouping of "elites" into luxury consumers versus ascetic aristocrats. The latter he defined as academics or public sector executives who, because they held less economic capital and presumably more cultural capital, were orientated towards "the least expensive and most austere leisure activities and towards serious . . . cultural practices" (p. 286). In contrast stood the luxury consumers—"members of the professions" whose "luxury tastes" led them to "amass the (culturally or economically) most expensive and most prestigious activities, reading expensive glossy magazines, visiting antique-dealers, galleries and concert-halls, holidaying in spa towns, owning pianos . . . works of art . . . foreign cars . . ." (p. 286).

Collectively, these theories and studies by Veblen, Simmel, Goffman, and Bourdieu (re)created assumptions that access to wealth determined access to luxury, and luxury was "conspicuous consumption," a "squandering," and "destruction of wealth" vested with a desire to exhibit economic power (Bourdieu 1984, p. 55). In subsequent studies, scholars and practitioners grouped luxury consumers according to the interaction of these two effects: those higher in wealth consumed luxury to *maintain* status and group affiliation, and those lower in wealth consumed luxury to *obtain* status and group affiliation.

These dominant views held sway over much of the marketing literature until the early 1990s when academics expanded their surveys to probe for nuances in consumer motives for luxury consumption (Dubois & Duquesne, 1993). Contrasting the perspectives of Allérès (1991) with Dubois and Duquesne (1993) demonstrates this shift. Although Allérès (1991) highlighted a fragmenting market, he still denoted his multiple tiers of consumer segments by income-related attributes: Classe Nantie, the wealthy class whose consumption was a maintenance of their privileges; Classe Intermédiarie, the intermediate class whose consumption was social mimicry; and Classe Moyenne, the middle class whose consumption was consumer greed. Dubois and Duquesne (1993), on the other hand, studied not only income-related motives akin to Veblen's conspicuous consumption, but also cultural motives, such as symbolic and self-expressive purposes as revealed in the works by McCracken (1988), Hirschman and Holbrook (1982), and Belk (1988). They found that both types of motives operated, with some luxury consumers driven more by one motive and others by both. Consumers categorized as buying luxury for "income" related purposes predominately viewed luxury brands as the standards of excellence and guarantees of authenticity that aligned with their socioeconomic status. Consumers described as buying luxury for "cultural" reasons used luxury brands as hedonic and self-expressive symbols of accomplishment and demonstrations of adaptation to cultural trends.

This shift in perspectives paved the way for future studies to interrogate a variety of consumer motives. Although the income-culture dichotomy could be critiqued for ignoring the importance of the social milieu, or obscuring the interrelation of status and self-expressive motives (see for instance works that extend Bourdiean theory such as Holt, 1998; Allen, 2002; and Arsel & Bean, 2013), it gained prominence in luxury studies. The addition of cultural motives, such as luxury being symbols of accomplishment, aligned with what sociologists Peterson and Kern (1996) noted as generational shifts in elites' highbrow tastes: younger generations consumed music more indiscriminately, replacing snob-like tastes with an open-minded approach that demonstrated an aptitude for recognizing cultural trends. Moreover, Dubois and Duquesne's theory encouraged scholars to note the effects of the growth of luxury: its democratization. As Dubois and Laurent (1995) argued, no longer was the market polarized between the "Excluded" (for whom luxury was at best a dream) versus the "Affluent. . . Old money [and] Nouveaux Riches" (for whom luxury was an "art de vivre"); rather, there was a third consumer segment emerging—the "Excursionists" whose consumption of luxury, while intermittent and linked to exceptional circumstances, was plausible (p. 69–70).

Luxury Consumers in a Democratized Marketplace

The effects of democratization called into question who was a luxury consumer and what luxury entailed, especially as luxury consumption started to grow exponentially in Japan, China, and Russia (see, for example, concerns voiced in Powell, 1990; Dubois & Laurent, 1995; Barnier, Rodina & Valette-Florence, 2006; Chadha, 2006; Thomas, 2007). As Baudrillard (1998) described, Veblen's conspicuous consumption could be seen across all consumer levels, regardless of income. Consumer society, since it was organized around the consumption and display of goods, meant that the higher the prestige of the good (fashion, houses, cars, etc.), the higher its sign value, and the higher one's standing would be in society. In a recursive manner, consumer demand pushed the companies to expand their product offerings, and companies pushed new product offerings to expand customers' consumption practices and preferences. The emergence of affordable but superpremium products (e.g. a cup of Starbucks coffee with a 40% premium over a more generic cup of coffee) and masstige products (mass produced prestige products), combined with a downward stretch by luxury brands to capture more of the market through brand extensions (e.g. sunglasses or perfume), contributed to what Silverstein and Fiske labeled in 2002 as the "Trading Up" phenomenon. Middle-market consumers selectively traded up to premium or affordable prestige products while trading down on categories less meaningful to them (Silverstein, Fiske, & Butman, 2008). Silverstein and Fiske (2003) aptly concluded, "people's buying habits do not invariably correspond to their income level" (p. 50). Consequently, "luxury" for some categories was becoming decoupled from income, Veblen's notions of conspicuous "waste" was transitioning to conspicuous "taste," and "luxury," and "premium" brands and their consumers were increasingly becoming blurred. As Twitchell (2003) stated in his examination of the American market, the movement since the 1980s to "move more and more objects up into luxury brands" had strained the credibility of the category (p. xiii). In an attempt to gain clarity on what luxury actually entailed, and to help marketers maintain value in the sight of their globally expanding consumer groups, academics undertook studies to assess consumers' perceptions, attitudes, behaviors, and motives related to luxury (often delineated by brand name goods) and then to cluster them based on these perspectives (Vigneron & Johnson 2004).

The Segmentation of Consumers: Perceptions, Attitudes, Behaviors, or Motives?

In the scramble to segment consumers, academics proposed a myriad of scales. As described below in detail, one can see how this reflected a fragmentation of the meaning of luxury and an extension of who was a luxury consumer. For example, in delineating luxury, scales differed in their approach: was luxury to be measured based on attributes of luxury in general or attributes of brands, or was it to be measured based on consumers' underlying motives? These differences in defining what was under study led to variances in how consumers would be segmented (e.g. along their perceptions of luxury or luxury brands or based on their personal motives). Important to note, however, is that most of the studies emanated from Western scholarship. As such, the scales and segmentations reflected Western-based individualistic traditions and sociocultural beliefs about luxury consumption, which came under challenge as luxury brands extended into Asian markets.

One of the preliminary studies that moved beyond an income-based segmentation model was completed by Kapferer (1998). He clustered consumers based on aspects of luxury brands that appealed to them. Drawing from a pool of students at HEC School of Management in France, Kapferer used student responses to draw up a list of why brands deserved the "appellation of luxury" (p. 44). He uncovered 16 brand attributes, including international reputation, uniqueness, craftsmanship, and quality, and also less recognized attributes such as the sense of magic, beauty, fashionability, and creativity. Based on the top five attributes respondents selected, Kapferer grouped respondents into four segments and aligned these with representative brands. The prototypical consumer held beauty of the object, excellence quality, magic and uniqueness of great importance (e.g. Hermes). The second group held creativity, the product's sensuality, then beauty and magic as imperative (e.g. Gucci). The third segment attached greater importance to beauty, magic, the brand's classical value yet ability to stay fashionable (e.g. Louis Vuitton). The fourth segment, driven by conspicuous purposes, sought exclusivity yet international reputation (e.g. Chivas). Although some of these clusters overlapped, there were demarcations between groups based on overriding affinities (e.g. beauty and craftsmanship versus creativity versus fashionability versus status symbols). Many of the brand attributes Kapferer identified found resonance in other studies. (Refer to Vigneron and Johnson (2004) for a summary of how Kapferer's (1998) attributes were applied in subsequent studies). However, key subjective attributes, although widely appealing—magic, the importance of beauty and creativity—became lost in much of the literature going forward. Rather, the focus shifted towards more objective attributes that companies could more readily control, such as quality, and motives that could be used to denote consumers who wanted luxury goods versus those who wanted premium products. Forming a basis for this latter stream of segmentation variables was Vigneron and Johnson's (1999) classifications of prestige-seeking consumers.

Vigneron and Johnson's (1999) article, based on a review of the literature, classified consumer motives into five major themes. These included: Veblenian motives, where conspicuous value appealed; snob motives, where tendencies to engage in social comparisons

(Festinger, 1954) resulted in consumers seeking exclusivity of brands to maintain distinctions; bandwagon effects, where the symbolic value of luxury brands and their use as a marker of group membership made the social value important (Solomon, 1983; McCracken, 1988; Belk, 1988); hedonism, where emotional desire and subjective intangible benefits (e.g. sensory pleasure) came to the fore (Hirschman & Holbrook, 1982; Sheth, Newman, & Gross, 1991); and perfectionism, where the superiority and quality of the good mattered (Roux 1995). They took these themes forward in their development of the "Brand Luxury Index" (BLI)—an index that could be used to gauge why consumers sought certain luxury brands and how they perceived the value of a luxury brand (Vigneron & Johnson, 2004). The BLI divided the valuation consumers attributed to brands into two groupings: non-personal aspects, which reflected extrinsic factors, such that luxury brands were valued based upon their conspicuous, unique/exclusive and high-quality merits; and personal aspects, which measured hedonic and extended-self attributes, such as luxury brands being viewed as "glamorous" and "rewarding" (p. 502). It was hypothesized that consumers could be clustered based upon their different perceptions of luxury brands. Hudders, Pandelaere, and Vyncke (2013) eventually repeated a similar brand-centric approach, clustering consumers according to whether they valued luxury brands for their expressive (e.g. conspicuous, exclusive), functional (e.g. excellent quality, craftsmanship), or emotional (e.g. elegance, comfort, creativity) qualities. Their findings resulted in three consumer segments: the impressive group who consumed for self-indulgence rather than to fulfill extrinsic needs; the expressive group who sought to impress others or express their identity to or disassociation from others; and the mixed segment (the largest grouping) that rendered both the indulgent and distinctive attributes of brands as important.

Taking a different approach, Dubois, Czellar, and Laurent (2005) decoupled the segmentation of luxury from brand attributes by segmenting consumers based on attitudes and self-reported practices regarding luxury in general. Their questionnaire, for example, asked: "In my opinion, luxury is flashy"; "Truly luxury goods cannot be mass produced"; "I almost never buy luxury products" (p. 117). Additionally, taking into account the globalizing market, they sought to assess the diversity of luxury attitudes by testing the scale in 20 countries (Dubois, Laurent, & Czellar, 2001). Their findings, although limited by the scale's Western cultural biases, were used to segment consumers into three groupings (comparable to Dubois and Laurent's (1995) previous work). These included: elitists, who held luxury to be an exclusive good reserved for refined people who can demonstrate true taste and appreciation; democratics, who believed luxury should be more widely available and that anyone should be able to consume it; and distants, who were not attracted to luxury and believed that a "fine replica" is a perfect substitute (Dubois et al., 2005, p. 122). In a similar vein, Deeter-Schmelz, Moore, and Goebel (2000) developed a scale to capture factors underlying consumer practices related to shopping for prestige clothing. The Precon scale assessed the importance of brand name, product quality, fashionability, store atmosphere, and social acceptability of the store. Both of these scales, created based on exploratory interviews, were argued to help managers position their upscale brands and to create positioning strategies to target prestige or luxury consumers.

In parallel, Tsai (2005), in an attempt to understand what other motives besides "buying to impress" lay beneath consumers' purchase intentions, started to expand into motives that might explain purchases of not only Western consumers but also the growing base of Asian consumers (p. 442). In his "Personal Orientation towards Luxury Brand" model, he added the motives of: self-directed pleasure (the purchase of luxury for hedonic purposes without emphasis on whether it pleases others); self-gift giving (the purchase of luxury for celebratory or emotionally compensatory purposes); congruity with internal self (the purchase of brands because they align with their self-perceived image); and quality assurance (the choice of goods based on the superiority of quality over prestige or other people's opinions). Although Tsai did not create customer segments, the robust results achieved in testing the questionnaire in eight countries, including geographical representations from Asia Pacific, Western Europe and North America, provided further impetus for marketers and academics to recognize that "social motives of displaying status, success, and distinction" were only part of the picture, and that non-Western traditions and perspective were imperative if marketers were to build and strengthen brand loyalty.

In taking a step back to develop a broader and cross-culturally relevant perspective of luxury consumers, Wiedmann, Hennigs, and Siebels (2009) and Hennigs et al. (2012) assessed the merits of the various scales, and combined three of these scales (Vigneron and Johnson 2004, Tsai 2005, and Dubois et al. 2005) with themes and questionnaires from literature streams outside of the luxury domain, such as Sheth et al.'s (1991) taxonomy of consumer motives and Richins and Dawson's (1992) materialism scale. Wiedmann et al. (2009) conceived that their resulting conceptual model, which divided antecedent motives into four types of value—social, individual, functional, and financial—could determine consumers' perceptions of luxury and be used to ascertain why consumers valued different luxury brands. Social value captured conspicuous and prestige motives (e.g. "I am interested in determining what luxury brands I should buy to make good impressions on others"). Individual value included self-identity, hedonistic, and materialistic motives (e.g. "I view luxury brand purchases as gifts for myself to celebrate something I do and feel excited about"). Functional value measured for the importance of quality, usability, and uniqueness (e.g. "I place emphasis on quality assurance over prestige when considering the purchase of a luxury brand"). Financial value considered price (e.g. "Luxury products are inevitably very expensive") (Hennigs et al. 2012, p. 1026). Based on preliminary empirical results with European consumers, Wiedmann et al. (2009) clustered consumers as: Materialists, where quality and usability of goods mattered; Rational Functionalists, where quality value and personal preferences/self-identity was of importance; Extravagant Prestige-Seekers, where prestige value and hedonistic extravagance were imperative; and Introvert Hedonists, where personal pleasure and the way luxury enhanced their quality of life mattered. In extending the model to reflect a global market segmentation, Hennigs et al. (2012) tested the model with consumers from Asia, Latin America and Northern America, and Eastern and Western Europe. Their cluster analysis revealed four overarching groups: the Luxury Lovers, who viewed luxury's exclusivity, uniqueness, social recognition, and fit with self-image as important; the Status-Seeking Hedonists, who valued luxury for its ability to impress people and to bring personal pleasure; the Satisfied Unpretentious, who held more individual versus social reasons, including quality assurance (versus prestige), buying luxury only when needed; and the Rational Functionalists, who, having a significant knowledge of the luxury world purchased luxury because of its superior product quality. Based on their analysis, Hennigs et al. (2012) concluded that since the basic motivational drivers of luxury consumers remained vested in financial, functional, personal, and social values of luxury—regardless of country of origin (e.g. Asia versus Western Europe)—and although these motives could fluctuate in their relative importance, it was better for marketers to "use groups of consumers rather than countries as a basis for identifying international segments" (p. 1020).

This finding contradicted the cultural recognitions that other scholars had argued were imperative to understand the Asian market. Wong and Ahuvia (1998), for example, raised concerns over the overly-Western individualistic rationales (upon which many of these scales were built). They hypothesized that the social orientation of Southeast Asian Confucian traditions, which led to an interdependent (versus Western independent) self-concept, a respect for hierarchies, and pressures to conform, would shift the motives from an internal, self-centered focus to motives vested in gaining external approval through publicly visible goods. Thus, the purpose of acquiring luxuries was to fit in or for gift exchanges, not for self-indulgences. The symbolic value of goods represented social positions within hierarchies versus self-expression. Indeed, in testing for these cultural nuances, Christodoulides, Michaelidou, and Li (2009) found that Vigneron and Johnson's (2004) BLI scale items of conspicuousness and uniqueness had low reliabilities. Li and Su (2007) found support for variances between Chinese and American consumers, demonstrating that Chinese consumers were motivated to consume luxury for social pressures related to face, that is, a "favourable social self-worth that a person wants others to have of her or him in a relational and network context" (p. 239). Unlike the Western notion of prestige, face relates less to personal successes and more to the maintenance of individual and familial honor. As Li and Su (2007) ascertained, Chinese consumers were more likely to purchase luxury for reasons related to conformity, a need to maintain a distinctive identity that matched their social status, and in order to show honor to others (i.e. gift giving). (For similar findings see: Phau and Prendergast, 2000; Wang, Sun and Song, 2011; Bian and Forsythe, 2012; Walley and Li, 2015.)

Trends and Gaps of the Segmented Consumer View

We see from the previous summary how, over the course of a decade, the boundaries between prestige and luxury products became blurred, and the segmentations of luxury consumers shifted from income-centric groupings, towards a combination of intrinsic and extrinsic motives. This trend became more entrenched as scholars affirmed the power of scales through comparative analysis (Barnier, Falcy & Valette-Florence, 2012; Husic & Cicic, 2009), and expanded explanatory models for luxury consumption to include self-esteem (Truong and McColl, 2011) and the internal motives (versus merely external factors) driving consumers to engage in bandwagon consumption (Kastanakis and Balabanis, 2012).

Additionally, underlying many of the studies was the need to understand how to navigate the growing demand for luxury in China, Russia, Japan, and India, and a consumer market that was increasingly becoming well-informed and less loyal to a single brand (Okonkwo, 2007). Scholars demonstrated how companies could segment a globalizing consumer market in such a way that luxury brands could align their brand associations with their offerings and retail and marketing strategies to maintain consistency and appeal in the eyes of consumers, or attempt to subtly recognize cultural variances. (See for example: Phau & Prendergast, 2000; Barnier et al., 2006; Chadha, 2006; Okonkwo, 2007; Atwal & Williams, 2009; Fionda & Moore, 2009; Chernev, Hamilton & Gal, 2011; Atwal & Jain, 2012; Kapferer & Bastien, 2012.)

These studies, however, vested in assumptions that marketing managers could shape the value and associations attributed to brands, tended to obfuscate the importance of social influence and the role other consumers played in determining a brand's association, despite the existence of a large body of literature (as detailed in Wood & Hayes, 2012). Indeed, as other academics found, symbolic meanings consumers attribute to brands are influenced by the consumer "types" who buy the brands (Muniz & O'Guinn, 2001) and whether other consumers use the brands conspicuously (Ferraro, Kirmani & Matherly, 2013). Secondly, the attempts to put consumers into segments resulted in placing too much emphasis on "why" individual consumers valued or purchased luxury, which overshadowed questions around "what" social groups consumers, through their symbolic consumption, were attempting to join or seek distance from, or how groups determined, enforced, or adjusted valuations of, and beliefs attached to, luxury and consumption practices. Thirdly, by treating consumers as objects, they failed to recognize the role that consumers played in co-creating value—a theme that would become increasingly imperative as technology allowed consumers to connect with each other and provided quick access to information that once used to be the cultural capital and markings of a privileged upbringing. In a parallel stream of literature, other researchers started to address these gaps by delving into how various groups responded to the democratization of luxury and how consumers and social structures interact to create or preserve social hierarchies and groupings.

The Luxury Consumer: Framed by Social Structures and Recognized as an Agentic Subject

To identify social structures or the agency of consumers as it relates to luxury, academics have pulled from literature on social comparison theory (Festinger, 1954), symbolic interactionism (Solomon, 1983), and the multiplicity of possible selves (Markus & Nurius, 1986). Although some of these theories had been used to develop the scales noted previously (such as social comparison and symbolic interactionism), the structured format of the scales muted the way consumers enacted or contradicted these theories. Applying these themes to study consumers' lived experiences reveals that luxury consumers were not easily categorized. Before delving into how these have been applied in more qualitative, exploratory studies, a brief recap of each theory is provided.

Social Comparison Theory reveals how consumers' self-evaluations and self-esteem, motives and ultimately their consumption preferences and behavior are influenced by comparisons either to those in their affiliated group (Bearden & Etzel, 1982; Phau & Prendergast, 2000), those in a group whom they aspire to be like (Escalas & Bettman, 2005; O'Cass & McEwen, 2004) and/or those they seek to avoid or disassociate (Berger & Heath, 2007; White, Argo, & Sengupta, 2012; Mazzocco, Rucker, Galinsky, & Anderson, 2012).

Symbolic Interactionism advocates that attention be brought to how consumers use products, language, and gestures to make sense of and interact with their physical and social world. In particular, perceptions of oneself are based on "a projection of how one appears to others—seeing oneself as others do" (Solomon, 1983, p. 232) (see also: Levy, 1959; Sirgy, 1982; Mick, 1986). Consumers are postulated to use goods that symbolically match the role society expects them to play, at times using goods to communicate new identities and at other times using goods to maintain established identities. As such, product symbolism allows social identities to be communicated between consumers and also internalized by consumers (Solomon, 1983).

Multiplicity of Possible Selves: A perspective on the multiplicity of possible selves argues that consumers should be viewed dynamically (rather than statically as the scales encourage). Possible selves represent "individuals' ideas of what they might become, what they would like to become, and what they are afraid of becoming" (Markus & Nurius, 1986, p. 954). It recognizes how consumers can hold converging and diverging goals, motives, aspirations, fears and perceptions of threats, and how they have real selves, ideal selves they seek to obtain, and undesired selves from which they seek distance (Ogilvie, 1987).

Status Contestations and the Rise of Counterfeits and (In)conspicuous Consumption

These three theoretical angles, often weaved together with theories on social status and distinctions (i.e. Bourdieu, Goffman, and Simmel), allow luxury consumers to be viewed as active participants, though influenced by pressures from social groups and norms. Studies in this vein, although they often risk muting the role of the marketer, reveal how consumers enact taste regimes, engage in status games, or how their consumption and discourse reflect desires to protect social distinctions. For example, Arsel and Bean's (2013) work on taste regimes—a concept central to Bourdieu's theory of elites' preference and ability to consume luxury—plots out how the emergence and reproduction of taste regimes are facilitated through: (i) the production and sharing of meaning brought about by mediated or face-to-face exchanges (e.g. knowing what luxury products to purchase); (ii) performances that enact and "conform to community-specific rules" (p. 901) (e.g. using luxury products in the approved manner); and (iii) "the embedding of objects in practice" (p. 902) (e.g. the use of luxury in ritualistic activities, or consciously contemplating or adopting (in)appropriate uses). Although this is a simplistic overview of the acculturation process that surrounds consumers' acquisition or maintenance of identities, Üstüner and Thompson (2012) offer a more nuanced view, noting how identity projects may result in interdependent status games and uneasy acquisitions of Bourdieuan modes of capital. Based on Turkish elites and their service providers (hairdressers), Üstüner and Thompson describe the subtle power plays that manifest when hairdressers attempt to acquire higher levels of cultural capital and perform and enact new identities. The elite reinforce what Bourdieu describes as symbolic domination (i.e. hairdressers internalizing and accepting their lower status in society) and protect the social hierarchy by: maintaining emotional and physical distance; severing ties when hairdressers transgress protocols or fail to defer authority; and denigrating and delegitimizing hairdressers' symbolic and cultural capital (e.g. their mode of dress or abilities to achieve hairstyles). Holt's (1998) earlier work noted similar tactics. Explaining how high cultural capital (HCC) American consumers maintain class boundaries in a mass-consumer society, Holt draws parallels between Bourdieu's theory of cultural capital, social comparison and discourse-based symbolic interactionism. Similar to Goffman's (1951) description of moral restrictions and Bourdieu's (1984) theories of vulgarization tactics, Holt concludes that HCC's privileged position not only allows them to determine prestigious practices but also to denigrate the practices of those who attempt to emulate them with pejorative terms, such as "materialistic," "showy," "ostentatious," "unrefined" (1998, p. 20). Over a decade later, Roper et al. (2013) recorded similar themes in their analysis of luxury consumers' discourse: it became the "other" luxury consumers who depended on luxury brands to validate social identities and relations; the respondents, on the other hand, overtly mocked luxury brands, even ones they purchased, or acted "moderately dispassionate" in attempts to distance themselves from being labeled as "brand dupes" (p. 393). More specifically, Arsel and Thompson (2011) expand upon tactics consumers use to prevent the devaluation of their cultural capital when burgeoning popularity of their lifestyle or of a preferred brand leads to cultural clichés. As they note, the tactics consumers use is predicated on their cultural authority and community status. Those high in status can call into disrepute clichés by classifying the clichés as being views of uninformed outsiders. Those low in status, however, must navigate the lines between being a legitimate community member versus a cultural junkie. As such, they stress the ways their consumption habits reflect the true spirit of the community. Although Arsel and Thompson's (2011) study is based on the experiences of Indie musicians and artists, it draws parallels to the experiences of luxury consumers and the clichés they must navigate (see e.g. Steinfield, 2015).

Collectively, these articles reveal how social comparisons and normative pressures clearly shape people's perspectives of each other and their own motives and behaviors. They also reflect a navigation of undesirable possible selves as consumers attempted to distance or deny their luxury behavior that could be construed as a social *faux pas*. The prominence of sociocultural forces and consumer reactions continues to grow in the literature as scholars and practitioners grapple with the implications of counterfeits, masstige products, the proliferation of branded goods, and the dominance of the Asian market. As described next, research focused on these marketplace dynamics has ranged from psychological experiments and hypothesized models to qualitatively rich descriptions.

Counterfeits: Studies on counterfeits distinguish them as inauthentic luxury-branded goods (versus non-branded items), that are used to obtain social group affiliation within reference groups (Turunen & Laaksonen, 2011). Unlike luxury goods, studies have found that consumers do not tend to use them to gain admiration because they fear social backlash and public ridicule from other social groups who might be able to distinguish between the genuine and the fake (Wiedmann, Hennigs, & Klarmann, 2012). In order to avoid these negative consequences and feelings of shame, consumers use counterfeits in private or when with friends (Penz & Stöttinger, 2012). Penz and Stöttinger (2012) have also demonstrated that consumers who purchase significantly and slightly cheaper counterfeits view themselves favorably as smart shoppers. Although Penz and Stöttinger do not relate these findings to the multiplicity of selves, many of their descriptions exemplify cognitive dissonance between possible selves: the celebrated real self of the smart shopper stands in contrast to the undesirable self of the poser who risks being shamed. Applying a social comparison perspective, Wilcox, Kim, and Sen (2009) showed that consumers are more likely to purchase counterfeits with logos if they view luxury brands as status symbols, important for helping them to fit in to a social situation; authentic luxury brands are likely to be purchased if consumers view the brands as part of fulfilling self-expressive functions. In contrast, Francis, Burgess, and Lu (2015) recorded that younger generations are pursuing counterfeit luxuries not for social comparison purposes, but for more symbolic and self-expressive reasons. As part of a "cool" anti-brand trend, counterfeits are equated to ideals of rebellion, fun, and being a bit bad by going against the mainstream. Symbolic consumption practices were also found by Gentry, Putrevu, Goh, Commuri, and Cohen (2002) in their study of tourists who knowingly seek out and purchase counterfeits: counterfeits under this guise become symbolic tokens of an authentic travel experience.

Inconspicuous Consumption: More recently, studies have started to examine consumers who choose inconspicuous consumption of luxury or rejection of luxury altogether. Berger and Ward's (2010) experiments conducted with fashion experts and normal students, demonstrated that those with high levels of cultural capital (i.e. knowledge of fashion) prefer subtle and inconspicuous signals on goods as long as these signals can be decoded by others in the know. This allows them to differentiate themselves from normal consumers and also to signal aspects of their identities to like-others. Berger and Ward concluded that similar results could be extrapolated onto luxury consumers: in order to avoid resemblance to middle-status individuals, high-status consumers may choose high-end options with subtle or absent logos even at the risk of resembling low-end options, (a result convergent with Holt, 1998). Findings from Geiger-Oneto, Gelb, Walker, and Hess (2012) also supported this proposition: respondents low in social status (measured by occupational prestige) and favoring status consumption were inclined to choose counterfeits. However, as social status increased, authentic luxury (an LV bag) was chosen over counterfeits, and, at higher levels of social status, respondents selected non-luxury items.

Status Games and Compensatory Consumption: Numerous experimental studies have specifically explored how consumers use luxury as part of status-related games. Han, Nunes, and Drèze (2010), for example, revealed that some consumers high in affluence but who have a low need for status use quiet signals (the patricians), while other wealthy consumers, who have a high need for status but lack the connoisseurship or culture necessary to interpret subtle signals, use loud signals (the parvenus). Consumers low in wealth who have a need for status mimic the parvenus often through the purchase of counterfeits (the poseurs), while those with a low need for status refrain from attempting to signal with luxury altogether (the proletarians). Rucker and Galinsky (2008) found that compensatory motives (compensation for a lack of power) cause low-status groups to choose high-status luxury goods, while Mazzocco et al. (2012) clarified that these higher levels of conspicuous consumption depend on the level of identification with a low-status group and the ego threat that arises from this identification. As Mazzocco et al.'s (2012) tests showed, although blacks (the low-status group) exhibited greater conspicuous consumption desires than whites, blacks who highly identified with their racial group held even greater conspicuous consumption desires, and whites, when made temporarily to identify with a low-status group, likewise had higher conspicuous consumption desires. Similarly, Sivanathan and Pettit (2010), in proposing an alternative explanation for low-income consumers' costly social signaling, demonstrated that low income consumers' purchase of status goods is motivated by compensatory behaviors aimed to restore or protect self-integrity and self-worth.

In contrast to the experimental studies, interpretive research by Gbadamosi (2015) captured how ethnic minority youth in the UK, in managing their various selves, use symbolic consumption to gain acceptance in society. Likewise, Steinfield (2015), who conducted interviews with South African luxury consumers, found that the emerging middle and upper class of black luxury consumers employ luxury as a loud or quiet signal depending on the social context and the identity respondents need to project to ward off undesirable stereotypes. For example, when attempting to instill confidence to secure tenders with black government officials, prestigious luxury items (bling watches) were often employed, or, when socializing with fellow blacks, the use of loud luxury (yellow suits) was encouraged as creative expressions of identity and success; however, when engaging with whites, blacks attempted to fit into the socialization restrictions and distanced themselves from perceptions of tainted wealth by wearing "safe black suits" (p. 33).

Collectively, these studies reveal that the assumed linkages between conspicuous consumption and status do not always hold (see also findings by O'Cass & McEwen, 2004; Truong, Simmons, McColl, & Kitchen, 2008). As Eckhardt, Belk, and Wilson (2015) contend, status – denoted by "high quality, luxury, and perhaps class"—needs to be decoupled from conspicuousness—associated with "recognisability, image and appearance" (p. 811). A high price may indicate a high status, but can also represent lower levels of conspicuousness (Berger & Ward, 2010). Moreover, as the growing body of research on young consumers indicates, compensatory consumption of luxury is being driven more by peer influence or sense of uniqueness or "coolness" rather than the achievement of higher levels of status (Francis et al., 2015; Gentina, Shrum, & Lowrey, 2016).

Comparing the "East" versus the "West" versus the Rest of the World: In offering a counterpoint to many of the Western-centric studies, a stream of literature has emerged to reflect upon differences between "East" and "West" luxury consumption. For example, in addition to the previously mentioned studies (e.g. Li & Su, 2007; Wong & Ahuvia, 1998), Phau and Prendergast (2000) demonstrated that the Confucian values of respect for authority and desire for harmony, affects the explanations given for the conspicuous consumption of Asian luxury consumers. As they argued from a social comparison perspective, the referent group shifts away from higher or lower social groups to members of the same group, leading to pecuniary emulations for conformity purposes. In contrast, Western consumers tend to use (in)conspicuous consumption for invidious purposes, as they seek to distinguish themselves from social groups. Although Han et al.'s (2010) study found that Western consumers also exhibit tendencies to engage in pecuniary emulations, the underlying motives were vested more in achieving individual prestige and distinction rather than saving face. Similarly, Jiang and Cova's (2012) and Lin's (2011) study on counterfeit consumption found that Chinese consumers' purchase of counterfeits was driven by attempts to meet sociocultural demands within financial limitations: the need to save face results in conformity to the brands approved by peers and by social group, which means that a counterfeit version is better than no brand if financial resources cannot be secured to purchase legitimate luxury. Yet Jiang and Cova (2012) also found that consumers driven by a low need for status were likely to purchase counterfeits as part of a hedonically gratifying experience (enjoyable and fun shopping), and internally satisfying accomplishment (obtaining fashionable goods at lower prices).

Although India is often classified as part of the East, research on luxury consumers reveals different social pressures, self-expressive motives, and consumer behaviors than East Asians (Eng & Bogaert, 2010; Atwal & Jain, 2012). For example, luxury is framed more akin to the Western mindset as being symbolic of individual wealth and achievement. Luxury gifts are likewise viewed as a mode of creating distinction: gifts bought for social functions, such as wedding gifts, become markers of people's wealth and success. However, luxury consumption is influenced by a strong pull towards preserving tradition and a preference to base luxury choices on local reference groups, such as Bollywood stars. As a result, foreign luxury becomes blended with traditional Indian clothes and creative designer wear (Eng & Bogaert, 2010).

As the research on India typifies, although initial forays have been made into the study of emerging markets in other areas of the world (India, Brazil, Russia, and wealthy markets in Africa) these studies tend to focus on how consumers are the same or different from the Western norm, often with a slant towards helping marketers understand and maneuver the landscape (Atwal & Bryson, 2014). Research that sheds light on the results of consumer agency (such as status games) remains limited (for notable exceptions see Steinfield (2015) and Üstüner and Thompson (2012) as discussed before).

The Luxury Consumer of the Future: Emerging Trends and Areas for Future Study

Demands for sustainability, the growth of luxury experiences and the sharing economy, and a globally and digitally connected market, are impending trends that will inevitably redefine luxury and the luxury consumer. Although research exists on some of these trends, their implications are still not fully understood and merit further consideration.

For example, Kapferer and Michaut-Denizeau (2013) and Joy, Sherry, Venkatesh, Wang, and Chan (2012), deliver convincing arguments that the luxury industry is well-aligned to address consumer demands for sustainability. However, as Kapferer and Michaut-Denizeau (2013) found, the sustainable focus taken by most companies to ensure properly sourced materials and environmentally friendly products, matter little. Moreover, it misaligns with human welfare concerns more heavily supported by consumers (i.e. exploitation of workforce). Questions remain regarding the generalization of these views: Kapferer and Michaut-Denizeau's (2013) work was with French consumers; Joy et al.'s (2012) was based on consumers from Canada and Hong Kong. Studies thus need to probe for cultural or generational differences. Consumer reactions to social or environmental transgressions require consideration for unsustainable luxury goods *and* luxury experiences (most research is still heavily focused on luxury goods, negating the environmental impact of experiences and services such as luxury travel, spas, sporting events, etc.). Additionally, a potential shift to more animal- and environmentally friendly materials raises questions regarding effects on the perceived authenticity of the luxury goods, and thus raises questions for whether elements valued as status symbols are changing. Similar to how consumers currently use inconspicuous luxury to denote higher status, consumers may use sustainable luxury products to engage in different forms of social comparison games or to communicate real or ideal identities of an eco-friendly self. The questions raised are thus not only what motivates sustainable luxury consumers, but also how the non-sustainable luxury consumers may navigate potentially undesirable identities. Luedicke, Thompson and Giesler's (2010) analysis of Hummer owners' response to a backlash website sheds light on one dimension—discourse tactics. They note how these morally tainted consumers use culturally prominent mythological scripts (e.g. American war hero or American exceptionalism) to navigate criticisms of excessive and wasteful consumption. However, group and individual practices or tactics, especially in regard to face-to-face confrontations or behaviors, require further consideration.

Secondly, technology and hyper-connectivity may be redefining consumer and producer roles. Although the implications of social media as it relates to luxury brand management has benefited from numerous studies (see for example the special issues edited by Ko, Phau, and Aiello (2016), Chandon et al. (2016), and Phan and Park (2014)), further considerations are still needed on topics related to how a hyper-connected world affects consumers' roles. Kapferer (2015), for instance, sheds light on numerous disruptive trends, including how online luxury, which lacks the traditional retail interactions and sensory components, will alter customer engagement, not only between luxury brands' representatives and consumers, but between consumers themselves. Studies by Tynan et al. (2010) and Zhang (2015) have started to reveal how consumers employ networks and social media to shift their roles from a consumer to value co-creator (consumers who work collaboratively with companies to produce innovations that can expand the value proposition) or a prosumer (a consumer who has an increased involvement in content production, often working independently). Tynan et al. (2010) found that companies and consumers can leverage co-creation processes to offer a better, overall luxury brand experience, including giving certain consumers access to a company's key designer or introducing them to artists doing cutting edge designs. Zhang (2015) critically examines Chinese women prosumers who use social media to engage in transnational reselling of Western luxury (i.e. they advertise goods by posting pictures on blogs featuring purchased luxury and then mail luxury goods to clients in China who place orders online). On one hand, Zhang lauds how this entails a form of agentic and participatory power that allows women to redefine boundaries between work and consumption, the commercial and the personal. On the other hand, she questions how this plays into maintaining divisions in societies along class, race, nationality and gender, and how this fosters a commoditization of the prosumer. Although these studies attest to inroads being made, questions remain. How will co-creative consumers and prosumers navigate the resulting multiple selves? And what implications will co-creation and prosumption have on the value proposition and symbolic value of luxury goods and experiences, especially as the prosumer starts to subsume the position of the advertiser and retailer?

Thirdly, luxury experiences, while being identified and shaped into a taxonomy (Atwal & Williams, 2009), connected to the retail space (Dion & Arnould, 2011), and studied at selective venues, such as hotels (Walls, Okumus, Wang & Kwun, 2011), have yet to be fully understood, especially with the rise of the hyper-connected, sharing economy. As Andjelic (2015) summarized, "Traditional luxury imagery may have been a reflection of our identity, but experiential luxury is our identity." This new "memorandum of understanding" of the sharing economy may mean that rented luxury creates experiences that play to social expectations (e.g. yachts, high-end artworks, gowns, watches) and allows consumers to build unique identities through amassed global vacation swaps (e.g. a weekend in a NYC townhouse for a weekend on a private island). The shared economy, although still in a nascent research state in the consumer behavior literature (Belk, 2014; Bardhi & Eckhardt, 2012), clearly has the potential to disrupt the market, redefining goods that we once owned as goods that we merely experience for a rented time. Companies like Project Runway are taking the market to the next level of democratization. What are the implications of these for status games, the demarcation of luxury consumers, and the symbolic value of goods and experiences? Luxury, in this experiential world, may evolve to align more with groups built around desired lifestyles and sociocultural preferences than groups built around socioeconomics and owned status symbols.

In conclusion, while our understanding of luxury consumers has come a long way, much remains to be uncovered if we are to understand the way market changes affect status symbols, and in turn, the implications these have on the way they are used to shape, maintain, and communicate consumer identities.

References

Allen, D. (2002). Toward a Theory of Consumer Choice as Sociohistorically Shaped Practical Experience: The Fits-Like-a-Glove (FLAG) Framework, *Journal of Consumer Research*, 28 (4), 515–32. doi:10.1086/338202.

Allérès, D. (1991). Spécificités et Stratégies Marketing Des Différents Univers Du Luxe, *Revue Française Du Marketing*, 132/33, 71–95.

Andjelic, A. (2015). The Devil Shares Prada: Consumers Want Experiences, Not Products, July 29, http://adage.com/article/digitalnext/devil-shares-prada-sharing-economy-boosts-luxury/299725/.

Arsel, Z., & Bean, J. (2013). Taste Regimes and Market-Mediated Practice, *Journal of Consumer Research*, 39 (5), 899–917. doi:10.1086/666595.

Arsel, Z., & Thompson, C. J. (2011). Demythologizing Consumption Practices: How Consumers Protect Their Field-Dependent Identity Investments from Devaluing Marketplace Myths, *Journal of Consumer Research*, 37 (4), 791–806.

Atwal, G., & Bryson, D. (Eds.). (2014). *Luxury Brands in Emerging Markets*. New York: Palgrave Macmillan.

Atwal, G., & Jain, S. (Eds.). (2012). *The Luxury Market in India : Maharajas to Masses*. Basingstoke: Palgrave Macmillan.

Atwal, G., & Williams, A. (2009). Luxury Brand Marketing – The Experience Is Everything!, *Journal of Brand Management*, 16 (5), 338–46. doi:10.1057/bm.2008.48.

Barbon, N. (1905). *Nicholas Barbon on A Discourse of Trade (1690)*. J. H. Hollander (Ed.). Baltimore: John Hopkins Press.

Bardhi, F., & Eckhardt, G. M. (2012). Access-Based Consumption: The Case of Car Sharing, *Journal of Consumer Research*, 39 (4), 881–98. doi:10.1086/666376.

Barnier, V., Falcy, S., & Valette-Florence, P. (2012). Do Consumers Perceive Three Levels of Luxury? A Comparison of Accessible, Intermediate and Inaccessible Luxury Brands, *Journal of Brand Management*, 19 (7), 623–36. doi:10.1057/bm.2012.11.

Barnier, V., Rodina, I., & Valette-Florence, P. (2006). *Which Luxury Perceptions Affect Most Consumer Purchase Behavior? A Cross Cultural Exploratory Study in France, The United Kingdom and Russia*. Retrieved from www.escp-eap.net/conferences/marketing/2006_cp/Materiali/Paper/Fr/DeBarnier_Rodina_ValetteFlorence.pdf.

Baudrillard, J. (1998). *The Consumer Society: Myths and Structures*. Thousand Oaks: SAGE.

Bearden, W. O., & Etzel, M. J. (1982). Reference Group Influence on Product and Brand Purchase Decisions, *Journal of Consumer Research*, 9 (2), 183–94. doi:10.1086/208911.

Belk, R. (1988). Possessions and the Extended Self, *Journal of Consumer Research*, 15 (2), 139–68.

Belk, R. (2014). You Are What You Can Access: Sharing and Collaborative Consumption Online, *Journal of Business Research*, 67 (8), 1595–1600. doi:10.1016/j.jbusres.2013.10.001.

Berger, J., & Heath, C. (2007). Where Consumers Diverge from Others: Identity Signaling and Product Domains, *Journal of Consumer Research*, 34 (2), 121–34. doi:10.1086/519142.

Berger, J., & Ward, M. (2010). Subtle Signals of Inconspicuous Consumption, *Journal of Consumer Research*, 37 (4), 555–69.

Berry, C. (1994). *The Idea of Luxury: A Conceptual and Historical Investigation*. Cambridge: Cambridge University Press.

Bian, Q., & Forsythe, S. (2012). Purchase Intention for Luxury Brands: A Cross Cultural Comparison, *Journal of Business Research*, 65 (10), 1443–51. doi:10.1016/j.jbusres.2011.10.010.

Bourdieu, P. (1984). *Distinction: A Social Critique of the Judgement of Taste*. (R. Nice, Trans.). Cambridge, MA: Harvard University Press.

Chadha, R. (2006). *The Cult of the Luxury Brand : Inside Asia's Love Affair with Luxury*. London: Nicholas Brealey.

Chandon, J., Laurent, G., & Valette-Florence, P. (2016). Pursuing the Concept of Luxury: Introduction to the JBR Special Issue on "Luxury Marketing from Tradition to Innovation." *Journal of Business Research*, 69 (1), 299–303. doi:10.1016/j.jbusres.2015.08.001.

Chernev, A., Hamilton R., & Gal, D. (2011). Competing for Consumer Identity: Limits to Self-Expression and the Perils of Lifestyle Branding, *Journal of Marketing*, 75 (3), 66–82. doi:10.1509/jmkg.75.3.66.

Christodoulides, G., Michaelidou, N., & Li, C. H. (2009). Measuring Perceived Brand Luxury: An Evaluation of the BLI Scale, *Journal of Brand Management*, 16 (5–6), 395–405. doi:10.1057/bm.2008.49.

Deeter-Schmelz, D. R., Moore, J. N., & Goebel, D. J. (2000). Prestige Clothing Shopping by Consumers: A Confirmatory Assessment and Refinement of the "Precon" Scale with Managerial Implications, *Journal of Marketing Theory and Practice*, 8 (4), 43–58.

Dion, D., & Arnould, E. (2011). Retail Luxury Strategy: Assembling Charisma through Art and Magic, *Journal of Retailing*, 87 (4), 502–20. doi:10.1016/j.jretai.2011.09.001.

Dubois, B., Czellar, S., & Laurent, G. (2005). Consumer Segments Based on Attitudes Toward Luxury: Empirical Evidence from Twenty Countries, *Marketing Letters*, 16 (2), 115–28. doi:10.1007/s11002-005-2172-0.

Dubois, B., & Duquesne, P. (1993). The Market for Luxury Goods: Income versus Culture, *European Journal of Marketing*, 27 (1), 35–44. doi:10.1108/03090569310024530.

Dubois, B., & Laurent, G. (1995). Luxury Possessions and Practices: An Empirical Scale. In F. Hansen (Ed.), *European Advances in Consumer Research*,, 2, 69–77, Provo, UT: Association for Consumer Research.

Dubois, B., Laurent, G., & Czellar, S. (2001). Consumer Rapport to Luxury : Analyzing Complex and Ambivalent Attitudes, *Les Cahiers de Recherche*, 736, Paris: HEC. http://ideas.repec.org/p/ebg/heccah/0736.html.

Eckhardt, G. Belk, R., & Wilson, J. (2015). The Rise of Inconspicuous Consumption, *Journal of Marketing Management*, 31 (7–8), 807–26. doi:10.1080/0267257X.2014.989890.

Eng, T., & Bogaert, J. (2010). Psychological and Cultural Insights into Consumption of Luxury Western Brands in India, *Journal of Customer Behaviour*, 9 (1), 55–75. doi:10.1362/147539210X497620.

Escalas, J., & Bettman, J. (2005). Self-Construal, Reference Groups, and Brand Meaning, *Journal of Consumer Research*, 32 (3), 378–89. doi:10.1086/jcr.2005.32.issue-3.

Ferraro, R., Kirmani, A., & Matherly, T. (2013). Look at Me! Look at Me! Conspicuous Brand Usage, Self-Brand Connection, and Dilution, *Journal of Marketing Research*, 50 (4), 477–88.

Festinger, L. (1954). A Theory of Social Comparison Processes, *Human Relations*, 7 (2), 117–40. doi:10.1177/001872675400700202.

Fionda, A., & Moore, C. (2009). The Anatomy of the Luxury Fashion Brand, *Journal of Brand Management*, 16 (5–6), 347–63. doi:10.1057/bm.2008.45.

Francis, J., Burgess, L., & Lu, M. (2015). Hip to Be Cool: A Gen Y View of Counterfeit Luxury Products, *Journal of Brand Management*, 22 (7), 588–602.

Gbadamosi, A. (2015). Brand Personification and Symbolic Consumption among Ethnic Minority Teenage Consumers: An Empirical Study, *Journal of Brand Management*, 22 (9), 737–54.

Geiger-Oneto, S., Gelb, B., Walker, D., & Hess, J. (2012). "Buying Status" by Choosing or Rejecting Luxury Brands and Their Counterfeits, *Journal of the Academy of Marketing Science*, 41 (3), 357–72. doi:10.1007/s11747-012-0314-5.

Gentina, E., Shrum, L. J., & Lowrey, T. M. (2016). Teen Attitudes toward Luxury Fashion Brands from a Social Identity Perspective: A Cross-Cultural Study of French and U.S. Teenagers, *Journal of Business Research*, 69 (12), 5785–92. doi:10.1016/j.jbusres.2016.04.175.

Gentry, J., Putrevu, S., Goh, J., Commuri, S., & Cohen, J. (2002). The Legitimacy of Counterfeits: Consumers Choosing Counterfeit Brands and Tourists Seeking Authentic Counterfeits, *Macromarketing Conference Proceedings*, 226–41.

Goffman, E. (1951). Symbols of Class Status, *The British Journal of Sociology*, 2 (4), 294–304. doi:10.2307/588083.

Han, Y. J., Nunes, J. C., & Drèze, X. (2010). Signaling Status with Luxury Goods: The Role of Brand Prominence, *Journal of Marketing* 74 (4), 15–30. doi:10.1509/jmkg.74.4.15.

Hennigs, N., Wiedmann, K., Klarmann, C., Strehlau, S., Godey, B., Pederzoli, D., . . . Oh, H. (2012). What Is the Value of Luxury? A Cross-Cultural Consumer Perspective, *Psychology & Marketing*, 29 (12), 1018–34. doi:10.1002/mar.20583.

Hirschman, E., & Holbrook, M. (1982). Hedonic Consumption: Emerging Concepts, Methods and Propositions, *Journal of Marketing*, 46 (3), 92–101. doi:10.2307/1251707.

Holt, D. (1998). Does Cultural Capital Structure American Consumption?, *Journal of Consumer Research*, 25 (1), 1–25.

Hudders, L., Pandelaere, M., & Vyncke, P. (2013). The Meaning of Luxury Brands in a Democratized Luxury World, *International Journal of Marketing*, 55 (3), 391–412.

Husic, M., & Cicic, M. (2009). Luxury Consumption Factors, *Journal of Fashion Marketing and Management: An International Journal*, 13 (2), 231–45. doi:10.1108/13612020910957734.

Jiang, L., & Cova, V. (2012). Love for Luxury, Preference for Counterfeits –A Qualitative Study in Counterfeit Luxury Consumption in China, *International Journal of Marketing Studies* 4 (6). doi:10.5539/ijms.v4n6p1.

Joy, A., Sherry Jr, J.F., Venkatesh, A., Wang, J., & Chan, R. (2012). Fast Fashion, Sustainability, and the Ethical Appeal of Luxury Brands, *Fashion Theory*, 16 (3), 273–95. doi:10.2752/175174112X13340749707123.

Kapferer, J. (1998). Why Are We Seduced by Luxury Brands? *Journal of Brand Management*, 6 (1), 44–49. doi:10.1057/bm.1998.43.

Kapferer, J. (2015). *Kapferer on Luxury: How Luxury Brands Can Grow Yet Remain Rare*. Philadelphia: Kogan Page Publishers.

Kapferer, J., & Bastien, V. (2012). *The Luxury Strategy: Break the Rules of Marketing to Build Luxury Brands*. Philadelphia: Kogan Page Publishers.

Kapferer, J., & Michaut-Denizeau, A. (2013). Is Luxury Compatible with Sustainability? Luxury Consumers' Viewpoint, *Journal of Brand Management*, 21 (1), 1–22. doi:10.1057/bm.2013.19.

Kastanakis, M. N., & Balabanis, G. (2012). Between the Mass and the Class: Antecedents of the "bandwagon" Luxury Consumption Behavior, *Journal of Business Research*, 65 (10), 1399–1407. doi:10.1016/j.jbusres.2011.10.005.

Ko, E., Phau, I., & Aiello, G. (2016). Luxury Brand Strategies and Customer Experiences: Contributions to Theory and Practice, *Journal of Business Research*, 69 (12), 5749–52. doi:10.1016/j.jbusres.2016.04.170

Levy, S. (1959). Symbols for Sale, *Harvard Business Review,* July-August, 117–24.

Li, J. J., & Su, C. (2007). How Face Influences Consumption - a Comparative Study of American and Chinese Consumers, *International Journal of Market Research*, 49 (2), 237–56.

Lin, Y. J. (2011). *Fake Stuff: China and the Rise of Counterfeit Goods*. New York: Routledge.

Luedicke, M. K., Thompson, C, J., & Giesler, M. (2010). Consumer Identity Work as Moral Protagonism: How Myth and Ideology Animate a Brand-Mediated Moral Conflict, *Journal of Consumer Research*, 36 (6), 1016–32. doi:10.1086/644761.

Markus, H., & Nurius, P. (1986). Possible Selves, *American Psychologist*, 41 (9), 954–69. doi:10.1037/0003-066X.41.9.954.

Mason, R. (1993). Cross-Cultural Influences on the Demand For Status Goods, In W. F. Van Raaij & G. J. Bamossy (Eds.). *European Advances in Consumer Research*, 46–51. Provo, UT: Association for Consumer Research.

Mazzocco, P. J., Rucker, D. D., Galinsky, A. D., & Anderson, E. T. (2012). Direct and Vicarious Conspicuous Consumption: Identification with Low-Status Groups Increases the Desire for High-Status Goods, *Journal of Consumer Psychology*, 22 (4), 520–28. doi:10.1016/j.jcps.2012.07.002.

McCracken, G. D. (1988). *Culture and Consumption: New Approaches to the Symbolic Character of Consumer Goods and Activities*. Bloomington: Indiana University Press.

Mick, D. G. (1986). Consumer Research and Semiotics: Exploring the Morphology of Signs, Symbols, and Significance, *Journal of Consumer Research*, 13 (2), 196–213. doi:10.1086/209060.

Muniz, A., & O'Guinn, T. (2001). Brand Community, *Journal of Consumer Research*, 27 (4), 412–32. doi:10.1086/319618.

O'Cass, A., & McEwen, H. (2004). Exploring Consumer Status and Conspicuous Consumption, *Journal of Consumer Behaviour*, 4 (1), 25–39. doi:10.1002/cb.155.

Ogilvie, D. M. (1987). The Undesired Self: A Neglected Variable in Personality Research, *Journal of Personality and Social Psychology*, 52 (2), 379–85. doi:10.1037/0022-3514.52.2.379.

Okonkwo, U. (2007). *Luxury Fashion Branding: Trends, Tactics, Techniques.* New York: Palgrave Macmillan.

Penz, E., & Stöttinger, B. (2012). A Comparison of the Emotional and Motivational Aspects in the Purchase of Luxury Products versus Counterfeits, *Journal of Brand Management*, 19 (7), 581–94.

Peterson, R. A., & Kern, R. M. (1996). Changing Highbrow Taste: From Snob to Omnivore, *American Sociological Review*, 61 (5), 900–7. doi:10.2307/2096460.

Phan, M. & Park, S. (2014). Introduction: Social Media Marketing and Luxury Brands, *Journal of Global Fashion Marketing*, 5 (3), 195–96. doi:10.1080/20932685.2014.908528.

Phau, I., & Prendergast, G. (2000). Consuming Luxury Brands: The Relevance of the "Rarity Principle," *Journal of Brand Management*, 8 (2), 122–38. doi:10.1057/palgrave.bm.2540013.

Powell, B. (1990). Flaunting It, Japan Style, *Newsweek*, 7 (116), 46–47.

Richins, M., & Dawson, S. (1992). A Consumer Values Orientation for Materialism and Its Measurement: Scale Development and Validation, *Journal of Consumer Research*, 19 (3), 303–16.

Roper, S., Caruana, R., Medway, D., & Murphy, P. (2013). Constructing Luxury Brands: Exploring the Role of Consumer Discourse, *European Journal of Marketing*, 47 (3/4), 375–400. doi:10.1108/03090561311297382.

Roux, E. (1995). Consumer Evaluation of Luxury Brand Extensions, In *Proceedings of the European Marketing Academy*, 1971–80. Cergy-Pontoise, France: ESSEC.

Rucker, D., & Galinsky, A. (2008). Desire to Acquire: Powerlessness and Compensatory Consumption, *Journal of Consumer Research*, 35 (2), 257–67.

Sheth, J., Newman, B., & Gross, B. (1991). Why We Buy What We Buy: A Theory of Consumption Values, *Journal of Business Research*, 22 (2), 159–70. doi:10.1016/0148–2963(91)90050–8.

Shukla, P. (2011). Impact of Interpersonal Influences, Brand Origin and Brand Image on Luxury Purchase Intentions: Measuring Interfunctional Interactions and a Cross-National Comparison, *Journal of World Business*, 46 (2), 242–52. doi:10.1016/j.jwb.2010.11.002.

Silverstein, M., & Fiske, N. (2003). Luxury for the Masses, *Harvard Business Review*, April: 48–57.

Silverstein, M., Fiske, N., & Butman, J. (2008). *Trading Up: Why Consumers Want New Luxury Goods—and How Companies Create Them.* New York: Penguin.

Simmel, G. (1957). Fashion, *American Journal of Sociology*, 62 (6), 541–58.

Sirgy, J. (1982). Self-Concept in Consumer Behavior: A Critical Review, *Journal of Consumer Research*, 9 (3), 287–300. doi:10.1086/208924.

Sivanathan, N., & Pettit, N. (2010). Protecting the Self through Consumption: Status Goods as Affirmational Commodities, *Journal of Experimental Social Psychology*, 46 (3), 564–70. doi:10.1016/j.jesp.2010.01.006.

Solomon, M. (1983). The Role of Products as Social Stimuli: A Symbolic Interactionism Perspective, *Journal of Consumer Research*, 10 (3), 319–29.

Steinfield, L. (2015). *Consumer Types versus Stereotypes: Exploring Social Tensions in the Luxury Market of South Africa.* SSRN Scholarly Paper ID 2612830. Saïd Business School Working Paper. Rochester, NY: Social Science Research Network.

Thomas, D. (2007). *Deluxe: How Luxury Lost Its Luster.* New York: Penguin Press.

Truong, Y., & McColl, R. (2011). Intrinsic Motivations, Self-Esteem, and Luxury Goods Consumption, *Journal of Retailing and Consumer Services*, 18 (6), 555–61. doi:10.1016/j.jretconser.2011.08.004.

Truong, Y., Simmons, G., McColl, R., & Kitchen, P. (2008). Status and Conspicuousness – Are They Related? Strategic Marketing Implications for Luxury Brands, *Journal of Strategic Marketing*, 16 (3), 189–203. doi:10.1080/09652540802117124.

Tsai, S. (2005). Impact of Personal Orientation on Luxury-Brand Purchase Value: An International Investigation, *International Journal of Market Research*, 47 (4), 427–52.

Turunen, L. L. M., Laaksonen, P. (2011). Diffusing the Boundaries between Luxury and Counterfeits, *The Journal of Product and Brand Management*, 20 (6), 468–74.

Twitchell, J. (2003). *Living It Up: America's Love Affair with Luxury.* New York: Simon and Schuster.

Tynan, C., McKechnie, S., & Chhuon, C. (2010). Co-Creating Value for Luxury Brands, *Journal of Business Research*, 63 (11), 1156–63. doi:10.1016/j.jbusres.2009.10.012.

Üstüner, T., & Thompson, C. J. (2012). How Marketplace Performances Produce Interdependent Status Games and Contested Forms of Symbolic Capital, *Journal of Consumer Research*, 38 (5), 796–814. doi:10.1086/660815.

Veblen, T. (2009). *The Theory of the Leisure Class.* Martha Banta (Ed.). Oxford: Oxford University Press.

Vigneron, F., & Johnson, L. (1999). A Review and a Conceptual Framework of Prestige-Seeking Consumer Behavior, *Academy of Marketing Science Review*, 3 (1), 1–17.

Vigneron, F., & Johnson, L. (2004). Measuring Perceptions of Brand Luxury, *Journal of Brand Management*, 11 (6), 484–506. doi:10.1057/palgrave.bm.2540194.

Walley, K., & Li, C. (2015). The Market for Luxury Brands in China: Insight Based on a Study of Consumer's Perceptions in Beijing, *Journal of Brand Management*, 22 (3), 246–60.

Walls, A., Okumus, F., Wang, Y., & Kwun, D. J. (2011). Understanding the Consumer Experience: An Exploratory Study of Luxury Hotels, *Journal of Hospitality Marketing & Management*, 20 (2), 166–97. doi:10.1080/19368623.2011.536074.

Wang, Y., Sun, S., & Song, Y. (2011). Chinese Luxury Consumers: Motivation, Attitude and Behavior, *Journal of Promotion Management*, 17 (3), 345–59. doi:10.1080/10496491.2011.596122.

White, K., Argo, J., & Sengupta, J. (2012). Dissociative versus Associative Responses to Social Identity Threat: The Role of Consumer Self-Construal, *Journal of Consumer Research*, 39 (4), 704–19. doi:10.1086/664977.

Wiedmann, K., Hennigs, N., & Klarmann, C. (2012). Luxury Consumption in the Trade-off between Genuine and Counterfeit Goods: What Are the Consumers' Underlying Motives and Value-Based Drivers?, *Journal of Brand Management*, 19 (7), 544–66.

Wiedmann, K., Hennigs, N., & Siebels, A. (2009). Value-Based Segmentation of Luxury Consumption Behavior, *Psychology and Marketing*, 26 (7), 625–51. doi:10.1002/mar.20292.

Wilcox, K., Kim, H. M., & Sen, S. (2009). Why Do Consumers Buy Counterfeit Luxury Brands? *Journal of Marketing Research*, 46 (2), 247–59. doi:10.1509/jmkr.46.2.247.

Wong, N., & Ahuvia, A. (1998). Personal Taste and Family Face: Luxury Consumption in Confucian and Western Societies, *Psychology and Marketing*, 15 (5), 423–41.

Wood, W., & Hayes, T. (2012). Social Influence on Consumer Decisions: Motives, Modes, and Consequences, *Journal of Consumer Psychology*, 22 (3), 324–28. doi:10.1016/j.jcps.2012.05.003.

Zhang, L. (2015). Fashioning the Feminine Self in "Prosumer Capitalism": Women's Work and the Transnational Reselling of Western Luxury Online, *Journal of Consumer Culture*, February, 1469540515572239. doi:10.1177/1469540515572239.

PART XIII

Subcultures

25

COMMUNITY LOST: THE UNREALIZED COLLABORATIVE MARKET POTENTIAL OF CREDIT UNIONS

Hope Jensen Schau[1] *and Albert M. Muñiz Jr.*[2]

[1]UNIVERSITY OF ARIZONA, TUCSON, AZ, USA
[2]DEPAUL UNIVERSITY, CHICAGO, IL, USA

No, but you . . . you . . . you're thinking of this place all wrong . . . Well, your money's in Joe's – right next to yours. And in the Kennedy House, and Mrs. Macklin's house, and, and a hundred others. Why, you're lending them the money to build, and then, they're going to pay it back to you . . .
> *(George Bailey, explaining collective financing of home ownership well before the share economy in Frank Capra's It's a Wonderful Life)*

Introduction

Consumption communities. Collaborative consumption. Collaborative marketplaces. Peer-to-peer markets. Sharing. The access economy. These are some of the hottest buzzwords in the marketplace, powered by a wave of consumer-driven trends toward a new way of consuming. The access economy is a global movement away from private or traditional ownership, toward communal, collaborative, collective consumption, or put simply, sharing. Entrepreneurs are capitalizing on this trend to offer consumers worldwide access to pools of products and services inspiring them to own less and share more—with family, friends, and loosely linked community members—nearly strangers. The B2C (business-to-consumer) model of production/consumption is giving way to the C2C (consumer-to-consumer) model, often now called peer-to-peer, in which the business institution exists in order to enable resource access, or the sharing of resources between consumers linked to one another through often nebulous ties (Bardhi and Eckhardt 2012).

The access economy accounts for $15B in the US with an estimated 90 million active sharers, most of whom are Generation X with Millennials close behind (Pew Research). From transportation access via Zipcar (autos) and Spokefly (bicycles), to food cooperatives (LocalHarvest), to Airbnb (peer-to-peer accommodations), to Spinlister and Gear Shed (peer-to-peer sports gear)—more and more resources are accessed rather than owned, or available on a communally shared basis in an access-oriented economy.

In *Time Magazine* (February 9, 2015), Joel Stein titles his article "Baby You Can Drive my Car" with the subtitles "And Stay in My Guest Room. And do my Errands. And Rent my Stuff." Stein highlighted the access-oriented, shared resource models that are in many ways challenging our traditional ownership paradigms. In fact, the sharing economy is a misnomer; the more appropriate title is the access economy where consumers pay to access resources, rather than buy them outright (Eckhardt and Bardhi 2015). Access is granted via payment within a membership of consumers, who often have the ability, indeed obligation, of rating one another on their interactions. Interestingly, the most prevalent qualms expressed by individuals participating in the access economy are based on trust: distrust of others in the access community, distrust about how the rented item will be treated, distrust of the quality of the items accessed, distrust over private information being leaked, and a general distrust that the resources required to participate in the access network exceeds the value exchanged. This expressed distrust supports Eckhardt and Bardhi's (2015) assertion that this is not a sharing economy. It also belies a concern that access networks fall short of any community ethos with members acting more as networks of loosely linked members who feel no familial bond with one another.

The new access economy has taken established businesses, brands and institutions by surprise, and many are racing to catch up—working to create peer-to-peer opportunities and join the world of collaborative consumption. For example, Ford, the oldest surviving auto manufacturer, is starting an access car service (Risen 2015). However, Ford's efforts to reinvigorate its market presence may not be successful as traditional firms and institutions are disadvantaged in the shared access business model. Rachel Botsman, Collaborative Lab founder, asserts that trust has shifted in this new collaborative marketplace from institutions to individuals (Botsman 2015). As such, Ford will have to faithfully and authentically practice the access model to win over the collaborative market segment.

One market that has lagged the farthest behind in the access economy is the traditional financial market. However, one of the five companies in the collaborative consumption space that Forbes called out was LendingClub—a peer-to-peer company practicing a community ethos where individual members lend to other individual members. In the time frame reported, LendingClub had successfully rolled out an IPO raising $870 million dollars and its valuation was $3 billion (Forbes 2015, Thenexttechstock.com 2015). An example of non-traditional financial companies taking measures to keep pace with these changes, Santander Bank sends its non-qualifying borrowers to FundingCircle, which, like LendingClub, is a peer-to-peer enterprise (Botsman 2015).

Interestingly, credit unions were onto this "new" trend in the finance world in the 1800s, when farmers first combined resources to cooperatively acquire equipment, on credit, before the harvest season. Credit unions have continued in a member-to-member, collaborative financial model that is, in light of the access economy we see today, extremely far-sighted. However, when talking about the access economy financial models, credit unions are not mentioned in popular or business press. This most likely reflects deeply embedded biases toward new technologies and the supposedly revolutionary new practices they spawn. Instead, relatively new, technology-centered companies, like Kickstarter and GoFundMe, with a member-to-member lending model, much like credit unions, steal the limelight of the shared access economy. Also relevant is that, despite being early entrants in the peer-to-peer financial sphere, credit unions' financial instruments have not kept pace with the changing world. For example, financial instruments, even in the credit union sphere, are based on traditional forms of government sanctioned and recognized kinship ties. Credit unions have not capitalized upon their inherent member-to-member organizational structure to be the market leader in the shared access financial sector. Surprisingly, although they have been member-to-member financing for more than a century, not even credit unions refer to themselves as part of the collaborative consumption movement. Thus our primary research questions are: (1) are shared access networks, market-oriented communities as claimed in popular and business press? and specifically, (2) if shared access networks are community based and credit unions were founded to be community focused, why are credit unions omitted in the access economy discourse?

Theoretical Foundation

Collaborative Consumption

Despite the theoretical dominance of the economic rational man and micro psychological notions of motives and goals, little consumption is truly individual and independent of other social actors (e.g., purchased by one person for the sole and private use of one person). Rather, consumption is most often performed in social collectives. Collectives can take the form of dyads, families, neighborhoods and local municipalities, local affinity groups, professional organizations, brand communities, nations, and even the human race. Your family is your first consumer collective. Your neighbors and co-workers provide the next most common collectives. Then, there are those collectives that are based on affinity (e.g., the running subculture) and often center on brands themselves (brand communities, like Nike Run). These networks can be on-ground, at-a-distance, online, or hybrid.

Collaborative consumption is more than mere collective consumption. It is when the collective works together to create value that would not be there if the consumption were performed individually (Botsman and Rogers 2010). Collaborative consumption takes place in social networks where value is added in synchronous, as well as asynchronous sequential, collaboration. With the help of technology like social media, collaborative consumption can extend beyond the confines of a single locale or proximal relationships, maximizing the collaborative capacity.

Collaboration can range from input on product attributes, acquisition influence, collective bargaining, simultaneous use, sequential use streams, co-use, and collective simultaneous and sequential product and/or service modification and innovation (see Muñiz and Taillard this volume). As it becomes easier to communicate, collaborate, and share costs, we expect that larger groups will collaborate in more significant ways than ever to reduce costs and enhance value.

Collective and collaborative consumption and production are prevalent and qualitatively different from individual consumption and firm-centered production. Collaborative consumption often leads to increased, potentially unanticipated value creation and ultimately collaborative production (Botsman and Rogers 2010). Firms can realize value by understanding collective behaviors and harnessing collaboration.

We identify four types of collaborative relationships in business today:

1 **Business-to-consumer**, where businesses encourage collaboration with their current consumers to promote value propositions to new and existing consumers, increase brand awareness, and enhance consumer-brand engagement. For example: Doritos' consumer-created Super Bowl commercial contest or Amazon's review system where consumers review products and buyers and sellers review one another.

2 **Consumer-to-consumer**, where consumers collaborate with other consumers to realize enhanced value through brand use. For example: Harry Potter fan fiction forums or aftermarket customization "parties" for Apple's iWatch.

3 **Business-to-business**, where businesses collaborate to produce increased value to one another and to end users. For example: just-in-time resource allocation arrangements or supply chain backhaul agreements where costs are reduced by contracting cargo for delivery trucks' return trips rather than run them empty on the back trip.

4 **Consumer-to-business**, where consumers collaborate with businesses on their own initiative to enhance value. For example: consumer-initiated and firm supported Mini Cooper or Harley Davidson rallies.

The access economy, collaborative consumption, collective consumption, and peer-to-peer are all terms that refer to the movement toward consumer-to-consumer sharing of assets, with new businesses and institutions that facilitate this access model.

Airbnb, one of the most famous collaborative consumption market successes, is called by John Mildenhall, the company's CMO, "a community-drive super-brand" (Botsman, 2015). Indeed, there are now Airbnbs listed on producthunt.com promoting access to products beyond accommodations, extending to driveways and even restrooms. This might lead one to think of the access economy as a passing fad or trivial; however, the access economy is a formidable economic force crossing many industries (Figure 25.2 later). In fact, five of the 15 startups Forbes ranked as "fastest growing valuations over time between funding rounds in 2014" were part of this new shared access economy: Uber and Lyft (peer-to-peer taxi services), RelayRides (peer-to-peer auto rentals), LendingClub (peer-to-peer financial lending), and Airbnb (Forbes 2015). All of these access networks have distinct membership directives including personal information stored for accountability and markers of belonging. All have specified practices. All inspire moral obligation to rank and even comment on interactions. In essence, these exemplars all have markers of brand and market-oriented communities: consciousness of kind, rites and traditions, and moral responsibility (Muñiz and O'Guinn 2001). Community scaffolds the access economy by enabling members to trust one another.

Financing Ownership in the Share Movement

The access economy is often thought of as synonymous with the end of ownership but in practice access models exist alongside traditional ownership models (Bardhi and Eckhardt 2012). In fact, consumers in a given day or week may buy or use traditionally owned goods and sequentially or simultaneously use accessed goods and services. For example, a person heading out for a night with friends may use his personally owned smartphone to request an access-based car via Lift or Uber.

The access economy is uniquely poised to solve consumer challenges such as affording and storing special occasion use products. Girl Meets Dress (Davidi 2014) offers women the ability to essentially rent luxury gowns worn for special and often single use occasions. This is a highly desirable value proposition, as the business model allows shared access to a set of luxury dresses for a short term at a dramatically reduced price compared to outright ownership and removes the necessity of storage. Women need never wear the same special occasion dress twice. Similarly, LoanATool is a tool access library where consumers pay to access tools they rarely need, ensuring that they have the specialized tool they need without the financial obligation and storage concerns associated with ownership on demand. Still, ownership continues to be desirable for many products and for many consumers who participate in collaborative consumption (Rifkin 2001).

Business models are emerging to accommodate and facilitate shared ownership and access libraries in nonkinship networks:

* transportation cooperatives (bicycle and automobile sharing),
* homes (time shares and communes),
* cloud computing where data is stored in a shared cloud not in the personal computer.

Such arrangements portend changes for the ownership of traditional assets like automobiles and real estate. Changing ownership models of these assets most likely will affect their financing, as consumers demand financial instruments that fit their life. Credit unions are uniquely poised to facilitate shared ownership systems, if they can become part of the access economy discourse and modify their financial instruments to capitalize on their member-member origins. Unfortunately, before the current access movement, traditional financial institutions had moved far away from this collaborative financing. Even credit unions, which should be members lending to members by charter, use FHA loans for housing, require family relationships for shared banking accounts, and have no provision for shared, communal assets in financial instruments.

Family Only! Obstacles to Entry into the Share Economy Marketplace

In the United States, financial instruments are predominantly offered to collectives that meet the legal definition of family or other sanctioned contractual relationships (legally recognized partnerships, cooperatives and corporations). Kornhauser (1993) examines the underpinnings of the "only for family and married couples" joint tax return rules. The IRS, banks, credit unions, insurance companies and other traditional financial institutions seem not only tethered to old conventions of private ownership, but also tethered to legally sanctioned definitions of "family" that are not reflective of the kinship structures seen today. Blended families, step families, multi-generational households (adult children with spouses and children moving back with parents), friends banding together to share expenses—many of these relationships and more show a definition of family that is morphing.

While the nuclear family seems like a fundamental concept, anthropological data reveal it as a recent development. The American notion of the nuclear family, living independently, headed by a breadwinning man and homemaker wife is a modern phenomenon. Even with the strict definition of family as

> . . . a social group characterized by common residence, economic cooperation and reproduction. It contains adults of both sexes, at least two of whom maintain a socially approved sexual relationship, and one or more children, own or adopted, of the sexually cohabiting adults.
>
> *(Murdock 1949, p. 1)*

Many individuals identify at least two nuclear families in their lives—family of origin and family of procreation. Before the idea of nuclear family, the extended family was the dominant family configuration. Industrialization, early capitalism, and WW2 brought mobility to many Western countries that disrupted extended families, and allowed a new definition of the financially independent nuclear family to take hold.

However, across cultures, people live in myriad family and kinship groupings. The dominant form of family in the global context is the extended families (Widmer 2010). In the United States, immigration, economic hardships, cooperative philosophies, eco-footprint concerns, and legitimizing social reforms have allowed for many different family structures to be recognized socially. The financial world seems ripe for a move away from instruments that build upon a socially constructed view of "family" to the sharing economy, and credit unions are a logical place to find this instigated.

In an advertisement for its "Friends and Family" plan for cell phone service, Sprint used the term "framily" to describe the collaborative consumption aspect of their new plans. Unlike traditional cell phone contracts, theirs supported up to ten different people sharing the plan, the discount, and the bills. Although this may sound like a traditional family plan where parents add extra lines and phones for children, Sprint's version separated out the bills for each member—and there is no family requirement to be a part of this collective. Framily is an important term, because it highlights one of the obstacles that the share economy finds when it meets financial institutions: the "family" requirement. Sprint's plan ended up being short-lived, but it was a clever attempt at eliminating obstacles for nontraditional groups of people who wanted to share.

The sharing economy is global, and although the Sprint plan seems progressive, it is actually behind other parts of the world. Steenson and Donner (2009), write about cell phone sharing in India. Not only are plans shared, but phones are:

> Arundathi is a college student in Bangalore. As she sits in one of the city's many new popular coffee shops, her mobile rings. Although the young woman on the other end of the line is not looking for Arundathi, she has not misdialed, either. The caller asks if Arundathi's friend Neema is there. Indeed, she is, and Arundathi happily passes over the handset. The caller was trying to locate Neema but did so by contacting *someone* else, not *someplace* else.
>
> *p. 231*

Credit Unions are stifled by the dominance of legal definitions in creating financial products that exclusively recognize these sanctioned relationships (i.e., marriage and dependent status). CUs may opt to be on the leading edge of political discussions and legal definitions to create innovative financial products for collectives not necessarily recognized by the legal systems (i.e., multi-generational households and domestic partnerships not sanctioned by a governing body). Members are the credit union, the credit union is the members, and members decide what products the credit union offers and sells. In essence, the origins of credit unions are aligned with the access economy models. Changing their financial offerings to leverage the member-to-member ethos and being a part of government reformation to recognize a wider set of social relationships and obligations, credit unions can lead the charge in creating a sustainable access economy. As members grow as part of the access economy, the credit union would be a natural partner to offer products that move with them.

The Shared Access Economy is Not New

In current American and world economies, within family-and-friend networks have exhibited "quasi-credit" (Fafchamps 2004) zero-interest informal loan structures and pure transfers. This has been studied by academics in rural settings, global settings, inner city settings, and in times of economic hardship (Sagner and Mtati 1999). Historically weddings were sources of financial prosperity perpetuation, homesteads were often multi-generational lands. Wills remain collective asset flows. The credit union difference is that they aggregate member assets and turn them directly into enhanced wealth and access to financial instruments—for members not for profit.

However, over time, the meaning of ownership for specific items changes, and one of the major impacts of the shared access economy is changing these. For instance, automobiles began as part of a nuclear family identity, where the car demonstrated the affluence of the family and their status in the community (Flink 1990). From there, the automobile became one of the most prototypical "possessions as extension of self" (Belk 1988). The car one owned, drove, and parked in the driveway could be used to measure much about oneself and for others to judge. In the shared access economy, however, automobiles are shared or borrowed (Zip Car) and the meaning of car ownership is changed (Bardhi and Eckhardt 2012). The meaning of home ownership is on the cusp of a meaning change as well. Like the automobile, the house was a sign of family prosperity; however, the family identity was beyond the nuclear family to include the extended family, where estates and homesteads were the sign of the larger family identity (Ronald 2008). Ownership was shared under the umbrella of family and kinship. Legalities concerning estates were based on legitimate kinship (Spring 1997).

Shared ownership has been used in England, as the UK government tries to bring ownership into the realm of affordability for more of the population. Under shared ownership the meaning attached to the home itself in the ownership structure has been undergoing a transformation, not without hiccups (Bright and Hopkins 2011). The authors come to the conclusion that shared ownership stretches the concept of home ownership passed its breaking point. Here, a dweller pays a mortgage for 25–75% of the property's value at the time of contract and then up to 3% rental of the balance of the bank or community held value. The dweller is able to modify/improve/personalize the property within contractual specifications and to continuously inhabit the property. Tenancy rights can be transferred within a kinship network subject to a new valuation of the property. In essence, it is never owned outright and the rights associated with the shared ownership are lean and akin to access rights. As such, Bright and Hopkins (2011) suggest that more nuanced meanings are necessary for the concept of home ownership. They also argue that for shared ownership to continue, change is needed in the populace for home owning expectations. The time might well be here as many move forward to a sharing economy with collaborative consumption and collective assets that is more reminiscent of past times.

Method

A multi-method approach to examining our research questions was used. We are curious to see if shared access networks are market-oriented communities and if they are community based, why credit unions are omitted in the access economy discourse. First, secondary sources were examined and scanned for emerging trends. Next, credit union web presences were analyzed to determine if and how they referenced their member-to-member ethos and if they linked their mission to the peer-to-peer access market discourse. Then, interviews with credit union executives were conducted. Lastly, focus groups of dedicated credit union managers with an expressed interest in exploring how credit unions might leverage peer-to-peer collaborative consumption to create new products and services were facilitated.

Extant Literature Review and Market Trend Analysis

First, a review of the extant academic literature on collective and collaborative consumption was performed. This consists of examining all scholarly articles related to the topic of collaborative consumption and the access economy. Eighty-six articles that in some way addressed the central phenomenon were reviewed.

Next, a market summary of the latest trends in collaborative consumption across industries, including the financial services sector was conducted. Here, database searches for business press and general news venues were utilized. Key words identified relevant articles. Key words included: collaborative consumption, value co-creation, peer-to-peer markets, sharing, access, shared access, collaborative markets, and so on.

Credit Unions Web Presences

Credit unions' online presences were analyzed for references to community ethos and flexible financial offerings. Special attention was paid to a few that were incorporating collective collaborative consumption. From these data two case studies are presented.

Interviews

Interviews were conducted with 18 credit union executives from the United States and Canada, who self-identified as grappling with collaborative collectives beyond the nuclear family and how credit unions can better position themselves to offer new and relevant financial instruments. Interviews were semi-structured and followed a protocol that focused on trends facing credit unions, the shared access economy and how credit might create new product offerings that would fit into the shared economy ethos. Interviews were conducted in person and over the phone to maximize reach. The average interview duration was 42 minutes. Email exchanges with the interview participants were used for clarification and to develop key themes. An additional set of six email based interviews regarding some specific topics were solicited.

Focus Group Discussions

In a 2015 meeting of credit union leaders, collective, collaborative consumption was afforded a small working session. Here, a set of 21 participants were asked to ponder the impact increasingly collaborative consumers might have on financial markets and how credit unions might best structure new flexible financial instruments that would allow for collective utilization beyond the nuclear family. Participants got into small working groups of 3–5, and fleshed out ideas. Passionate discussions emerged. Each member had examples of how current financial instruments let them down. The groups toiled away the afternoon creating financial solutions. The groups were audio-recorded and transcribed. Their work products were collected and archived.

Data Analysis

Data were captured and analyzed iteratively (Schwandt 1997), and triangulating methods were used (extant literature content analysis, web presence content analysis, interviews and focus groups). Data analysis was guided by grounded theory as advocated in Glaser and Strauss

(1967) and elaborated by Strauss and Corbin (1998). We used the constant comparative method of analysis (Spiggle 1994), coding the data and distilling thematic patterns. Initial data were analyzed separately and then reinterpreted comparatively, while subsequent data were analyzed in light of previous data, or a hermeneutic circle of understanding (Schwandt 1997).

Taken together, this represents a robust corpus of data from which we can examine the manner in which credit unions fit into the access market discourse.

Findings

Context: Credit Unions Go Back to the Future

Bringing the access economy mindset to traditional financial instruments is not a new concept. In fact, credit unions were founded to aggregate financial resources among those with little capital, in order to collectively buy prohibitively expensive farm equipment in the 1800s (Moody and Fite 1984). The credit union model is member-owned, member-financed, a peer-to-peer structure rare in the financial world. Past research has suggested that credit union members appear to feel that they have a sense of community and trust in their credit unions, and do not feel this attachment to large financial institutions (Schau and DuFault 2015). Schau and DuFault (2015) find that credit union members talk about their financial institutions in terms of community ethos (belonging, moral obligation, and shared purpose) passionately referencing the credit unions' for members not for profit mission.

Credit unions achieve their competitive advantage over traditional banks because they are founded upon a premise of member collaboration. Resource advantage theory (Hunt, 2000) postulates that better competencies are the basis of competitive advantage. Currently, credit unions do not promote their competitive advantages (Cahan 2015). Credit unions' advantages come through a combination of competitive loan instruments, service, and the relationship with and between their members. The source of competitive advantage of a credit union stems from the collaboration with members that creates a sense of belonging and the feeling of being "taken care of." This gives credit unions a competitive advantage in meeting the needs of its members that is distinct from traditional banks and other financial institutions. Unfortunately, rather than touting their member-centered mission, most credit unions spend their marketing dollars telling the market that they are "just like banks"—specifically in reference to their breadth of financial offerings (Cahan 2015).

Neighborhood banks can approach the credit union distinction of being community focused but generally are banks that reserve a small percentage of their profits for community enhancement. Credit unions are member-owned and member driven, practicing of membership rituals, and communicating shared goals. This has potential to give credit unions a competitive advantage in the shared access economy because they strive to meet the needs of members with pooled membership resources. Because credit unions are owned by members and their profits are plowed back into membership resources, credit union members see their credit union as a trustworthy partner in financial matters. Our findings suggest that credit unions that leverage their forward market-facing position, their relationship with members, their mission, and their shared resources have higher member ratings and more active member accounts.

Credit unions' impression management practices include evangelizing the member-to-member model, touting the "for members not for profit" mission, and promoting outreach like the financial literacy programs. The social networking practices include governing activities like standardizing vocabulary, for example "member" rather than "customer." Community engagement practices include as participating in the educational events, sponsoring local youth teams, member fairs, acknowledging membership anniversaries (bank account openings, first car loans), and cultural rituals (e.g., new driver or graduation). Examples of brand use practices are financial services, member education, and loan choices. These practices align with operant resource focus. Practices are "value-in-context" in addition to "value-in-use" (Akaka et al. 2015).

Credit unions are communities of practice, creating value collaboratively. Although credit unions appear to be in the business of selling financial instruments, they are by charter and in actuality members providing service to each other. The core mission of credit unions is to continue to align with members in a shared sense of mission and community. Credit unions are participating in a co-created community with their members and focusing on relationships, trust, and personal service. Their financial instrument sales build off of this community of relationships. A significant number of credit union members recommend the credit union to their family, friends, and neighbors.

The credit union and each member co-creates a value proposition that relies on the credit union being a trustworthy institution, one that operates "for members not for profit" and is distinct from banks—a value that is, in large part, communicated to others via member evangelism.

A next step offering could well be collective financial instruments to participate actively in the access economy with their members. The collaborative structure and pro-member, anti-profit message of credit unions, in addition to their community and pro-social focus, position them as instruments of financial change. Customers who have defected from large banks to credit unions, whether to make a statement or just to exercise personal choice, appear to have a discourse that closely matches the discourse of the collaborative consumption movement (Schau and DuFault 2015).

Credit unions, as local, grass-roots movements, have the opportunity to connect local entrepreneurs with community members who can provide funding. A crowd-funded local business is more likely to be successful, leveraging the support of the members of the community that founded the business. Credit unions are in a unique position to connect these small business entrepreneurs and many savers in the local community, who may be willing to accept some risk in return for higher returns and the knowledge that they are supporting local businesses.

Our findings suggest that more engaged memberships are found in credit unions with more emphasis on their community ethos, suggesting that the time has come to reexamine the way credit unions communicate, offer financial services, and do business in an access-oriented versus an ownership-oriented world. A forward-looking perspective toward reinventing member-to-member financing may allow credit unions to be the financial institution of choice for the shared access economy.

Ironically, credit union executives assert that one reason for the egregious omission of credit unions in market discourse is that are old—they have aged out of our understanding of new financial models. Their very presence for generations negates their ability to assert novelty as part of this access economy (Geobey 2015). Still, all executives concede that the omission of credit unions in the market discussion of the access economy is due to their rigid adherence to financial institution norms and their assertions that credit unions offer the same products and services as big banks. In essence, credit union executives assert that they have traditionally overstated credit union similarities to banks and have been notoriously reluctant to be trailblazers in offering new financial instruments that better suit social relationships and access markets. The most successful credit unions in our study have been willing to innovate.

Trends: Credit Union Impetus to Create New Products and Services Consistent with Shared Economy

The credit union executives participating in this study cited an overarching desire for their credit unions to be flexible enough to effectively address nontraditional families, extended kinship groups, friends, and family networks ("framilies"), and multi-generational asset transfer. Four major reasons trends emerged for why credit unions should consider new collaborative product offerings:

1 Extension of adolescence.
2 Reluctance toward private homeownership.
3 Expansion of resource-dependent kinship and friendship households.
4 Desire to "make good" on the credit union mission ("for members by members").

Extended Adolescence. The first theme underscores the social reality of many first world nations: extended adolescence. Where historically in many cultures, adulthood began at the onset of reproductive capacities, and later high school graduation marked the end of childhood, current generations are opting to extend adolescence through the college years and even until the thirtieth birthday. Elongated childhoods mean postponing life milestones like moving out, marriage, home ownership, committing to career paths, and child bearing. These milestones correspond to many of the financial instruments a credit union member will purchase and utilize.

For example, interviewees discuss members delaying moving out and marriage, where families of origin include parents and children over 21 living in a family home and postponing savings goals like purchasing a home and home furnishings. With extended adolescence in the nuclear family home comes increased disposable income without the prior earmarked savings. It has implications for career trajectories. If a person delays milestone assets (home, furnishings, durables), then they may be more inclined to make decisions to pursue passion jobs not necessarily career-enhancing positions.

Nearly all the interviewed leaders describe an increasing percentage of member families consisting of parents (biological or blended) living together with under-employed, graduate student, or unemployed children over 21. These members seek insurance to cover these children, loans to help fund their postgraduate degrees, loans to invest in passion projects (small scale entrepreneurship ventures), and larger family homes of family compound options. The adult children, or *adulkids*, are slow to save for their own durables and real estate, favoring experience purchases like travel and restaurants.

Reluctance toward Private Homeownership. Respondents point to less institutional financial responsibility attributable to extended adolescence, and a fiscally conservative backlash from the mortgage crisis is making more credit union members reluctant to buy homes. Those in the middle of extended adolescence have little motivation to save for and invest in a permanent, privately owned residence. It is easier to live at home or in rentals that can be divested in favor of moves, job transitions, and the freedom to travel at whim. Conversely, the mortgage crisis left some aspiring homeowners homeless, some financially unstable and some afraid to invest precious nest eggs in now volatile real estate markets. Both result in a decreased demand for home ownership among US citizens.

Interestingly, immigrant and recent immigrant members have no noticeable change in their desire for homeownership and a piece of the American Dream. Informants cite these recent immigrants as eager to qualify for and thrilled to take on mortgages.

More Resource-dependent Kinship and Friendship Households. When childhood is elongated in an economy that favors a college degree, nuclear families are staying resource-dependent longer. Additionally, lifespans are increasing and families with older, resource-dependent relatives are increasing as well. In the United States, nearly half of households headed by people aged 40–59 include financial responsibility for a child, adult child, and/or parent over 65 (Parker and Patten 2013). "Sandwich generation" middle-aged credit union members often live in households with older children and aging relatives financially dependent upon them. These members live in extended kinship collectives.

Challenges and opportunities abound for college funding, multi-generational asset transfer, family auto fleets, and more flexible insurance offerings. Members are likely to demand auto purchasing across family members and geographical spaces, linked savings accounts, and insurance bundles that gather together resource-dependent groups.

The nuclear family is fundamentally different than it has been historically defined. Issues of marriage and remarriage in parenthood complicate family making. And the lived reality is almost unrecognizable from the mid-century ideal and further complicates the financial instruments that enable lifestyles. Households might find families funding college experiences for some members, real estate for the extended collective, and eldercare for the aging relatives. This means rethinking the single- or married-with-children models that underscore most financial instruments.

"Make Good" on the Credit Union Mission. Through the course of the conversations, credit union executives expressed the deep desire to get back to the roots of credit unions and their mission of "for member by member," "for people, not for profit," "responsible financing," and ultimately the collective collaborative nature of credit unions. Echoing Cahan (2015), interviewees expressed a sense of lost mission and often concern about credit unions that "tried to act like banks, not leverage the strengths of credit unions." A few participants referenced Bank Transfer Day as an impetus to return to the underlying mission of credit unions and as an opportunity to engage with consumers as a pro-social, nonexploitive financial services alternative to corporate, "greedy" banks.

Envisioning Collective Financing Products

Members of the focus groups actively considered innovative products and services for the shared access economy. The following collaborative multi-family/multi-generational financial instruments were put forth as potentially feasible and important in this new sharing economy:

- Mortgages
- Insurance
- Car purchases
- Savings accounts
- Vacation destinations
- Loans

They spoke of the importance of concepts such as family fleet cars, "framily" college funds and loans, and member-funded business ownership and development.

Three groups created products that allowed for collaborative real estate ownership, specifically among extended families and "framily" collectives. These groups considered ownership arrangements that included single and multi-unit configurations, multi-owner risk and obligations, and the flow of real estate within these collectives that shielded them from the legal and financial ramifications of probate.

Co-Funding Education

One group worked out logistics for a collective education vehicle where multiple contributors could pool funds for multiple recipients to meet educational aspirations, like college and trade school. As envisioned by the group, these collaborative college funds would bypass asset and gift taxes. Of course, the legal environment may not support these innovations at present but public policy can be reimagined to make innovative asset pooling a reality.

CU Crowdfunding

Participants also envisioned member-funded online communities where entrepreneurial ideas would be presented to the credit union community. Other members would vet the ideas, directing money to fund some while passing on others. This inter-credit union crowdfunding could strengthen member ties to the credit union community and foster better member-to-member connections.

Shared Services

Lastly, the focus group discussed building shared resource libraries for members. These asset libraries would include tools, sports equipment and even event rentals (tables, chairs, awnings, flatware, stemware, and other dishes needed for events such as weddings, reunions, and holiday parties). The credit union, as a trusted intermediary, would host these resource libraries ideally on site at branches in order to bring members in more frequently, and increase exposure to credit union products and financial literacy programs.

Best Practice Case Study: Crowdsourcing Meets Credit Union

The web site "True North Strong Communities" (www.truenorthstrong.ca)—a creation of $700M asset Northern Credit Union in Ontario, Canada—shows a unique blend of Kickstarter, credit union community, and traditional financial institution. The credit union hosts a crowdsourced funding community to fund various charitable ventures in the credit union's local communities (see Figure 25.1). The "About" page explains the concept and mission, and firmly embeds Northern Credit Union into the share economy and collaborative financing space:

> What is True North Strong Communities?
>
> It's the first initiative of its kind here in the North—a gathering place to donate to local projects, programs and charities across our region. Here, you can lend your support to a number of worthwhile causes, create a campaign of your own or learn more about becoming a Delegate.
>
> Launched by Northern Credit Union, True North Strong Communities is an opportunity for us to all come together and do some good, right here at home. Because together, we can do more than we ever could alone.

The site pages include highlights of current campaigns, one to create a campaign, and one for becoming a delegate. On the Campaigns page, pictures relevant to each campaign are shown, along with a Kickstarter style project description, a progress line showing funds collected and

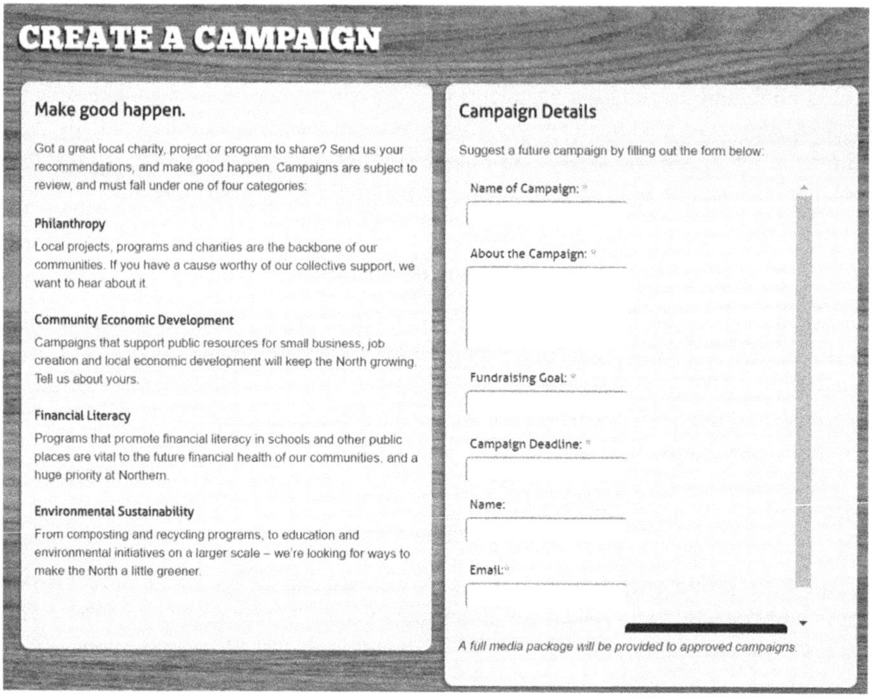

Figure 25.1 Northern Credit Union's True North Strong: Create a Campaign

goal, and a button to click to donate. Donations can be taken at any Northern Credit Union branch office. Anyone can use the button to donate—even if not a credit union member. When clicked, the user is prompted to log in with Facebook or Google, but they can also create an account. At log in, an email is received welcoming the user to the True North community. Donations can be made by standard credit cards or PayPal account, meaning payment from one's own credit union account are possible if that is linked to PayPal via debit card or account number.

Upon donating, givers receive an email saying, "Your contribution was a success! Thanks for your contribution, and for making <name of campaign> a success! Best regards, the True North Community" emphasizing the community aspect of the campaigns and contributions.

Campaigns range from supporting curling in the region, to supporting the Special Olympics Ontario Winter Games, to supporting a local program that gives lifelong learning experiences to disabled adults, among others. Northern Credit Union matches funds on some campaigns, bringing the entire credit union community into the shared space, not just individual donors.

On the "Create a Campaign" page, users are encouraged to create campaigns.

Active campaigns appear on the website like Figure 25.2.

Credit union membership is not required to create a campaign.

Below this text is a form to submit, headed by the phrase "Join the Movement." There is a video showing a 23-minute informational piece on the credit union's history and governance model. Northern Credit Union is using its market-facing operant resources to create a new Kickstarter-type crowdsourcing community, to bring its entire membership

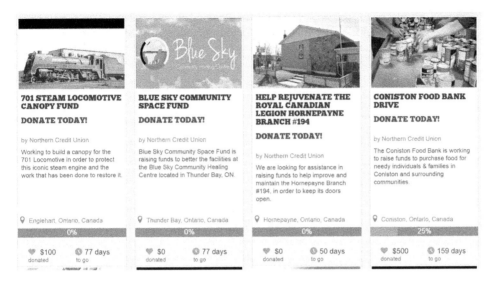

Figure 25.2 Northern Credit Union's True North Strong: Featured Campaigns

into this space by matching funds, and to encourage its members and others in the community to join together in collaborative finance. The credit union is using the practices that create and promote brand community to leverage its operant resources as it moves into the shared space. The "Welcome!" page after donating invites donors (credit union members and non-members) into the credit union's crowdsourcing community. Exchange and resource-integration practices are shown by educating members about the credit union's mission and difference from banks. The credit union is using representation practices by giving members an opportunity to show support for community needs, start campaigns for causes they are interested in. It is leading to evangelizing practices, where not only their members, but those who are a part of the campaigns they help, can act as its best sales people and increase its membership. By highlighting members' pro-social behaviors, this web presence also creates normalization practices related to helping the community, volunteering to be a delegate and become part of the credit union's governance structure, and the discourse of community. As described previously, practices are "value-in-context" in addition to "value-in-use" (Korkman et al. 2010; Vargo et al. 2008; Vargo and Akaka 2012). Further, resource-integration includes resource-embeddedness and is necessarily practice dependent. These practices work together to cocreate the credit union's market, and increases the market-facing value, especially as it aligns with the share economy's focus on collaboration and collectivities. Northern Credit Union is not only a financial institution, but is also now very plainly a community of individuals helping individuals, members financing other members, and serving their community at large. This type of program has the power to enhance trust within the membership and promote the shared access economy goals.

Best Practice Case Study: Inter-Credit Union Collaborative Opportunities

In the share economy, trust is shifting "from centralized institutions to decentralized networks and communities" (Botsman 2015). Credit unions are decentralized financial communities—each its own community of members loaning to other members and contributing to their local community as well. This partners well with the share economy, collaborative consumption mindset. Taking this collaborative financial consumption model out more broadly, a paradoxical opportunity to be more member-friendly exists by credit unions banding together in joint ventures to share resources and risk.

Rachel Botsman writes of the collaborative consumption mindset that one of the major places ripe for disruption in the financial market: "Remove redundant intermediaries to directly match wants and haves." For example, Arizona State Credit Union requires a physical purchase order for potential car loan applicants, and a physical copy of a Kelly Blue Book estimate, both of which applicants must hand carry to the branch during branch hours to initiate a car loan. Contrast that with CarMax over the phone or online car loan verification that requires no hand carried physical documents and takes less than 15 minutes from start to finish. The CarMax website and representatives have integrated Kelly Blue Book information, credit report data, and purchase order information for the cars they sell. Collaboratively working to streamline processes and share resources to decentralize these services and make them jointly available to a cooperative of credit unions has the promise of improving the credit unions' position in the new economic marketplace.

A number of forward-thinking credit unions are marching into this space. In the mortgage loan area, for instance, credit unions are partnering to develop and own title companies. Mortgages are an important area for credit unions as the economy morphs and changes. Says Jay Johnson, Execute Vice President of Callahan and Associates, in their 4th Quarter Trendwatch webinar about credit unions' performance in the mortgage market:

> First mortgage originations fell 20% compared to the previous year, but credit unions still performed better [than] the overall market, which dropped 40% during the same period," Johnson said. "A decade ago, we talked about credit unions moving from 2% of the mortgage market to 10%, and we're almost there.
>
> *(Muckian 2015)*

To be in position to provide alternative financial instruments as credit unions enhance their presence in the mortgage market, and to be more member friendly during the mortgage lending process, credit unions can take control in a number of ways by collaborating. By banding resources together, credit unions can become financial institutions where members can find, regularly and consistently, leading edge collaborative consumption instruments and the latest regulatory and compliance information.

David Birky, Executive Vice President and Chief Strategy Officer of Interra Credit Union, speaks to this in talking of a joint venture between two credit unions and an independent title company when we spoke with him in March, 2015:

> We are owners of a de novo joint venture title called CU Title Services with Teachers Credit Union in South Bend, IN and Meridian Title Company. We started CUTs in order to provide an improved member experience and exercise some additional control over the mortgage process. Since title searches are a volume driven business, it made perfect sense to do something collaborative with TCU. We do not view other credit unions as competitors. Our primary competition is banks. This was the first formal collaborative initiative we embarked on and it has gone very well. We are also an owner in Members Development Corp, a national research and development company that researches shared priorities for the owners, which I believe is invaluable.

Q: In an ideal world, what collaborative offerings or structures would you like to see offered by credit unions, and specifically by your credit union? Why?

> The biggest opportunities for collaboration appear to be in the back office arena. Areas like compliance are so complex and difficult to keep up with, that it would seem to make perfect sense not to duplicate those areas at every credit union. Marketing, business development and purchasing also present opportunities for shared knowledge and resources. Services that often end up in CUSOs like investments, insurance and trust services also represent good opportunities for collaboration given their highly specialized nature.

Q: Do you see any of these are realistic, viable options that you believe may transpire? Why?

> We have had multiple conversations with TCU and other credit unions about a partnership in offering property and casualty insurance at both of our credit unions. While that has yet to transpire, I believe it is still a real possibility. Particularly for smaller credit unions, I believe there is a demonstrated need [for] assistance on the compliance front and if we don't find a way to work together on this, many credit unions will simply not be able to keep up. I also believe in the power of the network – that we can do much more together than any of us can do on our own. I think we have an obligation to consider working together just so we have a chance to gain consideration from the majority of the population that doesn't even know about credit unions.

Q: What obstacles do you face in implementing collaborative offerings? What obstacles is the credit union industry as a whole facing on this front?

> Ego is generally the biggest stumbling block to collaboration. The ego of CEOs, Boards and credit unions in general that say we developed this, why should we share it with you?

Q: Which do you think are better poised to offer these collaborative solutions: banks, credit unions, or another institution? Do you see this potentially changing over the next few years? Why?

> Clearly, credit unions have an advantage given our cooperative nature and charter. Banks operate from a profit motive and which I don't expect to change any time soon. There are international cooperative models like Desjardins which is significantly ahead of where we are and that we could learn from. Credit unions by definition are designed to work together, and it is imperative to our survival that we bring collaboration to the forefront.

Other credit unions are similarly collaborating. Reads a local news report:

> Subsidiaries of two Knoxville-area credit unions have launched a "groundbreaking collaboration" to form a jointly owned title company.
>
> ORNL Federal Credit Union and Y-12 Federal Credit Union, both headquartered in Oak Ridge, have teamed up to launch CU Community Title Co. effective Jan. 2,

2015. The joint venture is officially owned by their subsidiaries, CU Community and Credit Union Services of East Tennessee.

CU Community Title, with eight employees, will continue to operate from its Knoxville office. "We have the capacity to bring on new business, and I don't see any changes there unless we bring on additional business," said Larry Jackson, CU Community's president.

Mark Ziegler, CEO of Y-12 Federal Credit Union, said the partnership reflects a national trend as credit unions collaborate to compete with larger players. "The credit union industry is a small percentage of the financial services industry so by collaborating we generate more volume, have better pricing and offer more member services," he said.

(Nolan 2014)

Title insurance is a crucial part of the mortgage loan process. Because credit unions, unlike banks, are not competing with each other, by sharing resources, the credit unions acquire an economy of scale. Careful adherence to regulations is vital, but credit unions could also share resources to achieve regulatory insight and in instituting best practices.

Just as people are shifting from a trust in institutions to a trust in peers, credit unions themselves can move to trust in their own credit union peers and rely on cooperatives for many redundant services.

Managerial Implications

Recommendations for Credit Unions

Feudal societies relied on collective financing and asset holdings (family/kinship, ethnicity, religious, geographic). Both assets and debts were collective in nature. Both assets and debts transcended a single life—descendants paid debts and enjoyed the assets of their ancestors. This can still be seen in places like Africa. It is traditional for the elderly to share their pensions with family and kin. In the United States, immigrant banking has historically been collective (family/kinship, ethnicity, religious, geographic).

The current economic climate has brought to the fore the need for nontraditional financial instruments with collective financing and asset holdings. Haider and McGarry (2005) found that private money transfers and shared living arrangements were a key source of support for low-income populations over the two preceding decades. This has only increased since that time, with the practices creeping up income levels as both the economy worsened, and the sharing movement grew.

Student loans, another growing issue in our society, has similarly affected a large portion of the population. Back-to-the-future financial instruments are needed to reflect the desire by many for friends and relatives beyond the traditional nuclear family to have the ability to participate in funding college educations.

- Recommendation: Review "family" requirements in financial instruments.
  In 1962, Sussman and Burchinal addressed the "unheralded structure" of kin and family relationships amidst current conceptualization, and found the nuclear family a difficult social construct for classification. Five decades later, kin and family structures have continued to morph into areas where the boundaries between family, kin, and friends make

it almost impossible to define what is a "family." Financial instruments that have strict family definitions and requirements not only rule out all sorts of alternative household arrangements, but restrict financial products catered to these arrangements. The spirit of credit unions is member wealth aggregation and wealth access. Moving beyond legally sanctioned collectives aligns with the CU Mission.

- Recommendation: Embrace and publicize the original credit union mission

  Credit unions can capitalize on the access economy's growing message surprisingly easily. The original charter for the creation of credit unions aligns almost identically with the share economy's ethos and goals. CUs should trumpet their roots as member-to-member wealth aggregators and member-to-member lending as the basis of the CU Mission. CUs were the first peer-to-peer lending institutions far before Kickstarter. Remind the market of the CU ethos.

- Recommendation: Acknowledge the threat and opportunity posed by peer-to-peer lending companies

  First, there is a need to disrupt the personal loan market and near-term value chains. Peer-to-peer lending companies like Lending Club and Prosper have become the face of the sharing economy's financial market. They are being touted as market disrupters. This is a great threat to credit unions, as one of the ways they are distinguished from traditional banks is the member-to-member structure. This distinction is in danger of being co-opted by these new companies. However, this also poses an incredible opportunity. As these companies ARE being touted as the financial face of the share economy, credit unions can target their messaging to capture this market segment.

Conclusion

The "credit union movement" after Bank Transfer Day in 2011 was a marker of dissatisfaction with big banks. Even while the transfer movement is slowing, credit unions can leverage popular excitement about peer-to-peer lending. By charter and mission credit unions reflect the access economy ideals supported by a community ethos. In essence, there is a potential to realize the power of collaboration and to take a place in the access economy.

To date, there has not been a well-articulated connection drawn between the new incarnation of the access economy, and the generations-old credit union movement. However, credit unions better represent the "sharing" sensibility of the new way of thinking about possessions than do any other traditional financial institutions, and their members feel a strong sense of trust in them. Many credit unions offer unique financial instruments that may allow the sharing economy viewpoint to extend to financial instruments and products. As credit unions progress into the arena of shared and collaborative financial instruments, the core mission of credit unions aligns with members in a shared sense of vision and community.

Credit Unions Participate in a Co-Created Community with their Members, and Focus on Relationships, Trust, and Personal Service

Credit unions are a co-created community of members and financial institution. According to our research, they create relationships, they engender trust, and they provide outstanding service. This makes sense, because they are already members helping members, in a collaborative financial consumption community. They have been at the forefront of social movements from their foundation in the 1800s, to funding loans for poor communities, to the place of refuge for consumers escaping large bank policies with which they disagreed on Bank Transfer Day. Credit unions are now poised to be at the forefront of what might be the most important social movement in their history—the sharing economy (Cahan 2015). If they can develop shared financial instruments that enable consumers to increase their dive into collaborative and shared ownership and community finance, credit unions themselves could become their own financial social movement. The share economy is the next frontier for consumers, and financing these shared communities may well be the next frontier of the financial industry, with credit unions leading the charge.

References

Akaka, M. A., S. Vargo and H. J. Schau (2015), "The Context of Experience," *Journal of Services Marketing*, 26(2): 206–223.

Bardhi, B. and G. M. Eckhardt (2012), "Access-based Consumption: The Case of Car Sharing," *Journal of Consumer Research*, 39 (December): 881–898.

Belk, R. W. (1988), "Possessions and the Extended Self," *Journal of Consumer Research*, 15 (September): 139–168.

Botsman, R. (2015), "Collaborative Finance: By the People, For the People," www.collaborativeconsumption.com/2014/07/31/collaborative-finance-by-the-people-for-the-people/.

Botsman, R. and R. Rogers (2010), *What's Mine Is Yours: The Rise of Collaborative Consumption*, New York, NY: Harper Business.

Bright, S. and N. Hopkins (2011), "Home, Meaning and Identity: Learning from the English Model of Shared Ownership." *Housing, Theory and Society* 28(4): 377–397.

Cahan, B. B. (2015), "Choosing Relevance: How Credit Unions Can Harness Transparency and Show Impact," Filene Report.

Davidi, A. (2014), "How Girl Meets Dress is Capitalising on the Demise of Ownership," *The Guardian*, (June 11) www.theguardian.com/media-network/media-network-blog/2014/jun/11/girl-meets-dress-anna-bance.

Eckhardt, G. M. and F. Bardhi (2015), "The Sharing Economy Isn't About Sharing at All," *Harvard Business Review*, (January 28), 125–130.

Fafchamps, M. (2004), *Rural Poverty, Risk and Development*, Cheltenham: Edward Elgar Publishing.

Flink, J. (1990), *The Automobile Age*, Boston: The MIT Press.

Geobey, S. (2015), "Peer-to-Peer Lending and the Future of Cooperation," Filene Research Institute Reports.

Glaser, Barney, and Anselm Strauss (1967), *The Discovery of Grounded Theory*, London, UK: Weidenfeld & Nicolson: 1–19.

Haider, S. J. and K. McGarry (2005), *Recent Trends in Resource Sharing among the Poor*. No. w11612. National Bureau of Economic Research.

Hunt, S. D. (2000), "The Competence-Based, Resource Advantage, and Neoclassical Theories of Competition: Toward a Synthesis," in A. Heene and R. Sanchez (Eds.), *Competence-Based Strategic Management: Theory and Research*, Toronto: John Wiley & Sons, pp. 177–208.

Korkman, Oskar, Kaj Storbacka and Bo Harald (2010), "Practices as Markets: Value Co-creation in E-invoicing." *Australasian Marketing Journal (AMJ)* 18(4): 236–247.

Kornhauser, M. E. (1993), "Love, Money, and the IRS: Family, Income-Sharing, and the Joint Income Tax Return." *Hastings Law Journal*, 45: 63.

Moody, J. C. and G. C. Fite (1984), *The Credit Union Movement: Origins and Development, 1850–1980*, Dubuque, IA: Kendall/Hunt Publishing Company.

Muckian, M. (2015), Credit Union Times. www.cutimes.com/2015/03/01/credit-unions-cash-in-on-improving-economy, accessed 10/20/2015.

Muñiz, A. M., Jr. and O'Guinn, T. C. (2001), "Brand Community," *Journal of Consumer Research* 27 (March): 412–432.

Murdock, G. P. (1949), *Social Structure*, New York: Free Press.

Nolan, A. (2014), "Local Credit Unions to Create Title Company", Knoxville News-Sentinel, Dec 2014, www.knoxnews.com/business/local-credit-unions-to-create-title-company_62470930 accessed 10/20/2015.

Parker, K. and E. Patten (2013), *The Sandwich Generation: Rising Financial Burdens for Middle-Aged Americans*, Pew Research Center.

Rifkin, J. (2001), *The Age of Access: The New Culture of Hypercapitalism Where All of Life is a Paid-For Experience*, Los Angeles, CA: Tarcher Penguin.

Risen, T. (2015), "Amid Rise of Zipcar and Uber, Ford Drives Into Car-Sharing Space," US News and World Report (June 25), www.usnews.com/news/articles/2015/06/25/ford-car-sharing-program-shows-demand-for-zipcar-uber.

Ronald, Richard (2008), *The Ideology of Home Ownership: Homeowner Societies and the Role of Housing*. Springer.

Sagner, A. and R. Mtati. (1999), "Politics of Pension Sharing in Urban South Africa," *Ageing and Society* 19: 393–416.

Schau, H. J. and B. L. DuFault (2015), *Bank Transfer Day and the Sharing Economy: Credit Union Practices Performing the Financial Market of a Collaborative Consumption Social Movement*, Working Paper.

Schwandt, Thomas A.(1997), *Qualitative Inquiry: A Dictionary of Terms*, Thousand Oaks, CA: Sage Publications, Inc.

Spiggle, Susan (1994), "Analysis and Interpretation of Qualitative Data in Consumer Research," *Journal of Consumer Research* 21(3): 491–503.

Spring, E. (1997), *Law, Land, and Family: Aristocratic Inheritance in England, 1300 to 1800 (Studies in Legal History)*, Chapel Hill: The University of North Carolina Press.

Steenson, M. and J. Donner (2009), "Beyond the Personal and Private: Modes of Mobile Phone Sharing in Urban India," in S. W. Campbell and R. Ling (Eds.), *Mobile Communication Research Annual* Piscataway, NJ: Transaction Books. Vol. 1, pp. 231–250.

Strauss, A. and J. Corbin (1998), "Basics of Qualitative Research: Techniques and Procedures for Developing Grounded Theory," in *Basics of Qualitative Research*, Thousand Oaks, CA: Sage.

Sussman, Marvin B., and Lee Burchinal (1962), "Kin Family Network: Unheralded Structure in Current Conceptualizations of Family Functioning," *Marriage and Family Living* 24(3): 231–240.

Vargo, Stephen L. and Melissa Archpru Akaka (2012), "Value Cocreation and Service Systems (re)Formation: A Service Ecosystems View," *Service Science* 4(3): 207–217.

Vargo, Stephen L., Paul P. Maglio and Melissa Archpru Akaka (2008), "On Value and Value Co-creation: A Service Systems and Service Logic Perspective," *European Management Journal* 26(3): 145–152.

Widmer, E. D. (2010), *Family Configurations: A Structural Approach to Family Diversity*, Surrey, UK: Ashgate Publishing Limited.

26

CO-CONSTRUCTING INSTITUTIONS ONE BRICK AT A TIME: APPROPRIATION AND DELIBERATION ON LEGO IDEAS

Albert M. Muñiz Jr.[1] and Marie Taillard[2]

[1]DEPAUL UNIVERSITY, CHICAGO, IL, USA
[2]ESCP EUROPE BUSINESS SCHOOL, LONDON, UK

The LEGO Group offers thousands of model kits for sale globally, and one source of ideas for new kits is LEGO consumers. Firms that want to use consumer ideas can actively partner with consumers, they can borrow ideas from them, or they can even steal ideas from them. Consumer research has recently begun exploring how firms can effectively partner with consumers to develop products and brand experiences, a phenomenon frequently labeled as "cocreation." In this chapter, we use the LEGO brand as a context to explore the rules and tensions of cocreation.

Consumer cocreation is a prominent topic in the contemporary marketing trade press and is commonly observed in the lives of brands and consumers. Technology has enabled the development of platforms on which different kinds of contributors can exchange ideas, and as a result, many firms have launched collaborative programs in which they encourage customers to suggest product ideas and other innovative inputs. While many firms understand the potential benefits of integrating external resources, they often confront significant challenges and obstacles in doing so. The logic motivating or guiding externally performed activities may be incompatible with internal processes, practices, and standards. The president of the crowdsourcing development firm Topcoder wrote for *Wired* magazine that a substantial number of firms will attempt and then abandon cocreation of innovation when it fails to engage consumers and/or improve firm innovation:

> At the onset of 2014 we find crowdsourcing where cloud was just a few short years ago – widely discussed, unevenly adopted and on the cusp of widespread industry impact. Similarly, we will see crowdsourcing experience hypergrowth but also leave some damaged bystanders that were caught up in the hype and mislead [*sic*].
>
> *(Singh 2014)*

As with many revolutionary changes, the hype might exceed practical understanding.

There are many potential sources of frustration in cocreation. Leveraging firm-led user communities is cost-intensive and difficult to manage, and it precipitates "a loss of control on the part of the producer firm" (Hienerth, Lettl, and Keinz 2014, 851). Managers may find customer ideas redundant, unattractive to mass markets, or otherwise impractical (Bayus 2013). They may find themselves overwhelmed by the volume of customer ideas (Gloor and Cooper 2007). Other challenges include designing appropriate interface mechanisms (Terwiesch and Xu 2008), recruiting qualified contributors (Jeppesen and Lakhani 2010), and managing the process (Füller, Hutter, and Faullant 2011; Singh 2014). It is not surprising that many of these ventures fail. Some prominent documented failures include the Campbell Soup Company (Phillips 2011), CrowdSpirit (Chanal and Caron-Fasan 2010), Genius Crowds (Crowdsourcing. org 2013), and Naked & Angry (Weingarten 2007). Many factors explain these failures, but a common element was creativity at the expense of marketability. Creativity does not necessarily translate into salability.

Despite the risks, however, ignoring cocreation opportunities is problematic for two reasons. First, customers tend to expect that their contributions to a brand or product will be met with gratitude or some form of recognition (Füller et al. 2009; Gebauer, Füller, and Pezzei 2013). This expectation may be more pronounced when contributions are made publicly and gather significant support from communities and other institutions (Muñiz and O'Guinn 2001). Second, evidence suggests that integrating stakeholders is favorable to change and innovation (Taillard et al. 2016; Von Hippel 2005).

Tension clearly exists between the drive to incorporate user input and the myriad challenges in doing so. A prerequisite to resolving this tension is a better understanding of the processes and outcomes of cocreation activities, particularly from an institutional perspective. In other words, we need a better understanding of how the two (or more) entities involved in the cocreation process operate and make decisions. Work on this front is progressing, albeit slowly.

The literature on cocreation is replete with examinations of cocreation practices (Schau, Muñiz, and Arnould 2009), their effects on community building, issues of control and fairness between consumers and firms (Cova, Pace, and Skålén 2015), the different roles that contribute to the cocreation of value (Hartmann, Wiertz, and Arnould 2015), and managerial approaches to cocreation (Payne, Storbacka, and Frow 2008). Much of the literature emphasizes the institutional nature of these activities, as they occur within communities of engaged consumers. What is missing is an account of how these communities emerge as institutions through their collaboration with firms and what these institutional processes mean for the firms and consumer communities.

In making a case for the endogenous role of consumers in cocreating value with a firm, much of the literature has glossed over the existing gap between the consumer community as an institution and the brand or firm as an institution. Consumer communities and firms operate separately, are driven by different purposes, and enact different practices (Skålén, Pace, and Cova 2015). However, evidence indicates that brands and consumers benefit from finding goal congruence (Healy and McDonagh 2013) or practice alignment (Skålén, Pace, and Cova 2015). These accounts are useful in discussing how collaborative practices develop, but they do not address the ongoing recursive effects of the institutionalization processes on the collaboration between consumers and firm (Barley and Tolbert 1997). In other words, while extant research recognizes more or less explicitly that two or more sets of institutional logics are at play, it does not provide a dynamic process-based account of the evolving relationship between the two institutions and their respective logics. This gap is significant: both consumer communities and firms (or their strategies) evolve as they collaborate with each other, and as a result, the consumer community and the firm can develop and exhibit new and/or different practices that, over time, can alter their relationship.

The LEGO Group has developed a strong reputation as a leader in community building and empowering fans to contribute their creativity and building skills to developing new products and fostering engagement (Antorini 2007; Antorini, Muñiz, and Askildsen 2012). In recent years, LEGO has developed a platform on which fans can propose their own models for production. In this chapter, we examine the evolution of practices on the LEGO Ideas platform by analyzing conversations about rules and purposes. These conversations constitute not just a representation of the ongoing collaboration but also the collaborative process itself (Phillips, Lawrence, and Hardy 2004). In other words, we use conversations and online posts as a source of data, a reflection of participants' intentions and actions, but we are also aware that these posts are actions themselves and, as such, constitute performances of the practices and contribute to the institutionalization process. Thus, we explore the institutionalization process itself by analyzing the effects of participants' posts on the overall evolution of practices.

Theoretical Foundations

The notion that consumers play a role in the cocreation of brands is well established in marketing. Muñiz and O'Guinn (2001, 412) note that members of brand communities affect perceived quality, brand loyalty, brand awareness, and brand associations: brand community members are coconspirators in the creation of the brand and "play a vital role in the brand's ultimate legacy." McAlexander, Schouten and Koenig (2002) build on this thinking and show the effect of other community members on creating excitement and a sense of community around a shared brand consumption event. Camp Jeep and H.O.G. Fests are cocreated between the respective marketers and brand enthusiasts. Kozinets (2002) shows how participants at Burning Man cocreate the event, going so far as to enforce the rules for performance, participation, and observation. Consider also the participants at Burning Man, who create a temporary community in which to practice divergent social logics and escape from aspects of the mainstream market. This sort of user cocreated experience has been soundly demonstrated (Muñiz and Schau 2005, 2007, 2011; Schau, Muñiz, and Arnould 2009).

Consumers can be particularly creative when embedded in communities, and marketers sometimes solicit and use the outputs of these activities (Antorini, Muñiz, and Askildsen 2012; Cova, Pace, and Skålén 2015). Sometimes, these consumers can help evaluate ideas that other consumers generate. Involving the community in the evaluation of consumer-generated ideas can have both positive and negative consequences. For example, the community can drastically reduce the number of ideas internal developers need to evaluate (Filieri 2013). At the same time, consumers might be evaluating ideas in a manner that is inconsistent with the criteria applied by internal developers. A host of positive and negative reactions can result from a community's satisfaction and/or dissatisfaction with a cocreative process (Kozinets et al. 2010). Hell hath no fury like a cocreative consumer scorned. This is an important consideration, as consumers can hold firm ideas about what is appropriate for the brand, and these ideas need not align with those of the marketer (Muñiz and O'Guinn 2001).

Epp and Price (2011) and Skålén, Pace, and Cova (2015) offer valuable direction here when they note that different parties are likely to have overlapping and distinct goals, potentially leading to both accord and discord. Communities have their own ways of doing things, as do firms. The larger, more developed, and older the community, the more likely it is to be set in its ways. The same goes for the firm. Such entrenched differences can be problematic when they do not align.

Cocreation activities at a process level have received some recent attention in the literature (Epp and Price 2011; Schau, Muñiz, and Arnould 2009; Skålén, Pace, and Cova 2015), but examination of the social aspect of cocreation is still limited (Skålén, Pace, and Cova 2015). Schau, Muñiz, and Arnould (2009) explore how members of nine brand communities created value through 12 practices. They demonstrate that these practices—"linked and implicit ways of understanding, saying, and doing things" (p. 31)—are intricate, pervasive, and organic, possessing trajectories or paths of development that play out over time. This is a valuable insight because it unpacks the cocreative social process, but it suffers from one noteworthy limitation: Schau, Muñiz, and Arnould (2009) treat brand community practices independent of the marketer. They do not consider how community practices might interface with firm practices. In their study, Epp and Price (2011) find that family member relational goals and integration processes affect consumption choices, but they never explore the marketer response. This is a significant gap.

Skålén, Pace, and Cova (2015) successfully bridge this gap. Their netnographic study of the interaction between Alfa Romeo and its fans, the Alfisti (see Alfisti.com), identifies groups of collaborative practices that develop in the cocreation efforts between the firm and consumers: interacting, identity, and organizing. These practices are compelling but, as are those in the work of Schau, Muñiz, and Arnould (2009), are contextually bound. Given that the primary activity on Alfisti.com at the time of the study was organizing the fledgling website as a site for collaboration and preparing for the brand centennial in the following year, it is not surprising that the organizing practice loomed so large here. This was the beginning of Alfa Romeo's more explicit efforts to cocreate with its consumers. The authors' assertion that cocreation succeeds when practices align is accurate for the context, but the three practice alignment strategies—compliance, interpretation, and orientation—do not lend themselves to a more established collaborative environment.

While the consumer community research stream shows that communities, as institutions, grow from cocreation actions, the nature of their institutionalization processes remains unclear. Collaboration between customers and firms is still a proverbial black box, with rather robust shortcomings across the disciplines that attempt to illuminate cocreation. This chapter aims to open the contents of that box. In doing so, we build on recent suggestions for further research on specific practices. For example, Schau, Muñiz, and Arnould (2009) suggest that research should attempt to discern and unpack the operation of a broader set of practices. Refining this understanding, they assert, will prove useful in creating novel strategies to further leverage the creative tendencies of marketplace actors.

Practices are routinized actions (Hartmann, Wiertz, and Arnould 2015), and they constitute an aspect of institutions. While the consumer community school addresses some institutionalization processes by showing how communities emerge from consumer practices, it focuses on consumers rather than their relationship with firms and thus fails to answer how practices emerge. We are interested in how institutions such as a firm, a team, a department, or a community, each with their own "institutional logics" or "organizing principles" (Friedland and Alford 1991, 248) of shared understandings and practices, guide and constrain the actions of their members while being "created, altered and reproduced" by these same actions (Barley and Tolbert 1997, 93). Evidence from the public and nonprofit sectors shows that cocreation across institutional boundaries (governments and communities of constituents) indeed fosters the development of new institutions (Lawrence, Hardy, and Phillips 2002). Inclusive public engagement practices by local government institutions can lead to the creation of new institutions (Quick and Feldman 2011). Phillips, Lawrence, and Hardy (2004) also show the role of discourse in institutionalization, a point that is particularly relevant when considering online communities, for which most of the actions of participants are indeed discourse based.

Visconti et al.'s (2010) study of street art and public space is instrumental here. They argue that goods such as public space precipitate contemporaneous, interactive, convergent, and divergent forms of agency because of the multiple entitlements potentially claimed with respect to such goods. There is certainly a parallel between collaborative consumption platforms and these types of public spaces. For example, multiple entitlements can be claimed; that is, the firm and the consumer can lay claim to the nexus of value contained therein. Drawing from the work of Aubert-Gamet (1997), Visconti et al. (2010) identify street artists' aesthetic space appropriation strategies to symbolically claim public spaces and prevent them from being appropriated by market forces. Similar appropriation strategies could be expected among consumers participating in firm-sponsored collaborative platforms. Consumers might develop strategies and practices that, in turn, allow them to stake a claim.

Method

Field Site

To address the research issues identified, we examine consumer and firm cocreation in an empirical context: the LEGO crowdsourcing platform LEGO Ideas (ideas.LEGO.com). The LEGO brand has been the subject of a great deal of analysis and theorizing. It has also been the topic of general-interest books (Baichtal and Meno 2011), blogs (LEGO.gizmodo.com), magazine articles (Koerner 2006), academic research (Antorini 2007), managerial books (Robertson and Breen 2013), and business school cases (Rivkin, Thomke, and Beyersdorfer 2013) and includes a massive library of design and technique-related writings. We assert that several aspects of the LEGO brand make it a compelling case for theoretical illumination.

First, it returned from the brink of failure by adapting to changes in the sociocultural environment and the ways children play (Robertson and Breen 2013). LEGO figured out how to market building blocks in the age of video games and widespread computing. Second, LEGO has inspired and fostered exceptional community and creativity among its users (Antorini 2007; Baichtal and Meno 2011). LEGO fans, adults in particular, congregate, collaborate, and innovate. They create a substantial amount of brand-related content in a variety of media. Third, LEGO has been successful in leveraging user creativity. Many observers have underscored the active and valuable work of adult LEGO users, supported by employees and managers at LEGO, as an example of successful cocreation (Antorini, Muñiz, and Askildsen 2012; Robertson and Breen 2013). LEGO's adroit integration of user contributions is atypical and therefore illuminating and allows us to elaborate theory and inform subsequent cocreation efforts.

LEGO Ideas (formerly LEGO Cuusoo) is one of the consumer collaboration efforts by LEGO and one of seven community support programs. In LEGO Ideas, contributors outside the firm are involved in two discrete tasks: idea generation and idea evaluation. LEGO Ideas seeks user ideas for new LEGO kits, and contributors post proposals for new model sets. These include pictures of the fully assembled kit as well as descriptive text and video. Members of the open registration site can comment on the model and vote on whether LEGO should produce the kit. Much of the vote-accumulating process plays out in social media, as various entities advocate for the kits and attempt to drive votes. Proposed kits that receive 10,000 votes are considered by LEGO for official production and evaluated for their commercial potential. Kits chosen for production by LEGO are typically modified to suit in-house preferences and then are manufactured and marketed by LEGO. In return, contributors of the kits chosen for production receive a percentage of sales. In the typology of customer cocreation developed by O'Hern and Rindfleisch (2010), LEGO Ideas represents codesigning, or what Kozinets, Hemetsberger, and Schau (2008) term "elicitation-evaluation." Analogous examples of codesigning/elicitation-evaluation include the open invention platform Quirky. com, the T-shirt platform Threadless, and watchmaker Tokyoflash.

Data

We drew methodological inspiration from prior work on cocreation practices (Epp and Price 2011; Schau, Muñiz, and Arnould 2009) and institutionalization processes (Barley and Tolbert 1997; Feldman 2004). We used the methods in these studies to structure and organize our observations and analysis. We sought data collection and interpretation approaches that would help us focus on processes and mechanisms. Similar to Schau, Muñiz, and Arnould (2009), we endeavored to move the unit of analysis away from the individual consumer and the firm to the practices and processes evident throughout cocreation activities. Our sampling frame consists of the site guidelines, terms of service, official comments, the site blog, and some relevant threads in social media. Our data include naturalistic observation of firm, consumer, and community activities and archival netnographic research on relevant forums. We observed the forums, downloaded messages, and postings. Because our focus is on the development of processes, we chose to limit our exploration to data that specifically refer to rules, guidelines, practices, and norms. Although other types of interactions among fans and with the LEGO Ideas staff also contribute to the development of processes, they went beyond the primary focus of our analysis.

Analysis

Our analysis of the data proceeded along two complementary tracks. Our first goal was to document the collaborative practices at play on LEGO Ideas, and the second was to explore the underlying recursive dynamics of institutionalization. We coded interactions on the LEGO Ideas platform from the time of the platform's inception to June 2016. The coding work was done both for fans and for platform administrators. In contrast with the typology of practices proposed by Schau, Muñiz, and Arnould (2009), this list goes beyond consumer practices to include practices performed by both platform users and administrators. As such, it is closer to the typology proposed in Skålén, Pace, and Cova's (2015) study, which recognizes the collaborative practices performed by members of both institutions. To understand and document the process of institutionalization that takes place as fans and the firm collaborate, we also performed a sequential analysis of interactions on the LEGO Ideas forum since its inception. This analysis was inspired by the methodology that Barley and Tolbert (1997) describe in their article on action and institutionalization.

Findings

Practices and their Trajectories

Our coding resulted in the compilation of a list of 13 practices (see Table 26.1). We identified ten main phases of development on the forum itself and two more critical phases (see Figure 26.1): one related to the posting of an R2D2 model on the LEGO Ideas platform (but not

Table 26.1 Cocreation practice typology

Practice category	Practice	Definition	Illustrative verbatim
Community Engagement	Challenging	Offering critiques of actions by TLG, particularly as they relate to LEGO Ideas and its operation. Challenging the fact that TLG is not playing by the rules that the community is developing and believes they have a right to expect. It is a form of appropriation. The consumer contributor feels they have a right to expect change and or/an answer from TLG.	Thanks for supporting anyway! I don't subscribe to the "Lego will never make a different UCS model on the same theme" view. The UCS Artoo was pretty small – besides it wasn't a Kenny Baker one :) - Besides they could just coin a new term/series if they wanted "Limited Edition Collectible" or whatever. That aside, this one's going to be a serious challenge for them."
Community Engagement	Clarifying	Seeking clarification of the rules and purposes of the site. This is similar to what Skålén et al (2015) called "Questioning and Answering."	The guidelines say you can't make level packs for lego dimensions, but can we make fun packs or team packs?
Community Engagement	Contributing	Submitting a kit, voting on a kit, commenting on a kit or promoting a kit. The trajectory of this practice has become more complicated. As LEGO Ideas and its attendant communities have developed, notions of appropriate contributions have evolved. For example, in terms of submitting a kit, designs have become more elaborate. There is more perceived pressure to make something grandiose so as to get social media buzz to drive votes. There is also more pressure to support kits and not be critical. The trajectory of this practice is creating problems for LEGO Ideas.	The Kenny Baker Artoo is about 16,000 bricks. Wow! Think about that when supporting, it's not going to be cheap. This will be the most expensive Lego set by far, but we all know how much fans want this set. Don't hesitate to sell your car (or at least your spouse's car) droids are better!
Community Engagement	Deliberation	Frequently co occurs with documenting. Has different categories subsumed within it, these include: 1) the rules of the game, 2) the purpose of the platform 3) justice (is it fair or not)? 4) which of these models is relevant to LEGO's market? 5) suggest specific additions to the platform. There is a trajectory within this practice to resolve some of the inherent conflicts/ ambiguities in Lego Ideas.	

Table 26.1 (continued)

Practice category	Practice	Definition	Illustrative verbatim
	Rules of game	Deliberating and debating the rules of the game	One question. I have some ideas that are based on certain series and reality shows. The characters in them - at times - curses, smokes and drinks. The TV series and reality shows aren't themed around cursing/smoking/drinking, but centers around the lives, ups-and-downs, and career advancement of these professionals. Understand that these are not allowed, but is there a way around it? For instance, not featuring cigarettes/ cigars and the liquors in the sets?
	Purpose of platform	Deliberating and debating the purpose of the platform	Why not take some small losses in the name of fun and engagement? Because they are a for-profit business. Making money is their primary purpose. They are all for fun and engagement, but only if they can make a profit doing it.
	Justice	Deliberating and debating the fairness of the outcomes for particular sets	Still think it is crap the corvette didn't get picked. That was an awesome model and they have nothing right now that compares. I'm not burying a big technic car. I don't like rvs or minis. How about something for a sports car enthusiast that isn't a super car? They even have a license deal with GM. Wtf!?
	Which models	Deliberating and debating the merits of a proposed model. This differs from evaluating in that rather than offering a set evaluation, the poster seeks to start an open ended discussion of the merits and faults of a propsed kit. As such, it might result in evaluating.	While I agree with some of these new guidelines, they leave a lot of overlooked details, as well as inconveniences and problems. First of all I suggest they remove the piece limit, as Lego has, on several occasions, made official sets with 3000-6000 pieces. these include; 2 Death stars, UCS Star Executor, UCS Millenium falcon, Taj Mahal, UCS merry go round and others.
	Additions to platform	Deliberating and debating potential additions to the platform	How about we all ask Lego Ideas for a Creators Forum where we can exchange tips and ideas? We could all send them an email. There's been a lot of discussion happening recently within some of the comments about what's appropriate/not appropriate, how to get more supporters, how to do good renderings, etc, and that would work WAY better if Ideas had a forum. (I know of a few external places, but that's not the same and not everyone participates in each one)

(Continued)

Table 26.1 (continued)

Practice category	Practice	Definition	Illustrative verbatim
Social Networking	Documenting	As defined by Schau, Muñiz and Arnould (2009), detailing the brand relationship journey in a narrative way anchored by and peppered with milestones. Here it includes efforts at relaying facts and information.	Think this is the project you are talking about: 1966 Batmobile 50th Anniversary- https://ideas.lego.com/projects/63116 Archived due to overlap with 76052 Batman™ Classic TV Series – Batcave
Social Networking	Evaluating	Offering critiques of user submitted kits, offering critiques of other comments on kits.	But theres just so much of it that it drowns out everything else on Ideas.
Social Networking	Milestoning	As defined by Schau, Muñiz and Arnould (2009), noting seminal events in brand ownership and consumption, it operates a little differently in this context. LEGO created several milestones for submitted projects. At 1,000 votes, a submission can no longer be deleted. At 5,000 votes, a project gets an additional six months to reach 10,000 votes. At 10,000 votes, the project is submitted for internal review	Congratulations on 5,000 supporters! You've earned an extra 182 days. Wow! By passing 5,000 supporters, you've made it into the upper ranks on LEGO Ideas. Since you've passed the halfway point, here's another 6 months (182 days) to reach the final milestone of 10,000 supporters. Best of luck as you aim to finish your journey strong. Contributors have accepted the value of these milestones and work toward them and congratulate others on reaching them
Social Networking	Supporting	Related to what Schau, Muñiz and Arnould (2009) called empathizing; Lending emotional and/or physical support to other members, including support for brand-related trials (e.g., product failure, customizing) and/or for non-brand-related life issues (e.g., illness, death, job).	I've been meaning to write something like this for a while. You've totally hit the nail on the head. At least 50% of what gets 10k votes has no chance of ever being made and it's a complete waste of everyone's time.

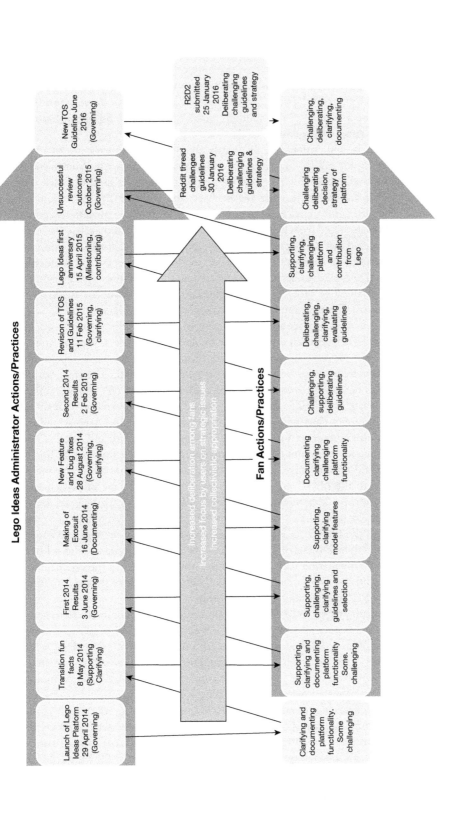

Figure 26.1 Cocreation practice process (adapted from Barley and Tolbert, 1997)

on the forum per se) on January 25, 2016, and one related to a Reddit post on January 30, 2016, vehemently challenging the guidelines in effect for LEGO Ideas at that time. Significantly, these two "nonforum" posts were the only ones originated by fans. Both triggered significant subsequent conversations and acted as catalysts for additional forum conversations. Together, these 12 phases reflect the evolution of the collaborative process on LEGO Ideas and provide an understanding of the resulting recursive process of institutionalization.

Practices are dynamic and follow a certain trajectory as they are enacted (Boulaire and Cova 2013; Schau, Muñiz, and Arnould 2009; Warde 2005). We found evidence of 13 practices. Two (documenting and milestoning) were identified previously by Schau, Muñiz, and Arnould (2009) in their list of 12 practices. Another, supporting practice was similar to their practice of empathizing. One was similar to what Skålén, Pace, and Cova (2015) term questioning and answering. The other nine practices were new practices that we discerned in this context. We validated practices proposed by Schau, Muñiz, and Arnould (2009) and Skålén, Pace, and Cova (2015) but discovered that neither of these extant typologies fully captured the complex reality of the interactions herein. One user practice stands out for its frequency, and because it has not been documented in the extant literature; we labeled it as "deliberating." Deliberating involves contributing to a collective problem-solving exercise, whether it is about crafting new rules, finding solutions to a dilemma, questioning fairness, or establishing purpose.

On LEGO Ideas, practices are authored by various actors at differing levels of aggregation and occupying diverse roles with respect to the brand and the market. We documented posts by two LEGO Ideas administrators, one of whom has a particularly strong reputation among fans. Other posts were by long-term fans whose reputation and influence are apparent. Some posts are the work of one-time participants who want to weigh in on a relevant topic. Others can be found repeatedly opining on one topic or another. Here, we note that the idea of a single brand community centered on the brand (Schau, Muñiz, and Arnould 2009; Skålén, Pace, and Cova 2015) obscures a great deal of community diversity and detail. There is not just one LEGO brand community; there are myriad collectives, temporary ad hoc communities that form and then dissolve, enduring tribes, and subcultures all interacting to create and realize value in the LEGO ecosystem. As a result, the landscape of participants on the LEGO Ideas platform is fragmented and complex. Whereas most participants are probably members of one or more LEGO-related communities, there is no one fan community specifically tied to the LEGO Ideas platform. Coupled with the lack of a LEGO Ideas forum per se (users can only comment on proposed models and in response to official LEGO Ideas blog posts), this fragmentation makes for an interesting paradox: on the one hand, users are acting independently; on the other hand, some have the power of strong fan communities behind them. This is an important consideration in our analysis.

Because our main purpose is to explore the institutional effects of interactions between the firm and consumers from a process perspective, we follow the lead of relevant extant literature. Channeling Warde (2005), Schau, Muñiz, and Arnould (2009) note that practices have trajectories, that is, a history and path of development. They are socially constructed (Warde 2005) and evolve toward greater institutionalization. As Schau, Muñiz, and Arnould (2009) note, practices that begin informally (e.g., creating Xena cosplay costumes) can evolve from simple actions (repurposing found items of clothing to fashion a crude outfit resembling a character) into complex actions (creating from scratch elaborate creative efforts that stress increasing levels of accuracy and professionalism). Their socially constructed nature makes these trajectories both autonomous from direct management efforts and indirectly responsive to management practices and the strategy they reflect. While the trajectory of these practices can be indirectly affected by individual or collective decisions (e.g., whether to allow a dialogue on the platform), they are the by-product, rather than the deliberate outcome, of the social processes of cocreation. As such, these trajectories could either create problems for firm/consumer cocreation or foster ever greater efficiency and harmony in the cocreation process. In the context of LEGO Ideas, we observed a clear evolution in the degrees and types of creativity on display, with both outcomes (increased friction and increased harmony in the cocreation process) resulting.

Figure 26.1 represents the time line from the inception of LEGO Ideas to June 2016, when a new set of guidelines was announced on the platform. We treated each of the identified phases as a specific event that included both an initial post and the conversation that ensued, either among fans or, at times, between fans and the LEGO Ideas administrators. While the administrators often do not actively engage in these conversations, their presence is strongly felt in several ways: they are often addressed or mentioned directly, and their selective responses are meaningful. By responding only to very specific questions, the administrators are clearly communicating their policy not to participate in broader conversations.

The sequential analysis reveals three overall trajectories in the practices of fans. First, fans gradually shift their deliberations more toward each other rather than the administrators. Together, the fans in the community consider issues such as how the platform should evolve. Second, fans gradually tend to address more strategic issues. They shift their concerns from evaluating particular proposed models to discussing how the LEGO Group should use the LEGO Ideas platform. Third, fans gradually exhibit greater evidence of appropriation—that is, they increasingly view the platform, and the contributions it yields, as theirs.

At the same time, our analysis of the two administrators shows three general responses. First, administrators gradually engage less in general conversations about the platform and its strategy. Over time, official comments shift toward specific models and particular posting rules rather than the platform itself. Second, administrators tend to respond only to very specific and direct questions. Over time, responses focus less on general issues and more on very discrete ones. Third, administrators strongly favor responding to model-specific questions.

These actions suggest that the two institutions of fans and administrators are evolving in opposite directions; whether this phenomenon is causal, however, is unclear. Our sequential analysis is based on Barley and Tolbert's (1997) methodology, but it exhibits one crucial difference from their study—namely, we work across different institutions, the firm, and its fans. We suggest that users of the LEGO Ideas forum do not start out with much of an institutional logic and are, at first, loosely organized, if at all. Our claim is that through their interactions on the LEGO Ideas platform, fans form institutional bonds with one another. In other words, over time, an institution centered on LEGO Ideas forms among fans who follow and contribute to LEGO Ideas. Their discursive interactions (Phillips, Lawrence, and Hardy 2004) among themselves and with the LEGO Ideas platform and its administrators shape their practices. Effectively, then, we are demonstrating the institutionalization process that takes place through the actions and interactions of platform users and administrators.

A relevant point on this trajectory also comes from Schau, Muñiz, and Arnould (2009), who note that practices endow participants with cultural capital. In the context of LEGO Ideas, the adroit performance of practices is a way for participants to claim status and have their voices heard. This could explain the drive toward increasingly complex and creative designs and greater deliberation. The competitive game surrounding the accrual of field-specific cultural capital can lead to a one-upmanship or ratchetting of efforts. This might explain a trend we have observed toward increasingly elaborate kits proposed on LEGO Ideas. Larger and more elaborate models are becoming more common. Members may be creating and submitting these increasingly sophisticated models as a way to compete with and top those that came before them, rather than creating models that LEGO can effectively sell to the mass market. This tendency seems to be a powerful driver in the movement to revise the platform rules, as some communities' members recognize the tendency toward overcomplexity and resent it.

The adroit performance of practices is also a way of being heard, appropriating the space, and even staking a claim as a cobuilding partner. The fans are becoming increasingly vocal. The LEGO Group is also evolving in its practices (stated formally in its terms of service) to balance community preferences and practices with firm goals and practices. In the two-and-a-half years that LEGO Ideas has been running, the terms of service and guidelines have been revised multiple times. The most recent revision appears to respond to recent calls from the community.

Deliberating the Rules and Purpose of the Platform

One of the phases we identified functioned as a precipitating event in the deliberations over the rules and purpose of the LEGO Ideas platform. In late January 2016, a user proposed a model featuring a life-sized replica of the Star Wars robot R2D2. As an extreme instance of the trend toward larger and more complex models, this event triggered deliberation among LEGO Ideas followers and participants. The discussion on the proposed model's LEGO Ideas page and a resulting off-site (Reddit.com) thread contribute to the three-pronged trajectories we described previously of increased deliberation, increased appropriation, and increased focus on strategy by fans. These discussions also represent a very real and sincere effort by fans to determine the purpose and rules of the site, including the best strategy for LEGO to follow. These threads represent an increased sense of appropriation of the site by fans.

Considering its size, the proposed R2D2 model would consist of thousands of bricks, it would be very expensive to package and ship, and consequently it would be impractical for most consumers. The designer recognizes this in his posting about the model (contributing practice):

> The Kenny Baker Artoo is about 16,000 bricks. Wow! Think about that when supporting, it's not going to be cheap. This will be the most expensive LEGO set by far, but we all know how much fans want this set. Don't hesitate to sell your car (or at least your spouse's car) droids are better! The only way we have to let LEGO know that we're willing to buy sets of this scale is to share like mad and get 10K supporters faster than any project has ever done. We can do it! Even so, it's likely going to have to be a very limited edition (& premium) run.

The creator of the proposed model knew it would be impractical and expensive but also believes that there is some real fan demand for such an elaborate model.

This model produced polarized reactions in the LEGO Ideas comments accompanying the proposal: users either loved the model ("supporting" practice) or challenged its viability and appropriateness ("challenging" practice). As one poster opined, "This, in its current size, will never be approved. The price would be outrageous. If it gains 10,000 votes, only a fraction of the supporters would ever be able to buy it. LEGO Ideas isn't intended to cater to niche markets. The design is incredible and stunning. However, this is the wrong platform to showcase it." Another poster summed up the naysayers' position as follows: "It's not going to happen, ever. This IDEAS platform seems to support the spread of false hopes." Around the same time, this poster also initiated an off-platform discussion on Reddit that was highly critical of the current state of the LEGO Ideas platform and proposed sweeping guideline changes.

As the discussion about this proposed model continued, posters linked to other examples of indulgent, high-brick-count models, essentially "documenting" other excesses. The R2D2 model was viewed as symptomatic of a few broad trends. As one contributor posted,

> I agree, something needs to be done. There should at least be a preliminary [evaluation to determine] 'Is this even an idea' step done by LEGO ... I've seen some over the top submissions but I didn't even realize that lord of the rings [sic] one even existed. How does the person ever expect to get that approved? How would anyone even begin to make instructions for that thing? ... I just looked at the actual updates for the Rivendell one. The actual set is just 7 buildings and not his giant diorama? That seems super deceptive. The pictures should only be what he includes in the set.

Here, the poster is "deliberating" both the rules of the game and the purpose of the site. The Lord of the Rings set mentioned in this post is similarly large and complex, and the poster is taking issue with it. There is some similarity to previously documented practices of "governing" and "managing" (Schau, Muñiz, and Arnould 2009; Skålén, Cova, and Pace 2015), but here, the governing and managing are debated by users on behalf of LEGO.

Despite acknowledging its impracticality, the R2D2 designer is sincere in wanting to send a message to LEGO that fans are interested in larger models. In this way, he is actively engaging in the "challenging" practice. He responded defensively to questions by commenters regarding its impracticality.

> Thanks for supporting anyway! I don't subscribe to the 'LEGO will never make a different UCS model on the same theme' view. The UCS Artoo was pretty small— besides it wasn't a Kenny Baker one :)—Besides they could just coin a new term/series if they wanted 'Limited Edition Collectible' or whatever. That aside, this one's going to be a serious challenge for them.

Here, the designer is justifying his model relative to other models produced by the LEGO Group while recognizing the difficulty his model would present. This reaction only served to energize opponents of his model and the trend they felt it represented. The critical conversation moved off-site.

One of the more critical contributors to the R2D2 discussion simultaneously initiated a Reddit discussion titled "LEGO Ideas Sucks Right Now." This thread was noteworthy for several reasons. It was initiated off-site because LEGO Ideas does not include an open forum. It also demonstrates the propensity of the users to think and reason ("deliberating") on behalf of LEGO more prominently than in the R2D2 thread. The creator of this thread begins his first post with the following:

> LEGO Ideas is a wonderful idea, giving fans a chance of getting their own set into production. However, LEGO is backing themselves into a corner with how things are going. This 'everyone is a special little snowflake' attitude that is widespread in the site shouldn't be there, it let's people post almost anything on the site. It has gone to the point where if you post actual valid criticism, stating facts such as "this set already exists" and "this is the size of a LEGOLAND display piece," people will call

you a hater and threaten you by saying you will get banned or flagged with that attitude … People seem to have forgotten that the platform is a place where you pretty much put up an essay to get your submission onto store shelves. Now it's like a forum to post your builds (whatever they are), and humongous MOCs [My Own Creation, designating user-created LEGO models]. LEGO.com and other forums are for that kind of stuff, not LEGO IDEAS.

Multiple practices are evident in this quote, including "challenging," "contributing," and "deliberating." The user wants LEGO Ideas to thrive and the LEGO Group to succeed as a business. His critique of rules, operation, and purpose is intended to be collaborative.

The post goes on to deliberate the rules and purpose of the platform and to offer some possible solutions:

So what the heck can we do about this? Here's 3 things that should be done: -1- Put some actual quality control on the submission page. Besides the obvious stuff, you can post ANYTHING if the picture meets the guidelines. Stuff like this happens often, not as bad, but to a certain degree. -2- Implement a size limit. I can't stress this enough, look at this and this, and tell me with a straight face that these have a chance. Do they look awesome? Yes. Would I like to have one? Yes. Will I get one? Probably not. When you click support, you get possible price options for: | 10-49 | 50-99 | 100-199 | +200$ | I think it should look a bit more like this: | 10-40 | 40-70 | 70-100 | +100$ | -3- Prohibit submissions from current licences LEGO is using. This goes along nicely with 2#, because there is so much stuff, mostly from Star Wars that is just HUGE, and even if they weren't huge, If they have a licence, and you suggest something from that licence, chance is they have a prototype/project for it, and suggesting a possible set already in development isn't going to take you far. It hasn't worked so far for any LEGO Ideas project, and it will never work.

This poster is proposing new rules and procedures and clarifying the role of LEGO Ideas for both LEGO and users. He is fully supportive of LEGO's commercial motives, and his proposed changes aim to eliminate the most common problematic elements.

This thread produced a vigorous conversation with more than 200 comments over the course of two weeks. Most comments are surprisingly supportive of LEGO's efforts to encourage product marketability. This is interesting because it is at odds with the distancing-from-the-market practice that Schau, Muñiz, and Arnould (2009) describe. One responder wrote the following, evincing the "supporting" practice:

Reading all this ranting and arguing makes my soup [sic] feel good! I agree that Ideas needs to be overhauled again. All the crap is keeping the real good ideas from being made. And it should be clear to people now what kind of sets will get made: ones that there is a substantial market for, ones that are between $20-$70 and between 200–700 pieces, and ones that don't interfere with license that LEGO already holds (no star wars, super heroes, or lotr). Also if your idea is for a non-licensed set and it meets all the criteria I just listed, then you will have even better chances. All this seems so obvious to me. How is everyone having such a hard time not realizing that they won't make a $600 sandcrawler or $1000 Rivendell? Or that, much as I would love one, they will not make a Legend of Zelda set! People just need to be more original with their submissions.

The poster proposes criteria consistent with ensuring the LEGO Group's success and expresses amazement that all participants do not understand these criteria. This posting was not atypical. Most contributors to this thread expressed similar views.

Appropriation and Official Response

The conversations excerpted here show fans engaging in sophisticated deliberation over questions such as product relevance, marketability, positioning, community strategy, and more. Fans are claiming their role as comanagers of LEGO Ideas and want to appropriate the space (Visconti et al. 2010). Their practices indicate increasing appropriation of the process and its rules, an increasing focus on the rules of the game, the purpose of the platform, and the modes of communication. In other words, through their deliberative practices, fans are increasingly asking for a "way in," for an opportunity to participate in a democratic process.

This finding echoes the work of Visconti et al. (2010), in that appropriation can take the form of either a dialectical or a dialogical process, depending on the individualist or collectivist appraisal each group of stakeholders has of the space. In the case of LEGO Ideas, we observe a collectivist appraisal by most of the fans who contribute and a somewhat ambivalent appraisal by LEGO Ideas administrators. While the very premise of the platform as a place of cocreation is collectivist, many of the administrator posts we analyzed are more individualist in nature. When the administrators provide clarifications or support, they tend to prefer addressing individual members; they discourage broad conversations. Indeed, such preference is built into the system. The platform does not provide a forum but rather a blog on which all conversations are initiated by administrators. By virtue of these actions, LEGO Ideas is managed primarily by its administrators as a platform on which individual fans interact with LEGO by submitting projects. Even the voting process constitutes an individual exercise in "representational democracy" rather than in the collective exercise of "deliberative democracy" (Guttman and Thompson 2004; Ozanne, Corus, and Saatcioglu 2009) that the users are trying to implement.

LEGO has adjusted its terms of service and site guidelines for LEGO Ideas several times over the course of its existence. In addition, both the terms of service and the guidelines changed from those used by the predecessor to LEGO Ideas, LEGO Cuusoo, a crowdsourcing experiment that ran from 2008 to April 2014 (LEGO Ideas Blog 2014). The terms of service and the guidelines for LEGO Ideas were designed with feedback from the Cuusoo experiment in mind. The greatest changes were giving projects one year to reach 10,000 supporters, extending submission eligibility to contributors ages 13–18 years, creating Clutch Power points (which facilitated the practices of milestoning and badging [Schau, Muñiz, and Arnould 2009]), eliminating edits after submission, and disallowing mock-ups of LEGO product boxes. Reactions to these changes were mostly positive, with most commenters trying to clarify their understanding of the new rules.

The most recent changes, announced in June 2016, nearly six months after the R2D2 and Reddit threads, represented the largest set of changes ever to the LEGO Ideas guidelines and its terms of service and closely reflected some of the changes advocated by community members in those threads. The principal change sought, in congruence with the Reddit thread, was to limit "submissions from current licenses LEGO is using." Because many commenters had responded positively to this suggestion, this is perhaps not surprising. Changes also included a limit of 3,000 pieces per model, consistent with user suggestions to "implement a size limit." Again, many commenters, on both the Reddit and the R2D2 threads, responded affirmatively to this suggestion, focusing on cost/price considerations.

Discussion and Conclusion

We have demonstrated clear evidence of institutionalization processes through practice trajectories that are themselves tied to the collaborative processes among fans and with the firm. Fans want in. They contribute a wide range of resources and are increasingly claiming a piece of the public space and an opportunity for democratic deliberation. However, while our time line starts at the inception of LEGO Ideas, we cannot ignore the overall context of a brand with a historically highly engaged and broad ecosystem.

A crucial aspect of the practice trajectories we have documented is users' increasing focus on clarifying the purpose of the platform. This is appropriation gone strategic. Users deliberate issues such as pricing, go-to-market strategy, and licensing, virtually usurping the role of LEGO senior marketers. For LEGO and its LEGO Ideas team, this strategic appropriation process poses its own crucial strategic challenges. As fans engage in more deliberative practices, should LEGO embrace the democratic deliberative processes or maintain the platform's more traditional mode of participation?

In the context of public policy management, a distinction has been made between two dimensions of public engagement: participation and inclusion (Quick and Feldman 2011). Participatory practices involve accessing a broad range of inputs, whereas inclusive practices facilitate the diversity and the strategic nature of inputs. In particular, inclusive practices exhibit three characteristics: they allow "different ways of knowing" (to include diverse participants), they "coproduce the process and content of decision making" (thereby adding strategic input), and they acknowledge "temporal openness" (accepting the long-term involvement of the community in a process that will continue to evolve over time) (Quick and Feldman 2011, 282). A comparative study of four public management projects with high/low participatory practices and high/low inclusive practices found that the highest levels of participant satisfaction were experienced under high-inclusive-practice conditions, with high participation scoring higher than low participation (Quick and Feldman 2011). While the public management study does not address the question of institutionalization, we can assume that the three facets of inclusive practices are conducive to institutionalization.

Our findings suggest that involvement at a strategic level not only meets user expectations but also may be beneficial in terms of customer satisfaction. While LEGO Ideas administrators refrain from explicit deliberation, we observe that they are both very attuned and responsive to fan deliberations, particularly when it comes to more strategic matters such as guidelines. As such, we could see a pattern develop in which fans continue to deliberate publicly until they get the attention of administrators. Fans make their case over time, patiently, with no real validation by LEGO, and then one day, a change is posted that addresses some of their points. They understand that LEGO operates according to a certain corporate machinery, and they simply try to find ways to make their case over time.

The issue is a broader one from simply a strategic perspective. Scholars have noted concerns about the fairness of cocreation. Cova, Pace, and Skålén (2015) consider two perspectives on consumer involvement and cocreation. One perspective views cocreating consumers as empowered and enabled in their efforts—it is a good thing because consumers are liberated. The critical perspective views cocreating consumers as being shaped and disciplined through marketing discourses—in this view, cocreating consumers are being exploited. We side with the former perspective because we consider the actions of appropriation evidence of awareness and agency. We believe that the critical perspective still relies on the trope of the consumer as a cultural dupe. It presupposes no self-awareness at either the individual or the institutional level, and it fails to take into account the very effects of institutionalization we have documented here.

In their work on community-embedded creative consumers, Schau, Muñiz, and Arnould (2009) suggest that future research should attempt to discern and unpack the operation of a broader set of practices. Refining such understandings, they assert, will prove useful in creating novel strategies to further leverage the creative tendencies of marketplace actors. We have responded to this call and proposed inclusion as a novel strategy. While we validated the practices proposed in Schau, Muñiz, and Arnould (2009) and Skålén, Pace, and Cova (2015), we also discovered that neither of these two extant typologies fully captures the complex reality of the interactions on the LEGO Ideas platform at this moment in time. This may reflect a reality that the identification of practices is an inherently idiosyncratic affair in which new contexts will require the divination of new practices.

Schau, Muñiz, and Arnould (2009, 41) also assert that "ceding control to customers enhances consumer engagement and builds brand equity." However, we believe that there is more complexity to this. Not only are the practices of the firm and consumers different, but crucially, they are constantly changing as well. In other words, understanding practices is simply not enough. As institutional logics develop between a firm and its customers, some level of appropriation on the part of customers is to be expected. The question for firms is whether they want to get ahead of the curve by adopting the collectivist, inclusive practices we have discussed. In either case, firms probably have much to gain from being transparent about some key strategic elements: the purpose of the cocreation activities or platform (e.g., product development, market research, customer engagement) and the degree and limits of customer involvement they are seeking. Acknowledging that these parameters may evolve would also be a positive signal.

Terwiesch and Xu (2008) note that one of the largest challenges in cocreation is designing appropriate interface mechanisms. Füller, Hutter, and Faullant (2011) and Singh (2014) similarly assert that another challenge is managing the process. We echo these concerns and unpack them. Managing the process involves establishing rules and expectations. We contend that a formidable approach would be to adopt the inclusive practices of public management by jointly and continually deliberating these points. This does not mean that the firm should abandon its goals or principles or, conversely, that members of the community should expect total and complete control. What we observe on the LEGO Ideas platform are highly appreciative and business-minded customers who have the best interest of the brand at heart; they are stakeholders in the truest sense. Of course, there are also risks: Schau, Muñiz, and Arnould (2009) assert that marketers should encourage greater diversity in practice. We agree, but with the following caveat: Be careful what you wish for. A proliferation of practices does not guarantee that the practices will be desirable to or compatible with the marketer.

References

Antorini, Yun Mi. 2007. "Brand Community Innovation: An Intrinsic Case Study." Doctoral dissertation, Department of Innovation and Organizational Economics, Copenhagen Business School.

Antorini, Yun Mi, Albert M. Muñiz Jr., and Tormod Askildsen. 2012. "Collaborating with Customer Communities: Lessons from the LEGO Group." *MIT Sloan Management Review* 53 (3): 73–95.

Aubert-Gamet, Véronique. 1997. "Twisting Servicescapes: Diversion of the Physical Environment in a Re-appropriation Process." *International Journal of Service Industry Management* 8 (1): 26–41.

Baichtal, John, and Joe Meno. 2011. *The Cult of LEGO*. San Francisco: No Starch Press.

Barley, Stephen R., and Pamela S. Tolbert. 1997. "Institutionalization and Structuration: Studying the Links Between Action and Institution." *Organization Studies* 18 (1): 93–117.

Bayus, Barry L. 2013. "Crowdsourcing New Product Ideas over Time: An Analysis of the Dell IdeaStorm Community." *Management Science* 59 (1): 226–44.

Boulaire, Christèle, and Bernard Cova. 2013. "The Dynamics and Trajectory of Creative Consumption Practices as Revealed by the Postmodern Game of Geocaching." *Consumption Markets & Culture* 16 (1): 1–24.

Chanal, Valérie, and Marie-Laurence Caron-Fasan. 2010. "The Difficulties Involved in Developing Business Models Open to Innovation Communities: The Case of a Crowdsourcing Platform." *M@n@gement* 13 (4): 318–40.

Cova, Bernard, Stefano Pace, and Per Skålén. 2015. "Brand Volunteering Value Co-creation with Unpaid Consumers." *Marketing Theory* 15 (4): 465–85.

Crowdsourcing.org. 2013. "Genius Crowds Closes Its Doors," accessed March 30, 2016, www.crowdsourcing.org/editorial/genius-crowds-closes-its-doors/25946.

Epp, Amber M., and Linda L. Price. 2011. "Designing Solutions Around Customer Network Identity Goals." *Journal of Marketing* 75 (2): 36–54.

Feldman, Martha S. 2004. "Resources in Emerging Structures and Processes of Change." *Organization Science* 15 (3): 295–309.

Filieri, Raffaele. 2013. "Consumer Co-creation and New Product Fevelopment." *Marketing Intelligence & Planning* 31 (1): 40–53.

Friedland, Roger, and Robert R. Alford. 1991. "Bringing Society Back In: Symbols, Practices and Institutional Contradictions." In *The New Institutionalism in Organizational Analysis*, edited by W. W. Powell & P. H. DiMaggio, 232–63. Chicago: University of Chicago Press.

Füller, Johann, Katja Hutter, and Rita Faullant. 2011. "Why Co-Creation Experience Matters? Creative Experience and Its Impact on the Quantity and Quality of Creative Contributions." *R&D Management* 41 (3): 259–73.

Füller, Johann, Hans Mühlbacher, Kurt Matzler, and Gregor Jawecki. 2009. "Consumer Empowerment Through Internet-Based Co-Creation." *Journal of Management Information Systems* 26 (3): 71–102.

Gebauer, Johannes, Johann Füller, and Roland Pezzei. 2013. "The Dark and the Bright Side of Co-Creation: Triggers of Member Behavior in Online Innovation Communities." *Journal of Business Research*, 66 (9): 1516–27.

Gloor, Peter, and Scott Cooper. 2007. "The New Principles of a Swarm Business." *MIT Sloan Management Review* 48 (3): 81–4.

Guttman, Amy, and Dennis Thompson. 2004. *Why Deliberative Democracy*. Princeton, NJ: Princeton University Press.

Hartmann, Benjamin J., Caroline Wiertz, and Eric J. Arnould. 2015. "Exploring Consumptive Moments of Value-Creating Practice in Online Community." *Psychology & Marketing* 32 (3): 319–40.

Healy, Jason C., and Pierre McDonagh 2013. "Consumer Roles in Brand Culture and Value Co-creation in Virtual Communities." *Journal of Business Research* 66 (9): 1528–40.

Hienerth, Christoph, Christopher Lettl, and Peter Keinz. 2014. "Synergies Among Producer Firms, Lead Users, and User Communities." *Journal of Product Innovation Management* 31 (4): 848–66.

Jeppesen, Lars Bo, and Karim R. Lakhani. 2010. "Marginality and Problem-Solving Effectiveness in Broadcast Search." *Organization Science* 21 (5): 1016–33.

Koerner, Brendan I. 2006. "Geeks in Toyland." *Wired* (February 1): 104.

Kozinets, Robert V. 2002. "Can Consumers Escape the Market? Emancipatory Illuminations from Burning Man." *Journal of Consumer Research* 29 (1): 20–38.

Kozinets, Robert V., Andrea Hemetsberger, and Hope Jensen Schau. 2008. "The Wisdom of Consumer Crowds Collective Innovation in the Age of Networked Marketing." *Journal of Macromarketing* 28 (4): 339–54.

Kozinets, Robert V., Kristine De Valck, Andrea C. Wojnicki, and Sarah J. S. Wilner. 2010. "Networked Narratives: Understanding Word-of-Mouth Marketing in Online Communities." *Journal of Marketing* 74 (2): 71–89.

Lawrence, Thomas B., Cynthia Hardy, and Nelson Phillips. 2002. "Institutional Effects of Interorganizational Collaboration." *Academy of Management Journal* 45 (1): 281–90.

LEGO Ideas Blog. 2014. "Welcome to LEGO Ideas!," accessed June 2016, https://ideas.LEGO.com/blogs/1-blog/post/1.

McAlexander, James H., John W. Schouten, and Harold F. Koenig. 2002. "Building Brand Community." *Journal of Marketing* 66 (1): 38–54.

Muñiz, Albert M., Jr., and Thomas C. O'Guinn. 2001. "Brand Community." *Journal of Consumer Research* 27 (4): 412–32.

Muñiz, Albert M., Jr., and Hope Jensen Schau. 2005. "Religiosity in the Abandoned Apple Newton Brand Community." *Journal of Consumer Research* 31 (4): 737–47.

Muñiz, Albert M., Jr., and Hope Jensen Schau. 2007. "Vigilante Marketing and Consumer-Created Communications." *Journal of Advertising* 36 (3): 35–50.

Muñiz, Albert M., Jr., and Hope Jensen Schau. 2011. "How to Inspire Value-Laden Collaborative Consumer-Generated Content." *Business Horizons* 54 (3): 209–17.

O'Hern, M., and Aric Rindfleisch. 2010. "Customer Co-Creation," in *Review of Marketing Research*, edited by Naresh K. Malhotra, 84–106. Bingley, UK: Emerald Group Publishing.

Ozanne, Julie L., Canan Corus, and Bige Saatcioglu. 2009. "The Philosophy and Methods of Deliberative Democracy." *Journal of Public Policy & Marketing* 28 (1): 29–40.

Payne, Adrian F., Kaj Storbacka, and Pennie Frow. 2008. "Managing the Co-creation of Value." *Journal of the Academy of Marketing Science* 36 (1): 83–96.

Phillips, J. 2011. "Open Innovation Typology." in *A Guide to Open Innovation and Crowdsourcing*, edited by P. Sloane, 22–35. London: Kogan Page.

Phillips, Nelson, Thomas B. Lawrence, and Cynthia Hardy. 2004. "Discourse and Institutions." *Academy of Management Review* 29 (4): 635–52.

Quick, Kathryn S., and Martha S. Feldman. 2011. "Distinguishing Participation and Inclusion." *Journal of Planning Education and Research* 31 (3): 272–90.

Rivkin, Jan W., Stefan H. Thomke, and Daniela Beyersdorfer. 2013. "LEGO (A): The Crisis." Harvard Business School Case 713–478, February 2013.

Robertson, David, and Bill Breen. 2013. *Brick by Brick: How LEGO Rewrote the Rules of Innovation and Conquered the Global Toy Industry*. New York: Crown Business.

Schau, Hope Jensen, Albert M. Muñiz Jr., and Eric J. Arnould. 2009. "How Brand Community Practices Create Value." *Journal of Marketing* 73 (5): 30–51.

Singh, Narinder. 2014. "Crowdsourcing in 2014: With Great Power Comes Great Responsibility," *Wired* (January): www.wired.com/insights/2014/01/crowdsourcing-2014-great-power-comes-great-responsibility/.

Skålén, Per, Stefano Pace, and Bernard Cova. 2015. "Firm-Brand Community Value Co-Creation as Alignment of Practices." *European Journal of Marketing* 49 (3–4): 596–620.

Taillard, M., L. D. Peters, J. Pels, & C. Mele. 2016. "The Role of Shared Intentions in the Emergence of Service Ecosystems." *Journal of Business Research* 69 (8): 2972–80.

Terwiesch, Christian, and Yi Xu. 2008. "Innovation Contests, Open Innovation, and Multiagent Problem Solving." *Management Science* 54 (9): 1529–43.

Visconti, Luca M., John F. Sherry, Stefania Borghini, and Laurel Anderson. 2010. "Street Art, Sweet Art? Reclaiming the 'Public' in Public Place." *Journal of Consumer Research* 37 (3): 511–29.

Von Hippel, Eric A. 2005. *Democratizing Innovation*. Cambridge, MA: MIT Press Books.

Warde, Alan. 2005. "Consumption and Theories of Practice." *Journal of Consumer Culture*, 5 (2): 131–53.

Weingarten, Mark. 2007. "'Project Runway' for the T-shirt Crowd." *CNN Business 2.0* (June 18), accessed December 2016, http://money.cnn.com/magazines/business2/business2_archive/2007/06/01/100050978/index.htm?postversion=2007061806

PART XIV

Social Class/Power

27

THE HIDDEN HAND OF SOCIAL CLASS

Paul Henry and Marylouise Caldwell

UNIVERSITY OF SYDNEY BUSINESS SCHOOL, SYDNEY, AUSTRALIA

> Position in the classification struggle depends on position in the class structure: and social subjects are perhaps never less likely to transcend the limits of their minds than in the representation they have and give of their position, which defines those limits.
> (conclusion to Bourdieu's *Distinction*, 1984, p. 484)

Social class remains one of most fundamental organizing principles that underpins all developed societies. Gender, ethnicity, and sometimes religion also play key roles in social organization. These organizing principles tend to interact in ways that result in hierarchies of (dis)-advantage. "Haves and have-nots" living in "good and bad" suburbs are plainly evident to even the casual observer. We often intuitively distinguish between people of our own social position and others through subtle cues of dress style, lifestyle activities and social behavior. At a more macro level we see systematic inequality in income and wealth across the Western world. For example, the wealthiest 20 per cent of households in Australia now account for 61 per cent of total household net worth, whereas the poorest 20 per cent account for just 1 per cent of the total (Douglas et al., 2014). We see similar patterns of (dis)advantage in terms of health-related outcomes. These span across virtually every measure of health, including obesity, smoking, diabetes, heart disease, physical activity levels, longevity, suicide, and on into consumption of sugar products and fatty foods. Differences in health outcomes suggest differences in lifestyle behaviors that can be only partially explained by ability to pay. Thus, multiple layers of inequality result in systematic difference in human potential for growth and ability to participate in the full range of social and material opportunities. Disadvantaged position constrains options and limits the chance to lead a fulfilling life. Disadvantage tends to reproduce into the next generation in ways where people are more likely than not to remain in their class of origin.

Given the profound implications of social class position on lifestyle, wellbeing and consumption patterns it is surprising to see that there has been relatively limited research focus in recent years on social class by consumer researchers. We suggest several underlying reasons for this. The first is the popular tendency to reduce social class to the economic dimension that highlights income, wealth, and ability to pay. The assumption here is that given the same amount of money that people of different classes will pursue similar consumption priorities that are driven by the same underlying motivations. However, we argue that distinctive sociohistorical conditions in childhood socialization molds class-specific worldviews. Bourdieu (1984) calls this *habitus*, but more on that next. These worldviews act as a lens that affects perceptions of self, place in the world, lifestyle preferences and consumption tastes. The second underlying reason relates to lack of conceptual understanding as to just what is social class. This creates questions as to exactly what researchers are aiming to capture when studying social class; and the question as to how best to classify people into class groups. One subsidiary problem here is that there are many classification schemes using different classifying variables and number of class groupings. A third underlying reason relates to the mistaken belief that class is an "outmoded" concept. More recent ideas such as postmodernity and liquid modernity supposedly driven by education, affluence, globalization, and heightened sense of individuality argue for a fragmentation of old social structures and greater diversity of tastes. We dispute this "outmoded" characterization of class. Consequently, a primary goal of this chapter is to address these three reasons for defocus on class. To this end we aim to illuminate the multilayered nature of social class and the underlying mechanisms that continue to shape social organization.

We start by sketching some history of class and consumer behavior. The conceptual foundations are built on the seminal contributions of Karl Marx and Max Weber. Marx highlighted "relations to the means of production" that distinguishes between factory owners, supervisors and workers. This classically delineates economic power that divides owner and workers. Of course, the means of production have changed dramatically from the industrial factory-based economies to that of more intangible means of production, such as services and technology that have come to dominate over old industries. We now see a reduction in blue collar workers in Western societies as well as a more educated society. However, it is unlikely that a contemporary service worker—retail check out, call center, data processor, or domestic cleaner—has any more security or autonomy than an industrial factory worker. In fact, we see new occupational divisions of domination that result from the internet revolution. These take the form of the division between the app-based delivery people that fulfil online orders for meals, groceries, and the like, to the often far more affluent purchasers of these services. It is rapidly becoming clear that the growing legion of app deliverers have very limited autonomy or security of income. Smiley (2016, p. 1) put it thus: "In the new world of on-demand everything, you're either pampered, isolated royalty—or you're a 21st century servant." We see the same occurring with Uber drivers whose supposed independence masks the piece-work reality of their "independent" worker conditions.

Weber expanded on Marx's economic notion proposing a tripartite concept of social class that integrates three separate but related mechanisms—economic class, social status, and power (party). In particular, Weber's idea of class position conferring differing levels of status introduces a social comparison aspect between self and other. This illuminated the idea of like clustering with like; that people of similar social status are more likely to feel comfortable socializing together and that distinctive lifestyles develop within these social groupings. It also points to barriers to mobility, in that higher status social groups are likely to be less accepting of people from lower status groups. This set the foundations for social distinction stemming from in-group socialization and development of distinctive mores and norms of behavior. Weber's notion of unequally distributed power is evident in the huge growth of unskilled jobs in the new service economy where individual authority and autonomy is low and oversight and control is high. Sustained experiences of powerlessness act to deflate self-esteem, confidence, and often increases frustration and feelings of hopelessness.

Lloyd Warner took up these Weberian ideas when studying the social organization of American life in the 1940s. His Yankee Town study painted a rich and nuanced story of everyday life in a suburban housing development that teased out the multidimensional character of social class in often mundane and inconspicuous consumption setting (Warner & Lunt, 1941). In this work, we start to gain a greater appreciation of the embodied character of class-distinctive world views. At the time this work attracted considerable attention from consumer researchers and professional marketers (Greyser, 1961; Larrabee, 1955; Newman, 1955; Rainwater et al., 1959). For example, Pierre Martineau (1958, p. 122) following research commissioned for the *Chicago Tribune* wrote dispelling the assumption that:

> A rich man is simply a poor man with more money and that, given the same income, the poor man would behave exactly like the rich ... *(it meant that)* ... the lower status person is profoundly different in his mode of thinking and his way of handling the world from that of the middle class individual.

Martineau then went on to summarize the findings into ten propositions that distinguish modes of thinking (worldviews) between lower- and middle-class people. It will be seen below that these modes of thinking are broadly supported by other researchers across different countries and endure into more recent time periods. Relative to lower status, middle-class people are characterized as:

- Being more future-oriented
- Having a viewpoint that embraces a longer expanse of time
- Having a better structured sense of perceiving
- Being more abstract and immaterial in thinking
- Having a greater stress on rationality
- Having greater urban identification
- Having more extended horizons; less limited
- Having greater sense of choice
- Having greater confidence and willingness to take risks
- Being less parochial.

The finding that class is more than just economic categories opened the door to the possibility that class groupings exhibit distinctive consumption motivations that generate conscious and non-conscious marketplace preferences. These preferences are shaped by more global worldviews that have been inculcated by within-class socialization processes (Coleman, 1983; Levy, 1966). These hold marketing implications in the areas of consumer segmentation and communications (Nickles, 2002; Wehner, 2002). Warner's ideas were introduced into the commercial environment through consumer research conducted by Social Research Inc. in the 1940s–1950s across diverse categories such as detergents and soaps, baby products, automobiles, clothing, telephone usage, feminine hygiene, toothpaste, hair products, financial management and credit, newspaper and magazine readership, television, radio, and food consumptions (Levy, 1966). Warner et al. (1949, p. 30) illustrates the applicability of distinctive motivations in consumer segmentation:

> Examination of the advertising displayed in various magazines demonstrates that advertising agencies and their clients often waste their money because they are ignorant of the operation of class values in their business ... frequently the manufacturer or retailer does not know how his product appeals to different classes. Sometimes the product will appeal to but one level, but often a product might appeal to, and be used

by all class levels, were the producer aware of how his product is valued at different social levels.

This fruitful program of research fell dormant by the 1970s. This was for a variety of reasons that can be summarized as (1) The overpowering myth of social equality and ideological disdain for class hierarchy, (2) Limited agreement on appropriate classification systems, (3) Conceptual confusion via reductionism of the concept down to surrogate indicators such as income levels, education, or occupation, and (4) Quantitative turn in consumer research that prized countable observations over qualitative nuance (see Henry & Caldwell, 2008). However, this is not to say that the findings are no longer relevant to contemporary society. On the contrary we see considerable parallels between the class distinctions identified in the 1940s with those found by contemporary researchers. We also argue that reading some of these earlier works can complement and add depth of understanding to more recent works. The similarity of finding between old and new periods points to a stability of fundamental class distinctions. We turn to the more contemporary research next.

Revival of Studies in Class and Consumption

Interest in social class saw a revival in the 1990s with work such as Holt's (1998) "Does Cultural Capital Structure American Consumption?" Part of the reason for the revival was the introduction of Bourdieu's (1984) theory of social practice into consumer research. This presented a novel means to explore class mechanisms and the impact of distinctive world-views on consumption. Bourdieu's theory has subsequently come to have significant influence in the study of consumption practices. Consequently, we first briefly sketch out the key elements of the theory. These include fields of social life, capitals, and habitus. For Bourdieu, the primary field is that of social class. However, people can also operate in other kinds of fields. For example, the gendered field of family and domestic life or the religious field. Individuals are positioned in a field in ways that attract varying degrees of social distinction. This is akin to Weber's status dimension. People that cluster around similar points in the field tend toward similar lifestyles, expectations, norms and values and consumption preferences. Position in the field derives from distribution of capitals (economic, cultural, and social). Cultural capital has received particular attention by consumer researchers because of the embodied form it often takes in taste formation (via habitus). However, cultural capital also takes the form of institutionalized capitals (e.g. credentials, titles, and degrees), and objectified capitals (ownership of consumer objects that mark taste). Each of these capital types can facilitate advantaged position in a field. Bourdieu employs three dimensions of capital mix to analyze distribution of participants across the field. These include total volume of capitals, composition of capitals (e.g. primarily economic or cultural) and trajectory of capital accumulation (e.g. change versus stability over lifetime). Note that this opens up the possibility that different individuals may hold quite different mixes of capitals. So, it is possible that a person may have high cultural capitals, yet also have limited economic resources. Likewise, the converse may apply. It is likely that in both these conditions that the person is experiencing class mobility (downward in the former and upward in the latter). As will be discussed next, these imbalances generate frustrations in terms of blocked lifestyle preferences or lack of social fit.

The final theoretical element—habitus—is probably the trickiest of the three. Habitus refers to the set of embodied dispositions and preferences that evolve through socialization and remain relatively stable across the life course. This implies that people reared in a particular position in the field of social class share a (reasonably) common habitus. It is important to emphasize the embodied nature of habitus. These dispositions are largely unconscious and we tend to first react on an emotional level where preferences are impeded. Habitus is said to be field-neutral; an individual orients to multiple fields from the point of view of a single habitus. To this point, Bourdieu likens habitus to that of a "generative grammar." Crossley (2001, p. 94) elaborates on how "the habitus schema acts like an underlying grammar, which allows a multitude of innovative forms of expression." This implies that the kinds of dispositions that qualify as habitus sit at a relatively abstract level. It also implies that dispositions embodied in habitus are not simply deterministic. Rather, consumers can seek to realize dispositions in a large variety of ways. This means that researchers seeking to classify class groups based solely on observable purchases will find it difficult to discern clear class distinctions for many product categories. For example, the upper-class person seen dressed in jeans and tee shirt is often indistinguishable from a working class person. The difference is that the upper-class person is likely to have a greater range of clothing to suit a more nuanced set of occasions.

So, what exactly are these embodied dispositions that indirectly guide consumptions? Probably the most comprehensive explication of interrelated dispositions in the consumer research literature is found in Holt (1998). Holt describes the consumption styles of six dimensions of taste that are inscribed in habitus. The six include material versus formal aesthetics; referential versus critical interpretations; materialism versus idealism; local versus cosmopolitan tastes; communal versus individual form subjectivity; and autotelic versus self-actualizing leisure. These dimensions exhibit strong parallels with Bourdieu's (1984) findings in 1960s French society. In *Distinction*, Bourdieu illustrates how underlying (class-based) systems of habitus influence a wide range of taste and lifestyle outcomes. It is also enlightening to compare the findings of Bourdieu and Holt with that of Warner's findings regarding class-based dispositions found within 1950s American society (summarized in Martineau, 1958). Collectively, the work of these researchers shows that similar class-based systems of dispositions are found across time period and geographic location (Henry & Caldwell, 2008).

Holt's (1998) six dimensions operate as a system of decontextualized understanding. People disposed to formal aesthetics and critical interpretation will also tend to exhibit preference for idealism, cosmopolitan tastes, individualism, and self-actualization. Additionally, Henry (2005) highlights that (dis)empowerment is a central feature of habitus. Empowerment stems from greater capacity for abstract thought, planning and problem solving ability, task persistence, ambitiousness, openness to diversity, and more extended time orientation. These capacities that dispose toward empowerment are directly related to Holt's dimensions of taste that inhabits an upper-class habitus. For example, Bourdieu (1984) describes how the upper-class capacity for abstract thinking translates into appreciation for more intellectually complex art forms or more sophisticated storylines in plays, movies, and literature. This parallels Holt's dimension regarding critical interpretation. Henry found that empowerment influences saving and financial management practices that advantage the upper classes.

Holt (1998) illustrates how class-based habitus influences housing and furniture choices in that lower classes (LCCs) focus on function and durability, while higher classes (HCC's) also prize these qualities as a base level. However, on top of this base they also value aesthetic qualities that appeal to sensibilities. HCCs consume media forms differently in more critically abstracted ways. LCC media interpretations tend to be more concrete and literal to the text. The materialism of LCCs stems from financial limitations that constrain their material desires—for example, better housing or more luxurious holidays. This causes them to focus on object luxury. On the other hand, HCCs who are less materially constrained deemphasize that which they already have and focus more on consumption of ideas and experiences.

So, for example, HCCs emphasize the quality of the food and experience in a restaurant, over the quantity of food. The cosmopolitan bent of HCCs prompts greater interest in the unusual and exotic. This may manifest in a greater variety of international food choices, musical styles, travel, and interest in global news. This prompts greater product experimentation. Appeal to individuality among HCCs stems from greater confidence and sense of choice. This manifests in rejection of products that are perceived as being mass produced and standardized. HCCs seek out products that mark their individuality; that have an artisanal quality. This reflects in clothing and home decoration. The drive toward individuality is one way that visibly distinguishes HCCs. All of these differences tend to add up to HCCs engaging in a much more diverse set of interests and activities than LCCs. Bourdieu refers to this as "omnivore" behaviors. This also fits with Warner's earlier ideas of a more limitless worldview and Henry's ideas of greater empowerment that facilitates confidence in possibilities.

Bourdieu's theory allows for change in position in the field—class mobility. This can happen when an individual's quantity and mix of capitals changes. Loss of job, natural disaster, and divorce often result in loss of economic capital and changes to desired lifestyle. Conversely educational opportunity can result in access to better jobs and increase in economic capital. However, most people remain in their class of origin and it appears that the greatest barrier to mobility lies in cultural capital inscribed in habitus (worldview). This internalized barrier self-limits an individual's potential. For example, when children from upper-class and lower-class schools were questioned about what are the good jobs, both groups replied in similar ways—doctors, lawyers, managers. Yet when asked what they themselves expect to become the upper-class kids replied that they expected to enter such professions, whereas the lower-class kids replied that they expected to enter far lower paid, menial jobs. This reflects a lower sense of potential and more limited sense of place in the world. Allen (2002) went on to demonstrate how class-based habitus constrains educational choices and life chances. He proposed the Fits-Like-A-Glove (FLAG) framework of choice in which chronically inculcated preferences are directed more by feelings than rational mechanisms. In Allen's study, working class students' choice of college was largely driven by experience of "fit" where they felt more comfortable at lower level campuses catering for a largely working class student population. This contrasted with relative discomfort with visits to more elite college campuses. Allen argues that such choices to attend lower level educational institutions constrains educational and subsequent career potential.

Henry (2005) demonstrates how habitus constrains potential for financial growth via differences in budgeting and money planning that stem from higher class people engaging in a more deliberative approach that encompasses greater discipline, problem solving, calculation, control, goal setting, and longer term planning. These allow higher class people to advance financial security from baseline income levels that are often similar to that of young working class people. Bernthal, Crocket, & Rose (2005) examined credit card usage and found embodied cultural capital facilitating and signaling distinctive lifestyle objectives. For example, LCCs see the card as protection against emergencies such as car breakdowns. Whereas HCCs emphasize credit cards as facilitators of lifestyle aspirations, for example holiday experiences, interior design or further education. The LCC perspective is primarily driven by security, while the HCC perspective is driven by opportunity. Again, these distinctive practices appear to be ingrained and act as a source of class reproduction. We see layering of disadvantage in poorer suburbs where inability to pay confines lower classes. Yet, there is also the social psychological constraint where sense of fit with like people comes into play. The metaphor "birds of a feather flock together" applies here where people with similar ways of thinking attract to like others and experience an instinctual comfort. One implication of interpersonal fit is that people with a lower social class social network will have less opportunity to accrue the kinds of social capital that higher class people are able to leverage. This is because lower-class social networks comprise people with less power and influence.

Ustuner & Holt (2007, 2010) have studied class in a less industrialized country—Turkey. This work seeks to explore applicability of Bourdieusian theory that has been primarily developed in Western nation settings. In line with Bourdieu they find a distinction between class fractions where LCCs emphasize conspicuous material display, and HCCs emphasize cultural sophistication. However, they find that the content of embodied taste varies from that found in Western nations. For example, they find HCCs trying to emulate Western lifestyle ideas in a scripted yet not embodied manner. The taste expressions they seek to emulate are not inscribed in habitus but are consciously mimicked with mixed success and "self-conscious doubt." This is contrary to Allen's (2002) fit-like-a-glove qualities of Western HCC experience. On the other hand, Turkish LCCs disdain the Western lifestyle myth and embrace local symbols of economic status. Vikas, Varman, & Belk (2015) also studied changes in relationships among the social hierarchy due to Westernized marketization in the North Indian context. The new economic order has upended old sources of distinction—particularly that of caste. Sitting at the most disadvantaged end of the Turkish economic scale, Ustuner & Holt (2007) studied poor women who have migrated from the rural areas. They find that absence of economic, social and cultural capital confines them to a dominated position at the bottom end of the class structure. They are found to respond in several ways, such as reinforcing the old village ways or alternatively trying to embrace modern consumer culture. The problem for the latter strategy in such attempts to break out from old ways is that it often results in failure—and "shattered identity projects." Interestingly though, Ustuner & Thompson (2012) do identify pathways for upward mobility in Turkish society via acquisition of social and cultural capital. This can occur when lower-class service workers (such as hairdressers) interact regularly with more elite customers. These workers are found to sometimes take on the consumption tastes of HCCs and form relationships beyond the workplace with clients. This leads to a reconfiguration of habitus, social practices, and position in the field.

Much of the contemporary work takes an intersectional approach where class is considered along with a range of other social classifications, such as gender, family role, and life stage. In particular, the interaction between gender and family role with class has been subject to considerable debate. Many traditional classification systems have employed occupation as a proxy for status. Yet, this presents a problem as to where to place the stay-at-home mother—an unpaid job that appears to hold little economic value. Then there is the question of placement of stay-at-home fathers. The solution has usually been to classify at the household level and use the highest status occupation in the household as the proxy. Still, the lived experience of the corporate executive and stay-at-home carer will be a world apart in terms of power relations, respect, everyday consumption practices and lifestyle priorities. Bourdieu (1984) points to the primary role of social class in shaping habitus. However, while he does acknowledge contributions of other factors such as gender it has been left to other researchers to take up this issue. In particular feminists have argued for a gendered aspect of habitus that imbues additional dimensions of habitus to that described above (Lovell, 2000; McCall, 1992; McNay, 1999; Silva, 2005). For example, habitus is shaped by combinations of life experiences that differentiate working class women from working class males. In this regard, Allen (2002) points to the particular experience of working class women's exposure to domestic violence in shaping preferences for welcoming and secure tertiary education environments.

More fundamentally, Skeggs (1997) argues for a feminine habitus that embodies "caring" dispositions. This contrasts with a male habitus that tends more toward competitive dispositions.

Caring dispositions focus on interpersonal relationships, communality, and affiliation, whereas competitive dispositions focus on individuality and autonomy (Thompson, 1996). Conflicting dispositions of gender and class are illustrated in Thompson's (1996) depiction of the "juggling" lifestyle of professional working mothers. In this study gendered responsibility for family and domestic organization coexists with the competitive nature of career-oriented professionalism. Skeggs (1997) argues that outside the field of family and domestic life caring dispositions provide limited access to potential forms of institutional power. Caring dispositions primarily manifest in unpaid work aimed at provisioning, maintaining and holding the family together. This is more than just a functional division of family labor. Thompson (1996, p. 400) notes that mothers in his sample "had thoroughly internalized an ethos of personal responsibility" (for family wellbeing).

Given the intersectional nature of social structures, recent work has employed Bourdieusian theory to include study of conditions that blend or control for class, gender, nation, race and religion. For example, Thompson's (1996) work considers class and female gender roles. Coskuner-Balli & Thompson (2013) flip the subject of analysis around to focus on middle-class fathers who take on the traditional female role of household carer, while the mother becomes the primary breadwinner. The father enters a subordinated role. This has consequences for the applicability of the capitals that the father brings to the new field of domestic life. In effect these fathers seek to convert their stock of economic and social capitals to attain cultural legitimacy. Sandikci & Ger (2010) consider gender, religion, and class in their study of veiling practices among women in Turkey. They find that middle-class women adopting veiling are influenced by their classed habitus that emphasizes aesthetic fashion style and individuality. Middle-class women sought to mark themselves from poorer, more traditional women through individualization. This set up competitions for just what constitutes religiously appropriate veiling practices that divides along class lines. Of course, there is also the interaction between class and race where racial minorities who manage to attain professional occupations still accrue more limited social capital compared to the dominant ethnic or national group. To this point, Crocket & Wallendorf (2004) explore the role of normative political ideology in African-American provisioning choices. Bone, Christensen, & Williams (2014) explore minority experience of restricted choice on self-concept. They compare this with the experience of white consumers from similar educational and economic backgrounds in their search for financial loans. The minority journey is found to be more of an arduous uphill battle that saps self-confidence and reinforces subordination.

Current Issues and Future Directions

We suggest five areas for future research: How people experience class mobility and change of positions in fields of social life; How people manage to participate in multiple fields that necessitate different forms of capitals; Tightening conceptualization of habitus and understanding stability of habitus; Bringing economic and social capitals back into the capitals mix as equals with cultural capital; Understanding within-class differences in consumption. We elaborate next.

Experience of Class Mobility

Despite the high-profile exceptions that make it big, most people remain in their class of origin. This applies both at the intergeneration and intra-generational levels. However, a minority do experience either upward or downward mobility. Mobility results from change in economic, cultural, or social capitals. Importantly, though, mobility to a new (and unfamiliar) lifestyle position in the field of social class brings with it that "fish-out-of-water" discomfort that stems from moving outside of one's socialized comfort zone (Allen, 2002). This can be particularly distressing for downwardly mobile people who lose capacity to enact desired lifestyle. It can also be disorienting for the upwardly mobile. For example, researchers have examined working class experiences of upward mobility via participation in elite educational opportunities that credential them for high paying professional employment. Yet they still struggle in the new environment surrounded by people imbued with a HCC habitus of more extended horizons, self-confidence, and importantly, sophisticated aesthetic tastes and more refined norms of behavior. Friedman (2014, p. 48) reviews the "hidden costs of mobility" (i.e. emotional stress) that include status anxiety in interacting with people in the new class position, together with sense of regret at abandoning the past. Ingram (2011) refers to "psychic costs" of dislocation from past and not fitting with present condition. This dislocation of habitus harks back to Martineau's quote (cited before) debunking the assertion that a poor man would behave exactly like the rich man if only they had more money.

While upward mobility can attract discomfort, it also empowers the pursuit of a better life. On the other hand, downward mobility constrains economic capacity to pursue desired lifestyles. Newman (1999, p. ix) prefaces her book *Falling from Grace* with

> Hundreds of thousands of middle-class families plunge down America's social class ladder every year. They lose their jobs, their income drops drastically, and they confront prolonged economic hardship, often for the first time. In the face of this downward mobility, people long accustomed to feeling secure and in control find themselves suddenly powerless and unable to direct their lives.

Downward mobility can stem from critical incidents such as job loss and sustained unemployment, onset of chronic illness or injury, natural disaster and loss of home, or divorce and family breakup—that can also mean loss of home. Taken together this range of examples is relatively common across communities. For example, separated single mothers where the ex-partner had been the primary breadwinner often face significant financial diminution. Many face loss of well-appointed family homes and move into less salubrious rented accommodations where a Bourdieusian logic of necessity and insecurity now prevails. In such cases the old lifestyle of the newly single mother is often turned upside down. They obviously have to cut consumptions and engage in careful budgeting. However, the disconnects between socialized expectations and new reality takes an emotional toll. Old rituals such as family dinners fall apart with loss of participants and instrumental imperatives to get through the day dominate. Old social activities and entertaining that regularly occurred in the old home end. Old leisure activities such as regular gym attendance and coffee with friends are curtailed with the time impositions of paid work and lack of backup for household activities. Alternatively, they often face obstacles to paid work and rely on government welfare. Welfare dependence demoralizes. Severe budgeting pressures dominate. Then there is the sense of shame in perceived failure in performance of the "good mother" role that binds family together. Compounding these changes the dispositions and lifestyle preferences embodied in old habitus persist—yet remain unfulfilled.

The question for consumer researchers becomes—how do people who suffer these kinds of critical incidents adjust their consumptions to survive and seek to recover more secure lifestyle positions? There has been some work by consumer researchers. For example, Saatcioglu & Ozanne (2013) found that downwardly mobile consumers who have moved into marginalized accommodation seek to retain their social distinction from others in the new neighborhood via their morally oriented worldviews. The old morality emphasizing self-control and autonomy persists. Consequently, the loss is taken as personal failure. These people prioritize a return to their old position by placing great emphasis on discipline and carefully monitoring their spending. They seek to distinguish themselves from others through highlighting that their neighbors lack such discipline. Because they view their situation as only temporary, they spend little money on home improvements. They defer such spending till they can regain the kind of home they expect to return to. On the other hand, people that have been habituated into the same marginalized neighborhood, do indeed, allocate time and money to "prettying up" their homes in expectation that nothing will change. Another example drawn from outside the consumer research field comes from studies of natural disasters. For example, Fothergill (2004) examined the aftereffects of a flood that devastated a community in the USA. People who had previously felt secure in home, family and community life suddenly lost jobs, their homes, and old social networks were broken apart—precarity prevailed. In particular, Fothergill traced how survivors recreate or negotiate new versions of domestic life. The loss of home was keenly felt with many moving into cramped accommodation. However, despite the challenges many did consciously try to recreate family rituals such as evening meals—emphasizing that it required considerable effort to reconstruct such rituals. They lamented having to improvise in new accommodations, come up with cheaper substitutes for the kinds of food they had previously enjoyed, and having to use substandard equipment to complete household chores. The meaning of artifacts retrieved from the old home often took on heightened emotional attachment to that previously held and they resented many of the new household items because they were usually traded down and this acted to remind them of the world they had lost.

Conceptualizing Habitus

The idea that classes exhibit distinctive dispositions that are inculcated through socialization within a particular position in the field of social life has proven very useful for researchers. However, there do appear to be areas of concern in a lack of clear conceptual specification, and the role of habitus in unconscious behavioral direction and generating emotionality. Part of the specification problem lies in the multidimensional character of dispositions that potentially qualify as elements of habitus. Another complexity for class-based habitus lies in the intersectionality with other bases for habitus formation. These include other kinds of rearing conditions such as gender, race, and religion. Class is experienced differently depending on these other kinds of factors. We argue that there is potential for further research to illuminate the underlying structures of habitus that impact consumption. The most comprehensive cross-class work remains Bourdieu's (1984) *Distinction*. In the field of consumer research Holt's (1998) work probably remains the richest analysis that links underlying dispositions to a more complete range of consumption taste drivers. However, the work in consumer research has tended to focus in on particular aspects of habitus. For example, note the discussion above about moral aspects of habitus, financial implications for (dis)empowerment, and misfit with educational environment. Bourdieu refers to dispositions embodied in habitus as a "generative grammar." This implies there is some form of causal hierarchy where the more abstract and enduring aspects influences the more concrete and transient. So, a higher-order example is the suggestion that upper-class people exhibit greater capacity for abstract thinking. These capacities can be deployed across a broad range of life settings. More broadly they facilitate problem solving which may in turn support more sophisticated evaluations of product features and alternatives. This would come in particularly useful for more complex purchases such as financial products. In deriving taste implications, Bourdieu (1984, p. 44) used the example of differing reactions to a photograph of an old woman's deformed hands. Manual workers employed relatively concrete and conventional descriptions of the photo, whereas people in professional occupations employed increasingly abstract interpretations with higher-order metaphoric interpretations as to meanings of life. These kinds of abstractions reflect in aesthetic tastes that flow into reactions to consumption of performances, artworks, interior design and fashion. Consequently, the influence of abstract thinking as a dimension of habitus-based generative grammar impacting many domains is evident. Questions then arise as to just which other dimensions should be admitted as higher-order generative grammar? Then there are questions as to how each of these dimensions relates to the others. So, using the examples from earlier; how may capacity for abstract thinking relate to other possible dimensions such as empowerment and task persistence (hard-worker values)? Indeed, is there a linear progression in strength of capacities along a lower-upper-class continuum—akin to Martineau's ten propositions? In any case, if such a generative grammar is so fundamental to social class then it certainly deserves further study.

A second issue for habitus mentioned previously relating to the nature of embodiment, unconsciousness and segue into emotions has also received limited attention by consumer researchers (Allen, 2002 being a notable exception). It does appear surprising that if habitus generates emotional reactions to environments (e.g. educational spaces), experiences (e.g. theatrical performances), objects (e.g. artworks, interior designs) and other people (e.g. moral reactions) that there has been so little use of this concept by consumer researchers as a gateway to understanding consumers' emotional worlds. The trepidation of unfamiliar education institutions was previously discussed. However, a range of class-distinctive emotional reactions may be extendable into other service environments such as retail spaces, pubs, and restaurants—joy, excitement, anticipation. The capacity of a theatrical performance to emotionally move one class of consumers, yet irritate another, appears strongly related to habitus. Likewise, the joy derived from viewing an inspirational piece of artwork resonates for some yet bemuses others. Similarly, the disgust felt by some at the irresponsibility of others can resonate strongly as a result of moral positions entrenched in habitus. The variety of emotional types illustrated previously—trepidation, joy, irritation, disgust—suggest that (dis)-comfort of (mis)fit is more than just a unidimensional driver of comfort and attraction or discomfort and withdrawal. Rather class-based habitus can provide a useful window into understanding how the full range of consumption-related emotional reactions vary by social class. Given that it does appear that dispositions inscribed in habitus often parallel desires and motivations that elicit emotions, it does appear that consumer researchers could more fruitfully explore this avenue to map class-based emotional worlds. Interestingly, we are seeing recent moves in the field of Sociology to engage psychological theories of emotion and motivation, and psychoanalysis to better assimilate these affective, emotional, and bodily qualities of habitus (see Silva, 2016). Silva argues that such engagement can bring "fresher thinking" into the sociological domain. Likewise, we see opportunity for the consumption domain.

A third issue for understanding habitus lies in the questions as to the relative plasticity or rigidity of the concept. Once formed, habitus is characterized as being relatively fixed. Although note the qualifying word, "relatively." Bourdieu acknowledges that habitus can change under exceptional circumstances of habitus/field misfit. Adaptation can occur when habitus encounters unfamiliar fields where old strategies no longer work. In everyday life consumers either live with habitus/field misfit or in the case of Allen's (2002) informants they withdraw to environments where they feel more comfortable. Very often consumers have the option to select out of those fields where discomfort occurs. This acts as a basic mechanism for social reproduction. However, what then of cases where consumers have to live with conditions where the field in question drastically changes and they are compelled to live with a permanent habitus/field misfit and chronic discomfort? Bourdieu argues that habitus can change in response. He cites an example from his early research of premodern Berber tribesmen who were suddenly and inextricably tipped into modernity. However, Bourdieu has little to say about the specific conditions, process, and outcomes of habitus change. More broadly, there is a startling lack of work that examines the effects on habitus that stem from change in field positions that are predominantly involuntary, sudden, and highly disruptive. The question of habitus change is strongly related to the allied experience of downward mobility discussed previously. In the face of significant social upheaval in contemporary society this question takes on more urgent interest.

Incorporating Social and Economic Dimensions

In recent years, consumer researchers have largely examined social class through a cultural capital lens that encompasses habitus as embodied cultural capital. This has been for good reason, in that cultural capital reflects underlying taste motivations that drive consumption. However, there has been limited work that incorporates economic and social capitals as being equally important determinants of consumption. The primary issue is that people sharing similar dispositions can exhibit quite disparate mixes of money and wealth, together with size and type of social networks. These disparities may result in significantly different consumption patterns. The stereotypical distinction between "old" money and "new" money people presents an obvious but understudied example. These diverse types of people often experience significantly different life trajectories, yet end up with similar economic resources and overlapping social networks. It raises questions about taste assimilation via overlapping networks and resulting use of similar economic capacities. Some consumers remain frugal despite economic wealth, while others spend their wealth lavishly. Certainly, cultural capital contributes to the explanation. Yet, it still provides an incomplete account. Then there is the question as to how distinctive social networks influence an individual's consumptions. Again, taking another stereotypical distinction between working class people instilled with socially conscious and hard-worker ethics versus others with a disenfranchised and belligerent bent—same limited money yet possibly influenced by different social networks. How do they consume differently? As noted before, Saatcioglu & Ozanne (2013) found differing habitus within disadvantaged communities. They demonstrate that study of different mixes that incorporate economic and social capitals with that of the cultural can refine the analysis of consumption outcomes.

We encourage future research that combines all the forms of Bourdieusian capitals. In that spirit, such analysis should also incorporate objectified and institutionalized cultural forms, as well as differing types of economic capitals, such as absolute versus disposable capitals; and distinctive types of social networks. Indeed, our recommendation to incorporate the economic and social dimension back into consumer studies of cultural capital is theoretically consistent with Bourdieu's basic premise that lifestyle preferences are socialized via lived experience of particular position in the field of social life. He emphasized that position in a field is not simply defined by cultural capital, but operates as a "multidimensional space" where position is a product of mix, quantities, and life trajectories of all three capital types—not just cultural. A focus on one capital type can distort position and cloud the nuanced reality of social distinction. In particular, we believe that a more holistic study of class employing Bourdieusian multidimensional space can help distinguish supposedly intra-class differences that, so far, remain unexplained and are often used to rebuke the continuing significance of social class. Consequently, we argue that there is much fruitful work left to do in using this more holistic view of social class to illuminate social life and consumption in contemporary society.

References

Allen D. (2002). Towards a theory of consumer choice as sociohistorically shaped practical experiences: The fits-like-a-glove (FLAG) framework. *Journal of Consumer Research*, 28, 515–532.

Bernthal, M., Crocket, D., & Rose, R. (2005). Credit cards as lifestyle facilitators. *Journal of Consumer Research*, 32, 130–145.

Bone, S., Christensen, G., & Williams, J. (2014). Rejected, shackled, and alone: The impact of systemic restricted choice on minority consumers' construction of self. *Journal of Consumer Research*, 41, 451–474.

Bourdieu, P. (1984). *Distinction: A social critique of the judgement of taste*. Cambridge, MA: Harvard.

Coleman, R. (1983). The continuing significance of social class to marketing. *Journal of Consumer Research*, 10, 265–280.

Coskuner-Balli, G., & Thompson, C. (2013). The status costs of subordinate cultural capital: At-home fathers' collective pursuit of cultural legitimacy through capitalizing practices. *Journal of Consumer Research*, 40, 19–41.

Crocket, D., & Wallendorf, M. (2004). The role of normative political ideology in consumer behavior. *Journal of Consumer Research*, 31, 511–528.

Crossley, N. (2001). *The social body: Habit, identity and desire*. London: Sage.

Douglas, B., Friel, S., Denniss, R., & Morawetz, D. (2014). *Advance Australia fair? What to do about growing inequality in Australia*. Weston, ACT: Australia 21.

Fothergill, A. (2004). *Heads above water*. Albany, NJ: State University of New York.

Friedman, S. (2014). The price of the ticket: Rethinking the experience of social mobility. *Sociology*, 48, 352–368.

Greyser, S. (1961). The case of the befuddled brewers. *Harvard Business Review*, March–April, 136–154.

Henry, P. (2005). Social class, market situation, and consumers' metaphors of (dis)empowerment. *Journal of Consumer Research*, 31, 766–778.

Henry, P., & Caldwell, M. (2008). Spinning the proverbial wheel: Social class and marketing. *Marketing Theory*, 8, 387–405.

Holt, D. (1998). Does cultural capital structure American consumption?. *Journal of Consumer Research*, 25, 1–25.

Ingram, N. (2011). Within school and beyond the gate: The complexities of being educationally successful and working class. *Sociology*, 45, 287–302.

Larrabee, E. (1955). Rosebuds on the silverware. *Industrial Design*, 2, 62–63.

Levy, S. (1966). Social class and consumer behavior. In J.W. Newman (Ed.), *On knowing the consumer* (pp. 146–160). New York: John Wiley.

Lovell, T. (2000). Thinking feminism with and against Bourdieu. *Feminist Theory*, 1, 11–32.

Martineau, P. (1958). Social classes and spending behavior. *Journal of Marketing*, 23, 121–141.

McCall, L. (1992). Does gender fit? Bourdieu, feminism, and conceptions of social order. *Theory and Society*, 2, 837–867.

McNay, L. (1999). Gender, habitus and the field: Pierre Bourdieu and the limits of reflexivity. *Theory, Culture and Society*, 16, 95–117.

Newman, J. W. (1955). Looking around. *Harvard Business Review*, (Jan–Feb), 135–144.

Newman, K. (1999). *Falling from grace*. Berkeley, CA: University of California Press.

Nickles, S. (2002). More is better: Mass consumption, gender, and class identity in postwar America. *American Quarterly*, 54, 581–622.

Rainwater, L., Colemen, R., & Handel, G. (1959). *Working man's wife: Her personality, world and lifestyle*. New York: Oceania.

Saatcioglu, B., & Ozanne, J. (2013). Moral habitus and status negotiation in a marginalized working-class neighborhood. *Journal of Consumer Research*, 40, 692–710.

Sandikci, O., & Ger, G. (2010). Veiling in style: How does a stigmatized practice become fashionable?. *Journal of Consumer Research*, 37, 15–36.

Silva, E. (2016). Habitus: Beyond sociology. *The Sociological Review*, 64, 73–92.

Silva, E. (2005). Gender, home and family in cultural capital theory. *The British Journal of Sociology*, 56, 83–103.

Smiley, L. (2016). The shut-in economy. *Matter Magazine*. San Francisco, CA: Medium.

Skeggs, B. (1997). *Formations of class and gender: Becoming respectable*. London: Sage.

Thompson, C. (1996). Caring consumers: Gendered consumption meanings and the juggling lifestyle. *Journal of Consumer Research*, 22, 388–407.

Ustuner, T., & Holt, D. (2010). Towards a theory of status consumption in less industrialized countries. *Journal of Consumer Research*, 37, 37–56.

Ustuner, T., & Holt, D. (2007). Dominated consumer acculturation: The social construction of poor migrant women's consumer identity projects in a Turkish squatter. *Journal of Consumer Research*, 34, 41–56.

Ustuner, T., & Thompson, C. (2012). How marketplace performances produce interdependent status games and contested forms of symbolic capital. *Journal of Consumer Research*, 38, 796–814.

Vikas, R. M., Varman, R., & Belk, R. (2015). Status, caste, and market in a changing Indian village. *Journal of Consumer Research*, 42, 472–498.

Warner, L., & Lunt, P. (1941). *The social life of a modern community, Vol. 1 Yankee city series*. New Haven, CT: Yale.

Warner, L., Meeker, M., & Eells, K. (1949). *Social class in America: A manual of procedure for the measurement of social status*. New York: Harper and Row.

Wehner, P. (2002). No place like home: Media audience research and its social imaginaries, *MARIAL working paper Series 15*, The Centre for Myth and Ritual in American Life, Atlanta, GA: Emory University.

28

IMPOVERISHED CONSUMERS: WHAT WE KNOW, WHAT WE DON'T KNOW, AND WHAT WE SHOULD DO

Ronald Paul Hill

GEORGE WASHINGTON UNIVERSITY, WASHINGTON, DC, USA

Chapter Orientation

The poor will always be with us, or so it goes in many passages in the Judeo-Christian bible. Thus, we have had the problem of poverty for millennia without any real solutions coming from several quarters, including consumer scholars. Of course, our academic discipline does not have such a lengthy history, only going back to seminal work by Alan Andreasen (1975; 1993) and a few others who were primarily interested in the consumption rights of African Americans. More recent scholarship has moved to other subpopulations of poor consumers (Talukdar 2008) along with the base of the pyramid (Viswanathan, Rosa, and Ruth 2010). Together, they reveal a solid but very inconsistent pattern of research that involves a relatively few academic adherents. While it is possible to bring this work together, the goal here is to chronicle previous work with men, women, and children that I have worked with and studied over time. The chapter proceeds from theme to theme, showing what I have learned and, ultimately, what remains to be done. Each theme has a particular set of projects as a guide so that lessons can be made tangible for researchers and other readers.

The themes presented are in no particular order and, in many cases, are interrelated. The first deals with the emotional baggage associated with poverty, from their negative monikers to difficult affective states. For this theme, my research with two distinct homeless populations is used to inform its content. The second theme reveals restrictions faced by the impoverished as they seek to navigate marketplaces that disallow appropriate access. In this case, research with poor youths who are compared to their more affluent counterparts tell the story, along with teen felons from the same poor communities. The third theme shows that not all impoverished people fall into "learned helplessness" as they seek alternative ways to gain access to possessions that they cannot acquire through normal channels. Lengthy academic research with incarcerated teens and adult men shows how such acquisition happens by theft or underground economies. The fourth theme examines different ways that poverty plays out in affluent versus impoverished nations around the world. Data gathered across these countries to examine resulting quality of life is used to bolster these differences. The fifth and final theme recognizes the integrity of the poor despite circumstances that would make many people give up hope. My work with the rural poor and incarcerated men is used to bolster this perspective.

Emotional Reactions to Negative Circumstances

This first theme resonates within my research on poverty and consumption, and it comes in several varieties. Many readers might think that the first concern for anyone without access to needed goods/services for basic survival would be to turn his/her attention to physical versus mental suffering as a priority for reduction. Of course, people who are starving wish to eat, and people who are cold seek clothing and shelter. However, across a wide variety of circumstances, it has often surprised me how being considered "down-and-out" takes an emotional toll on those that find themselves at the bottom (not base) of the socioeconomic totem pole. The terms we use to describe them tell their own stories: welfare mothers, dead-beat dads, anchor babies, mentally ill homeless, and more. Discussions of healthcare have historically been described as Medi*caid* instead of Medi*care*. Even the global poor are given faint praise as the *base* of the pyramid, and their relative status, and our moral obligations to them, are couched in terms of their combined earning power.

The two articles on homelessness provide examples of how poverty takes a toll on the men and women who must endure its vagaries. The first was conceived in concert with a Ph.D. student in sociology who was fearless at going into difficult environs and gaining access to individuals who did not want to be found (Hill and Stamey 1990). This research uncovered a large group of men, women, and children who exist outside the typical social welfare system, fending for themselves in unique ways. These people fully realized that they were "homeless" and subject to the vagaries of the streets, woods, or tunnels. The second constituency included women and children who lived in a private shelter run by a group of Catholic sisters who came from all over the world. In most cases, they had moved from various forms of shelter with family and friends before landing at this (nearly) last resort (Hill 1991b). They were given basic goods to keep them in adequate conditions, but they often felt denigrated by treatment that disallowed any attempt to exert themselves as adults capable of making simple decisions.

Emotional reactions can be devastating, leaving people nearly comatose. I will never forget one woman with an infant daughter who was told her month at the shelter was "up" and that she would need to go someplace else starting that evening. She stared into space as I got on the phone and tried to find emergency housing for the two of them. My own children were young at the time, so I felt great empathy for her and the baby, who had not had her diaper changed in so long that her outfit was soaked. She did not cry or fuss; she just stared straight ahead like her mother. You might think that these reactions were responses to their physical circumstances but they were not. Instead, they were most likely a fear response to the lack of ability to direct their lives as many adults have the discretion to do. Such a reaction is also not learned helplessness. It is, instead, imposed by others who do not recognize adult authority to conduct one's life in ways that make sense to the people who are suffering. For example, why one month? Why are you forced to leave if there is no other reasonable option?

The homeless living outside the shelter system were a very different story. While many struggled with a variety of physical and emotional maladies, they often were determined to be left alone, sometimes out of fear of losing all of their worldly possessions by going inside (most places disallowed carts or other similar containers). As a consequence, they typically accepted the negative label of "homelessness" but suggested that they lived on their own terms. We met them in a number of places that could only be described as uninhabitable by most housing standards. However, they found a way to make them "homey" or at least sufficient to basic needs by finding connections to electrical outlets and powering heaters, microwaves, refrigerators, and other appliances. Living in snow embankments, under bridges, and within old subway tunnels, they went to extreme measures to fight off depression and anxiety associated with their living experiences. Drugs and alcohol also played a role and whether they were used to mask affective states or were the cause of homelessness in and of themselves was never really resolved.

So what do we know? Well, it is clear that the poor suffer greatly, both physically and emotionally. However, the emotional toll may be even greater, at least in circumstances where they are neither starving to death nor freezing to death. This negative affect is partially caused by the degradation they feel that emanates from other people they come in contact with as they navigate markets and public assistance to live even the most basic of existences. Fighting this negativity is difficult work, even among the hearty who reside outside the shelter and welfare systems. What we don't know is whether these emotional states already existed and were exacerbated by their poverty circumstances and subsequent treatment. It is clear that the poor feel more stress and suffer more anxiety and depression than more affluent citizens, but it is unclear if one leads to the other. If concerned citizens, nonprofits, and government policy makers could be sure of the direction of causality, they could do more to keep those who suffer mentally from descending into greater poverty or homelessness.

Restricted Access to Goods and Services

It should come as no surprise to anyone that the marketplaces navigated by the poor are without abundance and/or access. Therefore, the descriptor of "restriction" may appear simplistic since it gives no indication as to why. In some cases, the sense of restriction is self-imposed, with poor consumers uncomfortable leaving their neighborhoods for communities of greater affluence that contain retailers with more variety and better (lower) prices. This feeling of discomfiture likely comes from differences in race, dress, comportment, and access to credit that may signal higher socioeconomic status. As a result, they often experience alienation and lack of confidence when they are in these different environments. Additionally, impoverished consumers may not have adequate transportation, including public buses and subway systems to and from their homes. Even if they do, carrying a number of grocery bags from supermarkets to train or bus stations is cumbersome at best and impossible at worst. Other forms of restriction exist as well and in combination they may also lead to resentment and further negative, affective states.

The projects that inform this theme are with youths from impoverished communities. The first concentrated on poor teenagers incarcerated for felony crimes at a religious-affiliated lockdown facility (Ozanne, Hill, and Wright 1998). Most were caught selling drugs or stealing cars so that they could gain resources necessary to engage the material largess available in affluent communities. In fact, those involved in theft often went from their neighborhoods to high-end retail shopping environs to acquire cars later sold to chop-shops (illicit re-manufacturers that disassemble cars into parts for resale). The second study examined materialism among children from two disparate communities; one in extreme poverty and the other in extreme affluence (Chaplin, Hill, and John 2014). The former, despite their decided lack of resources, are more materialistic than their affluent counterparts due to socioeconomic class positions.

The irony is that children with the fewest resources are most interested in acquiring goods and services.

I remember vividly working with incarcerated youths individually as well as collectively. One day during a conversation with a young African American teen, I asked him what it would be like to walk up to the door of a nearby working-class/middle-class residence and knock. He had lived his whole life within a few decaying blocks of a run-down neighborhood and had never seen such homes or wide-open spaces. He noted, with apprehension in his voice that the person who answered the door would likely shoot him with a gun! I cannot image a greater sense of true alienation between socioeconomic classes. Additionally, his peers provided similar reactions to various conversations. Another young man who had a history of stealing cars asked if I had any male children. I told him that I had two young sons. Without hesitation, he made it clear that my boys will do the same thing at his age. However, a different teenager who was also part of the conversation wisely stated: "No he won't (my son steal cars)! When his kid turns 16, he'll buy him a car!" In fact, I did, further revealing differences in restrictions between us.

The comparison between rich and poor children was also personally revealing. The neighborhoods selected could not have been more different. The wealthy kids lived in homes valued at about $1,000,000, which were surrounded by upscale retailers and luxury car dealers. They went to schools with the latest technology and a full contingent of afterschool activities. In contrast, poor kids resided in homes worth about $30,000, which were located near liquor stores, pawn shops, and fast food restaurants. One would think that children without money or shopping options would eventually get the message and reduce desires for material things. However, we found the opposite to be true; they wanted items even more than those who were more likely to have them. The previous literature made clear that young people's self-esteem was tied to levels of materialism, and this is the case here. It seems that restriction does lead to greater desire if one does not have extracurricular activities to bolster a sense of self.

Once again, what do we know? Well, it is clear that a lack of opportunity does not fully suppress the desire to have goods and services. In fact, the ubiquitous nature of our society's treasure-trove marketplaces ensures that even the very poor know what is ultimately available. If you consider the damaging impacts of harmful labels and socioeconomic differences on self-esteem, then it seems possible that negativity noted in the previous theme may increase yearnings. In the case of the youthful felons, sense of restriction also led to cravings for material things that they naturally would not be able to access. What we do not know is how to solve the problem without damning more generations to low-end jobs, substandard schools, and dead-end futures. The combination of blight, family trauma, and lack of good opportunities for real change makes research questions and definitive answers difficult to discern. Consider issues surrounding self-esteem. Can we find ways of elevating self-esteem that can counteract some of the damage done elsewhere? Might the effects be: short- as well as long-term?

Rebelling Against Negativity

No one wants to be considered subpar relative to their societal peers, regardless of their living circumstances. There are a number of possible reactions to the resulting negative physical and emotional responses that include lapsing into regular use of intoxicating substances, finding illicit ways of engaging marketplaces, and coping mechanisms that may have short-term benefits like the homeless woman and her child discussed earlier. These short-term approaches do little or nothing to resolve underlying problems, as one reader of my book containing short stories about various groups of the poor aptly noted (Hill 2001). He asked where the "Horatio Alger" success story was that gave an uplifting "rags to riches" profile of the American Dream. My response to him is my response to you; it is more myth than reality since most stay at or near socioeconomic classes they are born into as part of their families of origin. Nonetheless, restricted material worlds do not mean that impoverished consumers give up their acquisition dreams.

I turn now to one new and one already discussed subpopulation. The new group includes incarcerated men in a maximum-security prison who are serving life sentences or other lengthy "bids" (Hill, Rapp, and Capella 2015). Typically, they committed crimes between their fourteenth and twentieth birthdays, with trials that involved public defenders who did little in the way of creating a compelling case. Many of the men I worked with over a four-year period were honestly trying to redeem themselves after lives spent "hustling" on the streets. For most, their sentences had little or no impact on them at the time of sentencing because they assumed their release would occur after serving a number of years. The fact that "life means life" in this state eventually dawned on them as a terrible burden. The other group is juvenile felons doing their time in a religious-affiliated lockdown facility noted previously (Ozanne et al. 1998). A second take on their material lives supports this theme.

The first few times I entered the maximum-security prison where I taught and did other forms of advocacy for incarcerated men left me unhinged for two or three days. It took me a month or two to understand why: I was looking at three generations of men of color who were languishing in prison despite one, two, three, or more decades of seeking higher ground through education, mentoring, religion, and a variety of other developmental opportunities. We spent time trying to determine how they got things they needed in order to live according to some of their desires as functioning adults, even though this environment stripped them of important, previous identifiers as individuals. The context is built on regimentation and depersonalization, and it requires diligence and cunning to find ways of acquiring goods and services that are no longer available to them. Surprising to some, the men could get virtually anything they want as long as they have the resources to buy it, and they often prefer the underground marketplace to licit forms of acquisition that serve the prison-industrial complex.

Part of the rationale for seeking things from the underground economy versus the DOC or the one allowed source of outside products referred to as the "commissary," is the sneaky thrill, which was first made known to me by the teen felons discussed previously. Several of the young men incarcerated and educated there not only understood that what was available in society was not available for them, but they also recognized that this largess could be forcibly taken from the rightful owners. They were happy to regale me with stories about taking buses from their homes to the affluent mall in the suburbs and selecting a sports car of choice for enjoyment and profit. One of the most exciting parts was taking it away from the rightful owner as s/he approached the car, forcing the "previous" owner to watch them speed away from the parking lot. They would then go back to their buddies, ride the expensive car around showing off to girls in the neighborhood, eventually selling it for a few hundred dollars to "resellers." When asked about the ethics of this behavior, many noted that owners simply called insurance companies and got a new one.

So, one more time, what do we know? We know that the poor do not necessarily accept the material world and its restrictions as given, despite the pervasive negativity and want that they must bear. Some readers may ask: Is it fair for incarcerated men to find illegal ways to get the things they want to avoid the depths of their punishments? I ask how many of you would be willing to go decades without many decent meals, safe housing, reasonable clothing, education and other forms of development, and sexual intimacy. When we deny the humanity of the poor and destitute, why are we surprised they want to eat at the table of plenty? What we do not know is how to make sense of their reactions using consumer behavior lenses of white, upper-middle-class, western males. Every consumer faces some forms of restriction, even the most wealthy. Are there differences in coping strategies and behaviors according to who imposes restrictions, how long they are expected to last, and the goods and services that are kept from them?

Poverty across Nations

If you were raised similarly to me, you were likely told to eat your vegetables because there are starving people in some far-off parts of the globe who wish they had them. Over the years, I have been able to actually look at impoverishment from a U.S. or developed nations' perspective juxtaposed against poor consumers living in developing countries. Intuitively, it is logical that many abundant markets that fail to cater to lower socioeconomic classes in western economies are different from penurious marketplaces that fail most citizens. Unfortunately, these subgroups, but mainly the latter, are rarely considered by consumer behavior scholars who spend time reflecting vagaries of WEIRD societies (*W*estern, *E*ducated, *I*ndustrialized, *R*ich, and *D*emocratic nations). Can they possible be the same? Do theories and practices successful in the former work equally well in the latter? For example, everyone washes their hair at some point; do we just need to sell the poor shampoo in smaller, more affordable quantities?

Thus, while much is written about global marketing, the vast majority of this research comes from a single perspective: Does culture matter to consumers? If so, then what types of impact might it have on various steps or stages in the consumption process? My work in this regard demonstrates a pronounced set of effects of poverty on this process that defies simple extension of WEIRD theory from the affluent west to everyone else. The first investigation looks at how social comparisons of material wealth differ between people living in poorer nations (e.g., Vietnam, Ghana, and Zambia) versus richer countries (e.g., Canada, Sweden, and Germany) (Hill, Martin, and Chaplin 2012). The second considers how saving behavior manifests with consumers who live in the same set of developing and developed countries (Martin and Hill 2015). Together, they reveal distinct patterns of results between affluent and impoverished consumers across hemispheres, color, and continents.

These studies involved thousands of people from around the world who either lived in affluent developed nations or impoverished developing countries. The principal goal was to look at the relationship between consumption restrictions and life satisfaction, using national poverty as a moderator. Not surprisingly, results show that individuals who made upward socioeconomic comparisons to their more affluent neighbors were much less satisfied with their lives than those persons who made downward comparisons. It seems that having greater access to goods and services than most community members makes people feel better about their overall lives. If one does not, dissatisfaction occurs that has a negative halo impact on their contentment. The real surprise was *where* it seemed to matter. While differences in life satisfaction were significant in both national categories, it was even greater for people living in poorer countries. Thus, in places where individuals have highly restricted access to products that allow them to survive or thrive, social comparisons that place them on a lower rung than peers have potentially devastating emotional effects as well as possible physical harm.

The other study also includes a large global sample but looked, instead, at the impact of saving behavior on individual wellbeing. Again, national poverty levels acted as a relationship moderator. Findings reveal that as societal poverty increases, wellbeing decreases. This result was expected, but it is *how* saving behavior was impacted by poverty that is the most interesting outcome. It turns out that the number of individuals who actually save is *higher* in nations where impoverishment is the norm, and saving has an even greater impact on wellbeing for them than for their wealthier nation counterparts. The rationale becomes more intuitive once lenses of the poor are substituted for the viewpoint of the affluent. For a moment, imagine living close to survival level in Sub-Saharan Africa. What is life like when meager incomes and other resources are disrupted by illness, economic downturns, or government policies? The consequences can be shattering and lead to starvation or even death.

As is always asked: So what do we know? We know that the condition of poverty is much worse in impoverished nations where survival is threatened by the lack of goods and services. While this possibility exists for some individuals in developed nations, the negative impact of being poor on the lives of citizens in developing nations is more pronounced. Interestingly, such effects jeopardize both physical and psychological health in ways that suggest they are more pronounced in more impoverished countries. As always, there is much that we do not know. For example, why is the form of comparisons between haves and have-nots more devastating at the base of the pyramid? Is it similar to the envy experienced by materialists in the developed world or does it have to do with different emotional reactions? It seems that poverty swamps the impact of culture, but are there differences that can be partially explained by a combination of cultural norms along with relative and/or absolute poverty?

Integrity and Humanity of the Poor

Nothing is more telling about people living in poverty than a simple conversation. As a dean in Florida, the faculty required every MBA student to consult in teams with a licit business in an area of our town that was adjacent to campus and where African American citizens were forced to live up until the 1960s. It has remained predominantly a Black community, with some of the problems associated with deteriorating neighborhoods. When my students first entered the commerce district, they assumed that firm owners/managers would jump at the chance of having business professionals provide free consulting. What they found was natural skepticism across races and a group of entrepreneurs who had many more skills and dedication to task than their preconceived notions allowed. The same can be said of the graduate students who came to the prison in support of inmate proposals to start legitimate businesses on release. An integrity of purpose and innate skill bases came through loud-and-clear during interactions with the men.

Research that informs this theme comes from investigations of the rural poor as well as incarcerated adults discussed earlier. The former was part of a dissertation at Virginia Tech that included me as outside member of the committee (Lee, Ozanne, and Hill 1999). The lead author spent months talking with and helping women living in an Appalachian community find ways of accessing local and regional healthcare. She joined a religious group that toured the locale and performed a variety of services from a well-equipped van. They also facilitated the use of more sophisticated resources at a hospital center that was difficult to navigate both physically and emotionally. The incarcerated men, of course, are located in a maximum-security prison that keeps them inside the thirty-foot walls with razor wire and armed guards in the four corners. Nearly every move they make is scripted and they live under the greatest possible supervision that is consonant with total institutions. Yet, they find ways of individuating/developing the self.

The first investigation clearly shows that a majority of people in this Appalachian town were income poor and, at best, worked part-time at menial jobs since the closing of coal mines. Many luxuries that were once affordable, like newer model cars or home repairs/furnishings, were no longer possible, and the entire town appeared to sag. However, what they lacked in monetary resources were often supplemented by other resources, most especially social capital. As a consequence, the women in the town, who were the center of family along with community life, often came together to share their stories and energy to support one another through their most difficult times. This form of sharing is typically reciprocal, and the women often gave the most to those in greatest need. This generosity notwithstanding, their efforts can only go so far in replacing other goods and services that are sometimes necessary and urgent. In those cases, the input of outside resources like the healthcare workers in the mobile unit are used to increase the total pool of capital available to solve serious health issues.

In many respects, the men face similar circumstances. Their identities are changed by their surroundings, which negate their personhood at every turn. Because of long sentences or life-in-prison designations, many of the ordinary goods and services, from training programs to educational opportunities, are denied these men because of the mandate to support others who may be getting released in shorter timeframes. Thus, they continuously fight in courts of law for the right to have a reasonable share of negligible resources. The DOC lacks funds for most things except building new prisons, and any and all amenities that might make their lives palatable are unavailable in order to be "tough on crime." Yet, somehow, these men find outlets that serve to support healthcare, personal grooming, food consumption, education, religion, and other needs. Once again, their social capital comes into play, as they find creative ways to trade goods and services that are made or are imported into the institution by the men.

So, we ask, what do we know? Despite the most difficult situations imaginable, some people facing disadvantage and forced poverty are able to rise above what occurs around them and find ways of coping with the dearth of goods and services. In most cases, they are not after products that would be considered out of the ordinary to most consumers, and they just seek to have what would ordinarily be described as below standard treatment or fare. They may even be willing to take different paths to acquisition and usage than happen through most marketplaces. What don't we know? With this information in mind, we know little about how individuals and communities make decisions about alternative (and often risky) paths to take and how to bring such groups of people together to gain access to needed commodities, respectively. What also separates these two groups is their willingness to find licit and illicit methods of acquisition; but how do such ideas arise and who is likely to take various roles to ensure reasonable access?

Closing and Summary Remarks

I hope the reader has an understanding of the lives of at least some individuals who are plagued with poverty, often for a lifetime. The courage and tenacity to overcome the resulting difficulties acquiring and using needed and desired goods and services would overwhelm many among the more affluent if they were forced into the same circumstances. Because we often are not, it is easier and even seems logical to use our "lenses" of abundance and find their consumer strategies wanting. For example, why would one of the juvenile felons risk his life selling drugs on the streets versus seeking licit employment that promises a "better" long-term future? When asked what they thought life would be like five-years after interviews, the modal answer was "I could be dead." So why put off today by working at a meaningless job that goes nowhere only to never participate in the marketplace of plenty? I now turn to the five themes and suggest what we should do given the perspective of consumption adequacy (Martin and Hill 2012).

As noted earlier, the discussion also turns to what we should do as a community of scholars. For the most part, our contributions to society are the accumulation of information that often permeates various constituencies from academic peers and students to managers, consumer advocates, policy makers, and others in the larger society. The impact we have is important, but it often assumes that we are focused on the "right" issues and subpopulations. The fact that most of the truly vulnerable in this ever-present material culture are left out is of little interest, despite their sheer numbers and difficult lives. Is ignoring them, for the most part, a moral failure of the consumer field? Given the imbalance between interests in WEIRD societies relative to others, it may be the case. More importantly, however, the failure to find a moral compass to understand and navigate differences in consumption possibilities and sharing between haves and have-nots should be of concern to the scholarly and other communities. The introduction of consumption adequacy as a paradigmatic guide may provide an introductory solution to help frame next steps.

This concept has been employed in several of my previous writings but was applied for the first time to global data in Martin and Hill (2012). It is simply a dividing line between having enough goods and services to exist in a particular culture and not having enough. The tendency may be to concentrate solely on marketplace transactions, but acquisition and utilization of some products for the poor may come about through alternative routes such as governments, collective sharing, illicit transactions, and other means. Thus, in its totality, consumption adequacy detects the tipping point between poverty and a lack of poverty. It is made up of the following bundle of basic commodities: safe and secure housing; clothing for the physical environment and society; nutritious and culturally appropriate food and drink; preventative and remedial healthcare across gender and age; and opportunities for human development like education, training, and options for employment. Without them, the problems faced by the poor as noted are likely to occur.

Consider the negative emotional reactions to not having reached at least the consumption adequacy threshold. I remember interviewing children at a shelter for women and their children (Hill 1991a), speaking to them individually in the chapel while their mothers watched my son. At very young ages, their eyes were filled with wonder concerning the cornucopia of toys and other things, especially around the holidays. However, as they aged their emotional reactions seemed to move from joy/anticipation to some form of emotional deadening. Since these children were under 12 years of age, the work with juvenile felons was an extension to see how these emotional responses matured. For the most part, it moved to alienation and anger at the material culture that failed to give them what might best be viewed as a reasonable share. What should we do? It is important that we understand the fuller range of emotional reactions to lack of consumption adequacy across ages, societies, and cultures so that we are better able to predict and ameliorate this negativity and improve impoverished consumers' emotional quality of life.

Restricted access is at the very center of major problems associated with poverty, and some may feel it is a root cause of the negative affect described in this chapter. I tend to agree and it does not matter if the restriction is self-imposed because of fear or alienation or if it is other-imposed such as discrimination, lack of options, or locational challenges. I remember clearly volunteering at the donation room associated with the homeless shelter for women and children. A man came up and took a couch that he planned to carry from the shelter to his home several blocks away. He moved it one end at a time and it likely would have taken him hours to get to his home. I jumped in my old truck and we loaded it in for delivery. When we arrived, he took his child and the mother aside, opening the internal (now family) bed that became the very center of their living quarters. What we should do is discover ways that restriction manifests across internal and external sources and look at how they interact to drive feelings and behaviors.

Rebelling against poverty is consonant with other forms of fighting discrimination that disadvantages one group relative to others. My work has convinced me that impoverishment has profound effects that cancel out other factors as important as culture. At one point in my career, we hosted a feminist conference for faculty and students, with speakers from several business disciplines. An economist told the audience that she spent her entire career showing that gender was more important than any other variable as an explanation for wage differences between men and women. If we can say the same thing about poverty and the ability to reach consumption adequacy, what are the poor expected to do? Look on but not partake? Accept their position as second-class material citizens? What we need to do is look at emotional strategies and behavioral actions taken by the poor to better their consumption circumstances. Given their perspectives, what are incentive structures for acquisition methods that are licit versus illicit?

The final two themes of global poor and the integrity of poor come together in a nice way to close this chapter. My research allowed me to travel to Australia to discuss impact of material white culture on Aboriginal people. Even though it was over twenty years ago, I remember the tragedy of so many lives lost to desperation, alcoholism, and abuse. Nonetheless, it was inspiring to meet men and women who were taking stock in their lives and trying to exert their influence over their affairs by melding old cultural ways with the benefits of modern society. Leadership that formed was determined to make sure the upcoming generations were spared atrocities that plagued older generations, using traditional and formal education, alternative occupations that blended the old with the new such as ecotourism, and governing bodies that reclaimed their land and its governance. What should we do? Consumer researchers must ensure that the dignity of the totality of consumers' lives is considered when we examine how various products meet or fail to meet their needs, with a special focus on those who suffer from the many ills of poverty.

References

Andreasen, A. R. (1975). *The disadvantaged consumer*. New York: The Free Press.

Andreasen, A. R. (1993). Revisiting the disadvantaged: Old lessons and new problems. *Journal of Public Policy & Marketing, 12,* 270–275.

Chaplin, L. N., Hill, R. P., & John, D. R. (2014). Poverty and materialism: A look at impoverished versus affluent children. *Journal of Public Policy & Marketing, 33,* 78–92.

Hill, R. P. (1991a). Homeless women, special possessions, and the meaning of "home." An ethnographic case study. *Journal of Consumer Research, 18,* 298–310.

Hill, R. P. (1991b). Health care and the homeless: A marketing-oriented approach. *Journal of Health Care Marketing, 11,* 14–23.

Hill, R. P. (2001). Surviving in a material world: Evidence from ethnographic consumer research on people in poverty. *Journal of Contemporary Ethnography, 30,* 364–391.

Hill, R. P., Martin, K. D., & Chaplin, L. N. (2012). A tale of two marketplaces: Consumption restriction, social comparison, and life satisfaction. *Marketing Letters, 23,* 731–744.

Hill, R. P., & Stamey, M. (1990). The homeless in America: An examination of possessions and consumption behaviors. *Journal of Consumer Research, 17*, 303–321.

Lee, R. G., Ozanne, J., & Hill, R. P. (1999). Improving service encounters through resource sensitivity: The case of health care delivery in Appalachia. *Journal of Public Policy & Marketing, 18*, 230–248.

Martin, K. D., & Hill, R. P. (2012). Life satisfaction, self-determination, and consumption adequacy at the bottom of the pyramid. *Journal of Consumer Research, 38*, 1155–1168.

Martin, K. D., & Hill, R. D. (2015). Saving and well-being at the base-of-the-pyramid: Implications for transformative financial services delivery. *Journal of Service Research, 18*, 405–421.

Ozanne, J. L., Hill, R. P., & Wright, N. (1998). Juvenile delinquents' use of consumption as cultural resistance: Implications for juvenile reform programs and public policy. *Journal of Public Policy & Marketing, 17*, 185–196.

Talukdar, D. (2008). Cost of being poor: Retail price and consumer price differences across inner-city and suburban neighborhoods. *Journal of Consumer Research, 35*, 457–471.

Viswanathan, M., Rosa, J. A., & Ruth, J. A. (2010). Exchanges in marketing systems: The case of subsistence consumer-merchants in Chennai, India. *Journal of Marketing, 74*, 1–17.

Bibliography

Botti, S., Broniarczyk, S., Haubl, G., Hill, R. P., Huang, Y., Kahn, B., Kopalle, P., Lehmann, D., Urbany, J., & Wansink, B. (2008). Choice under restrictions. *Marketing Letters, 19*, 183–199.

Hill, R. P. (1992). Homeless children: Coping with material losses. *Journal of Consumer Affairs, 26*, 274–287.

Hill, R. P. (1992). Criminal receiving: The fence as marketer. *Journal of Public Policy & Marketing, 11*, 126–134.

Hill, R. P. (1994). Bill collectors and consumers: A troublesome exchange relationship. *Journal of Public Policy & Marketing, 13*, 20–35.

Hill, R. P. (1994). The public policy issue of homelessness: A review and synthesis of existing research. *Journal of Business Research, 30*, 5–12.

Hill, R. P. (1995). Blackfellas and Whitefellas: Aboriginal land rights, the Mabo Decision, and the meaning of land. *Human Rights Quarterly, 17*, 303–322.

Hill, R. P. (1995). Researching sensitive topics in marketing: The special case of vulnerable populations. *Journal of Public Policy & Marketing, 14*, 143–148.

Hill, R. P. (2002). Compassionate love, agape, and altruism: A new framework for understanding and supporting impoverished consumers. *Journal of Macromarketing, 22*, 19–31.

Hill, R. P. (2002). Consumer culture and the culture of poverty: Implications for marketing theory and practice. *Marketing Theory, 2*, 273–294.

Hill, R. P. (2002). Service provision through public-private partnerships: An ethnography of service delivery to homeless teenagers. *Journal of Service Research, 4*, 278–289.

Hill, R. P. (2002). Stalking the poverty consumer: A retrospective examination of modern ethical dilemmas. *Journal of Business Ethics, 37*, 209–219.

Hill, R. P. (2003). Homelessness in the United States: An ethnographic look at consumption strategies. *Journal of Community and Applied Social Psychology, 13*, 128–137.

Hill, R. P. (2005). Do the poor deserve less than surfers? An essay for the special issue on vulnerable consumers. *Journal of Macromarketing, 25*, 215–218.

Hill, R. P. (2008). Disadvantaged consumers: An ethical approach to consumption of the poor. *Journal of Business Ethics, 80*, 77–83.

Hill, R. P., & Adrangi, B. (1999). Global poverty and the United Nations. *Journal of Public Policy & Marketing, 18*, 135–146.

Hill, R. P., & Capella, M. L. (2014). Impoverished consumers, Catholic social teaching, and distributive justice. *Journal of Business Research, 67*, 32–41.

Hill, R. P., Felice, W., & Ainscough, T. (2007). International human rights and consumer quality of life: An ethical perspective. *Journal of Macromarketing, 27*, 370–379.

Hill, R. P., & Gaines. J. L. (2007). The consumer culture of poverty: Behavioral research findings and their implications in an ethnographic context. *Journal of American Culture, 30*, 81–95.

Hill, R. P., Hirschman, E. M., & Bauman, J. (1996). The birth of modern entitlement programs: Reports from the field and implications for welfare policy. *Journal of Public Policy & Marketing, 15*, 263–277.

Hill, R. P., Hirschman, E. M., & Bauman, J. (1997). Consumer survival during the Great Depression: A view from the field. *Journal of Macromarketing, 17*, 107–127.

Hill, R. P., & John Kozup, J. (2007). Consumer experiences of predatory lending practices. *Journal of Consumer Affairs, 41*, 29–46.

Hill, R. P., & Macan, S. (1996). Consumer survival on welfare with an emphasis on Medicaid and the Food Stamp Program. *Journal of Public Policy & Marketing, 15*, 118–127.

Hill, R. P., & Macan, S. (1996). Welfare reform in the United States: Resulting consumption behaviors, health and nutrition outcomes, and public policy solutions. *Human Rights Quarterly, 18*, 142–159.

Hill, R. P., & Martin, K. D. (2014). Broadening the paradigm of marketing as exchange: A public policy and marketing perspective. *Journal of Public Policy & Marketing, 33*, 17–33.

Hill, R. P., Peterson, R., & Dhanda. K. K. (2001). Global poverty and distributive justice: A Rawlsian perspective. *Human Rights Quarterly, 23*, 171–187.

Hill, R. P., Ramp, D. L., & Silver, L. (1998). The rent-to-own industry and pricing disclosure tactics. *Journal of Public Policy & Marketing, 17*, 3–10.

Hill, R. P., & Rapp, J. R. (2009). Globalization and poverty: Oxymoron or new policies. *Journal of Business Ethics, 85*, 39–47.

Hill, R. P., Rapp, J. R., & Capella, M. L. (2015). Consumption restrictions in a total control institution: Participatory action research in a maximum security prison. *Journal of Public Policy & Marketing, 34*, 156–172.

Hill, R. P., & Reed, R. (1998). The process of becoming homeless: An investigation of families in poverty. *Journal of Consumer Affairs, 32*, 320–332.

Hill, R. P., & Stephens, D. L. (1997). Impoverished consumers and consumer behavior: The case of AFDC mothers. *Journal of Macromarketing, 17*, 32–48.

Hill, R. P., & Szykman, L. (1993). A consumer-behavior investigation of a prison economy. *Research in Consumer Behavior, 6*, 233–262.

PART XV

Culture

29

MULTIPLE SHADES OF CULTURE: INSIGHTS FROM EXPERIMENTAL CONSUMER RESEARCH

Zeynep Gürhan-Canli,[1] *Gülen Sarial-Abi,*[2] *and Ceren Hayran*[1]

[1]COLLEGE OF ADMINISTRATIVE SCIENCES AND ECONOMICS
AT KOÇ UNIVERSITY, ISTANBUL, TURKEY
[2]MARKETING DEPARTMENT AT BOCCONI UNIVERSITY, MILAN, ITALY

> Even if you don't like colors, you will end up having something red. For everyone who doesn't like color, red is a symbol of a lot of culture. It has a different signification but never a bad one.
>
> *Christian Loubotin*

In the past couple of decades, research investigating the role of culture on consumer preferences and choices has gained increased attention. It is important to investigate the role of culture as culture influences perception, behavior, inter-personal communication, and relations, and even helps one to develop a personality. It influences one's way of thinking and living. With art, literature, language, and many other aspects, culture provides meaning to individuals. Hence, understanding the effects of culture on consumer behavior is important as it helps one to understand how different meaning makers in different cultures might influence the way consumers behave in the marketplace.

Our goal in this chapter is to provide a timeline for cross-cultural consumer research. We specifically suggest that cross-cultural consumer research has gone through three stages: (1) the introduction stage during the late 1990s, (2) a growth stage in the early 2000s, and (3) the maturity stage in the early 2010s. Acknowledging that there have been many different methods used to investigate the effects of culture on consumer behavior (e.g., qualitative research), in this chapter we only focus on experimental research conducted in these three time phases and suggest that there is still a lot of room for future research to investigate how culture might influence consumer preferences and choices.

Timeline of Cross-Cultural Consumer Research

Culture and Consumer Behavior Research in the Late 1990s and Early 2000s

In reviewing the literature on culture and its influences on consumer behavior, it is important to emphasize research that has been conducted by Hofstede (1984) and Triandis and Gelfand (1998).

In his influential work, Hofstede (1984) analyzed a database of employee value scores in IBM between 1967 and 1973. Analyzing data that covered more than 70 countries, he categorized country cultures based on four groups: power distance (i.e., the extent to which power is distributed unequally), individualism versus collectivism (i.e., the extent to which people in a society are integrated into groups), masculinity versus femininity (i.e., the extent to which there is a preference for achievement, assertiveness, material rewards for success or preference for cooperation, modesty), and uncertainty avoidance (i.e., the extent to which society has a tolerance for ambiguity). He named these four dimensions the dimensions of national culture, where each national culture would differ on these four different parameters. Although there have been additions to these dimensions (e.g., long-term orientation, indulgence versus restraint) in subsequent years, with more than 30,000 citations, Hofstede's work still remains one of the most influential frameworks for cultural researchers.

Furthermore, Triandis and Gelfand (1998) distinguished four dimensions of individualism and collectivism (i.e., vertical individualism, horizontal individualism, vertical collectivism, and vertical individualism). They defined vertical individualism as seeing the self as fully autonomous, but acknowledging there are inequalities that exist among individuals, while they have defined horizontal individualism as seeing the self as fully autonomous but believing that equality between individuals is the ideal. On the other hand, they have defined vertical collectivism as seeing the self as a part of a group but recognizing that there are inequalities within that group, while they have defined horizontal collectivism as seeing the self as a part of a group but believing that everybody in a group has equal rights. Hence, they have distinguished among different cultures on two dimensions: (1) whether people perceive themselves as part of a group or as being autonomous and (2) whether people acknowledge inequalities or they perceive everybody as equal. Distinguishing among vertical and horizontal individualism/collectivism, Triandis and Gelfand (1998) lead individuals in social psychology to investigate differences among different cultures.

Despite the growing interest in cross-cultural psychology in the 1990s with these two frameworks, relatively little was known about the processes by which culture affects consumer behavior. The literature that investigated the effects of culture was based on frameworks developed using participants from Western cultures, primarily the ones from the United States (Gergen, Gulerce, Lock, & Misra, 1996). In the late 1990s and early 2000s, researchers in consumer psychology started to pay attention to the effects of culture on consumer behavior (Aaker & Maheswaran, 1997; Maheswaran & Shavitt, 2000; Gürhan-Canli & Maheswaran, 2000). In this section, we review the early empirical work on culture and consumer behavior that began in the late 1990s. We suggest that most of the earlier work primarily focused on: (1) marketing communication content that would be persuasive across different cultures and (2) different information processing styles across cultures. In this section, we further demonstrate that the earlier work on cross-cultural consumer psychology mainly focused on individualism-collectivism dimensions of culture and neglected the other cultural orientations.

In one of the earliest empirical works on culture and its effect on consumer behavior, Han and Shavitt (1994) demonstrated that advertisements emphasizing individualistic benefits were more persuasive in the United States than in Korea, while advertisements emphasizing in-group benefits or family were less persuasive in the United States than they were in Korea. Following Han and Shavitt (1994), Aaker and Maheswaran (1997) investigated the effect of cultural orientation on persuasion. The authors tested the impact of motivation, congruity of persuasive communication, and the diagnosticity of heuristic cues on the processing strategies. In two studies, they demonstrated that there were cross-cultural variations in the perceived diagnosticity of heuristic cues. In their study 1, in the high-motivation and incongruent conditions, only the consensus information guided the evaluations for collectivist participants (i.e., participants from Hong Kong). In study 2, when processing new information, processing strategies adopted by individualist participants mirrored those adopted by the collectivists. This was the first evidence of how culture might influence consumer behavior through diagnosticity.

Extending the research by Aaker and Maheswaran (1997), Aaker and Williams (1998) investigated the role of emotional appeals on persuasion across cultures. Their results demonstrated that other-focused (e.g., empathy, peacefulness) emotional appeals led to more favorable attitudes for members of an individualist (i.e., participants from US) culture, while the ego-focused (e.g., pride, happiness) appeals led to more favorable attitudes for members of a collectivist (i.e., participants from China) culture. Aaker and Williams (1998) suggested that the persuasive effects found in their study 1 were due to the differences in the generation of and elaboration on a relatively novel type of thought. More specifically, because individual thoughts were more novel for the members of a collectivist culture and because collectivist thoughts were more novel for the members of individualist culture, ego-focused emotional appeals were more effective for the collectivists and other-focused emotional appeals were more effective for the individualists.

Reconciling her research on culture and consumer behavior, Aaker (2000) investigated the extent to which differences in perceived diagnosticity (vs. accessibility) that were embedded in persuasion appeals account for the attitudinal differences. More specifically, when information elaboration was low (i.e., participants were asked to spontaneously read a text and evaluate a brand), diagnosticity and accessibility were both high and this led to positive attitudes toward the brand. When instead elaboration was high (i.e., participants were asked to carefully read a text and evaluate a brand in detail), the effect of diagnosticity was high but the effect of accessibility was low and this led to negative attitudes toward the brand. Furthermore, in a series of three studies, Aaker and Sengupta (2000) demonstrated that when faced with information incongruity, consumers in an individualist culture (i.e., United States) followed an attenuation strategy (i.e., relying on the more diagnostic information and attenuating the impact of less diagnostic information), whereas consumers from a collectivist culture (i.e., Hong Kong) followed an additive strategy (i.e., pieces of information are combined to make evaluations).

While there has been some movement in understanding how culture influences consumer behavior, which was mainly in the area of persuasion, Maheswaran and Shavitt (2000) provided a research agenda in cross-cultural research. The authors discussed the fact that much of the earlier work showing the relationship between culture and consumer behavior mainly differentiated individualist versus collectivist cultures (Aaker & Maheswaran, 1997; Aaker & Williams, 1998; Han & Shavitt, 1994; Zhang & Gelb, 1996). However, they suggested that there might be other cultural categories that would deserve attention in cross-cultural research. They called attention to the distinction between societies that are horizontal (i.e., valuing equality; Sweden, Norway, Australia) and those that are vertical (i.e., emphasizing hierarchy; USA, France). They have further suggested that what was investigated up until the 2000s mostly reflected vertical forms, neglecting the horizontal cultures. Furthermore, they have suggested that there are other dimensions of cultural variation (i.e., power distance, uncertainty avoidance, and masculinity/femininity) that might explain several differences across cultures besides from individualism and collectivism.

Wang, Bristol, Mowen, and Chakraborty (2000) investigated the effects of connected versus separated advertising appeals on Chinese versus American consumers. Their results demonstrated that, while a connected advertising appeal that stressed interdependence and togetherness resulted in more favorable attitudes among Chinese and women consumers, a separated appeal resulted in more favorable attitudes among American and male consumers. This result could be also related to the gender differences in personality traits within cultures. McCrae and Terracciano (2005) have demonstrated in a study across 50 cultures that the personality traits between women and men might vary widely (e.g., women were more emotional and warm, and men were more assertive).

Although most of the earlier work on culture and consumer behavior has focused on how culture influenced information processing, Gürhan-Canli and Maheswaran (2000) extended the research on culture to country-of-origin effects. The authors showed that, in collectivist countries (e.g., Japan), evaluations for products from one's country of origin were more positive if they were familiar with the product, despite the superiority of it. This was mediated by vertical collectivism. On the contrary, in individualist countries (e.g., the US), the product from their country of origin got higher evaluations only if it was superior and innovative. Vertical individualism only mediated favorable product evaluations from their own country of origin. Following the research by Gürhan-Canli and Maheswaran (2000), other researchers started to investigate the effect of culture on different aspects of consumer behavior.

Summarizing the earlier work of cross-cultural consumer research, one might suggest that the earlier work on the effect of culture on consumer behavior could be explained through accessibility and diagnosticity accounts.

Culture and Consumer Behavior Research from the Early 2000s to the 2010s

The late 1990s experienced heightened interest in investigating the effect of culture on consumer behavior. While most of the research on this stream focused on how the content of the marketing communications should differ across cultures and how culture influences information processing, researchers started to get more interested in multiple methods (e.g., surveys, content-analyses) in cross-cultural research in the early 2000s, which led them to investigate different topics in consumer psychology besides information processing differences across cultures.

In this section, we review the literature on cross-cultural consumer research that was conducted between the early 2000s and 2010. We provide evidence that most of the cross-cultural consumer research in this time period focused on (1) the effects of other cultural orientations (e.g., horizontal versus vertical) on consumer behavior, (2) the effects of culture on goals and motivation, and (3) the effects of cultural orientations on brand and product evaluations as well as the development of culture-related phenomena (e.g., cultural icons). We further provide evidence that in this period, cross-cultural consumer researchers used multiple methods to test their predictions across different cultures.

In one of the earliest papers using multiple methods, Nelson and Shavitt (2002) predicted differences in achievement values across people from Denmark and the United States. Across multiple methods (i.e., qualitative interviews, surveys), people from the United States were found to be more vertically oriented than Danish people and people from Denmark were found to be more horizontally oriented than the Americans. More importantly, people from the US discussed the importance of achievement goals more frequently and evaluated achievement values more highly than Danes did.

In the beginning of the 2000s, researchers continued to understand the characteristics of different consumers across different cultures. Employing a content analysis method, Zhang and Shavitt (2003) examined 463 ads in China with respect to the cultural values emphasized in those ads. Results of the content analysis demonstrated that both modernity and individualism values predominated the ads in China. More importantly, revealing the shifting values among the Generation X, these values were more pervasive in magazine advertisements, which targeted the Chinese Generation X, than in television commercials. On the other hand, more traditional values such as collectivism were found to be more pervasive on television commercials as opposed to magazine ads.

In an attempt to understand how response styles might differ across cultures, Johnson, Kulesa, Cho, and Shavitt (2005) investigated the effects of four cultural orientations identified by Hofstede on extreme and acquiescent response styles. Data from approximately 18,000 participants across 19 nations were collected. Using hierarchical linear modeling, authors demonstrated that power distance and masculinity were positively and independently associated with extreme response style. This was because extreme response styles were clearer, more precise, and more decisive, characteristics that are highly appreciated in masculine and high power distance cultures. Individualism, uncertainty avoidance, power distance, and masculinity were negatively associated with acquiescent response behavior. The reasons for this were less clear and obvious. However, the authors suggested that cultures that reject ambiguity and uncertainty would use and prefer a less acquiescent response style, because that style would go against their cultural traits.

While the early 2000s experienced the use of multiple methods on cross-cultural consumer research, there has been an interest in experimental research designs in cross-cultural research as well. In the beginning of the 2000s, some researchers focused on differentiating characteristics across cultures and some others focused on understanding how culture might influence variables related with consumer behavior other than information processing. Aaker and Schmitt (2001) investigated how differences in self-construal (i.e., independent and interdependent self-construal) might affect consumption through the process of self-expression. There were differential levels of recall for similar and distinct items across culturally encouraged selves and there was higher recall for schema-inconsistent information. More specifically, memory for individuals with dominant independent and interdependent selves differed: individuals with a dominant interdependent self had better recall for distinct than similar self-relevant items, while individuals with dominant independent self had better recall for items indicating similarity with others.

In the early 2000s, other researchers also focused on the effects of culture on consumer behavior. More specifically, Kacen and Lee (2002) investigated the influence of culture on impulsive buying behavior. Conducting a multi-country survey with consumers from the United States, Hong Kong, Australia, Singapore, and Malaysia, the authors demonstrated that both regional level factors (i.e., individualism and collectivism) and individual cultural difference factors (i.e., independent and interdependent self-concept) influenced impulsive buying behavior. Similarly, Chen, Ng, and Rao (2005) investigated cultural differences in consumer impatience. Participants from the US may value immediate consumption more than participants from Singapore. Furthermore, Westerners may be more apt to expend their monetary resources to achieve the desirable outcomes, while Easterners could be more prepared to expend their monetary resources to prevent undesirable outcomes. This could be because Eastern culture is more driven to future (vs. present) thinking (Confucian dynamism dimension of Hofstede) and, thus, Easterners tend to be more patient than Westerners.

While most of the research on cross-cultural psychology focused either on individualism or collectivism in the early 2000s, limited research has also focused on bicultural consumers. In an attempt to understand how biculturals (i.e., the ones who are influenced by an East Asian and Western cultural orientation) respond to various types of persuasion appeals, Lau-Gesk (2003) demonstrated that biculturals tended to react more favorably toward both individually and interpersonally focused persuasion appeals. However, Lau-Gesk (2003) showed that this effect was more pronounced among those who integrated the two cultures compared to those who tend to compartmentalize each culture.

During the beginning of the 2000s, cross-cultural research in consumer behavior extended its interest into brands. More specifically, Aaker, Benet-Martinez, and Garolera (2001) investigated the association between brand personality and culture. Aaker (1997) has demonstrated that brands could have salient personality traits (i.e. Sincerity, Excitement, Competence, Sophistication, and Ruggedness) just like people do (i.e. Big-Five personality traits). Extending her work on brand personality, Aaker and colleagues (2001) demonstrated that a set of brand personality dimensions were common in both Japanese and American cultures (i.e., sincerity, excitement, competence, and sophistication), but some of them were culture-specific (e.g., peacefulness for the Japanese and ruggedness for the American). Sincerity, excitement, and sophistication were shared by both Spanish and Americans, while passion was more important for the Spanish and competence and ruggedness were more important for the American consumers. In short, Aaker and colleagues (2001) suggested that the symbolic meaning and value that brands carry were not only affected by the individuals' perceptions, but also by the cultural characteristics of the country where the consumers lived.

Similarly, Sung and Tinkham (2005) investigated brand personality structures in two different cultures (i.e., Korea and the United States). Passive likeableness and ascendancy were identified more with the Korean participants, which supported their prediction that the Confucian values of tradition and harmony were evident in Korean culture. On the other hand, white collar and androgyny were observed in participants from the United States, demonstrating that professional status and gender roles were more important for the Americans than for the Korean participants.

From 2005, research on culture and consumer behavior has accelerated. Researchers have not only focused on different information processing and response styles across cultures, but have also started to focus on the effects of culture on goals and motivations, on branding, and many other related consumer psychology variables. Briley and Aaker (2006a) first investigated the association between culture and motivation and goals, suggesting that subcultures should also be taken into consideration when considering the effects of culture on consumer behavior. Furthermore, they have argued that both cultural backgrounds and situational forces determine goals. More importantly, Briley and Aaker (2006a) demonstrated that culture influenced decision making as it influenced goal formation. Extending their research, Briley and Aaker (2006b) also demonstrated that culture-based differences in persuasion arose when individuals processed information in a cursory, spontaneous manner. However, the differences dissipated when one's intuitions were supplemented by more deliberative processing. Furthermore, their results showed that North Americans were more persuaded by promotion-focused information, and Chinese were more persuaded by prevention-focused information. However, this was only valid when initial, automatic reaction to messages was given.

While Aaker and her colleagues studied boundary conditions under which culture might be influential on consumers in the beginning of the 2000s, other researchers responded to the call by Maheswaran and Shavitt (2000) and have started to investigate other cultural dimensions (e.g., vertical, horizontal) apart from individualism and collectivism. Shavitt, Lalwani, Zhang, and Torelli (2006a) tested the importance of horizontal (i.e., valuing equality) and vertical (i.e., valuing hierarchy) dimensions of culture. They highlighted several sources of value for the horizontal and vertical distinction of cultural orientations. Following the commentaries by Aaker (2006), Meyers-Levy (2006), and Oyserman (2006), the authors further conceptualized a new research agenda on culture and how it could be studied from the perspective of horizontal and vertical dimensions (Shavitt, Zhang, Torelli, & Lalwani 2006b).

Starting from 2005, research on culture and branding has gained more attention. More specifically, researchers in cross-cultural psychology investigated how culture influenced brand extension decisions and also how consumers responded to brand failures across different cultures. Monga and John (2007) investigated how consumers from Eastern and Western cultures might differ in terms of their styles of thinking (i.e., analytic versus holistic) and how these different styles of thinking might influence brand extension evaluations. Western (Eastern) consumers primed to engage in holistic (analytic) thinking perceived higher (lower) brand extension fit and evaluated extensions more (less) favorably than would otherwise be the case. Extending their research on culture and evaluations of brand extensions, Monga and John (2008) further tested the effects of analytic versus holistic thinking on negative brand publicity. Analytic thinkers were more susceptible to negative publicity information than holistic thinkers. Furthermore, they were more likely to consider external context-based explanations for the negative publicity, which resulted in little or no revision of beliefs for the parent brand. In contrast, analytic thinkers were less likely to consider contextual factors, which led them to attribute the negative information to the parent brand and hence update their beliefs about the parent brand accordingly.

Ng and Houston (2006) compared the attitudes of American and Singaporean consumers toward well-known brands to test the impact of consumers' self-view on perception of consumer goods. Westerners, who tend to have a personality-oriented independent self-view, focused on the general qualities of the brand. However, Easterners, who tend to focus more interdependently on contextual factors and their relationship with others, associated a brand with its products. Swaminathan, Page, and Gürhan-Canli (2007) demonstrated that the self-concept connection and brand country-of-origin connection might vary based on self-construal. In a set of experimental studies, their results showed that under independent self-construal, self-concept connection was more important. However, under interdependent self-construal, brand country-of-origin connection was more important. Similarly, Ahluwalia (2008) tested the role of self-construal in enhancing a brand's stretchability potential. The results of a set of experiments demonstrated that an interdependent self-construal led people to distinguish relationships among the stimuli (e.g., distinguishing the extension from the brand) and hence enhanced the perceived fit of the extension and likelihood of its acceptance. However, these effects hold only for those who were motivated to elaborate extensively on the extension information.

Brands can become mirrors of the cultural traits of individuals in individualistic or collectivistic societies (Holt, 2004). This happens because consumers may link brands to cultural traits (Aaker et al., 2001). Aaker and colleagues (2001) have shown that culture could affect brand personality dimensions. Some brands in the United States (i.e., individualistic culture) were perceived as rugged (e.g. Marlboro), and some in Japan (i.e., collectivistic society) were perceived as peaceful. Research suggested that the brands that embraced more cultural values had higher chances of becoming icons (e.g., Harley Davidson, Nike, Apple, Vodka, etc.) because they created a strong connection with culture (Holt, 2004). Holt (2004) explained that "iconization" was not about the brand performance, but more about the symbolic meaning that is carried with its brand personality traits. Iconic brands, similarly to iconic people, are idealized by consumers and desired to become part of consumers' lives. Shavitt, Lee, and Johnson (2008) have summarized that culture could affect brand decisions. Their results showed that in individualistic cultures, consumers choose brands based on their attributes, advantages, and available information on the brand. In collectivistic cultures, instead, consumers are influenced by familiarity, friendliness, and perceived honesty of the brand.

Shavitt and colleagues (2006a) further proposed that consumers who belonged to the vertical individualistic culture might be more driven toward status symbols, such as prestige and possession, that transmit higher performance and achievement compared to others. In vertical-individualist societies or cultural countries (e.g., USA, Great Britain, France), individuals cared more about status, achievements, and demonstrating themselves to others. However, in horizontal-individualist societies or cultural countries (e.g., Sweden, Denmark, Norway, Australia), individuals were not prone to differentiation and they liked to view themselves as one group, with equal members (Nelson & Shavitt, 2002).

Apart from the research on brand evaluations, researchers also investigated the cultural influences on product evaluations. Hong and Kang (2006) tested the effect of country of origin (i.e., Germany or Japan) on judgments of quality and desirability of products. The results of their research demonstrated that when the product was typical of those manufactured in the country, identifying the country of origin increased its product evaluations regardless of whether industriousness or brutality was primed. The authors concluded that the animosity toward a product's country of origin had a negative effect on product evaluations only when the product was not one on which the country's reputation was based.

In short, research conducted between the early 2000s and 2010 mainly focused on (a) how different cultural orientations (e.g., horizontal vs. vertical) might influence consumer behavior, (b) product and brand evaluations across cultures, and (c) influence of culture on goals and motivations apart from their influence on information processing as well as development of culture-related phenomenon (e.g., cultural icons). Other than the diagnosticity and accessibility explanations, cultural norms, expectations, and motivation were also taken into account to explain the effects of culture on consumer behavior.

Culture and Consumer Behavior Research from the 2010s to Today

With the increasing trend for research investigating the effects of culture on consumer behavior in the early 2000s to 2010, the early 2010s experienced the maturity stage. Apart from a few papers on global and local branding and the effect of cultural orientation on brand extensions, in the early 2010s, researchers mostly focused on food consumption and spending tendencies as a function of cultural orientation.

Torelli and Shavitt (2011) demonstrated the influence of power (personalized vs. socialized) on information processing dependent on cultural orientation (individualism vs. collectivism). Vertical individualists had an increased tendency to stereotype products (i.e., recognize better information that is congruent to prior product expectations) when they were primed with personalized power. However, horizontal collectivists displayed a greater tendency to individuate products (i.e., recognize and recall better information that is incongruent with prior expectations), when they were primed with social power.

The early 2010s experienced the rise of cross-cultural consumer research on understanding global and local brands. Torelli, Özsomer, Carvalho, Keh, and Maehle (2012) focused on the impact of cultural traits on global brand concept. More specifically, the authors used the Schwartz's Value Survey (1992) to define a globally accepted brand concept. They made a distinction between the cultures based on horizontal and vertical individualism and collectivism, and linked this distinction with the branding concept. They suggested that a brand concept related to openness was more preferred by horizontal individualists. However, a brand concept related to self-enhancement was preferred more by vertical individualists.

Strizhakova, Coulter, and Price (2012) not only focused on how consumers' culture affected global brand preference, but also acknowledged the importance of global brands' identities in shaping the global identity of individuals. They investigated the mixture of global and local identities (referred to as "glocal" identity) and its effect on consumer behavior. The authors ended up identifying four groups of consumers: globally engaged, glocally engaged, nationally engaged, and unengaged consumer segments. Furthermore, they studied the effect of each one of these groups on involvement with local and global brands, use of local and global brands to signal their selves, and purchase of global and local brands. The results of their studies suggested that the globally engaged (vs. nationally engaged and unengaged) consumers had a stronger engagement and identification with both global and local brands. The globally engaged (vs. nationally) were more likely to purchase global brands. Moreover, the unengaged (vs. nationally engaged) consumer segments displayed lower interest for patriotic and national ideologies.

Research on brand extensions and the effect of culture on brand extensions have continued in the early 2010s. Torelli and Ahluwalia (2012) demonstrated that culture was important also in the congruity perceptions between a brand and a product as it could influence the evaluations over brand extensions. In a series of experiments, their studies showed that consumers had more favorable attitudes toward culturally congruent brand extensions (e.g., Sony electric car rather than Sony coffee machine) when both the parent brand and the product were culturally symbolic. Spiggle, Nguyen, and Caravella (2012) further suggested the brand extension authenticity (i.e., the extent that an extension carries the originality, uniqueness, heritage, and values of its parent brand) as a complementary concept to perceived fit in brand extension evaluations. They showed that authentic extensions enhanced consumers' attitudes, purchase likelihood, and recommendation intentions of the extended product to others.

Kubat and Swaminathan (2015) have studied the brand preference of bicultural consumers. Results demonstrated that among bicultural consumers, the degree to which a brand symbolizes a certain culture moderated the impact of bilingual advertising (vs. English advertising) on brand preference. More specifically, brands that were low in cultural symbolism enhanced brand preference among bilinguals when advertised bilingually. This happened when bicultural consumers perceived their host culture and their ethnic culture identities as compatible (vs. incompatible). Hence, at high levels of bicultural identity integration, bicultural consumers preferred a bilingual ad more, compared to an ad only in English, but only for a less symbolic brand. Relatedly, Torelli, Chiu, Tam, Au, and Keh (2011) showed that concurrent exposure to symbols of two dissimilar cultures (e.g., American Batman toys with a made-in China label) drew the consumer's attention to the defining characteristics of the two cultures. Hence, the authors suggested that this resulted in higher perceptibility of cultural differences for the same commercial product.

Research on culture and consumer behavior in the early 2010s has also focused on the way in which consumers considered the relation between the endorser in an ad and the content of it in terms of the fit between them. Kwon, Saluja, and Adaval (2015) empirically showed in a series of four studies that culture might affect the endorser-content fit perceived by the participants. More specifically, they showed that individuals in collectivist cultures expected a fit between the endorser's message and the endorser. If there was no fit, individuals in collectivist cultures tended to evaluate the ads less favorably. Individuals in individualist cultures did not have such expectations and they treated the message and the endorser as separate information. Hence, they were insensitive to incongruences between them.

Research on cross-cultural consumer behavior also focused on how consumers across cultures responded to unsatisfactory experiences (Ng, Kim, & Rao, 2015). Ng et al. (2015) demonstrated that collectivists were more likely to switch brands if they regretted their group for not taking action to prevent product failure. Individualists were more likely to switch brands if the regret and the inaction to prevent product failure came from the individuals, rather than the group of belonging.

Research in the early 2010s extended cross-cultural consumer research on aspects other than brand and product evaluations. For example, Gomez and Torelli (2015) demonstrated that making a particular culture salient (e.g., French vs. American) caused people to be more sensitive to the presence (vs. absence) of nutrition information in food labels. Moreover, French consumers were less likely to prefer foods that displayed (vs. did not display) nutrition information. Gomez and Torelli (2015) suggested that this was because the information was incompatible with the cultural norm of hedonic food consumption for the French consumers.

Research on cross-cultural consumer research in the early 2010s has also considered the effect of national culture on consumers' financial decision making. Petersen, Kushwaha, and Kumar (2015) showed that consumers' financial decisions depended not only on prior experiences or firm's characteristics, but also on cultural orientations. The authors focused on three of Hofstede's cultural dimensions: long-term orientation, uncertainty avoidance, and masculinity in the country of origin of the respondents, to understand the impact of those on savings rate tendency, credit card purchases, or general spending patterns. Their results demonstrated that individuals from countries with high long-term orientation were more affected by prevention-focused advertising messages to decide on their savings rate. Individuals from cultures with low uncertainty avoidance were more affected by promotion-driven ads and were more likely to use the credit card to make purchases. Finally, individuals from highly masculine cultures were more likely to overspend and react more positively to promotion-focused advertising addressed at extending their spending patterns.

More recently, DeMotta, Chao, and Kramer (2016) tested the effect of dialectical thinking on the integration of the contradictory information. Results demonstrated that low dialectical thinkers expressed more moderate attitudes when they processed contradictory information. Consumers low in dialectical thinking processed the contradictory product information less fluently, which reduced their judgmental confidence. As a result, these consumers had more moderate attitudes toward the contradictory information.

In short, research on cross-cultural consumer behavior has continued to investigate issues related with consumer behavior in the early 2010s. Although there has not been an increasing trend on cross-cultural consumer research in the early 2010s, most of the research focused on perception of global and local brands, brand extensions, and consumer behavior related with food consumption and spending tendencies. Furthermore, there has been some research investigating the other cultural orientations (e.g., masculinity, uncertainty avoidance, or strong national identity) apart from focusing only on individualism and collectivism orientations.

What Lies Ahead in Cross-Cultural Consumer Research

Throughout this chapter, we have proposed a timeline that the cross-cultural consumer research has gone through since its early findings in the late 1990s (see Figure 29.1). We have suggested that there have mainly been three phases that cross-cultural consumer research has gone through to the mid-2010s. Although the interest in cross-cultural consumer research has gained increased momentum in the 2000s, this increased momentum entered a maturity stage where there has been steady progress since. We suggest that researchers might further investigate the role of culture on (1) experiences, (2) coping with psychological threats, (3) consumption emotions, and (4) the use of digital and social media. In the following sections, we provide our call for research into each one of the previously mentioned concepts.

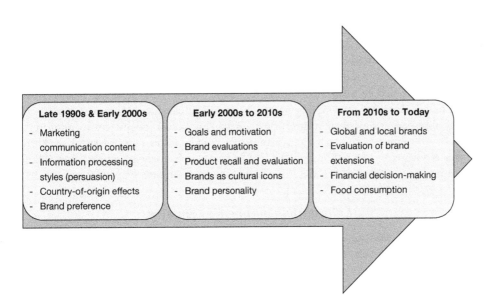

Figure 29.1 Timeline of cross-cultural consumer research

Culture and Experiences

Most of the research on culture has so far focused on branding and product evaluations (e.g., Hong & Kang, 2006; Kwon et al., 2015; Torelli & Ahluwalia, 2012). Culture surely has an important role in how consumers perceive the personality traits of brands (e.g., Aaker et al., 2001), or how responsive consumers are to marketing communications (Pauwels, Erguncu, & Yildirim, 2013).

However, most of the research seems to be driven toward the materialist side of what marketing offers (i.e., the product). We believe there is still a gap in the literature on culture and consumer behavior that might address the impact of culture on preferences for the materialistic versus experiential consumption. When would collectivists prefer experiential consumption to a materialistic one or a materialistic to an experiential one? Similarly, when would individualists prefer experiential consumption to a materialistic one, or a materialistic to an experiential one? Reviewing the literature, Gilovich, Kumar, and Jampol (2015) suggested that people get more satisfaction from experiential (vs. materialistic) purchases because: (1) experiential purchases enhance social relations, (2) experiential purchases develop a bigger part of one's identity, and (3) they are evaluated more on their own terms than material purchases. We suggest that future research might further investigate the role of cultural orientations on satisfaction from experiential purchases.

Culture and Psychological Threats

Literature on psychological threats suggests that culture might be a source of relief for threatened individuals. The reason for this is that culture enriches individuals with meaning in life (Becker, 1971; Van den Bos, 2009). According to Becker (1971), culture imposes a set of rules, customs, and goals to individuals, which may boost their self-esteem and mitigate the meaning threats the individual is experiencing.

Previous literature has demonstrated that when consumers experience mortality threats, their reaction and preference for brands will be affected by the fear of death (e.g., they would be willing to pay significantly more for prestigious brands in mortality threat condition versus no-threat condition; Mandel & Heine, 1999). Instead, when consumers experience intelligence threats, they reflect the effects of this threat not only on their academic results but also on the brands they use, by choosing brands that signal intelligence. Moreover, under social identity threats (e.g., racial discrimination to Afro-Americans), people try to mitigate the threat by choosing for their children names that convey status (e.g., Harvard or Alexus; Rucker & Galinsky 2008). We suggest that future research might investigate how cultural orientations might influence the way consumers cope with different types of meaning threats.

Culture and Consumption Emotions

Culture is an important factor to influence how one experiences emotions. It provides meanings to many different emotions such as happiness, sadness, anger, and fear. While one might wear black to a funeral in one culture (e.g., Western culture), another person from another culture (e.g., Asian culture) might wear white to a funeral. Hence, we suggest that how culture influences how different emotions are experienced is an important area that deserves future investigation. In this chapter, we mainly focus on happiness as a consumption experience.

Happiness is defined as "a state of well-being and contentment; a pleasurable or satisfying experience" (*Merriam-Webster's Collegiate Dictionary* 2016). Research has identified time and money as some of the strongest predictors of happiness (Mogilner, 2010). Time can be spent either working (hence increasing money), or building social relationships. Research has shown that although working hours in the US have increased, individual happiness levels have remained unchanged. In Europe, instead, working hours have decreased and this has led to an increase in happiness (Easterlin, 1995). Mogilner (2010) demonstrated that focusing on money motivated people to work more, but that did not lead to higher levels of happiness. Reminding individuals of time motivated them to spend more of it with important others rather than working and this made them happier. Hence, priming people with the thought of time emphasized social connections and enhanced happiness.

We believe that culture has a strong impact as a predictor of happiness. Culture shapes the focus of goals and rules individuals stick to (Becker, 1971). For instance, in individualistic cultures, since focus is more on inequality and on being superior to others (Oyserman, Coon, & Kemmelmeier, 2002), happiness might be achieved by spending time working for individual goals rather than socializing. On the contrary, in collectivistic cultures, emphasis is on being similar to the others in the group. This might lead to the prediction that in collectivistic cultures, happiness is achieved by spending time socializing rather than working. However, we suggest that the effect might attenuate if those people in collectivistic cultures work toward a collectivistic goal.

We might also predict culture to moderate the pursuit of happiness gained from excitement versus calmness. Aaker et al. (2001) demonstrated that culture influenced preference for brand personality dimensions. For instance, in research conducted in Spain on brand personality traits, only Sincerity, Excitement, and Sophistication overlapped out of the five brand personality traits (Aaker et al., 2001). In Japan instead, Ruggedness was substituted with Peacefulness (Aaker et al., 2001). We predict that specific cultural dimensions (e.g., excitement vs. peacefulness) can determine happiness pursued from products. More specifically, in a culture characterized by calmness and peacefulness (vs. excitement) consumers would be happier by consuming brands and products characterized by calmness and peacefulness (vs. excitement).

Culture and Digital and Social Media

In 2016, more than 3.4 billion users were registered online, more than 300 million from the number of online registered users in 2015 and almost 500 million more compared to 2014 (www.internetlivestats.com/internet-users/). Toubia and Stephen (2013) recognized that in order for a company to attract customers, it has to incentivize them to be active online.

Research on knowledge creation and knowledge sharing suggested that cultural values had an important role in determining the extent to which individuals are willing to share (Hofstede, 1984). Bhagat, Kedia, Harveston, and Triandis (2002) suggested that in individualistic cultures, people tend to process information by focusing on each piece of it, rather than the whole. For instance, individualists were more accepting of the written and the codified information, while collectivists tended to disregard the written information and focused more on non-verbal content (Bhagat et al., 2002; Hall, 1979). Moreover, individualists were more prone to asking questions and interacting. While individualists preferred formal ways of communication and knowledge sharing, collectivists preferred more the informal ways (Hwang, Francesco, & Kessler, 2003).

All these previous findings demonstrate that cultural aspects are crucial to information and knowledge sharing. Toubia and Stephen (2013) suggested that for companies that were active online, it was not only important to have many user followers, but also to engage them to interact with the company. Hence, finding ways to motivate users to engage online is fundamental. We predict that in individualistic cultures, consumers would interact more with the company in knowledge and opinion sharing, in liking or sharing company content if the message is mostly written and concise, and if it allows the individual to publicly show their knowledge and opinion. On the contrary, in collectivistic cultures, customers engage more if the content is mostly visual, if it does not require the user to "put their face in," and if it is designed in an informal and warm way. Hence, we expect a positive engagement of online users if the company takes into consideration the impact of culture on online content sharing.

Concluding Remarks

In this chapter, we have provided an overview of the development of cross-cultural consumer research since the late 1990s. We have reviewed the empirical work investigating the effects of culture on consumers. We have demonstrated that although there has been increased interest in investigating the effects of culture on consumer behavior in the early 2000s, cross-cultural consumer research has been in its maturity stage since 2010. We have provided calls for future research where researchers might investigate further topics in consumer behavior.

References

Aaker, J. L. (1997). Dimensions of brand personality. *Journal of Marketing Research, 34*(3), 347–356.

Aaker, J. L. (2000). Accessibility or diagnosticity? Disentangling the influence of culture on persuasion processes and attitudes. *Journal of Consumer Research, 26*(4), 340–357.

Aaker, J. L. (2006). Delineating culture. *Journal of Consumer Psychology, 16*(4), 343–347.

Aaker, J. L., Benet-Martinez, V., & Garolera, J. (2001). Consumption symbols as carriers of culture: A study of Japanese and Spanish brand personality constructs. *Journal of Personality and Social Psychology, 81*(3), 492.

Aaker, J. L., & Maheswaran D. (1997). The effect of cultural orientation on persuasion. *Journal of Consumer Research, 24*(3), 315–328.

Aaker, J., & Schmitt, B. (2001). Culture-dependent assimilation and differentiation of the self preferences for consumption symbols in the United States and China. *Journal of Cross-Cultural Psychology, 32*(5), 561–576.

Aaker, J. L., & Sengupta, J. (2000). Additivity versus attenuation: The role of culture in the resolution of information incongruity. *Journal of Consumer Psychology*, 9(2), 67–82.

Aaker, J. L., & Williams, P. (1998). Empathy versus pride: The influence of emotional appeals across cultures. *Journal of Consumer Research*, 25(3), 241–261.

Ahluwalia, R. (2008). How far can a brand stretch? Understanding the role of self-construal. *Journal of Marketing Research*, 45(3), 337–350.

Becker, E. (1971). *The birth and death of meaning: An interdisciplinary perspective on the problem of man*. 2nd Ed. Free Press.

Bhagat, R. S., Kedia, B. L., Harveston, P. D., & Triandis, H. C. (2002). Cultural variations in the cross-border transfer of organizational knowledge: An integrative framework. *Academy of Management Review*, 27(2), 204–221.

Briley, D. A., & Aaker, J. L. (2006a). Bridging the culture chasm: Ensuring that consumers are healthy, wealthy, and wise. *Journal of Public Policy & Marketing*, 25(1), 53–66.

Briley, D. A., & Aaker, J. L. (2006b). When does culture matter? Effects of personal knowledge on the correction of culture-based judgments. *Journal of Marketing Research*, 43(3), 395–408.

Chen, H., Ng, S., & Rao, A. R. (2005). Cultural differences in consumer impatience. *Journal of Marketing Research*, 42(3), 291–301.

DeMotta, Y., Chao, M. C. H., & Kramer, T. (2016). The effect of dialectical thinking on the integration of contradictory information. *Journal of Consumer Psychology*, 26(1), 40–52.

Easterlin, R. A. (1995). Will raising the incomes of all increase the happiness of all? *Journal of Economic Behavior & Organization*, 27(1), 35–47.

Gergen, K. J., Gulerce, A., Lock, A., & Misra, G. (1996). Psychological science in cultural context. *American Psychologist*, 51(5), 496.

Gilovich, T., Kumar, A., & Jampol, L. (2015). A wonderful life: Experiential consumption and the pursuit of happiness. *Journal of Consumer Psychology*, 25(1), 152–165.

Gomez, P., & Torelli, C. J. (2015). It's not just numbers: Cultural identities influence how nutrition information influences the valuation of foods. *Journal of Consumer Psychology*, 25(3), 404–415.

Gürhan-Canli, Z., & Maheswaran, D. (2000). Cultural variations in country of origin effects. *Journal of Marketing Research*, 37(3), 309–317.

Hall, E. T. (1979). *Au-delà de la culture, collection Points Essais*, éditions du Seuil.

Han, S. P., & Shavitt, S. (1994). Persuasion and culture: Advertising appeals in individualistic and collectivistic societies. *Journal of Experimental Social Psychology*, 30(4), 326–350.

Hofstede, G. (1984). *Culture's consequences: International differences in work-related values* (Vol. 5), Sage.

Holt, D. B. (2004). *How brands become icons: The principles of cultural branding*. Harvard Business Press.

Hong, S. T., & Kang, D. K. (2006). Country-of-origin influences on product evaluations: The impact of animosity and perceptions of industriousness brutality on judgments of typical and atypical products. *Journal of Consumer Psychology*, 16(3), 232–239.

Hwang, A., Francesco, A. M., & Kessler, E. (2003). The relationship between individualism–collectivism, face, and feedback and learning processes in Hong Kong, Singapore, and the United States. *Journal of Cross-Cultural Psychology*, 34(1), 72–91.

Johnson, T. P., Kulesa, P., Cho, Y. I., & Shavitt, S. (2005). The relation between culture and response styles: Evidence from 19 countries. *Journal of Cross-Cultural Psychology*, 36(2), 264–277.

Kacen, J. J., & Lee, J. A. (2002). The influence of culture on consumer impulsive buying behavior. *Journal of Consumer Psychology*, 12(2), 163–176.

Kubat, U., & Swaminathan, V. (2015). Crossing the cultural divide through bilingual advertising: The moderating role of brand cultural symbolism. *International Journal of Research in Marketing*, 32(4), 354–362.

Kwon, M., Saluja, G., & Adaval, R. (2015). Who said what: The effects of cultural mindsets on perceptions of endorser-message relatedness. *Journal of Consumer Psychology*, 3(25), 389–403.

Lau-Gesk, L. G. (2003). Activating culture through persuasion appeals: An examination of the bicultural consumer. *Journal of Consumer Psychology*, 13(3), 301–315.

Maheswaran, D., & Shavitt, S. (2000). Issues and new directions in global consumer psychology. *Journal of Consumer Psychology*, 9(2), 59–66.

Mandel, N., & Heine, S. J. (1999). Terror management and marketing: He who dies with the most toys wins. *NA-Advances in Consumer Research*, 26, 527–532.

McCrae, R. R., & Terracciano, A. (2005). Personality profiles of cultures: Aggregate personality traits. *Journal of Personality and Social Psychology*, 89(3), 407.

Merriam-Webster. Accessed July 30, 2016. www.merriam-webster.com/dictionary/happiness.

Meyers-Levy, J. (2006). Using the horizontal/vertical distinction to advance insights into consumer psychology. *Journal of Consumer Psychology, 16*(4), 347–351.

Mogilner, C. (2010). The pursuit of happiness time, money, and social connection. *Psychological Science, 21*(9), 1348–1354.

Monga, A. B., & John, D. R. (2007). Cultural differences in brand extension evaluation: The influence of analytic versus holistic thinking. *Journal of Consumer Research, 33*(4), 529–536.

Monga, A. B., & John, D. R. (2008). When does negative brand publicity hurt? The moderating influence of analytic versus holistic thinking. *Journal of Consumer Psychology, 18*(4), 320–332.

Nelson, M. R., & Shavitt, S. (2002). Horizontal and vertical individualism and achievement values: A multi-method examination of Denmark and the United States. *Journal of Cross-Cultural Psychology, 33*(5), 439–458.

Ng, S., & Houston, M. J. (2006). Exemplars or beliefs? The impact of self-view on the nature and relative influence of brand associations. *Journal of Consumer Research, 32*(4), 519–529.

Ng, S., Kim, H., & Rao, A. R. (2015). Sins of omission versus commission: Cross-cultural differences in brand-switching due to dissatisfaction induced by individual versus group action and inaction. *Journal of Consumer Psychology, 25*(1), 89–100.

Oyserman, D. (2006). High power, low power, and equality: Culture beyond individualism and collectivism. *Journal of Consumer Psychology, 16*(4), 352–356.

Oyserman, D., Coon, H. M., & Kemmelmeier, M. (2002). Rethinking individualism and collectivism: Evaluation of theoretical assumptions and meta-analyses. *Psychological Bulletin, 128*(1), 3.

Pauwels, K., Erguncu, S., & Yildirim, G. (2013). Winning hearts, minds and sales: How marketing communication enters the purchase process in emerging and mature markets. *International Journal of Research in Marketing, 30*(1), 57–68.

Petersen, J. A., Kushwaha, T., & Kumar, V. (2015). Marketing communication strategies and consumer financial decision making: The role of national culture. *Journal of Marketing, 79*(1), 44–63.

Rucker, D. D., & Galinsky A. D. (2008). Desire to acquire: Powerlessness and compensatory consumption. *Journal of Consumer Research, 35*(2), 257–267.

Schwartz, S. H. (1992). Universals in the content and structure of values: Theoretical advances and empirical tests in 20 countries. *Advances in Experimental Social Psychology, 25*, 1–65.

Shavitt, S., Lee, A., & Johnson, T. P. (2008). Cross-cultural consumer psychology. In C. Haugtvedt, P. Herr, and F. Kardes, (Eds.) *Handbook of Consumer Psychology*, 1103–1131. New York: Psychology Press.

Shavitt, S., Lalwani, A. K., Zhang, J., & Torelli, C. J. (2006a). The horizontal/vertical distinction in cross-cultural consumer research. *Journal of Consumer Psychology, 16*(4), 325–342.

Shavitt, S., Zhang, J., Torelli, C. J., & Lalwani, A. K. (2006b). Reflections on the meaning and structure of the horizontal/vertical distinction. *Journal of Consumer Psychology, 16*(4), 357–362.

Spiggle, S., Nguyen, H. T., & Caravella, M. (2012). More than fit: Brand extension authenticity. *Journal of Marketing Research, 49*(6), 967–983.

Strizhakova, Y., Coulter, R. A., & Price, L. L. (2012). The young adult cohort in emerging markets: Assessing their glocal cultural identity in a global marketplace. *International Journal of Research in Marketing, 29*(1), 43–54.

Sung, Y., & Tinkham, S. F. (2005). Brand personality structures in the United States and Korea: Common and culture-specific factors. *Journal of Consumer Psychology, 15*(4), 334–350.

Swaminathan, V., Page, K. L., & Gürhan-Canli, Z. (2007). "My" brand or "our" brand: The effects of brand relationship dimensions and self-construal on brand evaluations. *Journal of Consumer Research, 34*(2), 248–259.

Torelli, C. J., & Ahluwalia, R. (2012). Extending culturally symbolic brands: A blessing or a curse? *Journal of Consumer Research, 38*(5), 933–947.

Torelli, C. J., Chiu, C. Y., Tam, K. P., Au, A. K., & Keh, H. T. (2011). Exclusionary reactions to foreign cultures: Effects of simultaneous exposure to cultures in globalized space. *Journal of Social Issues, 67*(4), 716–742.

Torelli, C. J., Özsomer, A., Carvalho, S. W., Keh, H. T., & Maehle, N. (2012). Brand concepts as representations of human values: Do cultural congruity and compatibility between values matter? *Journal of Marketing, 76*(4), 92–108.

Torelli, C. J., & Shavitt, S. (2011). The impact of power on information processing depends on cultural orientation. *Journal of Experimental Social Psychology, 47*(5), 959–967.

Toubia, O., & Stephen, A. T. (2013). Intrinsic vs. image-related utility in social media: Why do people contribute content to Twitter? *Marketing Science, 32*(3), 368–392.

Triandis, H. C., & Gelfand, M. J. (1998). Converging measurement of horizontal and vertical individualism and collectivism. *Journal of Personality and Social Psychology*, *74*(1), 118.

Van den Bos, K. (2009). Making sense of life: The existential self trying to deal with personal uncertainty. *Psychological Inquiry*, *20*(4), 197–217.

Wang, C. L., Bristol, T., Mowen, J. C., & Chakraborty, G. (2000). Alternative modes of self construal: Dimensions of connectedness–separateness and advertising appeals to the cultural and gender-specific self. *Journal of Consumer Psychology*, *9*, 107–15.

Zhang, J., & Shavitt, S. (2003). Cultural values in advertisements to the Chinese X-generation – promoting modernity and individualism. *Journal of Advertising*, *32*(1), 23–33.

Zhang, Y., & Gelb, B. D. (1996). Matching advertising appeals to culture: The influence of products' use conditions. *Journal of Advertising*, *25*(3), 29–46.

30

THE CASE FOR EXPLORING CULTURAL RITUALS AS CONSUMPTION CONTEXTS

Cele C. Otnes

UNIVERSITY OF ILLINOIS AT URBANA-CHAMPAIGN, CHAMPAIGN, IL, USA

During the summer of 2016, the world's citizens were awash with opportunities to engage with and participate in many captivating cultural rituals, here defined as aesthetic, performative, and symbolic public events occurring on a grand scale that are broadly accessible to consumers via mass and/or social media. From weeks-long celebrations that marked the 90th birthday of Queen Elizabeth II throughout the Commonwealth, to the opening ceremony of the 2016 Rio Olympics, to regional events such as the Running of the Bulls in Pamplona, these symbol-laden, performative events connect consumers to sociocultural discourses, institutions, and values at the most macro level. Yet as popular as they can be (e.g., over 900 million people viewed or streamed the Opening Ceremony of the London Olympics; Ormsby 2012), ritual studies within consumer research overwhelmingly emphasize those occurring between dyads (e.g., gift giving; Belk and Coon, 1993; Otnes, Lowrey and Kim 1993), within family and/or friendship groups (e.g., Bradford 2009; Epp and Price 2008; Wallendorf and Arnould 1991; Wooten 2000), or within self-contained social units such as brand or consumption subcultures (Belk and Costa 1998; Bradford and Sherry 2015; Kozinets 2002).

These studies affirm that rituals can facilitate important individual and relational goals. For example, gift giving and receipt can signal changes in relationship trajectories (Ruth, Otnes and Brunel 1999), and help consumers express filial piety and support social order in kinship and friendship networks (Joy 2001). Ritualistic behavior within subcultures can help consumers escape from the strictures of daily life (Kozinets 2002; Schouten and McAlexander, 1995), or even foster survival in crisis contexts (Klein, Lowrey, and Otnes 2015). Equally revealing are studies of the downsides of ritual participation for dyads, families, or social groups – such as the social obligations that gifts of time and physical effort impose (Marcoux 2009), the ways ritual boredom or even "ritual death" can occur within the family (Otnes, et al., 2009) and how consumers resist ritual participation (Weinberger 2015). In short, Weinberger and Wallendorf's (2012) observation that most gift-giving research focuses on micro-level behavior and neglects the activity on a broader sociocultural level rings true about ritual scholarship in general.

Granted, exploring well-practiced rituals on micro- and meso- levels, especially those that link to calendric occurrences such as annual holidays – is typically easier than plumbing this behavior on a more macro level. This is because predicting and gaining access to cultural rituals may be difficult, since they may occur infrequently and unpredictably. For example, funerals for beloved citizens or leaders obviously occur on very short notice, and often in locales that may be difficult to access quickly. Nevertheless, I believe if ritual research is to remain salient to the consumer-behavior discipline, scholars must incorporate cultural rituals into the field of study. Stated more bluntly, with few exceptions (e.g., Weinberger and Wallendorf 2012), our field has effectively ceded the study of cultural rituals (sometimes described as "spectacles") to anthropology, cinema/media/visual studies, history, and sociology (Beeman 1993; Marshall 2002; Morreale 2000).

Recently, some scholars have begun to examine how understanding consumption rooted at the cultural level – and in particular, ritual-related topics – can inform marketing practice. For example, studies explore how marketers incorporate rituals into customer interactions and commercial offerings (e.g., Bradford and Sherry 2013; Dobscha and Foxman 2012; Otnes, Ilhan, and Kulkarni 2012). This cross-pollination of theoretical approaches toward ritual study and perspectives and problems emanating from retailing and services marketing are important to the field. Indeed, as events are often supported by substantial financial and human capital from commercial sources, cultural rituals afford scholars unique opportunities to continue deepening our understanding of applied consumer behavior.

I structure this chapter as follows: first, I make my case for the importance of broadening the scope of consumer scholarship to include cultural rituals, and for illuminating the impact of ritualized consumption on a sociocultural level. In doing so, I focus on recent cultural rituals staged by one institution – the British monarchy. After explicating how cultural rituals can illuminate our understanding of several key topics, I delve into the relevance of illuminating a key strategic marketing element – the brand. In sum, I seek to coax scholarship on rituals from within well-mined settings (e.g., under the Christmas tree; around the family dinner table), and into more public, spectacle-laden arenas.

Context: Monarchy and the British Royal Family Brand

Many cultural institutions, especially those embedded within the political and religious spheres, rely on rituals to remain viable and visible. Across the world, the institution of monarchy – or the political system that typically features one ruler – has retained its dominant cultural influence, even as the political power of many royal dynasties has dissipated. The creation myths of many monarchies emanate from ancient beliefs that those ascending to power do so through the will of divine providence. Most royal families also boast long lines of relatively continuous descent; for example, the Imperial House of Japan, which claims to be the longest monarchic dynasty, traces its roots to 660 B.C. Thus, monarchs and their families typically reside atop the apex of the social-class hierarchies within their realms.

For centuries, many of the world's royal families of Europe, Asia, and Africa have relied on lavish and public cultural rituals to reaffirm their power and status at home or abroad, and/or to instill or reignite national pride in their subjects, as typified here:

> In an overwhelming show of royal power, the procession of [France's] Henry II into Rouen in 1551 included 50 Norman knights, horse-drawn chariots [symbolizing] Fame, Religion, Majesty, Virtue, and Good Fortune, 57 armored men representing the kings of France, musicians, military and regional groups, six elephants and a band of slaves and captives, all of whom moved through the Roman Arch

of Triumph . . . [It also] included public shows at other arches, and an elaborate river triumph with mock battles, boats, and mermen with tridents riding fish.

(Cole 1999, 16–17)

Within their home countries, monarchs typically take center stage during cultural rituals that celebrate royal births, royal birthdays, investitures, coronations, lengths of reigns (e.g., Silver, Golden, and Diamond Jubilees), the ends of wars, and of course, royal weddings. Royal-rooted rituals also commemorate more somber occasions, such as acknowledging a nation's war dead, or commemorating the passing of monarchs. In October 2016, King Bhumibol Adulyadej of Thailand died after a 70-year reign. Cultural commemorations included a 30-day moratorium on entertainment by citizens, a yearlong mourning period during which citizens and even tourists were urged to wear "respectful colors," and a parade with hundreds of thousands of spectators as the King's body was transported to lie in state. Furthermore, "the government . . . set up a telephone hotline to help people cope . . . Google Thailand set its homepage to black and white . . . all TV channels . . . including . . . [foreign ones like] BBC and CNN, have been replaced with black-and-white royal broadcasts" (Holmes 2016).

Public-relations arms of monarchies often export carefully crafted spectacles to foreign shores, and participate in well-publicized events during their royal tours. Such occasions allow host countries both to valorize visiting monarchs and to shine the spotlight on their own locales, providing free exposure that can spark economic boosts. After the Duke and Duchess of Cambridge visited India in 2016, Travelocity saw a 25 percent increase in website bookings in the country, and a 200 percent boost in searches for hotel rooms in Mumbai, the royal couple's first stop on the tour (Lippe-McGraw, 2016).

To illuminate the importance of including cultural rituals in the stable of consumer research, I focus on the contributions of three recent events staged by the British Royal Family Brand (or BRFB; Otnes and Maclaran, 2015) from 2011 to 2016. These are: the Royal wedding of Prince William and Catherine Middleton, the celebration(s) of the Queen's Diamond Jubilee in 2012, and the Queen's 90th birthday celebration(s) in 2016. Balmer and his colleagues first conceptualized monarchy as a corporate brand, one specifically rooted in heritage and relying on pomp and pageantry to bolster equity (e.g., Balmer, Greyser and Urde, 2006). In our recent exploration of the role of the BRFB in consumer culture, we argue that the potency and appeal of the brand stems from its representation of five highly salient categories of brands – namely, global, family, heritage, human, and luxury. The BRFB is essentially devoid of political power; nevertheless, the touristic and heritage pull of the British monarchy, fueled by strong currents of Anglophilia around the world, is undeniable. VisitBritain asserts "the royal family generates . . . about $767 million every year in tourism revenue, drawing visitors to historic royal sites like the Tower of London, Windsor Castle, and Buckingham Palace" (Khazan, 2013).

These three BRFB exemplars differ in grandiosity and uniqueness from more "micro," but nevertheless anticipated and highly orchestrated, rituals associated with the monarchy. These range from daily events such as the Changing of the Guard ceremonies at Buckingham Palace and Windsor Castle, to annual pageants like the Queen's "Trooping the Colour" parade or the Opening of Parliament by the monarch in full regalia. Table 30.1 contains details on these three events. Two other hugely significant occasions to the BRFB during this period, the births of Prince George and Princess Charlotte in 2013 and 2015, also generated tremendous public excitement. But beyond palace officials placing the traditional notices of the births in the forecourt of Buckingham Palace, and quick public viewings of the families when they left the hospital, no widespread spectacles marked these occasions.

Table 30.1 Summary of BRFB cultural rituals: 2011–2016

Ritual	Date(s)	Principle figures	Venue(s)	Public activities	Audience (est.)	Cost (est.)	Revenues (est.)
The Royal Wedding	April 29, 2011	Prince William, Catherine Middleton, the BRFB, world leaders	London; UK (5,500 street parties)	Procession from palace to Westminster Abbey; wedding ceremony; carriage procession; balcony wave; RAF fly-past.	TV: 300,00–2 million; Internet: 27 Facebook posts/sec.	$34 million	$2 billion (tourism; street party supplies)
The Diamond Jubilee	June 2–5, 2012	Elizabeth II, the royal family, visiting royals	London & Windsor, UK; Commonwealth nations	London: Thames Diamond Jubilee Pageant (flotilla), BBC concert at Buckingham Palace, service of Thanksgiving; Balcony wave; RAF fly-past; museum exhibitions. Windsor: Horse Show, parade; Britain: 9,500 street parties; Big Jubilee lunches; royal tour; museum exhibits; Jubilee woods planting World: Jubilee beacons lighting, Big Lunches, Commonwealth visits by royal family members[1].	1.5 million (London); 17 million (UK viewers of BBC Jubilee concert); 3.5 m (France); 6.8 million (US); 2 mil visitors to Jubilee website;	£1.3–3.5 bn[2]	£409 million
The Queen's 90th Birthday Celebration	May and June, 2016	Elizabeth II, other BRFB members	Windsor & London	Windsor: Four nights of music, song, dances, and equestrian displays. London: Trooping the Colour parade; balcony appearance, RAF fly-past, Patron's picnic for 10,000	10,000 at Patron's picnic; 6000/night at Windsor gala; 10 million celebrants in Britain[3]	unavailable	£1.1 billion (by British celebrants)

[1] https://www.royal.uk/60-facts-about-diamond-jubilee-celebrations-uk

[2] http://www.telegraph.co.uk/news/interactive-graphics/9197527/Queens-Diamond-Jubilee-cost-of-the-celebrations.html

[3] http://www.cbc.ca/news/world/queen-elizabeth-90th-birthday-1.3620788

I leverage these three events, and occasional references to others, to demonstrate how cultural rituals can accomplish the following: (1) showcase the singularity of iconic elements and practices; (2) illuminate the efficacy of supporting sub-rituals; (3) probe linkages between consumption and emotional display; and (4) unpack the salience of spectacular showmanship. I follow the discussion of these benefits by deeply interrogating the reflexive relationship between brands and cultural rituals.

What Cultural Rituals Can Illuminate

Showcasing the Singularity of Iconic Elements and Practices

The three BRFB rituals in Table 30.1 all incorporate exceptional goods, services, and experiences in their design. Some of these clearly meet Belk, Wallendorf, and Sherry's (1989) definition of "quintessence," or elements that seem to embody all of the desired, "right" combination of elements within an entity, and in so doing transcend their commercial origins and rise to the status of the sacred and iconic. For example, Catherine Middleton's wedding gown by the British design firm Alexander McQueen reportedly cost around $400,000. It featured hand-sewn English and French lace, and a nine-foot train designed to imitate an opening flower (Moss 2011). Echoing the Queen's choice in 1953 to incorporate symbols of the Commonwealth members into the design of her coronation gown, Ms. Middleton's gown featured hand-appliqued symbols of the four nations within the United Kingdom. Likewise, the Queen's State Coach created for her Diamond Jubilee includes fragments from iconic British landmarks such as the Royal Yacht Britannia; St. Paul's, Canterbury, and Durham Cathedrals; Henry VIII's flagship the *Mary Rose;* No. 10 Downing Street, and a piece of the apple tree under which Isaac Newton purportedly discovered gravity (Abdulaziz 2014).

Even the world's wealthiest citizens would have difficulty competing with the BRFB in acquiring items possessing similar cultural caché, because they lack the requisite genetic and historic capital that contribute to the provenance and bolster the mystique of these artifacts. Such unattainability not only imbues these quintessential items with a singular cultural potency, but also enables them to extend the reach and resonance of the cultural rituals in which they are initially embedded. But to prolong these effects, these quintessential artifacts must themselves be emplaced within carefully crafted constructions of post-ritual display, in venues saturated with sacredness and singularity. For example, when Buckingham Palace exhibited Catherine, the Duchess of Cambridge's wedding gown during the summer of 2012, over 625,000 people bought tickets, contributing to a 50% increase in palace-tour sales over the prior year (Raynor 2012). Likewise, Princess Diana's bridal gown became the centerpiece of a multi-nation tour that conveyed her life story through photographs and possessions. Reminding visitors that Cinderella fairy tales can indeed come true, the 1981 Royal Wedding and the ensuing displays and discussions that followed reinvigorated consumers' desires for lavish wedding ceremonies (Otnes and Pleck, 2003) and contributed to Diana's glamorous image and elevation to the highest echelon of the fame-stratosphere.

Although these artifacts clearly wield cultural and commercial power, the scarcity and singularity of the rituals themselves are likely even more enticing than any particular artifact embedded within them. Rites of passage such as births, marriages, and deaths occur relatively infrequently within any social sphere, and when they do, they typically are marked as the most profound occurrences within the life history of a person or family. The ability to witness such rites as they incorporate pomp and pageantry, and within the context of what has historically been one of the most socially, economically, and politically powerful kinship networks in the world, means these events as a whole may also acquire a quintessence and once-in-a-lifetime aura. Consider too that certain factors of the human condition (e.g., longer life spans, fewer children) mean these occasions are becoming less frequent, while others (e.g., celebrating the 90th birthday of a monarch) spring up to meet the changing times. Thus, understanding what quintessence means with respect to cultural rituals as a whole, rather than with respect to their component parts such as artifacts, is an important research topic to address.

Illuminating the Efficacy of Supporting Sub-Rituals

Many cultural rituals feature myriad sub-rituals that emanate from focal artifacts or events. For example, the Christmas tree is often the center of gift giving, decorating and other family rituals (Otnes et al., 2009). As Table 30.1 demonstrates, the British monarchy devotes exorbitant sums to creating cultural rituals. While often garnering criticism as wasteful and elitist, there is no denying that these "one-off" events appeal to people wishing to witness history first-hand, and who enjoy the ensuing bragging rights associated with having done so. The amount of money spent on travel, hotels, meals, and royal commemoratives (from higher-end pieces sanctioned by the monarchy, to "tourist tat" like thimbles, pencils, bobbleheads, and so on) affirms the appeal of such occasions, and of their tangible representations. For the 2011 Royal Wedding, revenue from "memorabilia alone was estimated at £200m, with the total reaching £480m . . . when [adding] food and drink" (Gladwell 2011). Likewise, the Diamond Jubilee weekend contributed to an infusion of £120 million into the London economy (Martin 2012).

Yet often, financial assessments of cultural rituals do not accurately capture the impact of sub-rituals throughout the nation and the world that occur in conjunction with these occasions. In fact, some may acquire the status of becoming aspects of the focal iconic celebration. In particular, "street parties" began as part of the nationwide celebration within Britain in 1919 to mark the end of World War I. The website www.streetparty.org.uk describes these events as unique to the U.K., and notes they typically coincide with the occurrence of (happy) royal rituals. This event represents an interesting consumer-culture context because increasingly, participants rely on the marketplace to create specially prepared goods and services as core elements of the festivities. For the thousands of street parties held in the U.K. during the Diamond Jubilee (a period of deep recession in Britain), "Marks & Spencer . . . sold more than 200,000 jubilee teacakes, 50,000 commemorative cookie tins and . . . 31 miles of bunting" ("Queen's Jubilee a Fiesta . . . ," 2012). Commentators note that that because these events occur on a local level, they may accomplish more than offering communal expression of respect for the Queen, and in fact may reduce feelings of isolation associated with increasingly urban lifestyles.

Sub-rituals that spring up or become entrenched in larger cultural rituals are largely absent from the consumer-research landscape. As such, exploring the evolution of their meanings for participants, and the ties to the broader cultural ritual they support, represents ripe fodder for exploration. A related but broader topic pertains to understanding how consumers across the globe co-create, participate in, and communicate about cultural rituals when they live thousands of miles away from the focal event. Often, consumers may feel compelled to celebrate these events in real-time, altering their patterns of work or sleep as they navigate tricky time-zone adjustments to do so. Consider the activities of guests at the Ritz-Carlton in Washington, D.C., who gathered to watch the 2011 Royal Wedding:

> more than 200 Americans assembled in . . . the ballroom, where the dress code appeared to be Ascot-inspired. Breakfast [included] scones and clotted cream,

English rashers of bacon and a specially commissioned blend of tea with ingredients sourced in Berkshire, the county of the newly-titled Duchess of Cambridge.

(Geoghegan 2011)

In sum, exploring how sub-rituals enable participation in focal but distant occasions – especially in the age of Fear of Missing Out (FOMO; Hedges 2014) – could enrich our understanding of consumers' and practitioners' contemporary ritual engagement.

Probing Linkages between Consumption and Emotional Display

Engaging in shared celebration and commemoration means cultural rituals offer unique opportunities for scholars to explore how consumption-laden occasions spur the experience of emotions. In particular, Gopaldas (2014, 995) defines marketplace sentiments as "collectively shared emotional dispositions toward marketplace elements." Public outpourings of emotion during cultural rituals such as Princess Diana's funeral represent a unique and rare chance for citizens across the world to experience a shared sense of belonging to humanity – what Victor Turner (1975) terms "communitas" – in the broadest and often the most benign sense. Such sentiments may be increasingly important in a world where divisive and often hostile cultural, economic, social, and political differences dominate contemporary global discourses. At the very least, these occasions provide an opportunity to understand how emotional experiences occur outside of the more typical experimental contexts that dominate consumer research, and in more experiential ones.

The ways in which these visible and sensory-laden emotional displays impact consumers' experiences of these occasions is also worth exploring. Some personality types (e.g., introverts; Cain 2013), may find outpourings of marketplace sentiments overwhelming or even traumatizing. Others may become anxious or fearful when large and diverse crowds contribute to the inversion of rules that often occurs during ritual enactment – rules that typically govern order and social structure. Thus, the ways the emotional components of cultural rituals impact consumer well-being also should interest researchers whose work aligns with the Transformational Consumer Research paradigm (e.g., Mick et al. 2012).

In addition, how consumers experience marketplace sentiments in cultures unaccepting of, unaccustomed to, or unprepared for mass positive and negative expressions of emotion may prove to be an intriguing research topic. The public outpouring of grief after Princess Diana's death in Britain took many cultural observers by surprise, with scholars commenting on the incompatibility and incongruity of this experience in a nation whose character is perceived as synonymous with "keeping calm and carrying on" (Thomas 2008).

Unpacking the Salience of Spectacular Showmanship

Cultural rituals often showcase the best practices of spectacle creation, leveraging teams of talented culture-producers charged with dazzling audiences by orchestrating innovative, ludic, sensory-stimulating, and aesthetically-laden experiences. Consider the array of elements comprising the centerpiece of the Queen's Diamond Jubilee celebration, a 1000-strong flotilla down the Thames:

> Ten "music herald barges" will unite each section of boats . . . They'll include choirs, live bands and orchestras . . . the Ancient Academy of Music . . . will perform Handel's "Water Music" [on] 18th century instruments . . . the final barge

[contains] the entire London Philharmonic Orchestra [playing] pieces associated with [each building] it passes . . . [at] the headquarters of MI-6 . . . [its] maestro will cue James Bond's theme song. Loudspeakers will broadcast . . . to those standing on the banks . . . The flotilla includes . . . a replica of an 18th-century barge, and the Dim Riv, a half-size replica of a Viking longboat . . . Venetian gondolas, a Hawaiian war canoe, and about 15 specially decorated dragon boats. Tug boats will follow, as will some 70 passenger boats, about 60 motorboats from yacht clubs, and a fleet of amphibious DKUW . . . boats used in tourists' duck tours . . . . More solemn are the ships . . . that, in 1940 [helped] evacuate 385,000 Allied troops from Dunkirk. When the last boat sails under Tower Bridge . . . 1,800 energy-efficient LED lights and 2,000 meters of LED linear lights [on the Bridge] will gleam "diamond white" all weekend.

(Adams, 2012)

Given the often competitive aestheticism displayed in the celebration of meso-level consumer rituals (e.g., lavish weddings, bar/bat mitzvahs, quinceañera parties) it is surprising that ritual scholars have not paid more attention to the role of aesthetics within cultural rituals. In fact, few studies explore the benefits (e.g., experiencing positive emotions such as delight; Ball and Barnes, 2017), and consequences (e.g., sensory overload, guilt and regret from overindulgence) of consumer immersion in highly aestheticized cultural spectacles, although some research does explore the consequences of consumers being burdened by ritual preparedness (Wallendorf and Arnould, 1991).

Related to explaining how consumers capture, co-create, and cope with ritual aesthetics, attention should be paid to people's increasing tendency to use social-media platforms to create their "spatial selves" − or relying on online and offline resources to "document, archive, and display their experience and/or mobility within space and place . . . to represent or perform aspects of their identity to others" (Schwartz and Halegoua, 2014, 2). The 21st-century version of showing vacation slides to the neighbors manifests itself in people's ability to immediately disseminate their attendance at coveted cultural spectacles via social media, and bolster their social status, reaffirm their tastes, and flaunt their cultural and economic capital. However, we possess little understanding of how the ways consumer create spontaneous social selves impacts their experiences of the rituals unfolding before them.

Interrogating the Reflexive Relationship between Brands and Rituals

In the introduction to this chapter, I asserted that the relationship between brands and cultural rituals deserves special attention. Support for this claim is rooted in the fact that while rituals clearly act as conduits for culture, brands do so as well (Aaker, Benet-Martinez, and Garolera, 2001). Nevertheless, as is the case with ritual research, much of the research on consumers' use of brands focuses on the cognitive and affective outcomes of brand use for individuals (e.g., as aspects of their identities or signals of cultural and economic capital; Kirmani 2009; Nelissen and Meijers 2011) and for meso-level groups such as "brand communities" (e.g., McAlexander, Schouten, and Koenig, 2002). But as is evidenced by brand-sponsorship tactics of highly ritualized sporting and media events (e.g., the Olympics, the Super Bowl, awards-show ceremonies) many manufacturers and marketers often seize the opportunities to showcase brands within the context of cultural rituals, and even to try and make brands inextricable elements within these events. In sum, both rituals and brands owe much of their vitality to relying on and reflecting cultural heritage, discourses, iconicity, and myths. Focusing on how brands influence cultural rituals – and vice versa – can help strengthen linkages between the sociological, anthropological, or historical approaches to both phenomena, and can revitalize the relevance of cultural rituals to contemporary marketing strategy and practice.

In this section, I delve more deeply into the reflexive relationship between brands and cultural rituals by exploring the following: (1) ritual brands as ideological symbols; (2) cultural rituals as portals for human brands; (3) the role of brands in commercializing cultural rituals; (4) cultural rituals and place branding; (5) brands and ritual subversion; and (6) rituals as contexts for brand revitalization.

Ritual Brands as Ideological Symbols. Within cultural rituals, branded goods can serve as ritual artifacts, or items Rook describes as communicating "specific symbolic messages . . . integral to the meaning of the total experience" (1985, 253). Belk, Wallendorf and Sherry (1989) observe some ritual artifacts considered so sacred, only one or a few key players (e.g., shamans) may possess the authority to handle or use them. Marketers are keenly aware that products and brands often play focal roles in rituals. Indeed, a plethora of branded goods is available in the form of memorabilia, special foods and beverages, and products offered by companies that specialize in cultural commemoration.

Consider the Bradford Exchange, a U.S.-based firm that began operations in 1973. Its website homepage touts itself as "the premier source for a vast array of unique limited-edition collectibles and fine gifts that offer an exceptionally high level of artistry, innovation, and enduring value." Exploring the firm's website reveals offerings in porcelain, coins, dolls, and other materials that tangibilize events many people might find culturally, pop-culturally, or historically significant. In that vein, it has been quick to issue items that commemorate all of the major rituals and milestones that emanate from the BRFB. Among its offerings to commemorate the 2011 Royal wedding is the "Royal Wedding Jeweled Plate." Retailing for $49.95, it features a photo of the happy bride and groom exiting their ceremony at Westminster Abbey in the center, while its rim featured repeat motifs of the large blue sapphires and diamonds in the new Duchess of Cambridge's (formerly, Princess Diana's) engagement ring. Of course, one of the ultimate goals of commemorative firms such as the Bradford Exchange (and the brand of commemoratives actually produced by the British monarchy itself, the Royal Collection) is that ultimately, people will seek to collect the brand as well as the occasion. Such items may acquire their potency as harbingers of cultural rituals because they represent immediately recognizable and visible evidence that a person endorses and/or has indirectly or directly participated in a ritual. Furthermore, the growth of e-tailing means consumers who seek to engage with these rituals, but who live far from the focal events, can participate through commemorative consumption. Thus, these branded commemoratives that endure long after the streets have been swept of celebratory debris are proof positive that ritual observers have participated in, and perhaps even perceive themselves as a part of, history.

Cultural Rituals as Portals for Human Brands. At their core, cultural rituals often exist to celebrate or commemorate human brands (Thomson 2006). Typically, these are famous people (celebrities, politicians, sports figures) who retain professional image-managers and who themselves strive to become the focus or face of marketing or revenue-generating effort for their organizations or for advertisers. Exploring how heritage-based human brands such as monarchs, renowned spiritual leaders, beloved artists, and literary figures resonate with consumers affords researchers an opportunity to expand the understanding of their potency, as well as their interconnection to cultural rituals.

The British monarchy is the very definition of a human brand: at any given point in history (with the exception of the joint reign of William III and Mary II from 1689–1694), its face has been either *one* king or *one* queen since 1066. The outpouring of respect and admiration for the Queen during her 90th birthday celebration also served as a delayed commemoration (at her insistence) of her record as the U.K.'s longest-reigning monarch. As I will demonstrate, this event (among many others involving her and her family during her reign) reveals just how resonant human brands, especially those playing symbolic roles as harbingers of past and present cultural values, can remain within a culture.

Within the BRFB, one of the most famous human brands to emerge in recent years is Princess Diana – and her elevation to cult status still fascinates scholars two decades after her death. Like many successful human (Oprah Winfrey) and non-human brands (e.g., Apple; Volkswagen), Diana's narrative often focused on her triumph over adversity as an "underdog brand" (Paharia et al., 2011). In the same fashion, Kate Middleton's coal-mining ancestors and air-hostess mother became crucial threads within her own underdog narrative. Her propulsion from a young woman with a barely-there claim to the aristocracy into the stratosphere of the global social hierarchy wields a massive halo effect for most of the non-human brands she chooses to display (Logan, Hamilton, and Hewer 2013). Furthermore, her underdog narrative enabled commentators to capitalize incessantly on the similarities of her fairy-tale wedding to the Disney version of the Cinderella story – right down to the eerily-similar resemblances of William and Catherine to the animated Prince Charming and Cinderella.

However, one area of potentially fertile research for practitioners is exploring how to balance the two key elements of human brands – namely, the "human" and the "brand." Obviously, the massive budgets and scale cultural rituals entail require management by professional marketers, event planners, and image consultants, who promote their human brands through tried-and-true techniques. Yet a marketing-savvy and even cynical public may find many of these tactics to be too transparent, leading to a possible tainting of the occasion as more commercial than authentically cultural. For the BRFB, one key task is to balance the accessibility to the monarchy that cultural rituals and their incessant media/social media coverage provide, with maintaining the mystique of the monarchic brand. In other words, the BRFB's handlers must strive to maintain an appropriate distance for the brand from the "mere celebrities" that populate the pages of tabloid newspapers, magazines such as *Hello* and *People*, Facebook and Instagram pages, and Twitter feeds *ad nauseam*. If the distinction between royals and "mere" celebrities collapses, the legitimacy of maintaining (and funding) the brand may be threatened (even as technically, the BRFB now pays for itself through revenues it generates from the "Crown Estate"). However, other human brands could benefit from explorations of how to create and communicate brand mystique and charisma, and of how the public portrayals of human brands through ritual participation or social media contribute to or detract from desired brand outcomes.

Relatedly, associating established brands with iconic human variants clearly can drive sales – as the "Kate effect" (now expanded to the "Cambridge effect") clearly demonstrates. This term captures the impact of the Duchess of Cambridge and her children appearing in "High Street" (e.g., off-the-rack) brands that are accessible to many royal fans. After social-media images appear of the family wearing certain brands, sales of these items often skyrocket, and can even cause retailers' websites to crash, and merchandise stocks to quickly deplete. Although Catherine's choice of more mainstream brands no doubt exacerbates this effect, in truth the brand choices of the BRFB have spurred such emulative practices for decades. Consider that the corgi was a working dog breed found mainly on farms until Princess Elizabeth received her first one as a pet. However, the actual benefits for consumers of purchasing such mainstream brands that the BRFB endorses through usage remain undertheorized.

Roles of Brands in Commercializing Cultural Rituals. The typically off-the-chart media/social media exposure that cultural rituals enjoy means marketers often aggressively devise ways to insinuate their brands into these activities. These strategies range from serving as official sponsors of rituals and touting this status throughout the events (e.g., in myriad ads during the Olympic games; ensuring athletes wear apparel that prominently features branded logos) to merely appearing on lists of sponsors or suppliers of focal goods and services. The general public may even remain unaware of how extensively rituals such as the Queen's 90th birthday celebrations relied on commercial support. However, the official website for the event(s) names 29 sponsors, including high-end and stalwart British "heritage" brands such as Jaguar (actually owned by India's Tata Motors since 2008), Land Rover and the supermarket chain Waitrose.

Nevertheless, ritual organizers may find the concept of blatant brand connections undesirable, or even crass. Tasked with staging the flotilla for the Queen's Diamond Jubilee (described previously), Phil Smith described the delicate balancing act between creating an event designed to represent history, and enabling his sponsors to take visible parts:

> This isn't an ordinary opportunity for sponsorship. It has to be handled with decorum and taste, as well as sensibility. It won't be a question of a brand extravaganza on the river by festooning boats with brand names. The . . . overwhelming majority of brand-owners . . . appreciate that this is a national event with historic significance and that brands must behave with sensitivity.
>
> *(Barnes and Chapman, 2012)*

Interestingly, throughout history the British monarchy has demonstrated that it understands how branding practices can contribute to its salience and legacy. In a three-volume study of how different royal houses within Britain promoted themselves to its court and its subjects, the historian Kevin Sharpe (2009, 2010, 2013) traces such practices to the Tudor monarchy in the 1500s. For example, he describes how Elizabeth I relied on branding techniques (such as requiring members of her court to wear cameos with her image) to demonstrate their loyalty, and how she served as the model for the Virgin Mary in illustrations of the earliest printed Bibles. However, contemporary consumer scholars do not plumb the ways brands contribute to consumers' perceptions of cultural rituals. As noted earlier, many brands themselves rely on consumers' desires to tangibilize their memories of cultural rituals by acquiring key commemoratives.

Even ordinary brands, or those consumers encounter on a more everyday basis, often take center stage at cultural rituals. The Patron's Lunch for 10,000 held as part of the Queen's 90th birthday party (and modeled after the street-party sub-ritual) resembled a British "brandfest" (McAlexander and Schouten 1998) in many ways. It was replete with commemorative hampers provided by the mainstream retailer Marks & Spencer, products and volunteers from brands such as the now-global British pharmacy chain Boots, the iconic alcohol brand Pimm's, BT, and Unilever. Although the commercial success of these brands stems from their embeddedness into people's ordinary lives, participants and collectors clearly hungered for these limited-edition brand variants: unused picnic hampers from the event now fetch up to £250 on eBay (Wilgress, 2016).

Cultural Rituals and Place Branding. Since the inception of cultural rituals, both their creators, and spectators expect these events to be chockablock with aesthetics, and many times the ritual venue is a crucial contributor to achieving this outcome. Fortunately for the BRFB, it is inextricably tied to what is considered one of the most historic and picturesque cities in the world – London. Home to iconic sites that teem with royal heritage such as Westminster Abbey (site of all coronations, many royal weddings and monarchic tombs), the Houses of Parliament and those skillfully managed by the national charity Historic Royal Palaces (e.g., Tower of London, Hampton Court Palace, and Diana's former home Kensington Palace), London offers the perfect backdrop for monarchic cultural rituals. Citizens and tourists alike who experienced the three BRFB rituals discussed here could seamlessly experience an admixture of contemporary, historic, and perhaps even ancient traditions. For example, during the 2012 Diamond Jubilee, they could transition from watching a parade of military might on the Mall in front of Buckingham Palace, to visiting exhibits of Andy Warhol's portraits of the Queen at the National Portrait Gallery, to taking in theatrical productions about past, present, and even future monarchs in London's West End.

Many of London's retail establishments also contribute to and benefit from this fortuitous place branding by creating ties to the BRFB's rituals in the form of window displays, special menu items, and themed products and services (Figure 30.1). Place branding also extends to locations beyond London; during May and June 2016, the shops in Windsor, England – site of the Queen's favorite residence and epicenter of her 90th birthday celebration – were festooned with birthday messages and displays of attire such as the broad-brimmed, colorful hats the Queen favors on her ritual walkabouts through the town (Figure 30.2). Yet how such synergies between place and pomp impact consumers' experiences of cultural rituals – and their subsequent attitudes toward and experiences of the places where they are staged – remains undertheorized.

Figure 30.1 Diamond Jubilee merchandise window display, June 2012

Source: Photo by the author.

Figure 30.2   Queen's 90th birthday celebration store window, Windsor, England, 2016

Source: Photo by the author.

Brands and Ritual Subversion. Just as brands can serve as harbingers of unity during cultural rituals, they can also provide consumers with vehicles through which to express their displeasure with these occasions. With respect to BRFB-related rituals, countercultural branded goods enable consumers to embrace and express an anti-monarchical ideology when they display, refuse to display, purchase altered goods, or even alter branded goods themselves. As such, subversive ritual brands offer scholars opportunities to explore key discourses related to ideologies and values that rituals and or/brands can express.

At such times, people may create new products that particular subcultures may adopt to undercut what they perceive as an uncritical acceptance of cultural rituals. If successful, some of these one-off products may even result in the creation of a brand. Prior to the 2011 Royal Wedding, the artist Lydia Leith created her "Royal Wedding Sick Bag." Although initially created "as a joke around the dinner table," it became hugely popular with those disgusted and fatigued with royal rituals ("Royal Wedding Barf Bags . . . ," 2011). This variant sold so well that Leith expanded her line to include bags branded for the Diamond Jubilee and the births of Prince George and Princess Charlotte, allowing anti-royalists to thematically express their distaste for the BRFB (and no doubt spurring a new line of collectibles in the process). The success of Leith's new brand and its extensions points to the need for critical explorations of the sociocultural benefits and consequences of cultural rituals, and the roles of subversive brands within them. Put another way, while marketers may strategically arrange for brands to play active roles in these events, consumers may seek entrepreneurial output that enables them to leverage brands as they engage in activist roles.

Rituals as Contexts for Brand Revitalization. Like many rituals, the three BRFB variants I highlight represent rare historical occurrences that are widely anticipated and motivated by people who wish to have their "ritual longing" satisfied (Arnould, Price, and Curasi, 1999).

Such occasions can revitalize well-established brands by providing their manufacturers with opportunities to generate potentially cherished commemoratives, especially if these take the forms of luxury, limited editions that leverage their scarcity (Park, Jaworski, and MacInnis, 1986). As I note earlier, the often-irresistible pull of these cultural spectacles means heritage-brand variants can extend the time span and impact of ritual occasions to include times before and after the core performative activities of the rituals. Research on holidays supports the salience of brands as key ritual artifacts (Rook 1985), and the assumption that they can act as iconic tradition conduits at holiday meals (Wallendorf and Arnould 1991), or during annual gift-giving traditions (Otnes, Lowrey, and Kim 1993).

Yet what remains underexplored is the impact of embedding brands within cultural rituals on metrics such as short- and long-term brand image. One global advertising agency, BBDO, argues that embedding brands into cherished rituals can transform them into "fortress brands," making it less likely that consumers will forgo them during economic downturns (BBDO: The Ritual Masters, 2007).

In summary, contemporary branding theory recognizes these entities as harbingers of culture, and as repositories of key cultural constructs such as myths and discourses. However, conceptual linkages between brands and rituals remain undertheorized, beyond general observations that marketers can infuse brands with cultural elements such as myths and values to enhance their resonance for consumers (Atkin 2004; Holt 2004; McCracken 1990).

Contemporary Challenges Facing Cultural Rituals

In this final section, I explore how some macro-elements can shape – and disrupt – consumers' and practitioners' perspectives about cultural rituals. In recent years, the contemporary global landscape has become increasingly unsettled due to increases in global terrorism, economic uncertainly, political upheaval, and contested debates about human rights and social justice. The staging of public and therefore potentially vulnerable cultural rituals reflects these underlying currents. Security costs to protect the British Royal family and the 50 attending heads of state during the 2011 Royal Wedding was approximated at £20 million. The recent massacre during the Bastille Day celebrations in Nice, France in the summer of 2016 also should encourage exploration of a key question: How can cultural rituals remain viable in a world that faces increasing vulnerability to violence in the public sphere? On the meso level, reactions to such vulnerability have already contributed to the shifting of previously public rituals to more private (and ostensibly secure) spaces. Consider that American Halloween celebrations, traditionally rooted in the nighttime visitation of neighbors' homes, often now occur in more enclosed, supervised venues such as homes, and even retail stores.

The aesthetic competitiveness and cost of staging globally salient cultural rituals that bring status and regional-pride issues into high relief means debates about their salience increasingly incorporate issues pertaining to social justice and sustainability. Consider that the 2008 Beijing Olympic Games cost China $40 billion in new elements within the civic infrastructure, and renovations and removals of less desirable ones. Observers argue that an event lasting just over two weeks likens the Olympics to a modern-day potlatch (Broudehoux 2007) – one typified by a cycle of grand creation and display, followed by destruction, dismantling, and decay of its requisite components. Adopting a critical stance on cultural rituals – typically the purview of cultural-studies scholars – could also be of interest and value to scholars interested in the domains of sustainable, ethical, and civically responsible consumption.

Likewise, the impact of such viral social-media transmissions on the salience, efficacy and longevity of cultural rituals is an area ripe for exploration by scholars in communication and consumer research. The current grassroots movement of "Pantsuit Nation," which fostered ritual participation in the form of posting acquisitions and wearing of pantsuits (by men, women, and children) in support of Hillary Clinton's candidacy for U.S. president, offers an excellent example of a ritual that quickly achieved cultural status, but did not contribute to the desired outcome. In sum, even as the salience of causes or institutions that leverage cultural rituals may be questioned, what seems assured is that cultural rituals themselves will remain salient as viable enterprises involving focal institutions, consumers and commercial entities – and that these rituals retain meanings and importance for these stakeholders.

Conclusion

Incorporating the study of cultural rituals into consumer behavior scholarship is important because these events represent consumer culture writ large. They communicate the values of a culture to domestic and foreign audiences through sensory- and often luxury-laden spectacles, as their organizers seek to remind the world of revered accomplishments and icons entrenched within a specific heritage. Cultural-ritual orchestrators now include corporations that try and leverage the significance and visibility of these events to fulfill key marketing and public-relations goals. These ritual crafters offer up brands, celebrities, technologies, innovators/ entrepreneurs, and cultural producers to create memorable, emotion-inducing experiences for participants and observers. Likewise, the often-commemorative consumption choices that members of the ritual audience make signify their valorization of these events, iconicize key components of the ritual, and help them visibly express their allegiance or resistance to the ideologies and themes underlying these occasions.

I hope this chapter offers persuasive evidence that consumer scholars should consider cultural rituals – and the often-localized satellite sub-rituals they support – as important and illuminating research contexts. Besides enabling us to explore the meanings of rituals, they will help us better understand key dimensions of the interplay between these broad cultural (and often global) phenomena, and the roles of the marketplace in creating meaningful experiences for contemporary consumer-citizens.

References

Aaker, J. L., Benet-Martinez, V., & Garolera, J. (2001). Consumption symbols as carriers of culture: A study of Japanese and Spanish brand personality constructs. *Journal of Personality and Social Psychology, 81*(3), 492.

Abdulaziz, Z. (2014). *History on wheels: 5 things to know about the queen's new carriage.* Retrieved from www.today.com/news/history-wheels-5-things-know-about-queens-new-carriage-2D79756846.

Adams, W. L. (2012). *Diamond Jubilee river pageant: A thousand boats set sail in honor of Her Majesty.* Retrieved from http://content.time.com/time/specials/packages/article/0,28804,2114386_2114388_2116321,00.html?iid=sr-link1.

Atkin, D. (2004). *The Culting of Brands: When Customers Become True Believers.* New York, NY: Portfolio.

Arnould, E. J., Price, L. L., & Curasi, C. F. (1999). Ritual longing, ritual latitude: Shaping household descent. The Seventh Interdisciplinary Conference on Research in Consumption: Consumption Ritual.

Ball, J., & Barnes, D. (2017). Delight and the grateful customer: Beyond joy and surprise. *Journal of Service Theory and Practice, 27*(5), 250–269.

Balmer, J. M. T., Greyser, S. A., & Urde, M. (2006). The Crown as a corporate brand: Insights from monarchies. *Journal of Brand Management, 14*(1), 137–161.

Barnes, R., & Chapman, M. (2012). *Marketing the Queen: Brands face a Diamond Jubilee balancing act.* Retrieved from www.campaignlive.co.uk/article/1125369/marketing-queen-brands-face-diamond-jubilee-balancing-act.

BBDO: The Ritual Masters, Advertising Educational Foundation report, May 11, 2007, Retrieved from www.aef.com/on_campus/classroom/research/data/7000.

Beeman, W. O. (1993). The anthropology of theater and spectacle. *Annual Review of Anthropology, 22,* 369–393.

Belk, R. W., & Coon, G. S. (1993). Gift giving as agapic love: An alternative to the exchange paradigm based on dating experiences. *Journal of Consumer Research, 20*(3), 393–417.

Belk, R. W., & Costa, J. A. (1998). The mountain man myth: A contemporary consuming fantasy. *Journal of Consumer Research, 25*(3), 218–240.

Belk, R. W., Wallendorf, M., & Sherry, J. F., Jr. (1989). The sacred and the profane in consumer behavior: Theodicy on the odyssey. *Journal of Consumer Research, 16*(1), 1–38.

Bradford, T. W. (2009). Intergenerationally gifted asset dispositions. *Journal of Consumer Research, 36*(1), 93–111.

Bradford, T. W., & Sherry, J. F. (2013). Orchestrating rituals through retailers: An examination of gift registry. *Journal of Retailing, 89*(2), 158–175.

Bradford, T. W., & Sherry, J. F. (2015). Domesticating public space through ritual: Tailgating as vestaval. *Journal of Consumer Research, 42*(1), 130–151.

Broudehoux, A. (2007). Spectacular Beijing: The conspicuous construction of an Olympic metropolis. *Journal of Urban Affairs 29*(4), 383–399.

Cain, S. (2013). *Quiet: The power of introverts in a world that can't stop talking.* New York, NY: Broadway Books.

Cole, M. H. (1999). *The Portable Queen: Elizabeth I and the Politics of Ceremony.* Amherst, MA: University of Massachusetts Press.

Dobscha, S., & Foxman, E. (2012). Mythic agency and retail conquest. *Journal of Retailing, 88*(2), 291–307.

Epp, A. M., & Price, L. L. (2008). Family identity: A framework of identity interplay in consumption practices. *Journal of Consumer Research, 35*(1), 50–70.

Geoghegan, Tom (2011). *Royal wedding: Breakfast parties in the U.S.* Retrieved from www.bbc.com/news/world-us-canada-13232038.

Gladwell, A. (2011). *£200m to be spent' on royal wedding souvenirs.* Retrieved from www.bbc.co.uk/newsbeat/article/13157931/200m-to-be-spent-on-royal-wedding-souvenirs.

Gopaldas, A. (2014). Marketplace sentiments. *Journal of Consumer Research, 41*(4), 995–1014.

Hedges, K. (2014). *Do you have FOMO: Fear of Missing Out?* Retrieved from www.forbes.com/sites/work-in-progress/2014/03/27/do-you-have-fomo-fear-of-missing-out/#7bab33692391.

Holmes, O. (2016). *Thai king's funeral held at palace as mourners line streets of Bangkok.* Retrieved from www.theguardian.com/world/2016/oct/14/thailand-year-of-mourning-death-king-bhumibol.

Holt, D.B. (2004). *How Brands Become Icons.* Boston, MA: Harvard Business School Press.

Joy, A. (2001). Gift giving in Hong Kong and the continuum of social ties. *Journal of Consumer Research, 28*(2), 239–256.

Khazan, O. (2013). *Is the British royal family worth the money?* Retrieved from www.theatlantic.com/international/archive/2013/07/is-the-british-royal-family-worth-the-money/278052/.

Kirmani, A., (2009). The self and the brand. *Journal of Consumer Psychology, 19*(3), 271–275.

Klein, J. G., Lowrey, T. M., & Otnes, C. C. (2015). Identity-based motivations and anticipated reckoning: Contributions to gift-giving theory from an identity-stripping context. *Journal of Consumer Psychology, 25*(3), 431–448.

Kozinets, R. V. (2002). Can consumers escape the market? Emancipatory illuminations from Burning Man. *Journal of Consumer Research, 29*(1), 20–38.

Lippe-McGraw. J. (2016). *After Will and Kate's royal tour, travel interest in India has spiked.* Retrieved from www.travelandleisure.com/travel-tips/travel-trends/will-kate-boost-india-tourism.

Logan, A., Hamilton, K., & Hewer, P. (2013). Re-Fashioning Kate: The making of a celebrity princess brand. *NA-Advances in Consumer Research Volume, 41,* 378–383.

Marcoux, J. S. (2009). Escaping the gift economy. *Journal of Consumer Research, 36*(4), 671–685.

Marshall, D. A. (2002). Behavior, belonging, and belief: A theory of ritual practice. *Sociological Theory, 20*(3), 360–380.

Martin, M. H. E. (2012). *The Queen's Diamond Jubilee weekend brings £120 million cash boost to London.* Retrieved from www.standard.co.uk/news/london/the-queens-diamond-jubilee-weekend-brings-120-million-cash-boost-to-london-7819722.html.

McAlexander, J. H., & Schouten, J. W. (1998). Brandfests: Servicescapes for the cultivation of brand equity. *Servicescapes: The concept of place in contemporary markets,* 377–402.

McAlexander, J. H., Schouten, J. W., & Koenig, H. F. (2002). Building brand community. *Journal of Marketing, 66*(1), 38–54.

McCracken, G. D. (1990). *Culture and Consumption: New Approaches to the Symbolic Character of Consumer Goods and Activities.* Bloomington, IN: Indiana University Press.

Mick, D. G., Pettigrew, S., Pechmann, C. C., & Ozanne, J. L. (2012). (eds.). *Transformative Consumer Research for Personal and Collective Well-Being.* London, EN: Routledge.

Morreale, J. (2000). Sitcoms say goodbye: The cultural spectacle of Seinfeld's last episode. *Journal of Popular Film and Television, 28*(3), 108–115.

Moss, H. (2011). *Sarah Burton: Kate Middleton Wedding Dress Designer.* Retrieved from www.huffingtonpost.com/2011/04/29/sarah-burton-kate-middleton-wedding-dress_n_855299.html.

Nelissen, R. M. A., & Meijers, M. H. C. (2011). Social benefits of luxury brands as costly signals of wealth and status. *Evolution and Human Behavior, 32*(5), 343–355.

Ormsby, A. (2012) *London 2012 opening ceremony draws 900 million viewers.* Retrieved from http://uk.reuters.com/article/uk-oly-ratings-day-idUKBRE8760V820120807.

Otnes, C. C., Crosby, E., Kreuzbauer, R., & Ho, J. (2009). Tinsel, trimmings, and tensions. *Explorations in Consumer Culture Theory,* ed., John F. Sherry, Jr. and Eileen M. Fischer, London: Routledge, 171–189.

Otnes, C. C., Ilhan, B. E., & Kulkarni, A. (2012). The language of marketplace rituals: Implications for customer experience management. *Journal of Retailing, 88*(3), 367–383.

Otnes, C., Lowrey, T. M., & Kim, Y. C. (1993). Gift selection for easy and difficult recipients: A social roles interpretation. *Journal of Consumer Research, 20*(2), 229–244.

Otnes, C. C., & Maclaran, P. (2015). *Royal Fever: The British Monarchy in Consumer Culture.* Berkeley, CA: University of California Press.

Otnes, C. C., & Pleck, E. H. (2003). *Cinderella Dreams: The Allure of the Lavish Wedding.* Berkeley, CA: University of California Press.

Paharia, N., Keinan, A., Avery, J., & Schor, J. B. (2011). The underdog effect: The marketing of disadvantage and determination through brand biography. *Journal of Consumer Research, 37*(5), 775–790.

Park, C. W., Jaworski, B. J., & MacInnis, D. J. (1986). Strategic brand concept-image management. *The Journal of Marketing, 50*(4), 135–145.

Queen's Jubilee a Fiesta for Souvenir-Sellers. (2012). (AP) Retrieved from www.cbsnews.com/news/queen-elizabeth-iis-diamond-jubilee-a-fiesta-for-souvenir-sellers/.

Raynor, G. (2012). *Duchess of Cambridge's wedding dress helps raise £10 million as Buckingham Palace visitor numbers soar.* Retrieved from www.telegraph.co.uk/news/uknews/theroyalfamily/9409550/Duchess-of-Cambridges-wedding-dress-helps-raise-10-million-as-Buckingham-Palace-visitor-numbers-soar.html.

Rook, D. W. (1985). The ritual dimension of consumer behavior. *Journal of Consumer Research, 12*(3), 251–264.

Royal wedding barf bags made by graphic designer Lydia Leith. (2011). Retrieved from www.huffingtonpost.com/2011/02/16/royal-wedding-barf-bags-m_n_824304.html.

Ruth, J. A., Otnes, C. C., & Brunel, F. F. (1999). Gift receipt and the reformulation of interpersonal relationships. *Journal of Consumer Research, 25*(4), 385–402.

Schouten, J. W., & McAlexander, J. H. (1995). Subcultures of consumption: An ethnography of the new bikers. *Journal of Consumer Research, 22*(1), 43–61.5

Schwartz, R., & Halegoua, G. R. (2014). The spatial self: Location-based identity performance on social media. *New Media & Society,* 1643–1660.

Sharpe, K. (2009). *Selling the Tudor Monarchy.* New Haven, CT: Yale University Press.

Sharpe, K. (2010). *Image Wars: Promoting Kings and Commonwealths in England 1603–1660.* New Haven, CT: Yale University Press.

Sharpe, K. (2013). *Rebranding Rule: The Restoration and Revolution Monarchy 1660–1714.* New Haven, CT: Yale University Press.

Thomas, J. (2008). From people power to mass hysteria Media and popular reactions to the death of Princess Diana. *International Journal of Cultural Studies, 11*(3), 362–376.

Thomson, M. (2006). Human brands: Investigating antecedents to consumers' strong attachments to celebrities. *Journal of Marketing, 70*(3), 104–119.

Turner, V. (1975). *Dramas, Fields, and Metaphors: Symbolic Action in Human Society.* Cornell University Press, 1975.

Wallendorf, M., & Arnould, E. J. (1991). "We gather together": Consumption rituals of Thanksgiving Day. *Journal of Consumer Research, 18*(1), 13–31.

Weinberger, M. F. (2015). Dominant consumption rituals and intragroup boundary work: How non-celebrants manage conflicting relational and identity goals. *Journal of Consumer Research*, ucv020.

Weinberger, M. F., & Wallendorf, M. (2012). Intracommunity gifting at the intersection of contemporary moral and market economies. *Journal of Consumer Research*, *39*(1), 74–92.

Wilgress, L. (2016). *Picnic hampers from Queen's birthday street party go up for sale on eBay for more than £250*. Retrieved from www.telegraph.co.uk/news/2016/06/14/picnic-hampers-from-queens-birthday-street-party-go-up-for-sale/.

Wooten, D. B. (2000). Qualitative steps toward an expanded model of anxiety in gift-giving. *Journal of Consumer Research*, *27*(1), 84–95.

PART XVI

Applied Consumer Behavior

31

CONSUMER BEHAVIOR IN THE MARKETING INFORMATION ECOSYSTEM

John Wittenbraker[1] and Norbert Wirth[2]

[1]GFK, PHILADELPHIA, USA
[2]SUPERCRUNCH BY GFK, LONDON, UK

In this chapter, we...

- Illustrate the evolving development and use of marketing information in the digital era
- Provide a theoretical context and recommend a different, more human lens for thinking about and acting on marketing information
- Issue a call to action for advancements in data access and analytics, commercial marketing research and the science of consumer behavior to accelerate the wise development and sustainable use of digital marketing information.

Marketing in the Information Economy

The Rise of Marketing Technology (An Engine Driving the Growth of Digital Culture)

Marketing is undergoing a dramatic shift as both a cause and consequence of the accelerating digital transformation of our culture. Because commerce fuels the internet, marketing technology (MarTech) is an important driver of this digital transformation. The tools and platforms of this cybernetic marketing include the technology that manages digital advertising, other digital content and experience (interactive/web, apps, videos, search, and the systems that manage content), CRM and social engagement systems, eCommerce and digital sales systems and the data, analytic, and management technologies that support these activities (see Figure 31.1).

Bound up in the larger accelerating digital transformation, MarTech is growing at an exponential rate (see Figure 31.2). IDC estimates that the spending on MarTech will reach over \$32B per year by 2018, reaching a compound average growth rate so far of 12.4% (Columbus, 2015). Looking further forward, other analysts estimate that spending on marketing tech will reach \$120B by 2025 (Garg, 2016). Chiefmartech.com has been monitoring the competitive landscape of the MarTech business and finds an exponential growth with some very large

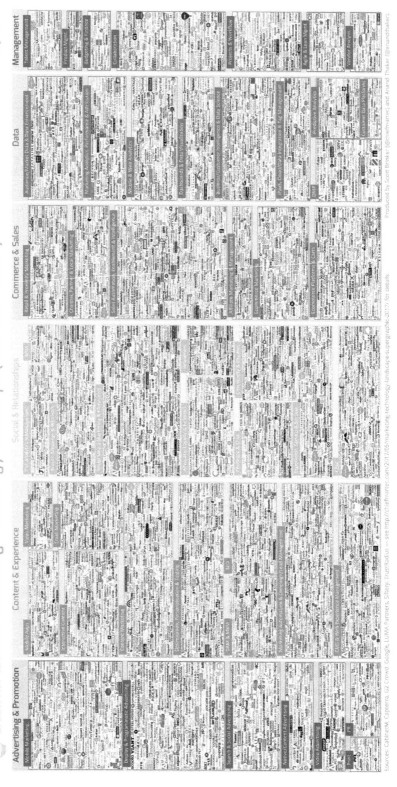

Figure 31.1 Evolution of the marketing technology landscape (Brinker, 2017)

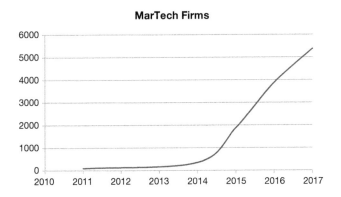

Figure 31.2 Growth curve for MarTech firms (Brinker, 2017)

players and a long tail of startups crowding the space (Brinker, 2016). Five years ago, there were around 150 firms in play, a number that has grown to over 5,000 in 2017.

Although marketing technology is rapidly growing, the effect on consumers is not always as intended. Consider the evolution of the digital advertising space, one of the largest and most active subsectors of MarTech. Although simple click-thru rates are low, the economics of digital advertising still produces a good ROI. At the same time, the aversive effects of some digital advertising, especially interstitial or pop-up ads, have been well-documented (Hong, 2014; Guadiano, Dolan, Gerrol, & McGarry, 2016). The interruption or impediment of consumers' natural experiential flow or goal-directed behavior while using the internet or a mobile device is considered a cardinal cause of advertising avoidance (Hoffman & Novak, 1996; Cho & Cheon, 2004; Edwards, Li, & Lee, 2002).

Behavioral retargeting of advertising can be also effective, but research into the collateral effects of targeting and personalization has shown that this can exacerbate already negative attitudes about digital advertising. Leave a pair of Jimmy Choo shoes in an online shopping cart and the same shoes follow you around on the internet for weeks (Helft & Tanzina, 2010). Even making a purchase online will not put an end to the annoyances of retargeting. If you shop several sites for a new backpack, retargeting cookies are dropped on your browser by each site. After you buy from one site, the others will continue to display ads for the backpack you just bought. As retargeting has evolved, it has moved beyond site-based approaches to drive conversion. And now, search-based retargeting is being used as way to market to new customers who show evidence of category interest (Hamon & Plomian, 2013).

An independent study of consumer attitudes shows that a vast majority hold negative attitudes about ad targeting and personalization (Turow, King, Hoofnagle, Bleakley, & Hennessey, 2009). There is a feeling among consumers that it's getting worse (Vizard, 2016). The winning essay for the 2016 Gold AdMap Prize calls current practice in this area "the uncanny valley of personalization," referring to a classic problem in robotics that near perfect facsimiles of humans evoke revulsion in observers that only increase as more detail is added (Fenwick, 2016).

Publishers are more sanguine, framing survey results based on a view that the issue is about balancing consumers' need for privacy with their need to see content that is personally relevant for them (Davidson, Wong, Cramer, & Weinberg, 2014). These practices can be effective. Catherine Tucker and her colleagues have explored the behavioral effects of the phenomenon in detail (Tucker, 2012). In a seminal study (Goldfarb & Tucker, 2011), using a large database of results of display ad campaigns, they found that the use of highly obtrusive ads (e.g., including audio, video, sometimes presented in an overlay on top of content) significantly increases purchase intent. They also found that ads that match (are targeted to) website content increase purchase intent. But ads that use both approaches (highly obtrusive *and* targeted) produce *lower* purchase intent than ads that use obtrusiveness or targeting alone. This negative effect was strongest for people who refused to report their income, an indication that privacy concerns may be a significant factor in inhibiting purchase intent. We speculate that ads that are both highly obtrusive and context-targeted come across as inappropriately intrusive for these privacy-minded consumers. In a follow-up study (Tucker, 2014), Tucker found in a randomized field experiment that when Facebook granted users control over personally identifiable information (managing privacy) in the middle of the experiment, the click-thru rate on personalized ads doubled compared to the period prior to granting this control.

The persistent stalking of retargeted advertising and clunky attempts at customized communication are beginning to produce a grassroots backlash against the industry. Coverage of retargeting in the mainstream press accelerated this popular anxiety (Angwion, 2010; Dunaway, 2010; Helft & Tanzina, 2010). The digital advertising industry recognized these challenges. Under pressure from the US Federal Trade Commission, leading industry trade groups banded together in 2015 to form the Digital Advertising Alliance and institute AdChoices (Digital Advertising Alliance, 2016), a button that appears on many digital ads. This button presents consumer the option to "Stop seeing this ad," and then asks to them to indicate whether it is because the ad was inappropriate, repetitive or irrelevant. Not surprisingly, this post hoc shifting of responsibility to the consumer has not been entirely effective. A recent survey from the Internet Advertising Bureau found that one in four consumers use an ad blocker on their computers and 15% block ads on their smartphones (Srugonis & Das, 2016). The incidence of ad blocking was corroborated by a survey by TRUSTe, an online privacy certifier (TRUSTe, 2016). The same survey shows that AdChoices may be effective in addressing privacy concerns. Awareness of AdChoices is at 42%, and 39% of respondents report that this program would make them feel more positive about targeted ads. But still, over half would not feel more positive, indicating that relying on consumers to self-curate display advertising will continue to be a persistent challenge.

Other subsectors of the MarTech industry also struggle to effectively capitalize on the promise of delivering a *personalized* consumer experience. Consider how Customer Relationship Management (CRM) systems fail to really understand relationships (Avery, Fournier, & Wittenbraker, 2014). CRM systems are carefully tuned to track customer contacts and purchase behavior. Combined with simple demographic data, these systems guide customer engagements and leave customers frustrated that the company is not able to meet their more complex relationship expectations. CRM algorithms that focus mainly on profitability may leave occasional customers looking to deepen their relationship feeling unappreciated and lose conversions. Customers with a more instrumental mindset are put off by attempts spawned by CRM systems to befriend them with chummy emails and chirpy pop-ups on the brand's website or app. Well executed, CRM systems should deliver compelling, personalized customer experiences that serve not just to make a sale, but to deepen that relationship over the longer run (Melvin, 2016).

Adapting for Market Success

With the rush of players, strategies and practices flooding the digital landscape, how do we know what works? How can we separate the effective tools from those that add no or only marginal value? So far, marketing technology, like most complex systems, evolves to become more and more effective each day mostly based on trial and error. Tim Harford, in his book *Adapt: Why Success Always Starts with Failure* (Harford, 2011) argues that using Darwinian principles of variation, testing, and selection are the most effective way for complex systems like economies and technologies to succeed. Practitioners in the MarTech field clearly subscribe to this approach, advising that "agile methodology is your savior" and there "is no such thing as a roadmap" (Wright, 2016). They use agile/lean practices to rapidly optimize their systems to maximize business outcomes.

Insights from Large-Scale Field Experimentation

This rapid optimization is accelerated by insights developed from field experimentation on digital behavior (Lambrecht & Tucker, 2013). Working with a large online retailer, Bleier and Eisenbiess (2015) found that personalization can influence the effectiveness of banner ads after a store visit, but the strength of this effect is highly contingent on the timing and placement of the ads. For example, highly personalized banners (showing only narrowly the specific products that were most viewed) produced more click-throughs just after the consumer left the online store, but this effect decreases rapidly and over time. But after 23 days, banners with a moderate degree of personalization (showing more broadly products from either the most viewed brand, or the most viewed category) begin to outperform the highly personalized banners. In a related lab study, the authors found that view-through (returning later to the store's website) was increased only by motive-congruent ads presented during goal-directed browsing. Motive congruence, however, does not affect consumers engaged in more free-range, experiential browsing.

Optimization Models from Clickstream Data

Other researchers and practitioners have undertaken a parallel track to develop models that can be used for the direct optimization of personalization and targeting. Early developments of "e-customization" models for content and configuration of email campaigns from clickstream data yielded significant improvements in click-throughs (Ansari & Mela, 2003). More recently, Urban, Liberali, MacDonald, and Hauser (2014) developed an automated banner morphing algorithm that applies a Bayesian updating and dynamic programming optimization to viewers' clickstream data to ensure the banner ad will maximize click-through rates, consideration, and purchase likelihood. Data scientists working at digital media agencies are in the most relevant position to work out even more dynamic applied systems. These applications use machine learning algorithms that process massive amounts of clickstream data in real-time, building thousands of models automatically to target display advertising (Dalessandro, Hook, Perlich, & Provost, 2015; Perlich & Dalessandro, 2014).

Where does the understanding and insight about *consumer behavior* contribute in this rapidly evolving, almost twitching system? Technologists recognize that the "human" must be at the center of the system, but the human is most often represented only by financial metrics (market share, share of wallet, and sometimes, lifetime value), or by discrete behaviors (trial, repeat, loyalty).

But, in practice there is often a systematic bias in the measures used by MarTech systems, extending the insight often attributed to Peter Drucker: what is easy to measure, is more likely to be managed (Bredenberg, 2012; Zak, 2013). Short-term measures like page views and click-through rates are the most accessible metrics and hence, the systems are often tuned to optimize them without regard to unintended consequences that could also impact the longer-term behavioral and financial outcomes. So, we have short-term, post hoc fixes like AdChoices that put the onus on the consumer to curate their own advertising.

Brands and marketers struggle to keep up with the exponential growth of this technology (Wright, 2016). And this struggle extends to the scientific study of consumer behavior. Part of this challenge is rooted in a fundamental difference in perspective on the "human." While both technologists and marketers agree about the outcome metrics, their approaches to optimizing the system to deliver those outcomes differ. Technologists tend to focus on information and data, reducing the complex to smaller, manageable bits. But humans focus on meaning, the assembly of these bits into more complex wholes that comprise their experience and guide their behavior. In the quest to leverage actionable information and data, algorithms treat context as noise and seek to control it or strip it away. The problem is that in the human experience of meaning, context is everything.

Marketing in the Information Ecosystem

So how should we reframe marketing and marketing technology to address this information/ meaning dilemma to make our technology more sustainably effective? Consumer behavior is influenced by a complex system of interactions among consumers, between consumers and products, brands and channels, all of which comprise consumer experience. Consumers process this experience by making meaning of this complex system of interactions, which guides their behavior over time in the system. By using only a short-term economic lens to understand and influence consumer behavior, we will fall short of producing a sustainable marketing enterprise.

Consumer Behavior in the Context of Information Ecology

In the face of the growing speed and complexity brought on by the acceleration of digital technology and the availability of more and more data on individual consumers, we suggest that a lens that considers the broader *information ecosystem* might inform a marketing enterprise that better serves both consumers and marketers. In his article "Information Ecology – a Viewpoint", Alexei Eryomin defines information ecology as the science concerned with the influence of information on systems:

> Information ecology is the science that studies the laws governing the influence of information:
>
> • on the formation and functioning of bio-systems, including that of individuals, human communities and humanity in general;
> • on the health and psychological, physical and social well-being of the human being; and
> • which undertakes to develop methodologies to improve the information environment.
>
> *(Eryomin, 1998)*

In this conception, the information economy or market is one example of a "bio-system" as it reflects a particular aspect of human communities. Balancing this, information ecology also focuses on the health and well-being of the human being. And finally, it does both in a way that improves the information environment, thereby making it self-sustaining.

Taken together, this reflects the concept of self-reference, or autopoiesis (self-generation) that the German sociologist Niklas Luhmann describes in *Social Systems* (Luhmann, 1984). The information ecosystem is part of what Luhmann calls the social system, where marketing is experienced as a form of communication, comprising utterance, information and understanding (Luhmann, 2013). The growth of digital culture adds a new twist to Eryomin's conception because individuals and communities are not only the recipients of communications and information, but also the producers of information. Consumers and marketers are becoming much more active, but not always well-tuned participants in the information ecosystem. Currently, the data, information technology and communications and influence methods available to marketers are in a developmental, "high variance" state. New technology and software is emerging and evolving at a rapid rate with solutions like programmatic advertising and chatbot customer engagement significantly disrupting the world of marketing. And what gets lost along the way is the human.

The concept of marketing information ecology suggests that consumers and marketing, with all its constituent components and stakeholders, are inhabitants of one ecosystem. The early days of marketing couldn't be portrayed in this way, since marketing had very limited knowledge about the individual consumers it would reach with a specific activity. Consequently, marketing information could only target average consumer segments. A print campaign could for example target the readers of a specific magazine or a TV ad the viewers of a specific channel at a given time. For the individual consumers, this information was noise that had to be interpreted.

In the digital environment, this has changed dramatically. Consumers leave traces about websites they've visited, about products purchased, content they've engaged with, and so on. All this information forms a growing repository of profile data, available in real-time to optimize marketing activities. Although there are legal restrictions regarding what data can be stored or used, regarding where and when real personal information can be processed, the amount of knowledge linked to cookies and advertiser IDs is unparalleled.

So technically, marketing information can be individualized to a degree (reflecting enough context) that should make it meaningful to the individual consumer. This enables marketers to interact with consumers on a level that goes far beyond noise – they can provide meaningful information and action opportunities at the individual level. This represents an enormous opportunity but at the same time calls for responsible use of the new possibilities. If the marketing information ecosystem can't be organized in a sustainable way, there is a significant risk of stakeholders opting out. If the fact that consumer profiles are getting richer and richer can't be leveraged to the consumers' benefit, if they don't have the option to give or withdraw permission regarding how their data is being used, if they can't actively express interests, then the sustainability of the ecosystem is at risk.

In its current state the system can't be described as sustainable. Targeting and retargeting often causes frustration or concerns and consumers find it suspicious to be exposed to ads that obviously relate to their recent behavior or demographic profile, but not in a positively stimulating way. Who wants to see an ad for the very product they just purchased a minute ago?

The Way Forward

There is significant opportunity here, but also significant risk. We are at a turning point. We need to close the gap between markets and brands and the marketing technology they use. Will the marketing enterprise keep pace with the digital reality and make positive contributions to the information ecosystem and social system at large? Or will the marketing enterprise be too slow to improve consumer experiences or too persistent in sub-optimizing to narrow, short-term metrics of success and attenuate the sustainability of the ecosystem?

A focus on the experience of the consumer is the key. To be a sustainable positive force, marketing in the digital age must better manage communication, focusing not only on what Luhmann calls utterance and information, but also on understanding. Marketing actions must reflect the context of the individual consumer so that they convey meaning that will extend the effects of that experience beyond each episodic action or point of contact.

We see three areas where the business, technology and academic communities can help formulate a more sustainable information ecosystem for marketing and consumer experience.

Better Data and Analytics

The first area of opportunity is to find ways to get better consumer data and smarter technologies for understanding and acting on it. The methods we use to capture consumer data must improve. It's not just that we need more data, but we need the kind of data that can help us more effectively account for the context of individual consumers in the touchpoints and marketing actions that are taken with them. Concerns about privacy, exacerbated by fairly common experiences of bad uses of consumer data make consumers reluctant to allow access to more or better data. Marketing practitioners need to innovate around the value exchanges they use to get these data. Amazon passively harvests its customers' shopping and purchase behavior to make recommendations. But even with its industry-leading recommendation engine, Amazon found the need to acquire GoodReads, a social cataloging service that allows readers to register and rate the books they read, share with friends and get customized recommendations. By fostering the development and return of social capital for better consumer context data, Amazon is in a position to provide even more relevant content marketing to drive traffic on its platforms.

Getting better data is not enough – we need better technology for processing and acting on those data. Deep learning algorithms are showing great promise as intelligent agents for producing individual behavior that is complex and nuanced, based on contextual data (Yakob & Sirhan, 2016). Companies that produce or manage digital goods and services like Spotify, Amazon, Netflix and Google have been at the forefront of this development. Marketing technology providers are beginning to take advantage of deep learning algorithms, adding them to their software stacks and engineering in ways to improve the quality of their classifiers and downstream action engines.

Better Commercial Marketing Research

The marketing research industry has been observing, monitoring, analyzing and interpreting consumer behavior for decades. The industry has changed substantially over time, enabled by new data sources and by new scientific approaches that allowed market researchers to analyze consumers' behavior more rigorously. Now, it's a $43 billion business worldwide, but the size of the industry is leveling off. At the same time, the spend on marketing technology will soon match marketing research and is projected to grow to $120 billion by 2025 (Columbus, 2015). How can marketing research transform itself to better contribute to the future sustainability of the marketing information ecosystem?

Since the early 1900s when Charles Coolidge Parlin conducted the first studies of what he called "commercial research," marketing research has been engaged in the "systematic gathering and interpretation of information about individuals or organizations using the statistical and analytical methods and techniques of the applied social sciences to gain insight or support decision making." (ICC/ESOMAR, 2008). For much of its history, marketing research has used *active* methods: interviews, ethnographic studies, focus groups, surveys, and consumer panels all involve the active engagement of consumers in the research process. Leveraging the quantitative and qualitative methodologies of social science, marketing researchers have been able to provide marketers and brands with not just information, but deeper, meaning-based insight into the causes and effects of products and marketing actions. This is valuable, but not at all scalable in its raw form for use by marketing technology.

But from the beginning, Parlin also employed *passive* methods. In his very first study conducted for the Campbell Soup Company, Parlin counted Campbell soup cans left in the trash in various neighborhoods of Philadelphia to better understand the target market for the product (Boone & Kurtz, 2008). He used the results to convince senior management that Campbell soup was being consumed not so much in high income households who were thought to be better able to pay for convenience, but rather by working class households who did not have servants to cook for them.

Use of passive methods in marketing research continued, mainly using observational or ethnographic research techniques. With the advent of measurement technology, passive measurement has grown and the amount of data collected has exploded. TV audience meters are an early example of this, where measurement devices are being installed in people's homes to capture the exact viewing behavior of all household members. The data revolution in marketing research began with these technologies as these systems provide granular data on minute-to-minute media consumption augmented with demographic profile data.

If we take this concept into a truly digital environment, the measurement technology changes from hardware to software, the number of potential stimuli grows radically, the concept of broadcasting schedules gets replaced by asynchronous and partially individualized, often dynamic content and the complexity of possible behavior patterns to be observed becomes boundless.

Marketing research, aiming to capture consumer behavior in a digital, multi-device environment calls for passive measurement technology that can be deployed to all forms of devices, to monitor how people behave in this non-physical world. Alternatively, the data are captured on a network or server level. Cookie technology, browser add-ons, metering software, and proxy server based approaches evolved in sync with the internet growing into the marketing "Eldorado" it is today. Advertisers need to understand how their marketing activities impact consumer behavior and market researchers need to sharpen their tools to provide this information.

Mobile is "just" the next evolutionary step. Mobile devices connect the digital and the physical world again – and marketers are starting to realize this. These devices give people access to digital content, and thus marketing stimuli. At the same time, they allow people to navigate the physical world and provide information about geo location, and with a little technical twist, even micro geo or indoor location. And even more interesting is the fact that mobile devices communicate with other devices and sensors via various protocols. All this provides a vast amount of data, which leads us to another significant transformation the market research industry is undergoing – maybe the most radical one in its history.

Marketing research will continue to be in demand – the need for context rich, clearly defined data, generated for a specific purpose, with known qualities and error margins will not go away. CMOs and brand teams will continue to need data-driven insights that inform marketing strategy and decisions. But there is a new use for context rich marketing research data emerging. And that is to serve as a reference layer to connect and enrich digital data from other sources, data that have often been produced as a by-product, in extremely large quantities. Market researchers today find themselves at the intersection of data from multiple sources, capturing different aspects of consumer behavior in the marketing information ecosystem.

Here lies an opportunity for significant contribution to the information ecosystem from marketing research. Using complex imputation, data fusion, and deep learning algorithms, marketing research has the unique capability to contribute the kind of rich, individualized context data that can imbue a marketing action with understanding and produce a more meaningful, relevant experience for the consumer.

Better Consumer Behavior Science

So far, practitioners have been on the defensive, lagging behind the rapid expansion of marketing technology. Practitioners are not the only stakeholders who have a responsibility to reformulate marketing through the lens of information ecology. Consumer behavior science also has significant contributions to make. Research and theory in the discipline is often at the forefront of a more consumer-centric view of the marketing enterprise (Rust, Moorman, & Bhalla, 2010), but the focus of consumer behavior science is only beginning to explore the deeper effects of cybernetic marketing on the consumer beyond click-throughs and view-throughs. Consumer behavior research is beginning to show how brand interacts with targeting and personalization to influence behavior (Anand & Shachar, 2009; Bleier & Eisenbiess, 2015; Summers, Smith, & Reczek, 2016).

More research like this is needed to understand how consumers interact with and respond to marketing technology. What is the longer-term impact on attitudes and behavior regarding the brand? How might marketing technology be used to deepen brand relationships and make them more sustainable over time? How might this affect consumer well-being, as well as sustainability of the marketing information ecosystem?

By improving our understanding of the dynamics of marketing automation on consumer behavior, research in the discipline can help marketing technology produce better consumer experiences. It can also serve as a foundation for innovation in the area that matches the inspiration provided by technological advances with inspiration in advances in understanding consumer experience in cybernetic contexts.

References

Anand, B. N., & Shachar, R. (2009). Targeted advertising as signal. *Quantitative Market Economics*, 7(3), 237–266.

Angwion, J. (2010, July 30). The Web's New Gold Mine: Your Secrets. *The Wall Street Journal*.

Ansari, A., & Mela, C. (2003). E-customization. *Journal of Marketing Research*, 4(2), 131–145.

Avery, J., Fournier, S., & Wittenbraker, J. (2014, July-August). Unlock the mysteries of your customer relationships. *Harvard Business Review*, 92(7–8), 72–81.

Bleier, A., & Eisenbiess, M. (2015). Personalized online advertising effectiveness: The interplay of what, when, and where. *Marketing Science*, 35(5), 669–688.

Bleier, A., & Eisenbiess, M. (2015). The importance of trust for personalized online advertising. *Journal of Retailing*, 91(3), 390–409.

Boone, L., & Kurtz, L. (2008). *Contemporary Marketing 2009 Update*. Mason, OH: Cengage Learning.

Bredenberg, A. (2012, December 2). *Who said, "What gets measured gets managed"?* Retrieved September 22, 2016, from A Thinking Person, a.k.a. Cogit8R: https://athinkingperson.com/2012/12/02/who-said-what-gets-measured-gets-managed/.

Brinker, S. (2016, March 21). *Marketing Technology Landscape Supergraphic (2016)*. Retrieved September 23, 2016, from chiefmartec.com: http://chiefmartec.com/2016/03/marketing-technology-landscape-supergraphic-2016/.

Brinker, S. (2017, May 10). *Marketing Technology Landscape Supergraphic (2017): Martech 5000*. Retrieved June 22, 2017, from http://chiefmartec.com/: http://chiefmartec.com/2017/05/marketing-techniology-landscape-supergraphic-2017/.

Cho, C.-H., & Cheon, H. J. (2004). Why do people avoid advertising on the internet? *Journal of Advertising*, 33(4), 89–97.

Columbus, L. (2015, January 15). *IDC Predicts CMOs Will Drive $32.3B In Marketing Technology Spending By 2018*. Retrieved August 1, 2016, from Forbes.com: www.forbes.com/sites/louiscolumbus/2015/01/17/idc-predicts-cmos-will-drive-32-3b-in-marketing-technology-spending-by-2018/#460d5d8d5bd9

Dalessandro, B., Hook, R., Perlich, C., & Provost, F. (2015). Evaluating and optimizing online advertising: Forget the click, but there are also good proxies. *Big Data*, 3(2), 90–102.

Davidson, J., Wong, E., Cramer, H., & Weinberg, L. (2014, May). *The balancing act: Getting personalization right*. Retrieved from yahoo.com: https://yahooadvertising.tumblr.com/post/97766688710/the-balancing-act-getting-personalization-right.

Digital Advertising Alliance. (2016, July 15). Retrieved from http://youradchoices.com/.

Dunaway, G. (2010, September 3). *What's So Creepy About Retargeting?* Retrieved from Adotas: www.adotas.com/2010/09/what-so-creepy-about-retargeting/.

Edwards, S. M., Li, H., & Lee, J.-H. (2002). Forced exposure and psychological reactance: Antecedents and consequences of the perceived intrusiveness of pop-up ads. *Journal of Advertising*, 31(3), 83095.

Eryomin, A. L. (1998). Information ecology - a viewpoint. *International Journal of Environmental Studies. Vol. 54*, 54(3–4), 241–253.

Fenwick, O. (2016). The uncanny valley of personalization. *Admap*.

Garg, A. (2016, July 15). *Martech and the decade of the CMO*. Retrieved August 1, 2016, from foundation-capital.com: https://foundationcapital.com/decadeofthecmo.

Goldfarb, A., & Tucker, C. (2011). Online display advertising: Targeting and obtruseiveness. *Marketing Science*, 20(3), 389–404.

Guadiano, P., Dolan, P., Gerrol, S., & McGarry, R. (2016). How annoyance impacts ad performance. *ARF Experiential Learning, Audience Measurement*. New York: Advertising Research Foundation.

Hamon, D., & Plomian, D. (2013, Q2). *Chango Retargeting Barometer*. Retrieved from Chango: www.scribd.com/document/278743505/Retargeting-Barometer-2013.

Harford, T. (2011). *Adapt: Why Success Always Starts with Failure*. New York: Farrar, Straus and Giroux.

Helft, M., & Tanzina, V. (2010, August 29). Retargeting Ads Follow Surfers to Other Sites. *The New York Times*.

Hoffman, D. L., & Novak, T. P. (1996). Marketing in hypermedia computer-mediated environments: Conceptual foundations. *Journal of Marketing*, 60(3), 50–68.

Hong, Y.-H. (2014, November). Which is more annoying? Comparing the cognitive, affective and conative effects of button ads and pop-up ads. *Journal of Business and Economics*, 5(11), 2074–2084.

ICC/ESOMAR. (2008). ICC/ESOMAR International Code on Market and Social Research. Retrieved July 31, 2016, from www.esomar.org.

Lambrecht, A., & Tucker, C. (2013). When does retargeting work? Information specificity in online advertising. *Journal of Marketing Research*, 50(5), 561–576.

Luhmann, N. (1984). *Soziale Systeme: Grundriß einer allgemeinen Theorie*. Frankfurt: Suhrkamp.

Luhmann, N. (2013). *Introduction to Systems Theory*. Malden, MA: Polity Press.

Melvin, E. (2016). Stop selling and start building. *Admap*.

Perlich, C., & Dalessandro, B. (2014). Machine learning for targeted display advertising: Transfer learning in action. *Machine Learning*, 95(1), 103–127.

Rust, R. T., Moorman, C., & Bhalla, G. (2010, January-February). Rethinking marketing. *Harvard Business Review*, 88(1–2), 94–101.

Srugonis, K., & Das, S. (2016, June). Retrieved from IAB: www.iab.com/wp-content/uploads/2016/07/IAB-Ad-Blocking-2016-Who-Blocks-Ads-Why-and-How-to-Win-Them-Back_2016.pdf.

Summers, C. A., Smith, R. W., & Reczek, R. W. (2016). An audience of one: Behaviorally targeted ads as implied social labels. *Journal of Consumer Research*, 43(1), 156–178.

TRUSTe. (2016, May 9). *Research Finds DAA Adchoices Icon Increases Favorability Toward Targeted Ads and Awareness has Risen to 42%*. Retrieved from truste.com: www.truste.com/about-truste/press-room/research-finds-daa-adchoices-icon-increases-favorability-toward-targeted-ads-awareness-risen-42/.

Tucker, C. (2012). The economics of advertising and privacy. *International Journal of Industrial Organization*, 30(3), 326–329.

Tucker, C. (2014). Social networks, personalized advertising and privacy controls. *Journal of Marketing Research*, 51(5), 546–562.

Turow, J., King, J., Hoofnagle, C. J., Bleakley, A., & Hennessey, M. (2009). *Americans reject tailored advertising and the three activities that enable it*. Retrieved from The New York Times: www.nytimes.com/packages/pdf/business/20090929-Tailored_Advertising.pdf.

Urban, G. L., Liberali, G., MacDonald, E., & Hauser, J. R. (2014). Morphing banner advertising. *Marketing Science*, 33(1), 27–46.

Vizard, S. (2016, September 14). Is digital advertising getting worse? UK consumers seem to think so. Retrieved from *Marketing Week:* www.marketingweek.com/2016/09/14/isdigitaladvertisinggetting worseukconsumersthinkso/.

Wright, T. (2016, May). Marketing technology growth – Piercing through the chaos. Inc. Retrieved from www.inc.com/travis-wright/marketing-technology-growth-piercing-through-the-chaos.html (accessed May 2017).

Yakob, R., & Sirhan, H. (2016). How personalisation needs to have its Ford moment. *Admap*.

Zak, P. (2013, July 4). *Measurement myopia*. Retrieved September 22, 2016, from Drucker Institute: www.druckerinstitute.com/2013/07/measurement-myopia/.

32

EMERGING TRENDS FOR CONSUMER BEHAVIOR PRACTITIONERS

Jim Multari

COMCAST CORPORATION, PHILADELPHIA, PA, USA

Data, Design, Decisions: A Marketer's Guide for Navigating the Intersection of Big Data and Market Research

In today's fast-paced, mobile, and always-on customer-centric world, marketers have more data at their disposal than ever before to help understand consumer behavior and trends while also informing critical business decisions. This stream of data can often times feel unending and overwhelming.

I've spent much of my ten years at Comcast, first with NBCUniversal and now within the XFINITY marketing and sales organization, working with project teams tasked with transforming vast amounts of data into an ongoing strategic storyline, providing business leaders with relevant and timely insights that drive results.

Today, our organization has entire teams dedicated to business intelligence; the company has rallied behind data driven decisions and making data actionable for everyone across the company.

A marketer's challenge is how to make sense of it all. As Stephen Few has said, "numbers have an important story to tell. They rely on you to give them a clear and convincing voice."

Take, for example, the many key performance indicators (KPIs) needed to run an effective sales and marketing organization:

- Media and media mix: effective advertising and branding should generate brand awareness and sales leads. In addition, understanding how your competition's media spend and marketing activities are impacting your performance is vital.
- Demand generation: are prospects and customers reaching out to you to do business? Are the phones ringing, are your digital portals generating traffic, are consumers coming into your retail stores, and so on?
- Conversion: how well are your various sales channels doing with converting leads into customers?
- Understanding your customers: what types of customers and consumer segments are doing business with the enterprise? Demographic profiles, propensity modeling and segmentation schemes are but a few of the critical inputs that need to be tracked.

- Base Analysis: How are customers interacting with your products or services? Are they upgrading to an additional line of business or subscribing to a premium service? How much are your customers using your products?
- Retention: how well is the enterprise doing at keeping its customers?
- Other critical market factors: inputs such as market share trends, economic indicators or even the weather can have an impact on business.

Phew. These examples contain hundreds of different data points to digest; many of which are often stored or generated using a variety of tools and sources. How can a marketer harness this information to make decisions? Does data alone really tell the entire consumer story? Where does market research fit in?

The Evolution of "Big Data"

Big data. I love big data. It's a term that's been around industry for a while now but one that I try to avoid. As we've demonstrated earlier, we already know we have a lot of data. Its "big," it's powerful, there's so much you can do with it. But the question remains: how do you truly harness it?

"Let's Build a Dashboard"

The first significant trend in big data's evolution was visualization. Many applications exist today that enable analysts to ingest large data sets (from tools like Excel, SAS, massive sources that sit on an SQL server, etc.) and create compelling analyses that graphically visualize and simply illustrate your data's main points. It's the age of the Infographic, and that can be a very good thing. "By visualizing information, we turn it into a landscape that you can explore with your eyes, sort of an information map," David McCandless has said. "And when you're lost in information, an information map is kind of useful."

There's nothing wrong with a well-done dashboard, however the issue today is there are simply too many dashboards. And dashboards all too often are less visual, more spreadsheet, making it difficult to tease out the right story. Today's business leaders receive multiple dashboards per day via e-mail, almost always tracking a particular piece of the business but rarely providing the full picture. These multiple points of communication have in some ways made it even more difficult for leaders to derive meaning, not easier. The big data may look nice but because dashboards are frequently independent of each other, getting a full enterprise view of performance remains challenging.

The 4 Ds of Insightful Data Design

Like an architect building a new skyscraper, we need a design plan to get from data to insights faster and easier. A simplified way of thinking about this is what I like to call the 4 Ds of Insightful Data Design (Figure 32.1).

Data

Big data, we've got it. Check. Yet there are still a few more critical things to think about here. Process automation is a must. Sources need to be connected and load times have to be minimized. A busy marketer can't spend their day manually uploading different data into different spreadsheets. It's just not sustainable.

Data by design

The 4 D's of insightful data design:

Figure 32.1   Data by design: The 4 Ds of insightful data design

A quality assurance mechanism is required to make sure your data loads are accurate and that there aren't any issues. You're going to need help here; if your organization doesn't have a business intelligence unit, talk to your information technology team. Many of the same processes used to manage hardware and other complex technical infrastructures can often be helpful with managing your data.

Detection

There are ways of making your data work for you so that significant trends or changes are spotted immediately, without manual analysis or investigation. Predictive modeling and other sophisticated approaches can help forecast what may happen in the future based on historical trends and market factors, but what if you simply want to know what's happening today? Think back to the list of marketing inputs we listed earlier; if foot traffic to a particular retail location has decreased 20% over the last week, use technology to automatically tell you about it. Excel or other widely available (and often free) tools give you the ability to set these thresholds to save time. Here's where a dashboard, data visualization or map can be quite effective; build an environment that's easy to use while also visually appealing. These sorts of interfaces are perfect for your marketing effectiveness war room, allowing teams to quickly spot changes, address issues, and celebrate wins.

Diagnosis

Here's another limitation to dashboards: you can't fit everything into one dashboard. Inevitably, your dashboard is going to spark questions that will require a deeper analysis; it's unavoidable and actually healthy for collaborative interaction in most instances. But how do you go back into your big data to answer these questions? If you have to rely on SQL coding experts to query what you need, you lose time and potentially miss out on an important business trend. A simple diagnosis tool is needed to go deeper into your data than your dashboard. Excel's slicer function and Tableau enable analysts to easily create *ad hoc* analyses from your source data in an easy to use drag and drop or pivot environment. Keep it simple so that when the questions come, you can get to the "why," quickly.

Dissemination

As we've demonstrated, true insights are more than just Excel spreadsheets and more than a dashboard. To bring it all together, you need a storytelling platform or information portal that breaks through. Consider the ten-second rule: you have less than 10 seconds to capture a recipient's attention via e-mail. If you can't get to the answer fast, you've lost them. Instead of sending an Excel spreadsheet or even a dashboard in a link or an attachment, send an alert that provides a compelling headline and the 3–5 key points that you want your business partners to know. Your message should be well designed and thought provoking. Include hyperlinks back to your portal where you can provide more detail and store your larger datasets or PowerPoint slides, making it convenient for a senior leader to get more detail later if they want it.

The 4 Ds can help with flipping the data dynamic in industry today. Instead of leading with your data, lead with the storyline. Why is this insight important for your leadership team to know? If they ask follow up questions, you've built detection tools that allow you to do additional investigation quickly. And you've connected your data sources and automated loads to save time. It's a winning formula.

The 4 Ds in Action

Consider the hypothetical scenario below that puts the 4 Ds to the test:

Dan is a marketing director in Comcast's customer acquisition unit. He's been tasked with tracking the impact of a new marketing campaign and promotional offer for each of the markets his campaign is targeting. Dan has multiple sources of data that can help tell the story and wants to bring things together into a simple summary to help senior leadership stay abreast of progress.

Data

Dan has multiple sources of information at his disposal, all of which are reported at a DMA level (DMA stands for designated market area, a Nielsen classification scheme that breaks the US into 210 different market segments; most media bought and sold in the US today is often done by DMA), total media spend, total customers acquired, connects by sales channel, market share and demographic characteristics.

Detection

Dan wants to know when his acquired units increase by 10% versus the prior day as well as monitor his sales channel activity daily to spot any significant changes that may be attributable to his marketing campaign. Dan works with his business intelligence partner, mapping out the different data points he's after and creating a wireframe of what he'd like his end product to look like. Business Intelligence takes Dan's feedback and quickly builds an automated tool that ingests Dan's different feeds and provides a dashboard that reports out on progress and alerts Dan when trends have moved in either a positive or negative direction.

Diagnosis

Dan knows that if he issues his new dashboard to senior leaders that they will come back with questions. Instead of relying on business intelligence for additional manual runs of analyses, Dan asks if the source data feeding his dashboard can be made available in Excel and set up using slicers, which give Dan the ability to dig deeper in a drag and drop environment that he is comfortable with.

Dissemination

Dan is ready to provide his leadership with reoccurring updates of progress. Instead of sending the team a large file of data or a complex dashboard, Dan takes his findings and packages them up in a narrative format and sends his e-mail with a compelling headline (i.e., "Latest Acquisition Campaign Generating Positive Results") and provides a link to the larger dashboard in case the team wants to dig deeper.

Dan feels really good about his analysis and storyline and thinks the campaign is making a difference for the business. The next day, Dan receives a note back from the head of acquisition marketing. The analysis that Dan crafted is useful but there are questions about what exactly is driving more customers to notice the campaign and take action. Dan has shown that his campaign is moving the needle but needs to dig deeper than the data to prove why.

What About Market Research?

So, with all this data, is there still room in a marketer's toolkit for market research?

The answer today, more than ever, is a resounding yes. While big data gets much of the attention it's more important than ever before to leverage both analytics and consumer insights to generate a true 360-degree view of consumer behavior.

At Comcast, we have a best in class Enterprise Business Intelligence (EBI) team. EBI brings together a variety of data sources from across the organization (utilizing many of the practices outlined in the previous section) to provide business units with a real time empirical view. But what happens when you want to know *why* a certain set of customers purchases a particular line of business or decides to upgrade service, or take a particular premium package? Your quantitative lens is sharp but you still need to get to the rational and emotional underpinnings that drive consumer behavior and decision making. Research is still required.

XFINITY Insights Community

One way Comcast is getting to the why is via our XFINITY Insights Community (XIC). The XIC is a representative panel of thousands of XFINITY customers and product users that have opted in to provide regular feedback about their customer experience. When a panelist opts in to participate, they select the topics that they are most interested in. This allows surveys to be targeted, which provides faster and more actionable results for business units and a more enjoyable feedback experience for XFINITY customers.

Panelists are incentivized via a points system and the XIC team diligently ensures the quality of the panel. The XIC is used by teams across the organization, including marketing and sales, product development, customer experience, and marketing/communications teams.

Back to Dan

Remember Dan from our previous section? He quickly realizes that he needs a deeper assessment to get at the whys of his campaign. He decides to partner with the XIC team to survey customers in the markets where his campaign ran. The XIC is large enough so that Dan can conduct analyses at an individual market level. Dan works with the XIC team to craft a survey that asks if customers saw the campaign, what they remembered about it and if it was a motivating reason why they decided to take action. Because the XIC also allows for images and video, Dan is able to show elements of his campaign to get an aided assessment of awareness and impact on action.

After a few days in field, Dan's XIC survey starts to bear fruit: he learns that while only a portion of customers saw the campaign, those that recalled seeing the digital elements were most likely to have pursued additional information as well as connected service. Customers also provided valuable feedback on the different campaign elements, giving Dan an opportunity to modify his digital and social campaign elements to further maximize their effectiveness.

Dan packages his findings (via his insights dissemination portal of course!) and gets back to marketing leadership with his perspective. This additional analytical depth hits the mark and gives leadership a holistic sense for the campaign's progress and sparks many conversations about new ideas for future initiatives.

Final Thoughts

As Dan has shown, operating effectively within a data driven culture requires good strategic perspective, technical know-how and the ability to partner across multiple groups to get things done.

A recent article by Bill Petti in my favorite baseball blog, "The Hardball Times" (www. hardballtimes.com/how-teams-can-get-the-most-out-of-analytics/), tells the story of the Pittsburgh Pirates, a team that combined good old fashioned scouting (qualitative) with deep data analytics and modeling (quantitative), to turn the franchise from a perennial loser to a regular competitor for division championships and postseason play. The article lists four must-have criteria for any data driven culture, regardless of industry:

1   The right metrics and insights: think back to our marketing KPIs. Petti suggests that metrics need to be predictive, reliable, and easily used by "all sorts of actors and decision-makers."
2   The right data and systems: Petti perfectly summarizes the 4 Ds:

> for organizations to fully apply their data driven insights, they must have the right infrastructure in place. The right metrics are based on "good" data (i.e. high fidelity, low latency, relevant data) and analysis is aided by efficient systems that make it easy to collect, merge, analyze and share the data and resulting insights. Usefulness in the field is based on systems that allow for the efficient organization, processing and timely reporting of relevant metrics. How data and insights are consumed is an area ripe for failure: as in advertising, the best messaging is meaningless if people don't see it or can't easily consume it.

3   The right people: Petti advocates for the right talent who appreciate data, are willing to learn, and are strategic.
4   Right culture: The enterprise, top to bottom, has to believe in and support the use of analytics and insights in every aspect of its operations.

At Comcast, we're working through these issues every day and are constantly fine tuning our data and insights recipe. Our key ingredients include the use of technology, a dash of smart design mixed with innovative research methods, all in an effort to fully understand consumer behavior.

References

Few, Stephen (2009). Perceptual Edge: Visual Business Intelligence Newsletter – *Statistical Narrative: Telling Stories with Numbers*. Retrieved from www.perceptualedge.com/articles/visual_business_intelligence/statistical_narrative.pdf

McCandless, David (2010). *The Beauty of Data Visualization – TED Talk*. Retrieved from www.ted.com/talks/david_mccandless_the_beauty_of_data_visualization/transcript?language=en

Petti, Bill – Hardball Times (2015). *How Teams Can Get the Most Out of Analytics*. Retrieved from www.hardballtimes.com/how-teams-can-get-the-most-out-of-analytics/

INDEX

Interra Credit Union 416–418
intersectionality 153–155, 451–452, 454
intrinsic goals 29–30
intrusions in narrative constructions 106
involvement 269

Kahneman, D. 106
Kaplan, Max 6
Kasser, T. 22, 23
key performance indicators 517, 521–522
kinship 405–407, 412
Kira, Alexander 7

labelling 72–74, 77
language *see* brand names; marketing language
learning, shopping as 50–51
LEGO Ideas: appropriation and response 437;
    cocreation and 422–424; practices 427–434;
    research methods 426–427; rules and purpose
    of platform 434–437; conclusions 438–439
Levy, Sidney J., works of 8–9
Levy's Academic Tree 9–11
Lewis, O., *Five families* 7
life cycle, values and 171
life satisfaction 28
List of Values (LOV) 166–167, 170–171
lists 103
literacy 135
local processing 110
Loftus, E. F. 106
logos 229–230
loneliness 29, 44, 91
luxury consumption: introduction 5, 380–381;
    agency and 388; compensatory consumption
    390–391; counterfeit goods 390; in
    democratized marketplace 383–384; future
    research 392–393; global studies 391–392;
    inconspicuous consumption 390; over time
    381–383; segmentation 384–388; social status
    388–391
lying: introduction 118–119; behavior 119;
    challenges of studying 122–124; consequences
    of 120; consumer to consumer 121–122;
    consumer to marketers 119–121; justifications
    for 120; manipulations 123–124; motivations
    122–123; by omission 121; relationships and
    124–125; social influences and 125–126;
    future directions 124–126

makeup 141
marginalized identities 153–155
market research 516–517, 525
Market Research Society (MRS) 350
marketability 436–437
marketing: future requirements 515–518;
    information ecosystem 514–515; rituals and
    490; technology 509–514

marketing language: bilingualism 271; contextual
    factors and 269–270; cross-modal sensory
    interactions 268–269; devices 263–268; future
    research and 272; personality traits and
    270–271; *see also* brand names
marketing technology: optimization of 512–514;
    rise of 509–512
marketplaces: access to 461–462; gender and
    338–341
Marx, Karl 446
masculinities: consumption and 338–341; research
    on 152–153; self-concept and 148
Maslow, A. 165, 167
material values scale 23, 32
materialism: introduction 21; antecedents 24–28;
    anthropomorphized products 87; class and
    449–450; conceptualizations 22–24;
    consequences 28–30, 31; critiques and further
    research 28–30; impoverished children
    461–462
McClelland, D.C. 7
McGuire, William J. 40–42
meaning: consumption and 134; sense of 27,
    41–42; through rejected choices 135
media: class and 449–450; materialism and 25–26;
    richness of 366
memory 102, 108–109
mental representations: conceptualizations
    100–102; declarative knowledge 102–107;
    procedural knowledge 107–113
merchandise 295
metaphor 263–264
metrics 513–514, 526
mimicry 88
mindsets 109
mobile devices: advertising and 234; data and 517;
    impact on pricing 204–205; social media 366
mobility of social class 450, 452–454
MODE model 252–253
monarchy 490–492
monitoring goals 176
mood: brand attitudes 246; repair 42; retail
    therapy and 39, 40
mortgages 416
motherhood 334–335
motivations: affective-growth motives 44–47;
    affective-preservation motives 42–44; attitude
    behaviors and 252–253; brand attitudes
    252–253; cognitive-growth motives 49–51;
    cognitive-preservation motives 47–49; for
    luxury consumption 384–388; materialism and
    29–30; to self-quantify 214–216, 220; for
    shopping 39; therapeutic utility and 40–42
mouth movements and brand names 279–281
movement 85, 104
multi-channel shopping 56
multifinality 179–180

For Product Safety Concerns and Information please contact our EU
representative GPSR@taylorandfrancis.com
Taylor & Francis Verlag GmbH, Kaufingerstraße 24, 80331 München, Germany